The Storytime Sourcebook II

Carolyn N. Cullum

Neal-Schuman Publishers, Inc.
New York London

Published by Neal-Schuman Publishers, Inc.
100 William Street, Suite 2004
New York, NY 10038-4512

Printed and bound in the United States of America.

The paper used in this publication meets the minimum requirements of American National Standard for Information Sciences - Permanence of Paper for Printed Library Materials, ANSI Z39.48-1992.

ISBN-13: 978-1-55570-589-3
ISBN-10: 1-55570-589-8

Library of Congress Cataloging-in-Publication Data

Cullum, Carolyn N.
The storytime sourcebook II : a compendium of 3500+ new ideas and resources for storytellers / Carolyn N. Cullum.
p. cm.
Includes bibliographical references and index.
ISBN 1-55570-589-8 (alk. paper)
1. Storytelling—United States. 2. Children's libraries—Activity programs—United States. I. Title.
Z718.3.C84 2007
027.62'51—dc22

2006035096

This book is dedicated to the
children who have attended my programs
throughout my years as a children's librarian
and most of all to
Theresa, Andrew, and Sean,
the next generation of readers in my family.

Contents

Preface

Children's librarians prepare and present storytimes for preschool children almost every day. Fundamental as this activity is, it can quickly become a burden. Finding enough time to dedicate to planning programs is never easy, particularly when working within the confines of an already demanding daily schedule. There are many excellent resources available that can lead you to the thousands of picture book titles and other media you might want to include in a program, and most local libraries have collections available to help storytellers produce great programs for children 2–8 years of age. More often than not, though, all these choices pose another challenge: How can a busy professional most effectively sort through and make selections from this "embarrassment of riches"?

Storytime Sourcebook has gone through an assortment of changes since its conception in 1990. The original work was developed when librarians were still using filmstrips as part of their presentations. In the 1999 update, filmstrips were deleted in favor of the videocassettes made available; picture book titles were increased from 10 to 15 titles per topic; and a song section was added providing cassette sources. Now in 2007, *The Storytime Sourcebook II* has been edited to provide many music and movement selections, craft, and activities that are original works. You will find increased numbers of videocassettes/DVDs, while picture books, crafts, and activities that have copyright dates older than 1995 have been replaced with more recently released material.

I created *The Storytime Sourcebook II* to provide both a unified listing of stellar resources and the means to locate them. For nearly 30 years, in my position as a school librarian, a teacher, and presently as System Coordinator for Children's Services for the Edison (New Jersey) Public Library System, I have had the opportunity to survey and select the best additions to children's education and entertainment. What a luxury, to be able to peruse, scrutinize, and evaluate piles of books! I conducted my search to help hardworking librarians master the sometimes unwieldy task of selecting the perfect combination of items to create seamless storytimes. Putting these years of work to use, I wrote *The Storytime Sourcebook II* to

- recommend more than 3,500 of today's best picture book titles, videos and DVDs, music and movement, crafts, activities, and songs;
- endorse outstanding resource books, guides, catalogs, and directories to locate materials easily and quickly; and
- bring into play nearly 150 possible combinations in ready-made themed programs with topical calendar tie-ins.
- as well as, to introduce an assortment of original music and movement activities, craft and activity ideas developed and used throughout my term as a children's librarian. (Note that source citations are not provided when the material is an original work provided by this author.)

The Storytime Sourcebook II was designed as a reference source to help you cull, locate, and match the right ideas or other elements needed for your own programs. While some music and movement activities will provide actual text because they are this author's work, others will simply offer you the source information to guide you to the book containing the text needed. This is done where other authors were not willing to provide permission to reprint their actual material. You can draw from the massive variety of valuable sources listed in these pages to develop programs that fit your own style of presentation, set of skills, and target audience.

While the Internet has made the research process a great deal easier, nothing can replace the old-fashioned method of sitting in the library with a stack of children's books in front of you. Samuel Johnson, the eighteenth-century English essayist and poet, once observed, "A man will turn over half a library to make one book." While writing the original *Sourcebook* and again while working on this one, I, too, turned over a large portion of many libraries' collections in search of superior titles to recommend.

Unique Tool of the Trade

The Storytime Sourcebook II presents a rich treasure trove of texts and titles, both updating the suggestions offered in the prior volume and racking up an impressive range of new materials. These pages will show you how to make great programs by choosing from:

- 2,222 books;
- 685 videos;
- 146 music and movements;
- 296 crafts, 292 activities, and 149 songs.

That makes for a grand total of 3,790 possible items! Included in that number are over 1,500 of the most recent sources—from picture book titles to crafts and music and movement activities to songs on CD that were added to the material in the original edition to form *The Storytime Sourcebook II*. To make room for this plethora of new materials, many older works from the original edition were culled. Readers with copies of the first book should find that the two make useful companions to one another.

Along with identifying and recommending sundry books, videos, music, and more, *The Storytime Sourcebook II* features a "Topical Events Calendar for Tie-in Storytime Themes" which links to the 146 themed topics. This can help you plan programs throughout the year by offering the event on, or around, the suggested date. Use the event to educate children about occasions such as Babysitter Safety Day, or, better yet, just have fun with such special happenings as International Goof-off Day or Talk Like A Pirate Day.

Book Organization

Part I, "Guides Storytellers Can Use Every Day," features four useful bibliographic selection tools needed to assemble some of the various building blocks of a successful storytime.

- Topical Events Calendar for Tie-In Storytime Themes
- Recommended Reference Books and Picture Books
- Recommended Videos and DVDs
- Classic "Not To Be Missed" Picture Book Titles

Part II, "Directories Storytellers Can Use Every Day," offers three companion files, providing ways to communicate with the people who publish, produce, or distribute the materials listed in the indexes.

- Publishers of Recommended Books
- Distributors of Recommended Videos and DVDs
- Distributors of Recommended Music and CDs

Part III, "Recommended A–Z Themed Programs," pulls together all of the possible combinations of the recommended materials into 146 individual storytime programs.

Part IV, "Finding Aids Storytellers Can Use Every Day" are complete alphabetical listings of all of the various elements of storytime, cross-referenced to the suggested programs in Part III.

- Index to Picture Book Authors
- Index to Picture Book Titles
- Index to Music/Movement Segments
- Index to Crafts
- Index to Activities
- Index to Song Titles

I hope you will feel free to draw from the abundance of valuable sources listed and rework them to create a personal program that fits your own personal approach. With the sheer volume of material offered in this edition, you can easily return to a topic used in a previous program and select different books, crafts, and activities to create another program on the same topic. The diversity of *The Storytime Sourcebook II* allows for the effective repetition of subjects crucial to the development of preschool children in ways that will make them enjoy the learning process.

Are you ready to design a program? Those with an intuitive feel for how the book is organized should feel comfortable diving right in. Others may want to consult the following "Starting Points to Program Planning" for suggestions and instructions on how to use the book effectively. Either way, I hope *The Storytime Sourcebook II* will be a valuable resource as you go about creating your own distinctive storytimes, helping you to let your imagination and inventiveness soar!

Starting Points to Program Planning

Depending on how you like to go about building your storytimes, there are two different approaches that you can take to using the resources laid out in the sections ahead.

Starting Point 1: Start with Selections and Build a Program

Construct a launching pad by browsing the resources of themes, topical calendar tie-ins, videos and DVDs, picture books, music and movement segments, crafts, activities, and songs until you find a selection or two that piques your interest. Even a single item can be developed in many interesting and unique ways.

I've come to call this process the "I love this ________________!" As you browse through possible selections in the guides and finding aids, stop when you hear yourself say...

- I love this Topical Calendar Tie-in!
  - Guide 1, "Topical Events Calendar for Tie-in Storytime Themes," arranged chronologically by date, matches the event to appropriate programs.
- I love this Picture Book!
  - Guide 2, "Recommended Reference Books and Picture Books," arranged alphabetically by author, provides the information needed to search a catalog to borrow the book or the publisher to buy it.
  - Guide 4, "Classic 'Not to Be Missed' Picture Books," arranged alphabetically by title, offers timeless masterpieces to consider including or mixing with the newer titles featured in the sourcebook.
  - Index 1, "Index to Picture Book Authors," and Index 2, "Index to Picture Book Titles," can be useful support tools. Each of these lists is also cross-referenced to suggested matching program topics
- I love this Video or DVD!
  - Guide 3, "Recommended Videos and DVDs," arranged alphabetically by title, presents the playing time, distributor name, and possible matching programs. (NOTE: Publisher and distributor contact information is listed in Part II.)
- I love this Music and Movement Segment, Craft, Activity, or Song!
  - Indexes 3, 4, 5, and 6, arranged alphabetically by name, match titles with programs. Turn to any of the suggested programs to find the source where you can locate the exact item.

Starting Point 2: Start with a Themed Program and Build It with Favorite Selections

For an alternate approach, begin by looking through the many themed programs offered in Part III. Turn to any engaging program, review all the possibilities from which to choose, pick out the ones you want, and then create your own distinct version. To explore more about the ideas or locate specific materials, use the tools in the first three parts of the book as described in Starting Point 1.

No matter which starting point you choose, you will find loads of fun-filled materials from which to choose and user-friendly, quick reference guides to help you locate materials.

A Word on Gathering Materials

After you have drawn together your selections, take this book to the library and locate the sources listed under the program's crafts and activities sections; these will provide additional details to help you select which you want to use.

Your local library should own or have access to most of the picture book titles. If it does not have a particular title listed, your local library can usually obtain it from other institutions through shared interlibrary loan procedures. Ask about this possibility at the reference desk.

Many libraries allow you to place reserves on picture book titles over the Internet. That will help you gather a group of books to determine your favorite from the list. Be sure to select a few more books than you actually require. Sometimes a book that goes over well with your group in the morning inexplicably bombs with the afternoon group, and you will want to have another title to read in its place.

For video or DVD titles be sure your library or school has obtained public performance rights to show these films. You can be compliant with U.S. Copyright Law by using such licensing companies as "Movie Licensing USA." See www.movlic.com/library for further guidelines on this issue.

Part I:

Guides Storytellers Can Use Every Day

1 Topical Events Calendar for Tie-in Storytime Themes

NOTE: These dates are based on the 2006 calendar. Since some event dates vary with the yearly calendar I've included information in the program section on how they move. Numbers in the righthand column are program numbers, not page numbers.

January

January 2	Happy New Year for Cats Day	7
January 6	Epiphany (Three Kings Day)	121
January 9	National Thank God It's Monday Day	50
January 14	Penguin Awareness Day	31
January 8–14	Universal Letter Writing Day	36
January 17	Customer Service Day	39
January 26	Australia Day	12
January 30	Bubble Wrap Appreciation Day	116

February

February 2	Groundhog's Day	82
February 6	Pay-a-Compliment Day	40
February 10–12	Gold Rush Days	144
February 12	Lost Penny Day	102
February 14	St. Valentine's Day	86
February 17	Great Backyard Bird Count	49
February 28	International Pancake Day	65
February 28	Mardi Gras	111
February 28	National Tooth Fairy Day	106

March

March	National Umbrella Month	141
March	Save Your Vision Month	75
March 1	National Pig Day	16
March 1–7	Returned the Borrowed Books Week	97
March 1–7	Write a Letter of Appreciation Week	100
March 2	Read Across America Day	1
March 3	I Want You to Be Happy Day	54
March 4	Babysitter Safety Day	20
March 6	Fun Facts about Names Day	107
March 6–12	National Cheerleaders Week	134
March 10–12	World's Largest Rattlesnake Roundup	119
March 11	Blizzard of '88 Anniversary	143
March 12	Salem Witch Trials	145
March 14	First National Bird Reservation in the United States	30
March 17	St. Patrick's Day	85
March 22	As Young as You Feel Day	110
March 22	International Goof-off Day	41
March 26	Make Up Your Own Holiday Day	26
March 27	Education and Sharing Day	25
March 27	Kite Flying Day	96
March 31	National "She's Funny that Way" Day	90

April

April	Appreciate Diversity Month	101
April	Foot Health Awareness Month	4
April	Straw Hat Month	45
April 1	National Love Our Children Day	18

(Continued)

April *(Continued)*

April 3	Birth of Jane Goodall	15
April 10	National Siblings Day	60
April 10–16	Young People's Poetry Week	115
April 13	International Plant Appreciation Day	114
April 15	Stories Day	21
April 16	Easter Sunday	80
April 16	Sechselauten	126
April 20	National Honesty Day	24
April 22	Earth Day	56
April 23	St. George's Day	52
April 24	National Playground Safety Week	122
April 28	Arbor Day	140
April 29	Anniversary of Casey Jones' Death	138

May

May	Clean Air Month	53
May 1	School Principals' Day	123
May 6	International Astronomy Day	133
May 12	National Hospital Week	88
May 13	International Migratory Bird Day	28
May 13	Mother Ocean Day	10
May 13	Preakness Frog Hop	70
May 19	National Children and Police Day	37
May 21–27	National New Friends, Old Friends Week	69
May 23	World Turtle Day	120
May 25	National Missing Children's Day	135
May 26–April 1	National Cleaning Week	38
May 28	Freeing the Insects Day	94

June

June 2	I Love My Dentist Day	34
June 10	Pandora's Arrival	48
June 15	Native American Citizenship Day	57
June 21	Summer Solstice	127
June 23–24	International Butterfly Festival	92
June 25	Log Cabin Day	89
June 27	Happy Birthday to You Composed	32
June 27	Birth of Helen Keller	132
June 28	Paul Bunyan Day	74

July

July	National Blueberries Month	71
July 1–23	Tour de France	27
July 1	First U.S. Zoo Anniversary	146
July 10	Don't Step on a Bee Day	93
July 15	Cow Appreciation Day	8
July 15–21	National Rabbit Week	17
July 17	Wrong Way Corrigan Day	23
July 20	Special Olympics Day	77
July 22	Pied Piper of Hamelin Anniversary (Maybe)	14
July 23	Gorgeous Grandma Day	76
July 23	Parent's Day	61
July 27	Walk on Stilts Day	130
July 31–August 5	National Clown Week	42

August

August	Get Ready for Kindergarten Month	95
August	National Inventors Month	98
August 9	National Underwear Day	44
August 11	Night of the Shooting Stars	108
August 11–September 9	People's Republic of China's Festival of Hungry Ghosts	73
August 14–20	National Aviation Week	139
August 14–18	Weird Contest Week	68
August 17	Sandcastle Day	124
August 23	National Hula-Hoop Championship Day	47
August 26	National Dog Day	9
August 26–27	Great American Duck Race	29

September

September 21	Elephant Appreciation Day	11
September 7	Grandma Moses Day	18
September 15	International Sing Out Day	105
September 16	Mayflower Day	33
September 17–23	National Farm Animals Awareness Week	62
September 22	Elephant Appreciation Day	55
September 23	Fish Amnesty Week	63
September 30	Family Health and Fitness Month	58
September 24	South Africa Heritage Day	66
September 10	Swap Ideas Day	91
September 19	Talk Like a Pirate Day	113
September 24	National Good Neighbor Day	104
September 30	Pumpkin Day	125

October

October	Adopt a Shelter Dog Month	2
October	Halloween Safety Month	83
October	Month of the Dinosaur	51
October	National Animal Safety and Protection Month	5
October 1–7	Mystery Series Week	129
October 4	Balloons Around the World	137
October 8	Great Chicago Fire Anniversary	35
October 14	First Official Flight to Break the Sound Barrier	109
October 15	Wishbone for Pets	112
October 16	Dictionary Day	3
October 18	Birthday of Confucius	67
October 19	Birthday of Winnie the Pooh's Friend Tigger	13
October 21	Reptile Awareness Day	118
October 21	Sweetest Day	131
October 22	National Color Day	46
October 27	Frankenstein Friday	103
October 31	Magic Day	99

November

November 2	Daniel Boone's Birthday	64
November 4	Sadie Hawkin's Day	72
November 14	Artifical Snow Introduced to America	142
November 14	National American Teddy Bear Day	6
November 19	Mother Goose Parade	59
November 19–25	National Game and Puzzle Week	117
November 22	What Do You Love About America Day	81
November 23	Turkey Free Thanksgiving	87

December

2 Recommended Reference Books and Picture Books

———. *Silly Shapes.* New York: Backpack, 2005; 10 pp., $4.98.
Aardema, Verna. *How the Ostrich Got Its Long Neck.* New York: Scholastic, 1995; 32 pp., $14.95.
Abercrombie, Barbara. *Michael and the Cats.* New York: Margaret K. McElderry, 1993; 32 pp., $13.95.
Adams, Cynthia G. *International Crafts and Games.* Grand Rapids, MI: Instructional Fair, 1997; 128 pp., $10.95.
Adler, David A. *I Know I'm a Witch.* New York: Henry Holt, 1988; 32 pp., $15.00.
Afanasyev, Alexander Nikolayevich. *The Fool and the Fish.* New York: Dial, 1990; 32 pp., $12.95.
Agee, Jon. *Dmitri, the Astronaut.* New York: HarperCollins, 1996; 32 pp. $14.95.
Ahlberg, Allan. *Monkey Do!* Cambridge, MA: Candlewick, 1998; 32 pp., $15.99.
Alborough, Jez. *Fix-it Duck.* New York: HarperCollins, 2001; 32 pp., $15.95.
Alborough, Jez. *Some Dogs Do.* Cambridge, MA: Candlewick, 2003; 32 pp., $15.99.
Alborough, Jez. *Tall.* Cambridge, MA: Candlewick, 2005; 32 pp., $15.99.
Alborough, Jez. *Watch Out! Big Bro's Coming!* Cambridge, MA: Candlewick, 1997; 32 pp., NA.
Alexander, Sally Hobart. *Maggie's Whopper.* New York: Macmillan, 1992; 32 pp., $14.95.
Aliki. *All by Myself.* New York: HarperCollins, 2000; 32 pp., $14.89.
Aliki. *Manners.* New York: Greenwillow, 1990; 32 pp., $15.93.
Aliki. *My Hands.* New York: Thomas Y. Crowell, 1990; 32 pp., $12.95.
Aliki. *My Visit to the Zoo.* New York: HarperCollins, 1997; 40 pp., $14.95.
Allard, Harry. *The Cactus Flower Bakery.* New York: HarperCollins, 1991; 32 pp., $14.89.
Allen, Janet. *Exciting Things to Do with Color.* New York: J.B. Lippincott, 1997; 45 pp., $4.95.
Allen, Judy. *Whale.* Cambridge, MA: Candlewick, 1992; 32 pp., $15.95.
Almond, David, and Stephen Lambert. *Kate, the Cat and the Moon.* New York: Doubleday, 2004; 32 pp., $15.95.
Ambrus, Victor. *What Time Is It, Dracula?* New York: Crown, 1991; 26 pp., $3.99.
Anderson, Adrienne. *Fun and Games for Family Gatherings.* San Francisco: Reunion Research, 1996; 140 pp., $12.95.
Anderson, Peggy Perry. *Time for Bed, the Babysitter Said.* Boston: Houghton Mifflin, 1987; 32 pp., $15.00.
Anderson, Peggy Perry. *To the Tub.* Boston: Houghton Mifflin, 1996; 32 pp., $13.95.
Anderson, Peggy Perry. *We Go in a Circle.* Boston: Houghton Mifflin, 2004; 32 pp., $15.00.
Andreae, Giles. *Dinosaurs Galore!* Wilton, CT: Tiger Tales, 2004; 32 pp., $16.95.
Andrews, Sylvia. *Rattlebone Rock.* New York: HarperCollins, 1995; 32 pp., $13.95.
Anholt, Catherine and Laurence. *One, Two, Three, Count with Me.* New York: Viking, 1996; 26 pp., $4.99.

Anholt, Laurence. *Leonardo and the Flying Boy*. Hauppauge, N.Y.: Barron's Educational Series, 2000; 32 pp., $13.95.

Anholt, Laurence. *The New Puppy*. New York: Western, 1994; 32 pp., $12.95.

Appelt, Kathi. *Bayou Lullaby*. New York: Morrow, 1995; 40 pp., $16.00.

Appelt, Kathi. *Bubbles, Bubbles*. New York: HarperCollins, 2001; 32 pp., $9.95.

Appelt, Kathi. *Watermelon Day*. New York: Henry Holt, 1996; 32 pp., $14.95.

Araki, Mie. *The Magic Toolbox*. San Francisco: Chronicle, 2003; 32 pp., $14.95.

Araujo, Frank P. *The Perfect Orange*. Windsor, CA: Rayve, 1994; 32 pp., $16.95.

Archer, Dash and Mike. *Looking After Little Ellie*. New York: Bloomsbury, 2005; 32 pp., $15.95.

Arden, Carolyn. *Goose Moon*. Honesdale, PA: Boyds Mills, 2004; 32 pp. $15.95.

Armstrong, Jennifer. *That Terrible Baby*. New York: Tambourine, 1994; 32 pp., $14.00.

Armstrong, Jennifer. *Wan Hu Is in the Stars*. New York: Tambourine, 1995; 32 pp., $14.93.

Arnold, Katya. *Meow!* New York: Holiday House, 1998; 30 pp., $16.95.

Arnold, Tedd. *Green Wilma*. New York: Dial, 1993; 32 pp., $13.89.

Arnold, Tedd. *More Parts*. New York: Penguin, 2001; 32 pp., $16.99.

Arnold, Tedd. *No More Water in the Tub!* New York: Dial, 1995; 32 pp., $14.99.

Arnosky, Jim. *Every Autumn Comes the Bear*. New York: Putnam, 1993; 32 pp., $5.95.

Arnosky, Jim. *Little Lions*. New York: Putnam, 1998; 32 pp, $15.99.

Arnosky, Jim. *Otters Under Water*. New York: Putnam, 1992; 32 pp., $14.95.

Arnosky, Jim. *Rabbits and Raindrops*. New York: Putnam, 1997; 32 pp., $15.99.

Arnosky, Jim. *Turtle in the Sea*. New York: Putnam, 2002; 32 pp., $15.99.

Asbjornsen, Peter. *The Three Billy Goats Gruff*. San Diego: Harcourt, 1998; 28 pp., $9.95.

Asch, Frank. *Barnyard Lullaby*. New York: Simon & Schuster, 1998; 40 pp., $15.00.

Asch, Frank. *Moonbear's Dream*. New York: Simon & Schuster, 1999; 32 pp., $15.00.

Asch, Frank. *Moonbear's Pet*. New York: Simon & Schuster, 1997; 32 pp., $15.00.

Asch, Frank. *Sand Cake*. New York: Parents Magazine Press, 1993; 48 pp., $5.95

Asch, Frank and Devin. *Baby Duck's New Friend*. San Diego: Gulliver, 2001; 32 pp., $15.00.

Asher, Sandy. *Princess Bee and the Royal Good-night Story*. Morton Grove, IL: Albert Whitman, 1990; 32 pp., $20.00.

Ashforth, Camilla. *Monkey Tricks*. Cambridge, MA: Candlewick, 1993; 32 pp., $15.95.

Ashley, Bernard. *Cleversticks*. New York: Crown, 1991; 32 pp., $10.99.

Ashley, Susan. *Bees*. Milwaukee, WI: Weekly Reader, 2004; 32 pp., $14.50.

Ashman, Linda. *Castles, Caves and Honeycombs*. San Diego: Harcourt, 2001; 32 pp., $16.00.

Auch, Mary Jane. *Monster Brother*. New York: Holiday House, 1994; 32 pp., $15.95.

Auch, Mary Jane and Herm. *The Princess and the Pizza*. New York: Holiday House, 2002; 32 pp., $16.95.

Ault, Kelly. *Let's Sign: Every Baby's Guide to Communicating with Grownups*. Boston: Houghton Mifflin, 2005; unpaged, $17.00.

Austin, Virginia. *Say Please*. Cambridge, MA: Candlewick, 1994; 28 pp., $12.95.

Avi. *The Bird, the Frog, and the Light*. New York: Orchard, 1994; 32 pp., $15.95.

Awdry, Christopher. *Tell the Time with Thomas.* New York: Random House, 1992; unpaged, $9.99.
Axelrod, Amy. *Pigs on a Blanket.* New York: Simon & Schuster, 1996; 32 pp., $13.00.
Axelrod, Amy. *Pigs Will Be Pigs.* New York: Simon & Schuster, 1994; 32 pp., $14.00.
Aylesworth, Jim. *The Completed Hickory Dickory Dock.* New York: Atheneum, 1990; 32 pp., $12.95.
Aylesworth, Jim. *Naughty Little Monkeys.* New York: Dutton, 2003; 32 pp., $15.99.
Bachelet, Gilles. *My Cat, the Silliest Cat in the World.* New York: Abrams, 2006; 32 pp., $16.95.
Baehr, Patricia. *School Isn't Fair!* New York: Simon & Schuster, 1991; 32 pp., $13.95.
Baer, Edith. *This Is the Way We Go to School.* New York: Demco Media, 1992; 40 pp., $10.80.
Baicker, Karen. *You Can Do It Too!* Brooklyn, N.Y.: Handprint, 2005; 32 pp., $13.95.
Bailey, Donna. *What We Can Do About: Litter.* Danbury, CT: Franklin Watts, 1991; 32 pp., $18.70.
Bailey, Guy. *The Ultimate Playground and Recess Game Book.* Camas, WA: Educators Press, 2001; 156 pp., $16.95.
Baker, Alan. *Benjamin's Balloon.* New York: Lothrop, Lee and Shepard, 1990; 32 pp., $12.95.
Baker, Alan. *Brown Rabbit's Day.* New York: Kingfisher, 1994; 32 pp., $7.95.
Baker, Alan. *Two Tiny Mice.* New York: Dial, 1990; 32 pp., $12.95.
Baker, Keith. *Hide and Snake.* San Diego: Harcourt, 1991; 32 pp., $12.95.
Baker, Keith. *More Mr. and Mrs. Green.* San Diego, Calif.: Harcourt, 2004; 332 pp. $16.00.
Baker, Keith. *Who is the Beast?* San Diego: Harcourt, 1990; 32 pp., $12.95.
Baker, Roberta. *Olive's Pirate Party.* New York: Little, Brown, 2005; 32 pp., $15.99.
Balian, Lorna. *A Garden for a Groundhog.* Nashville: Abingdon, 1985; 32 pp., $13.95.
Balian, Lorna. *Humbug Rabbit.* Nashville: Abingdon, 1997; 32 pp., $16.95.
Balian, Lorna. *Leprechauns Never Lie.* Nashville: Abingdon, 1994; 32 pp., $14.95.
Balian, Lorna. *Sometimes It's Turkey.* Nashville: Abingdon, 1994; 32 pp., $14.95.
Ball, Duncan. *Jeremy's Tail.* New York: Orchard, 1990; 32 pp., $14.99.
Ballard, Robin. *Good-bye, House.* New York: Greenwillow, 1994; 24 pp., $13.93.
Ballard, Robin. *Granny and Me.* New York: Greenwillow, 1992; 24 pp., $6.95.
Baltuck, Naomi. *Crazy Gibberish and Other Storyhour Stretches.* North Haven, CT: Linnet, 1993; 152 pp., $25.00.
Bancroft, Catherine. *Felix's Hat.* New York: Four Winds, 1993; 32 pp., $14.95.
Bang, Molly. *Goose.* New York: Blue Sky, 1996; 32 pp., $10.95.
Banish, Roslyn. *A Family Forever.* New York: HarperCollins, 1992; 44 pp., $14.00.
Banks, Kate. *And If the Moon Could Talk.* New York: Frances Foster, 1998; 34 pp., $15.00.
Banks, Kate. *The Great Blue House.* New York: Frances Foster, 2005; 32 pp., $16.00.
Banks, Kate. *The Night Worker.* New York: Frances Foster, 2000; 32 pp., $16.00.
Bany-Winters, Lisa. *Show Time! Music, Dance and Drama.* Chicago: Chicago Review Press, 2000; 190 pp., $14.95.

Barasch, Lynne. *A Winter Walk.* New York: Ticknor and Fields, 1993; 32 pp., $13.95.
Barber, Barbara E. *Allie's Basketball Dream.* New York: Lee and Low, 1996; 32 pp., $14.95.
Barbot, Daniel. *A Bicycle for Rosaura.* New York: Kane/Miller, 1991; 24 pp., $9.95.
Bare, Colleen Stanley. *Sammy, Dog Detective.* New York: Cobblehill/Dutton, 1998; 32 pp., $15.99.
Barkow, Henriette. *If Elephants Wore Pants . . .* New York: Sterling, Inc., 2004; 32 pp., $12.95.
Barner, Bob. *Bug Safari.* New York: Holiday House, 2004; 32 pp., $16.95.
Barner, Bob. *Parade Day: Marching through the Calendar Year.* New York: Holiday House, 2003; 32 pp., $16.95.
Barnes, Laura T. *Ernest and the Big Itch.* Sergeantsville, N.J.: Barnesyard, 2002; 32 pp. $15.95.
Barracca, Debra and Sal. *Maxi, the Hero.* New York: Dial, 1991; 30 pp., $14.99.
Barrett, Judi. *Animals Should Definitely Not Wear Clothing.* New York: Macmillan, 1989; 32 pp., $11.19.
Barrett, Ron. *Pickles to Pittsburgh.* New York: Atheneum, 1997; 32 pp., $16.00.
Bartalos, Michael. *Shadowville.* New York: Viking, 1995; 40 pp., $13.99.
Bartlett, Alison. *Cat Among the Cabbages.* New York: Dutton, 1996; 32 pp., $9.99.
Bateman, Teresa. *April Foolishness.* Morton Grove, IL: Albert Whitman, 2004; 32 pp., $15.95.
Bateman, Teresa. *Hamster Camp: How Harry Got Fit.* Morton Grove, IL: Albert Whitman, 2005; 32 pp., $15.95.
Bateman, Teresa. *Leprechaun Gold.* New York: Holiday House, 1998; 32 pp., $15.95.
Bauer, Caroline Feller. *Valentine's Day: Stories and Poems.* New York: HarperCollins, 1993; 95 pp., $15.95.
Bauer, Marion Dane. *Frog's Best Friend.* New York: Holiday House, 2002; 32 pp., $14.95.
Bauer, Marion Dane. *If Frogs Made Weather.* New York: Holiday House, 2005; 32 pp., $16.95.
Baumgaret, Klaus. *Laura's Secret.* Wilton, CT: Tiger Tales, 2003; 32 pp., $16.95.
Beach, Judi K. *Names for Snow.* New York: Hyperion, 2003; 32 pp., $16.99.
Beardshaw, Rosalind. *Grandpa's Surprise.* New York: Bloomsbury, 2004; 32 pp., $15.95.
Beaton, Clare. *Daisy Gets Dressed.* Cambridge, MA: Barefoot, 2005; 32 pp., $15.99.
Beaumont, Karen. *I Ain't Gonna Paint No More!* San Diego: Harcourt, 2005; 32 pp., $16.00.
Beck, Ian. *Emily and the Golden Acorn.* New York: Simon & Schuster, 1992; 32 pp., $14.00.
Beck, Ian. *Five Little Ducks.* New York: Henry Holt, 1992; 32 pp., $14.95.
Bedford, David. *The Copy Crocs.* Atlanta, GA: Peachtree, 2004; 32 pp., $15.95.
Bedford, David. *Touch the Sky, My Little Bear.* Brooklyn, N.Y.: Handprint, 2001; 32 pp., $15.95.
Bedford, David, and Peter Kavanagh. *Ella's Games.* Hauppauge, N.Y.: Barron's Educational Series, 2002; 32 pp., $12.95.
Beil, Karen M. *Grandma According to Me.* New York: Dell, 1994; 32 pp., $4.99.
Beil, Karen Magnuson. *Mooove Over!* New York: Holiday House, 2004; 32 pp., $16.95.

Bellows, Cathy. *The Grizzly Sisters.* New York: Macmillan, 1991; 32 pp., $14.95.
Bemelmans, Ludwig. *Rosebud.* New York: Random House, 1993; 32 pp., $8.99.
Bender, Robert. *The A to Z Beastly Jamboree.* New York: Lodestar, 1996; 30 pp., $14.99.
Bender, Robert. *A Most Unusual Lunch.* New York: Dial, 1994; 32 pp., $14.89.
Benjamin, Cynthia. *I am an Astronaut.* Hauppauge, N.Y.: Barron's Educational Series, 1996; 32 pp., $7.95.
Bennett, Kelly. *Not Norman: A Goldfish Story.* Cambridge, MA: Candlewick, 2005; 32 pp., $15.99.
Bentley, Nancy. *I've Got Your Nose!* New York: Doubleday, 1991; 32 pp., $12.99.
Berendes, Mary. *St. Patrick's Day Shamrocks.* New York: Child's World, 2000; 32 pp., $16.95.
Berenstain, Stan and Jan. *The Berenstain Bears Don't Pollute (Anymore).* New York: Random House, 1991; 32 pp., $8.99.
Berenstain, Stan and Jan. *The Berenstain Bears Go on a Ghost Walk.* New York: Harper Festival, 2005; 32 pp., $8.99.
Berg, Brook. *What Happened to Marion's Book?* Fort Atkinson, WI: Upstart, 2003; 32 pp., $16.95
Berg, Cami. *D is for Dolphin.* Santa Fe, NM: Windom, 1991; 32 pp., $18.95.
Berge, Claire. *Whose Shadow is This: A Look at Animal Shapes—Round, Long and Pointy.* Minneapolis, MN: Picture Window, 2005; 32 pp. $16.95.
Berkeley, Jon. *Chopsticks.* New York: Random House, 2005; 32 pp., $16.95.
Berlan, Kathryn Hook. *Andrew's Amazing Monsters.* New York: Atheneum, 1993; 32 pp., $13.95.
Berlin, Irving. *Easter Parade.* New York: HarperCollins, 2003; 32 pp., $16.89.
Bernasconi, Pablo. *The Wizard, the Ugly and the Book of Shame.* New York: Bloomsbury, 2004; 32 pp., $16.95.
Bernhard, Emery. *Ladybug.* New York: Holiday House, 1992; 32 pp., $14.95.
Bernhard, Emery and Durga. *How Snowshoe Hare Rescued the Sun: A Tale from the Arctic.* New York: Holiday House, 1993; 32 pp., $15.95.
Bernstein, Dan. *The Tortoise and the Hare Race Again.* New York: Holiday House, 2006; 32 pp., $16.95.
Bersma, Danielle, and Marjoke Visscher. *Yoga Games for Children.* Alameda, CA: Hunter House, 2003; 146 pp., $12.95.
Best, Cari. *Red Light, Green Light, Mama and Me.* New York: Orchard, 1995; 32 pp., $16.99.
Bianchi, John. *Spring Break at Pokweed Public School.* Buffalo, NY: Bungalo, 1994; 26 pp., $14.95.
Birdseye, Tom. *Look Out, Jack! The Giant is Back!* New York: Holiday House, 2001; 32 pp., $16.95.
Birchman, David Fran. *Brother Billy Brontos Bygone Blues Band.* New York: Lothrop, Lee and Shepard, 1992; 30 pp., $13.95.
Birchman, David F. *The Raggly, Scraggly, No-Soap, No-Scrub Girl.* New York: Lothrop, Lee and Shepard, 1995; 32 pp., $16.00.
Birney, Betty G. *Tyrannosaurus Tex.* Boston: Houghton Mifflin, 1994; 32 pp., $14.95.
Bittinger, Gayle (editor). *Best of Totline: Volume 2.* New York: Totline, 2003; 160 pp., $16.99.

Blackaby, Susan. *A Bird for You: Caring for Your Bird.* Minneapolis, MN: Picture Window, 2003; 32 pp., $16.95.
Blackstone, Stella. *Jump into January: A Journey Around the Year.* Cambridge, MA: Barefoot, 2004; 32 pp., $15.99.
Blackstone, Stella. *My Granny Went to Market: A Round-the-World Counting Rhyme.* Cambridge, MA: Barefoot, 2005; 32 pp., $16.99.
Blake, Jon. *Wriggly Pig.* New York: Tambourine, 1992; 30 pp., $3.99.
Blakey, Nancy. *Go Outside!* Berkeley, CA: Tricycle, 2002; 134 pp., $14.95.
Blakey, Nancy. *The Mudpies Activity Book: Recipes for Invention.* Berkeley, CA: Tricycle, 1989; 132 pp., $8.95.
Blankenship, LeeAnn. *Mr. Tuggle's Troubles.* Honesdale, PA: Boyds Mills, 2005; 32 pp., $15.95.
Blanco, Alberto. *Angel's Kite.* Emeryville, CA: Children's Book Press, 1994; 32 pp., $14.95.
Bledsoe, Karen E. *Hanukkah Crafts.* Berkeley Heights, NJ: Enslow, 2004; 38 pp., $22.60.
Bloom, Suzanne. *A Family for Jamie: An Adoption Story.* New York: Clarkson N. Potter, 1991; 24 pp., $13.99.
Bloom, Suzanne. *A Splendid Friend, Indeed.* Honesdale, PA: Boyds Mills, 2005; 32 pp., $15.95.
Blosser, Jody L. *Everybody Wins!: Non-Competitive Party Games and Activities for Children.* New York: Sterling, 1996; 144 pp., $16.95.
Boelts, Maribeth. *Summer's End.* Boston: Houghton Mifflin, 1995; 32 pp., $14.95.
Boelts, Maribeth. *A Kid's Guide to Staying Safe on the Streets.* New York: Powerkids, 1997; 24 pp., $13.95.
Boelts, Maribeth. *The Firefighters' Thanksgiving.* New York: Putnam, 2004; 32 pp., $15.99.
Boelts, Maribeth. *Little Bunny's Preschool Countdown.* Morton Grove, IL: Albert Whitman, 1996; 32 pp., $14.95.
Bogacki, Tomek. *Cat and Mouse in the Rain.* New York: Farrar, Straus & Giroux, 1997; 32 pp., $15.00.
Bond, Felicia. *Poinsettia and the Firefighters.* New York: Thomas Y. Crowell, 1984; 32 pp., $16.89.
Bond, Michael, and Karen Jankel. *Paddinton Bear: Goes to the Hospital.* New York: HarperCollins, 2001; 32 pp., $12.95.
Bonica, Diane. *Hand-Shaped Gifts.* Carthage, IL: Good Apple, 1991; 144 pp., $13.99.
Bonner, Lori. *Putting on a Party.* Layton, UT: Gibbs Smith, 2004; 63 pp., $9.95.
Bonsall, Crosby. *Mine's the Best.* New York: Harper and Row, 1997; 32 pp., $8.95.
Borden, Louise. *The Neighborhood Trucker.* New York: Scholastic, 1997; 28 pp., $3.95.
Bornstein, Ruth Lercher. *Rabbit's Good News.* Boston: Clarion, 1995; 32 pp., $13.95.
Boteler, Alison. *The Disney Party Handbook.* New York: Disney, 1998; 208 pp., $35.50.
Bottner, Barbara. *Be Brown!* New York: Putnam and Grosset, 2002; 32 pp., $10.99.
Bourgeois, Paulette. *Franklin and the Thunderstorm.* Tonawanda, NY: Kids Can, 1998; 32 pp., $10.95.
Bourgeois, Paulette. *Franklin and the Tooth Fairy.* Tonawanda, NY: Kids Can, 1995; 32 pp., $10.95.
Bourgeois, Paulette. *In My Neighborhood: Police Officers.* Tonawanda, NY: Kids Can, 1992; 32 pp., $12.95.

Bourgeois, Paulette. *In My Neighborhood: Postal Workers.* Tonawanda, NY: Kids Can, 1992; 32 pp., $12.95.
Bourgeois, Paulette, and Brenda Clark. *Franklin Rides a Bike.* New York: Scholastic, 1997; 32 pp., $3.99.
Bourgeois, Paulette, and Brenda Clark. *Franklin's Bicycle Helmet.* New York: Scholastic, 2000; 32 pp., $15.00.
Bowen, Anne. *Tooth Fairy's First Night.* Minneapolis, MN: Carolrhoda, 2005; 32 pp., $15.95.
Bradby, Marie. *More than Anything Else.* New York: Orchard, 1995; 30 pp., $15.95.
Bradman, Tony. *It Came from Outer Space.* New York: Dial, 1992; 26 pp., $12.00.
Branley, Franklyn. *Down Comes the Rain.* New York: HarperCollins, 1997; 32 pp., $14.89.
Bratun, Katy. *Gingerbread Mouse.* New York: HarperCollins, 2003; 32 pp., $13.89.
Braybrooks, Ann. *Winnie the Pooh: The Easter Bear?* New York: Random House, 1997; 32 pp., $12.95.
Breakspeare, Andrew. *Skating with the Bears.* New York: Dutton, 2004; 32 pp., $15.99.
Breathed, Berkeley. *A Wish for Wings that Work.* New York: Little, Brown, 1991; 32 pp., $14.95.
Brennan-Nelson, Denise. *Buzzy, the Bumblebee.* Chelsea, MI: Sleeping Bear, 1999; 32 pp., $15.00.
Brenner, Barbara, William Hooke, and Betty Boegehold. *Bunny Tails.* New York: Milk and Cookies, 2005; 32 pp., $15.95.
Brett, Jan. *Armadillo Rodeo.* New York: Putnam, 1995; 32 pp., $15.95.
Brett, Jan. *Christmas Trolls.* New York: Putnam, 1993; 32 pp., $15.95.
Brett, Jan. *Daisy Comes Home.* New York: Putnam, 2002; 32 pp., $16.99.
Brett, Jan. *The Hat.* New York: Putnam, 1997; 32 pp., $16.99.
Brett, Jan. *Trouble with Trolls.* New York: Putnam, 1992; 32 pp., $15.95.
Brett, Jan. *The Umbrella.* New York: Putnam, 2004; 32 pp., $16.99.
Bridges, Margaret Park. *I Love the Rain.* San Francisco: Chronicle, 2005; 32 pp., $15.95.
Bridges, Margaret Park. *Will You take Care of Me?* New York: Morrow, 1998; 32 pp., $22.95.
Bridges, Shirin Yim. *Ruby's Wish.* San Francisco: Chronicle, 2002; 32 pp., $15.95.
Bridwell, Norman. *Clifford's First Autumn.* New York: Scholastic, 1997; 32 pp., $8.19.
Bridwell, Norman. *Clifford's Thanksgiving Visit.* New York: Scholastic, 1993; 32 pp., $2.99.
Bright, Paul. *Nobody Laughs at a Lion!* Intercourse, PA: Good Books, 2005; 32 pp., $16.00.
Bright, Paul, and Ben Cort. *Under the Bed.* Intercourse, PA: Good Books, 2004; 32 pp., $16.00.
Briggs, Diane. *52 Programs for Preschoolers: The Librarians Year-Round Planner.* Chicago: ALA, 1997; 217 pp., $28.00.
Briggs, Diane. *101 Fingerplays, Stories and Songs to Use with Finger Puppets.* Chicago: ALA, 1999; 129 pp., $39.99.
Briggs, Raymond. *The Snowman Clock Book.* New York: Random House, 1991; 32pp., $7.99.
Brillhart, Julie. *Storyhour—Starring Megan!* Morton Grove, IL: Albert Whitman, 1992; 32 pp., $13.95.

Brillhart, Julie. *When Daddy Took Us Camping*. Morton Grove, IL: Albert Whitman, 1997; 24 pp., $13.95.

Brimner, Larry Dane. *The Littlest Wolf*. New York: HarperCollins, 2002; 32 pp., $15.89.

Brisson, Pat. *Benny's Pennies*. New York: Doubleday, 1993; 32 pp., $14.95.

Brochac, Joseph, and Gayle Ross. *The Story of the Milky Way*. New York: Dial, 1995; 32 pp., $14.99.

Brooks, Jennifer. *Princess Jessica Rescues a Prince*. Lake Forest, CA: NADJA, 1994; 48 pp., $15.95.

Brown, Alan. *Hoot and Holler*. New York: Knopf, 2001; 32 pp., $15.95.

Brown, Jo. *Where's My Mommy?* Wilton, CT: Tiger Tales, 2002; 32 pp., $14.95.

Brown, Laurie Krasny and Marc. *Dinosaurs Alive and Well!* New York: Little, Brown, 1990; 32 pp., $14.95.

Brown, Laurie Krasny and Marc. *How to be a Friend: A Guide to Making Friends and Keeping Them*. New York: Little, Brown, 1998; 32 pp., $14.95.

Brown, Marc. *D.W.'s Lost Blankie*. New York: Little, Brown, 1998; 32 pp., $13.95.

Brown, Marc. *D.W. Rides Again!* New York: Little, Brown, 1993; 32 pp., $11.15.

Brown, Marc. *Glasses for D. W.* New York: Random House, 1996; 32 pp., $11.99.

Brown, Margaret Wise. *The Dirty Little Boy*. Tarrytown, NY: Marshall Cavendish, 2005; 32 pp., $5.95.

Brown, Margaret Wise. *Little Donkey Close Your Eyes*. New York: HarperCollins, 1995; 32 pp., $13.89.

Brown, Ruth. *One Stormy Night*. New York: Dutton, 1992; 32 pp., $4.99.

Brown, Ruth. *Toad*. New York: Dutton, 1996; 32 pp., $15.99.

Brown, Ruth. *The World that Jack Built*. New York: Dutton, 1991; 32 pp., $13.95.

Browne, Anthony. *My Mom*. New York: Farrar, Straus & Giroux, 2005; 32 pp., $16.00.

Browne, Eileen. *Where's That Bus?* New York: Simon & Schuster, 1991; 28 pp., $13.95.

Bruchac, James and Joseph. *Native American Games and Stories*. Golden, Colo.: Fulcrum, 2000; 86 pp., $12.95.

Bruchac, Joseph. *Crazy Horse's Vision*. New York: Lee and Low, 2000; 32 pp., $16.95.

Bruchac, Joseph. *The Great Ball Game*. New York: Dials, 1994; 32pp., $14.89.

Bruchac, Joseph and James. Raccoon's Last Race. New York: Dial, 2004; 32 pp., $15.99.

Bruel, Nick. *Boing*. New York: Roaring Brook, 2004; 32 pp., $15.95.

Brumbeau, Jeff. *The Quiltmakers' Gift*. New York: Scholastic, 2000; 32 pp., $17.95.

Bryant, Raymond. *Fun Time Rhymes: On the Water*. Hauppauge, NY: Barron's Educational Series, 2003; 10 pp., $4.95.

Buckley, Helen E. *Moonlight Kite*. New York: Lothrop, Lee and Shepard, 1997; 32 pp., $16.00.

Bucknall, Caroline. *One Bear in the Hospital*. New York: Dial, 1991; 32 pp., $11.95.

Bunting, Eve. *Can You Do This, Old Badger?* San Diego: Harcourt, 1999; 32 pp., $15.00

Bunting, Eve. *In the Haunted House*. Boston: Clarion, 1990; 32 pp., $14.95.

Bunting, Eve. *Little Bear's Little Boat*. Boston: Clarion, 2003; 32 pp., $12.00.

Bunting, Eve. *My Red Balloon*. Honesdale, PA: Boyds Mills, 2005; 32 pp., $15.95.

Bunting, Eve. *Night Tree*. San Diego: Harcourt, 1991; 32 pp., $16.00.

Bunting, Eve. *Someday a Tree*. Boston: Clarion, 1993; 32 pp., $15.00.
Bunting, Eve. *Sunflower House*. San Diego: Harcourt, 1996; 32 pp., $15.00.
Bunting, Eve. *Sunshine Home*. Boston: Clarion, 1994; 32 pp., $16.00.
Bunting, Eve. *A Turkey for Thanksgiving*. Boston: Clarion, 1991; 32 pp., $13.95
Bunting, Eve. *Twinnies*. San Diego: Harcourt, 1997; 32 pp., $15.00.
Burden-Patmon, Denis. *Iwani's Gift at Kwanzaa*. New York: Simon & Schuster, 1992; 23 pp., $4.95.
Burg, Ann. *Autumn Walk*. New York: HarperCollins, 2003; 10 pp., $5.99.
Burke, Bobby, and Horace Gerlach. *Daddy's Little Girl*. New York: HarperCollins, 2004; 32 pp., $14.99.
Burrough, Tracy Stephen. *The Big Book of Kids Games*. Stamford, CT: Longmeadow, 1992; 184 pp., $4.99.
Burton, Marilee Burton. *My Best Shoes*. New York: Tambourine, 1994; 32 pp., $15.00.
Bush, Timothy. *Teddy Bear, Teddy Bear*. New York: Greenwillow, 2005; 32 pp., $14.99.
Butler, M. Christina. *One Snowy Night*. Intercourse, PA: Good Books, 2004; 32 pp., $16.00.
Butterworth, Nick, and Mick Inkpen. *Jasper's Beanstalk*. New York: Bradbury, 1993; 24 pp., $5.99.
Butterworth, Nick. *Jingle Bells*. New York: Orchard, 1998; 32 pp., $15.95.
Butterworth, Nick. *My Grandpa Is Amazing*. Cambridge, Mass.: Candlewick, 1992; 32 pp., $4.99.
Bynum, Janie. *Altoona Baboona*. San Diego: Harcourt, 1999; 32 pp., $13.00.
Calmenson, Stephanie. *Engine, Engine, Number Nine*. New York: Hyperion, 1996; 32 pp., $14.49.
Calmenson, Stephanie. *Good for You!: Toddler Rhymes for Toddler Times*. New York: HarperCollins, 2001; 64 pp., $16.96.
Calmenson, Stephanie. *Hotter Than a Hot Dog!* New York: Little, Brown, 1994, 32 pp., $14.95.
Calmenson, Stephanie. *Zip Whiz, Zoom!* New York: Little, Brown, 1992; 30 pp., $13.95.
Campbell, Andrea. *Perfect Party Games*. New York: Sterling, 2001; 192 pp., $9.95.
Cann, Jonathan V. *The Case of the Crooked Candles*. Milwaukee, WI: Steck-Vaughn, 1997; 32 pp., $22.83.
Cannon, Janell. *Stellaluna*. San Diego: Harcourt, 1993; 32 pp., $16.95.
Cannon, Janell. *Verdi*. San Diego: Harcourt, 1997; 32 pp., $16.00.
Capucilli, Alyss Satin. *Biscuit's Hanukkah*. New York: HarperCollins, 2005; 10 pp., $4.99.
Capucilli, Alyss Satin. *Biscuit's Snowy Day*. New York: HarperCollins,2005; 10 pp., $4.99.
Capucilli, Alyssa Satin. *Inside a Barn in the Country*. New York: Scholastic, 1995; 32 pp., $10.95.
Capucilli, Alyssa Satin. *Mrs. McTats and Her Houseful of Cats*. New York: Margaret K. McElderry, 2001; 32 pp., $16.00.
Carle, Eric. *The Grouchy Ladybug*. New York: HarperCollins, 1996; 32 pp., $15.90.
Carle, Eric. *Have You Seen My Cat?* Boston: Picture Book Studios USA, 1996; 21 pp., $6.99.
Carle, Eric. *Little Cloud*. New York: Philomel, 1996; 32 pp., $16.95.

Carle, Eric. *The Mixed-Up Chameleon.* New York: Harper and Row, 1998; 32 pp., $7.95.
Carle, Eric. *The Tiny Seed.* Boston: Picture Book Studio USA, 1998; 32 pp., $12.95.
Carlow, Emma, and Trevor Dickinson. *Kitty Princess and the Newspaper Dress.* Cambridge, MA: Candlewick, 2003; 32 pp., $16.99.
Carlson, Laurie. *Boss of the Plains: The Hat that Won the West.* New York: DK Publishing, 1998; 32 pp., $16.95.
Carlson, Laurie. *Days of Knights and Damsels: An Activity Guide.* Chicago: Chicago Review Press, 1998; 174 pp., $14.95.
Carlson, Laurie. *EcoArt!* Charlotte, VT: Williamson, 1993; 160 pp., $12.95.
Carlson, Nancy. *ABC I Like Me!* New York: Viking, 1997; 32 pp., $14.99.
Carlson, Nancy. *Arnie and the New Kid.* New York: Viking Penguin, 1990; 32 pp., $4.99.
Carlson, Nancy. *How to Lose All Your Friends.* New York: Viking Kestrel, 1994; 32 pp., $14.99.
Carlson, Nancy. *It's Going to Be Perfect.* New York: Viking, 1998; 32 pp., $15.99.
Carlson, Nancy. *Hooray for Grandparents' Day.* New York: Viking, 2000; 32 pp., $15.99.
Carlson, Nancy. *Take Time to Relax.* New York: Viking, 1991; 28 pp., $13.95.
Carlson, Nancy. *Think Big!* Minneapolis, MN: Carolrhoda Books, 2005; 32 pp., $15.95.
Carlstrom, Nancy White. *Barney Is Best.* New York: HarperCollins, 1994; 32 pp., $14.89.
Carlstrom, Nancy White. *Fish and Flamingo.* New York: Little, Brown, 1993; 32 pp., $14.95.
Carlstrom, Nancy. *I'm Not Moving, Mama.* New York: Macmillan, 1990; 28 pp., $13.95.
Carlstrom, Nancy White. *How Do You Say it Today, Jesse Bear?* New York: Macmillan, 1992; 30 pp., $15.00.
Carlstrom, Nancy White. *Let's Count it Out, Jesse Bear.* New York: Simon & Schuster, 1996; 32 pp., $15.00.
Carlstrom, Nancy White. *No Nap for Benjamin Badger.* New York: Macmillan, 1991; 28 pp., $13.95.
Carlstrom, Nancy White. *The Snow Speaks.* New York: Little, Brown, 1992; 32 pp., $15.95.
Carlstrom, Nancy White. *Swim the Silver Sea, Joshie Otter.* New York: Philomel, 1993; 32 pp., $5.95.
Carmine, Mary. *Daniel's Dinosaurs.* New York: Scholastic, 1990; 26 pp., $12.95.
Carr, Jan. *Splish, Splash, Spring.* New York: Holiday House, 2001; 32 pp. $15.95.
Carreiro, Carolyn. *Hand-Print Animal Art.* Charlotte, VT: Williamson, 1997; 144 pp., $14.95.
Carrick, Carol. *Valentine.* Boston: Clarion, 1995; 32 pp., $14.95.
Carter, Penny. *A New House for the Morrisons.* New York: Viking, 1993; 32 pp., $12.99.
Carville, James. *Lu and the Swamp Ghost.* New York: Atheneum, 2004; 32 pp., $17.95.
Caseley, Judith. *Grandpa's Garden Lunch.* New York.: Greenwillow, 1990; 24 pp., $12.89.
Caseley, Judith. *Harry and Willy and Carrothead.* New York: Greenwillow, 1991; 24 pp., $13.88.

Caseley, Judith. *Mr. Green Peas*. New York: Greenwillow, 1995; 32 pp., $15.00.
Caseley, Judith. *Slumber Party*. New York: Greenwillow, 1996; 32 pp., $14.93.
Caseley, Judith. *Sophie and Sammy's Library Sleepover*. New York: Greenwillow, 1993; 32 pp., $16.00.
Caseley, Judith. *Witch Mama*. New York: Greenwillow, 1996; 32 pp., $15.00.
Castaldo, Nancy Fusco. *Rainy Day Play!* Charlotte, VT: Williamson, 1996; 144 pp., $12.95.
Castaldo, Nancy Fusco. *Winter Day Play!* Chicago: Chicago Review Press, 2001; 160 pp., $13.95.
Cauley, Lorinda Bryan. *Things to Make and Do for Thanksgiving*. Danbury, CT: Franklin Watts, 1977; 48 pp., $7.90.
Cauley, Lorinda Bryan. *Three Blind Mice*. New York: Putnam, 1991; 32 pp., $14.95.
Cave, Kathryn. *That's What Friends Do*. New York: Hyperion, 2004; 32 pp., $15.99.
Cazet, Denys. *Born in the Gravy*. New York: Orchard, 1993; 32 pp., $15.95.
Cazet, Denys. *"I'm Not Sleepy."* New York: Orchard, 1992; 32 pp., $14.99.
Cazet, Denys. *Perfect Pumpkin Pie*. New York: Atheneum, 2005; 32 pp., $15.95.
Chamberlin, Mary and Rich. *Mama Panya's Pancakes: A Village Tale from Kenya*. Cambridge, MA: Barefoot, 2005; 32 pp., $16.99.
Chamberlin-Calamar, Pat. *Alaska's 12 Days of Summer*. Seattle, WA: Sasquatch, 2003; 32 pp., $16.95.
Chapman, Cheryl. *Pass the Fritters, Critters*. New York: Four Winds, 1993; 32 pp., $14.95.
Charles, Donald. *Calico Cat's Sunny Smile*. New York: Children's Press, 1990; 32 pp., $14.95.
Charles, Faustin, and Michael Terry. *The Selfish Crocodile*. Wilton, CT: Little Tiger, 1999; 32 pp., $14.95.
Charner, Kathy. *The Giant Encyclopedia of Theme Activities for Children 2 to 5*. Beltsville, MD: Gryphon House, 1993; 513 pp., $29.95.
Charner, Kathy. *The Giant Encyclopedia of Circle Time and Group Activities for Children 3 to 6*. Beltsville, MD: Gryphon House, 1996; 510 pp., $29.95.
Charmer, Kathy, and Maureen Murphy. *It's Great to be Three: The Encyclopedia of Activities for Three-Year-Olds*. Beltsville, MD: Gryphon House, 2002; 640 pp., $29.95.
Check, Laura. *Little Hands Paper Plate Crafts*. Charlotte, VT: Williamson, 2000; 128 pp., $12.95.
Chester, Jonathan, and Kirsty Melville. *Splash!: A Penguin Counting Book*. Berkeley, CA: Tricycle, 1997; 24 pp., $12.95.
Chesworth, Michael. *Rainy Day Dream*. New York: Farrar, Straus & Giroux, 1992; 32 pp., $14.00.
Child, Lauren. *But excuse Me that Is my Book*. New York: Dial, 2005; 32 pp., $16.99.
Child Lauren. *Who's Afraid of the Big Bad Book?* New York: Hyperion, 2002; 32 pp., $16.99.
Chinn, Karen. *Sam and the Lucky Money*. New York: Lee and Low, 1995; 32 pp., $14.95.
Chlad, Dorothy. *Playing Outdoors in the Winter*. New York: Children's Press, 1991; 32 pp., $10.95.
Chorao, Kay. *Shadow Night*. New York: Dutton, 2001; 32 pp., $15.99.

Chocolate, Deborah M. Newton. *Kwanzaa*. New York: Children's Press, 1990; 31 pp., $17.10.
Chocolate, Deborah M. *My First Kwanzaa Book*. New York: Scholastic, 1992; 32 pp., $10.95.
Chocolate, Debbi. *Kente Colors*. New York: Walker, 1996; 32 pp., $15.95.
Choldenko, Gennifer. *Moonstruck: The True Story of the Cow who Jumped over the Moon*. New York: Hyperion, 1997; 34 pp., $14.95.
Christelow, Eileen. *Don't Wake Up Mama*. Boston: Clarion, 1992; 32 pp., $15.00.
Christelow, Eileen. *Five Little Monkeys Bake a Birthday Cake*. Boston: Clarion, 1992; 32 pp., $5.95.
Christelow, Eileen. *Five Little Monkeys Play Hide and Seek*. Boston: Clarion, 2004; 32 pp., $15.00.
Christelow, Eileen. *Five Little Monkeys Sitting in a Tree*. Boston: Clarion, 1991; 32 pp., $15.00.
Christelow, Eileen. *Gertrude, the Bulldog Detective*. Boston: Clarion, 1992; 32 pp., $13.95.
Chrustowski, Rick. *Bright Beetle*. New York: Henry Holt, 2000; 32 pp., $15.95.
Chupela, Dolores. *Once Upon a Childhood: Fingerplays, Action Rhymes and Fun Times for the Very Young*. Lanham, MD: Scarecrow, 1998; 119 pp., $19.95.
Chupela, Dolores. *Ready, Set, Go!: Children's Programming for Bookmobiles and other Small Spaces*. Fort Atkinson, WI: Alleyside, 1994; 228 pp., $19.95.
Churchill, E. Richard. *Holiday Paper Projects*. New York: Sterling, 1992; 128 pp., $14.95.
Clark, Emma Chichester. *I Love You, Blue Kangaroo*. New York: Doubleday, 1998; 32 pp., $15.95.
Clark, Emma Chichester. *What Shall We Do, Blue Kangaroo?* New York: Doubleday, 2002; 32 pp., $15.95.
Clark, Sondra. *Wearable Art with Sondra*. Roseville, CA: Prima, 2000; 193 pp., $12.95.
Claybourne, Anna. *Summer*. North Mankato, MN: Thameside, 2001; 32 pp., $24.25.
Cleary, Beverly. *The Hullabaloo ABC*. New York: Morrow, 1998; 30 pp., $15.93.
Clement, Rod. *Grandpa's Teeth*. New York: HarperCollins, 1997; 32 pp., $14.95.
Cnojewski, Carol. *Kwanzaa Crafts*. Berkeley Heights, NJ: Enslow, 2004; 32 pp., $22.60.
Coats, Lucy. *One Hungry Baby*. New York: Crown, 1994; 32 pp., $9.99.
Cocca-Leffler, Maryann. *Mr. Taneen's Ties Rule!* Morton Grove, IL: Albert Whitman, 2005; 32 pp., $15.95.
Coffert, Nancy. *What's Cookin'? A Happy Birthday Book*. San Francisco: Chronicle, 2003; 32 pp., $14.95.
Cohen, Izhar. *A-B-C Discovery*. New York: Dial, 1998; 32 pp., $17.99.
Cohen, Peter, and Olaf Landstrom. *Boris's Glasses*. New York: R & S Books, 2003; 32 pp., $15.00.
Cole, Babette. *The Bad Good Manners Book*. New York: Dial, 1995; 32 pp., $13.99.
Cole, Babette. *Tarzanna*. New York: Putnam, 1992; 30 pp., $14.95.
Cole, Babette. *The Trouble with Uncle*. New York: Little, Brown, 1992; 32 pp., $14.95.
Cole, Henry. *Jack's Garden*. New York: Greenwillow, 1995; 24 pp., $16.00.

Cole, Joanna. *The Magic Schoolbus Inside a Beehive.* New York: Scholastic, 1996; 48 pp., $15.95.
Cole, Joanna, and Stephanie Calmenson. *Pin the Tail on the Donkey.* New York: Morrow, 1993; 48 pp., $15.00.
Cole, Joanna, and Stephanie Calmenson. *The Eensy, Weensy Spider: Fingerplays and Action Rhymes.* New York: Morrow, 1991; 64 pp., $13.95.
Cole, Joanna. *How I Was Adopted.* New York: Morrow, 1995; 48 pp., $16.00.
Cole, Joanna. *My Friend the Doctor.* New York: HarperCollins, 2005; 32 pp., $6.99.
Cole, Joanna, and Stephanie Calmenson. *Rain or Shine Activity Book: Fun Things to Make and Do.* New York: Morrow, 1997; 192 pp., $20.00.
Coleman, Michael. *Hank the Clank.* Milwaukee, WI: Gareth Stevens, 1994; 32 pp., $19.95.
Collicutt, Paul. *This Rocket.* New York: Farrar, Straus & Giroux, 2005; 32 pp., $15.00.
Collins, Pat Lowery. *Don't Tease the Guppies.* New York: Putnam, 1994; 32 pp., $14.95.
Collins, Pat Lowery. *Tomorrow, Up and Away!* Boston: Houghton Mifflin, 1990; 32 pp., $13.95.
Collins, Stanley H. *Family and Community.* Eugene, Ore.: Garlic, 1999; 32 pp., $14.95.
Collins, Suzanne, and Mike Lester. *When Charlie McButton Lost Power.* New York: Putnam, 2005; 32 pp., $15.99.
Coman, Carolyn. *Losing Things at Mr. Mudd's.* New York: Farrar, Straus & Giroux, 1992; 32 pp., $14.00.
Compton, Ken and Joanne. *Granny Greenteeth and the Noise in the Night.* New York: Holiday House, 1993; 32 pp., $14.95.
Cook, Deanna F. (editor). *Family Fun Boredom Busters.* New York: Disney, 2002; 224 pp., $24.95.
Cook, Monica Hay. *Kickin' Up Some Cowboy Fun.* Tucson, AZ: Monjeu Press, 1999; 144 pp., $14.95.
Cooper, Helen. *The Bear Under the Stairs.* New York: Dial, 1993; 32 pp., $5.99.
Cooper, Helen. *The Boy Who Wouldn't Go to Bed.* New York: Dial, 1996; 32 pp., $14.99.
Cooper, Jason. *Fire Stations.* Vero Beach, FL: Rourke, 1992; 24 pp., $10.95.
Cooper, Jason. *Police Stations.* Vero Beach, FL: Rourke, 1992; 24 pp., $10.95.
Cooper, Kay. *Too Many Rabbits and Other Fingerplays.* New York: Scholastic, 1995; 48 pp., 12.95.
Copage, Eric. V. *Kwanzaa: An African-American Celebration of Culture and Cooking.* New York: Morrow, 1993; 356 pp., $25.00.
Corwin, Judith Hoffman. *My First Riddles.* New York: HarperCollins, 1998; 24 pp., $9.95.
Corwin, Judith Hoffman. *Native American Crafts of California, the Great Basin and the Southwest.* Danbury, CT: Franklin Watts, 2002; 48 pp., $26.50.
Costanzo, Charlene. *A Perfect Name.* New York: Dial, 2002; 32 pp., $15.99.
Cote, Nancy. *Palm Trees.* New York: Four Winds, 1993; 40 pp., $14.95.
Costello, David. *Here They Come!* New York: Farrar, Straus & Giroux, 2004; 32 pp., $15.00.
Cottringer, Anne. *Ella and the Naughty Lion.* Boston: Houghton Mifflin, 1996; 32 pp., $14.95.
Coursen, Valerie. *Mordant's Wish.* New York: Henry Holt, 1997; 32 pp., $15.95.

Cousins, Lucy. *Hooray for Fish!* Cambridge, MA: Candlewick, 2005; 32 pp., $14.99.
Cousins, Lucy. *Maisy Goes to the Library*. Cambridge, MA: Candlewick, 2005; 32 pp., $12.95.
Cousins, Lucy. *What Can Rabbit See?* New York: Tambourine, 1991; 16 pp., $12.95.
Cowcher, Helen. *Jaguar*. New York: Scholastic, 1997; 32 pp., $15.95.
Cowcher, Helen. *Rain Forest*. New York: Farrar, Straus & Giroux, 1997; 32 pp., $16.95.
Cowen-Fletcher, Jane. *Farmer Will*, Cambridge, MA: Candlewick, 2001; 32 pp., $14.99.
Cowley, Joy. Gracias, *The Thanksgiving Turkey*. New York: Scholastic, 1996; 32 pp., $15.95.
Cowley, Joy. *The Rusty, Trusty Tractor*. Honesdale, PA: Boyds Mills, 1999; 32 pp., $14.95.
Cowley, Joy. *The Wishing of Biddy Malone*. New York: Philomel, 2004; 32 pp., $15.99.
Cox, Judy. *Go to Sleep, Groundhog!* New York: Holiday House, 2004; 32 pp., $16.95.
Crebbin, June. *Danny's Duck*. Cambridge, MA: Candlewick, 1995; 32 pp., $13.95.
Crebbin, June. *The Train Ride*. Cambridge, MA: Candlewick, 1995; 32 pp., $14.95.
Crews, Donald. *Inside Freight Train*. New York: HarperCollins, 2001; 32 pp., $9.95.
Crews, Donald. *Shortcut*. New York: Greenwillow, 1992; 32 pp., $6.99.
Crimi, Carolyn. *Henry and the Buccaneer Bunnies*. Cambridge, MA: Candlewick, 2005; 32 pp., $15.99.
Crimi, Carolyn. *Outside, Inside*. New York: Simon & Schuster, 1995; 32 pp., $15.00.
Cronin, Doreen, and Betsy Lewin. *Click, Clack, Splish, Splash*. New York: Atheneum, 2006; 32 pp., $12.95.
Cronin, Doreen. *Diary of a Spider*. New York: HarperCollins, 2005; 32 pp., $16.89.
Crozat, Francois. *I Am a Little Alligator*. Hauppauge, NY: Barron's Educational Series, 1993; 24 pp., $8.95.
Crume, Marion. *Do You See Mouse?* Parsippany, NJ: Silver, 1995; 32 pp., $18.95.
Cuetara, Mittie. *The Crazy Crawler Crane and Other Very Short Truck Stories*. New York: Dutton, 1998; 32 pp., $14.99.
Cummings, Pat. *Anansi and the Lizard*. New York: Henry Holt, 2002; 32 pp., $16.95.
Cummings, Pat. *Clean your Room, Harvey Room!* New York: Bradbury, 1991; 32 pp., $16.00.
Cuneo, Mary Louise. *What Can a Giant Do?* New York: HarperCollins, 1994; 32 pp., $14.89.
Curtis, Jamie Lee, and Laura Curnell. *I'm Gonna Like Me*. New York: HarperCollins, 2002; 32 pp., $17.89.
Curtis, Jamie Lee. *Where Do Balloons Go?: An Uplifting Mystery*. New York: HarperCollins, 2000, 32 pp., $16.99.
Curtis, Regina. *The Little Hands Playtime! Book*. Charlotte, VT: Williamson, 2000; 120 pp., $12.95.
Cushman, Doug. *The Mystery of King Karfu*. New York: HarperCollins, 1996; 32 pp., $14.95.
Cutler, Jane. *The Birthday Doll*. New York: Farrar, Straus & Giroux, 2004; 32 pp., $16.00.
Cuyler, Margery. *Please Say Please!: Penguin's Guide to Manners*. New York: Scholastic, 2004; 32 pp., $15.95.
Cuyler, Margery. *Skeleton Hiccups*. New York: Margaret K. McElderry, 2002; 32 pp., $14.95.

Cuyler, Margery. *Stop, Drop and Roll.* New York: Simon & Schuster, 2001; 32 pp., $16.00.

Czernecki, Stefan, and Timothy Rhodes. *The Singing Snake.* New York: Hyperion, 1993; 40 pp., $14.89.

Czernecki, Stefan. *The Cricket's Cage.* New York: Hyperion, 1997; 32 pp., $15.49.

Dahl, Michael. *Do Ducks Live in the Desert?* Minneapolis, MN: Picture Window, 2004; 32 pp., $16.95.

Dahl, Michael. *Pass the Buck.* Minneapolis, MN: Picture Window, 2004; 32 pp., $16.95.

Dahlstrom, Carol Field. *Easy Crafts to Make Together: 750 Family Fun Ideas.* Des Moines, IA: Meredith, 2004; 288 pp., $24.95.

Dale, Penny. *The Elephant Tree.* New York: Putnam, 1991; 32 pp., $14.95.

Dale, Penny. *Ten Out of Bed.* Cambridge, MA: Candlewick, 1996; 26 pp., $5.99.

Dale, Elizabeth. *How Long?* New York: Orchard, 1998; 32 pp., $14.95.

Dalgliesh, Alice. T*he Fourth of July Story.* New York: Aladdin, 1995; 32 pp., $5.99.

Daly, Niki. *Jamela's Dress.* New York: Farrar, Straus & Giroux, 1999; 32 pp., $16.00.

Danneberg, Julie. *First Day Jitters.* Watertown, MA: Whispering Coyote, 2000; 32 pp., $16.95.

Daning, Tom (editor). *Fun-to-Make Crafts for Easter.* Honesdale, Pa.: Boyds Mills, 2005; 64 pp., $7.95.

Daning, Tom (editor). *Fun-to-Make Crafts for Every Day.* Honesdale, PA: Boyds Mills, 2005; 64 pp., $15.95.

Danrell, Liz. *With the Wind.* New York: Orchard, 1991; 32 pp., $9.27.

Darling, Kathy. *Holiday Hoopla: Songs and Finger Plays.* Ashland, OH: Monday Morning, 1990; 64 pp., NA.

Darling, Benjamin. *Valerie and the Silver Pear.* New York: Simon & Schuster,1992; 32 pp., $14.95.

Davies, Aubrey. *Bone Button Borscht.* Tonawanda, NY: Kids Can, 1997; 32 pp., $15.95.

Davies, Nicola. *Big Blue Whale.* Cambridge, MA: Candlewick, 1997; 32 pp., $15.99.

Davies, Nicola. *One Tiny Turtle.* Cambridge, MA: Candlewick, 2001; 32 pp., $15.99.

Davis, Carl, and Hiawyn Oram. *A Creepy Crawly Song Book.* New York: Farrar, Straus & Giroux, 1993; 55 pp., $17.00.

Davis, Gibbs. *The Other Emily.* Boston: Houghton Mifflin, 1990; 32 pp., $4.95.

Davis, Katie. *Who Hops?* San Diego: Harcourt, 1998; 32 pp., $13.00.

Davis, Maggie S. *A Garden of Whales.* Buffalo, NY: Camden House, 1993; 32 pp., $16.95.

Davis, Robin Works. *Toddle On Over.* Fort Atkinson, WI: Alleyside, 1998; 95 pp., $12.95.

Davison, Martine. *Maggie and the Emergency Room.* New York: Random House, 1992; 32 pp., $5.99.

Davison, Martine. *Robby Visits the Doctor.* New York: Random House, 1992; 32 pp., $5.99.

Davol, Marguerite. *The Heart of the Wood.* New York: Simon & Schuster, 1992; 32 pp., $14.00.

Davol, Marguerite W. *How Snake Got His Hiss.* New York: Orchard, 1996; 32 pp., $14.95.

Deady, Kathleen W. *Out and About at the Zoo*. Minneapolis, MN: Picture Window, 2003; 32 pp., $17.95.

Dealey, Erin. *Little Bo Peep Can't Get to Sleep*. New York: Atheneum, 2005; 32 pp., $15.95.

deBrunhoff, Laurent. *Babar's Yoga for Elephants*. New York: Abrams, 2002; 32 pp., $16.95.

Deed, Carmen Agra. *The Library Dragon*. Atlanta, GA: Peachtree, 1994; 32 pp., $16.95.

Deetlefs, Rene. *Tabu and the Dancing Elephants*. New York: Dutton, 1999; 32 pp., $14.99.

DeFelice, Cynthia. *Casey in the Bath*. New York: Farrar, Straus & Giroux, 1996; 24 pp., $14.00.

Degen, Bruce. *Daddy Is a Doodlebug*. New York: HarperCollins, 2000; 32 pp., $15.89.

DeGroat, Diane. *Good Night, Sleep Tight, Don't Let the Bedbugs Bite!* New York: Sea Star, 2002; 32 pp., $15.95.

DeGoat, Diane. *Roses are Pink, Your Feet Really Stink*. New York: Morrow, 1996; 32 pp., $15.00.

Delacre, Lulu. *Nathan's Balloon Adventure*. New York: Scholastic, 1991; 32 pp., $12.95.

Delton, Judy. *My Mom Made Me Go to School*. New York: Delacorte, 1991; 32 pp., $13.99.

DeLuise, Dom. *Charlie the Caterpillar*. New York: Simon & Schuster, 1990; 40 pp., $15.00.

DeMarest, Christ L. *Firefighters A to Z*. New York: Margaret K. McElderry, 2000; 32 pp., $17.00.

Demarest, Chris L. *Fall*. San Diego: Harcourt, 1996; 16 pp., $4.95.

Demi. *Dragon Kites and Dragonflies: A Collection of Chinese Nursery Rhymes*. San Diego: Harcourt, 1996; 32 pp., $14.95.

Demi. *The Dragon's Tale: And Other Animal Fables of the Chinese Zodiac*. New York: Henry Holt, 1996; 32 pp., $16.95.

DePaola, Tomie. *Bill and Pete to the Rescue*. New York: Putnam, 1998; 48 pp., $15.99.

DePaola, Tomie. *Jamie O'Rourke and the Big Potato*. New York: Putnam, 1992; 32 pp., $14.95.

DePaola, Tomie. *Strega Nona Meets Her Match*. New York: Putnam, 1993; 32 pp., $15.95.

DePaola, Tomie. *Strega Nona Takes a Vacation*. New York: Putnam, 2000; 32 pp., $16.99.

DePaola, Tomie. *T-Rex is Missing!* New York: Grosset and Dunlap, 2002; 32 pp., $11.80.

DeRubertis, Barbara. *Deena's Lucky Penny*. New York: Kane, 1999; 32 pp., $4.99.

Desimini, Lisa. *My House*. New York: Henry Holt, 1994; 32 pp., $15.95.

Dibble, Carole H., and Kathy H. Lee. *101 Easy Wacky Crazy Activities*. Beltsville, MD: Gryphon House, 2000; 128 pp., $12.95.

Diller, Harriett. *The Waiting Day*. New York: Green Tiger, 1994; 32 pp., $14.00.

DiPucchio, Kelly, and Howard Fine. *Bed Hogs*. New York: Hyperion, 2004; 32 pp., $15.99.

DiPucchio, Kelly. *Dinosnores*. New York: HarperCollins, 2005; 32 pp., $16.89.

DiPucchio, Kelly. *Mrs. McBloom, Clean Up Your Classroom!* New York: Hyperion, 2005; 32 pp., $15.99.

DiPucchio, Kelly. *What's the Magic Word?* New York: HarperCollins, 2005; 32 pp., $1.89.
Dixon, Ann. *Winter Is.* Portland, OR: Alaska Northwest, 2002; 32 pp., $15.95.
Dodds, Dayle Ann. *The Color Box.* New York: Little, Brown, 1992; 28 pp., $14.95.
Dodds, Siobhan. *Grumble Rumble!* New York: DK Publishing, 2000; 32 pp., $5.95.
Dodson, Emma. *Badly Drawn Dog.* Hauppauge, NY: Barron's Educational Series, 2005; 32 pp., $14.95.
Donaldson, Julia. *The Gruffalo.* New York: Dial, 1999; 32 pp., $15.99.
Donaldson, Julia. *The Spiffiest Giant in Town.* New York: Dial, 2002; 32 pp., $5.99.
Dooley, Virginia. *I Need Glasses: My Visit to the Optometrist.* New York: Mondo, 2002; 32 pp., $13.95.
Downs, Mike. *You See a Circus, I See See . . . .* Watertown, MA: Charlesbridge, 2005; 32 pp., $14.95.
Dragonwagon, Crescent. *Annie Flies the Birthday Bike.* New York: Macmillan, 1993; 32 pp., $14.95.
Dubanevich, Arlene. *Calico Cows.* New York: Viking, 1993; 32 pp., $10.95.
Dubanevich, Arlene. *Tom's Tail.* New York: Viking, 1990; 32 pp., $13.95.
Dugan, Barbara. *Leaving Home with a Pickle Jar.* New York: Greenwillow, 1993; 32 pp., $12.05.
Dumbleton, Mike. *Dial-a-Croc.* New York: Orchard, 1991; 32 pp., $15.00.
Duncan, Lois. *The Longest Hair in the World.* New York: Doubleday, 1999; 32 pp., $15.95.
Dunbar, Joyce. *Lolopy.* New York: Macmillan, 1991; 32 pp., $14.95.
Dunbar, Joyce. *Shoe Baby.* Cambridge, MA: Candlewick, 2005; 32 pp., $15.99.
Dunn, Carolyn. *A Pie Went By.* New York: HarperCollins, 1999; 32 pp., $14.89.
Dupasquier, Philippe. *Andy's Pirate Ship: A Spot-the-Difference Book.* New York: Henry Holt, 1994; 32 pp., $11.95.
Duquennoy, Jacques. *The Ghost's Dinner.* New York: Western, 1994; 48 pp., $9.95.
DuQuennoy, Jacques. *The Ghosts' Trip to Loch Ness.* San Diego: Harcourt, 1996; 32 pp., $11.00.
DuQuette, Keith. *Cock-a-Doodle Moooo!: A Mixed-Up Menagerie.* New York: Putnam, 2004; 32 pp., $15.99.
Dyer, Heather. *Tina and the Penguin.* Tonawanda, NY: Kids Can, 2002; 32 pp., $14.95.
Eagle, Kin. *It's Raining, It's Pouring.* Watertown, MA: Whispering Coyote, 1994; 32 pp., $15.95.
Eagon, Robynne. *Game for a Game?* Carthage, IL: Teaching and Learning, 1995; 144 pp., $13.95.
Edwards, Pamela Duncan. *Dear Tooth Fairy.* New York: Katherine Tegen, 2003; 32 pp., $16.89.
Edwards, Pamela Duncan. *McGillycuddy Could!* New York: Katherine Tegen, 2005; 32 pp., $14.99.
Edwards, Pamela Duncan. *Roar!: A Noisy Counting Book.* New York: HarperCollins, 2000; 32 pp., $15.89.
Edwards, Pamela Duncan. *Rude Mule.* New York: Henry Holt, 2002; 32 pp., $15.95.
Edwards, Nancy. *Glenna's Seeds.* Washington, D.C.: Child and Family, 2001; 32 pp., $9.95.

Edwards, Pamela Duncan. *Warthogs Paint: A Messy Color Book.* New York: Hyperion, 2001; 32 pp., $14.99.

Edmonds, Lyra. *An African Princess.* Cambridge, MA: Candlewick, 2004; 32 pp., $15.99.

Edwardson, Debby Dahl. *Whale Snow.* Watertown, MA: Talewinds, 2003; 32 pp., $15.95.

Egan, Tim. *Chestnut Cove.* Boston: Houghton Mifflin, 1995; 32 pp., $14.95.

Ehlert, Lois. *Feathers for Lunch.* San Diego: Harcourt, 1990; 32 pp., $15.00.

Ehlert, Lois. *Pie in the Sky.* San Diego: Harcourt, 2004; 32 pp., $16.00

Ehlert, Lois. *Snowballs.* San Diego: Harcourt, 1995; 32 pp., $15.00.

Elliot, Marion. *My Party Book.* New York: Little, Brown, 1994; 96 pp., $14.95.

Elliot, Marion. *Paper Fun for Kids.* New York: Smithmark, 1994; 96 pp., $20.00.

Elliott, Dan. *Ernie's Little Lie.* New York: Random House, 1992; 40 pp., $4.95.

Elliott, George. *The Boy Who Loved Bananas.* Tonawanda, NY: Kids Can, 2005; 32 pp., $15.95.

Elliott, Laura Malone. *Hunter and Stripe and the Soccer Showdown.* New York: Katherine Tegen, 2005; 32 pp., $16.89.

Ellison, Sheila. *365 Games Toddlers Play.* Naperville, IL: Sourcebooks, 2003; 370 pp., $12.95.

Elschner, Geraldine. *The Easter Chick.* New York: North South, 2003; 32 pp., $16.50.

Emberley, Ed. *Go Away Big Green Monster.* New York: Little, Brown, 1992; 32 pp., $14.45.

Emberley, Michael. *Ruby.* New York: Little, Brown, 1990; 32 pp., $14.95.

Emberley, Rebecca. *My Mother's Secret Life.* New York: Little, Brown, 1998; 32 pp., $15.95.

Emberley, Rebecca. *Piñata!* New York: Little, Brown, 2004; 32 pp., $14.95.

Emmett, Jonathan. *No Place Like Home.* Cambridge, MA: Candlewick, 2004; 32 pp., $15.99.

Emmett, Jonathan. *Someone Bigger.* Boston: Clarion, 2003; 32 pp., $16.00.

Enderle, Judith Ross. *A Pile of Pigs.* Honesdale, PA: Boyds Mills, 1993; 32 pp., $10.95.

Enderle, Judith Ross, and Stephanie Gordon Tessler. *Where Are You, Little Zack?* Boston: Houghton Mifflin, 1997; 32 pp., $14.95.

Engel. Diana. *Eleanor, Arthur and Claire.* New York: Macmillan, 1992; 32 pp., $14.95.

Engelbreit, Mary. *Hey Kids! Come Craft with Me.* Des Moines, IA: Meredith, 1999; 112 pp., $19.95.

Engelbreit, Mary. *Queen of Easter.* New York: HarperCollins, 2006; 32 pp., $16.89.

Engelbreit, Mary. *Queen of Hearts.* New York: HarperCollins, 2005; 32 pp., $15.99.

Ericsson, Jennifer A. *The Most Beautiful Kid in the World.* New York: Tambourine, 1996; 32 pp., $16.00.

Erlbach, Arlene. *Happy Birthday Everywhere.* Minneapolis, MN: Millbrook, 1997; 48 pp., $23.90.

Erlbach, Arlene. *Sidewalk Games Around the World.* Minneapolis, MN: Millbrook, 1997; 64 pp., $23.90.

Ernst, Lisa Campbell. *The Bee.* New York: Lothrop, Lee and Shepard, 1986; 32 pp., $11.75.

Ernst, Lisa Campbell. *Bubba and Trixie.* New York: Simon & Schuster, 1997; 32 pp., $16.00.

Ernst, Lisa Campbell. *The Letters Are Lost*. New York: Viking, 1996; 32 pp., $14.99.
Ernst, Lisa Campbell. *Wake Up, It's Spring!* New York: HarperCollins, 2004; 32 pp., $16.89.
Ernst, Lisa Campbell. *Walter's Tail*. New York: Bradbury, 1992; 32 pp., $14.95.
Esche, Maria Bonfanti, and Clare Bonfanti Braham. *Kids Celebrate!* Chicago: Chicago Review Press, 1998; 300 pp., $16.95.
Evans, Lezlie. *Rain Song*. Boston: Houghton Mifflin, 1995; 32 pp., $14.95.
Evans, Story, and Lise O'Haire. *Hey Mom, I'm Bored!* New York: Three Rivers, 2000; 136 pp., $9.00.
Eversole, Robyn. *Flood Fish*. New York: Crown, 1995; 32 pp., $17.99.
Eversole, Robyn. *The Magic House*. New York: Orchard, 1992; 32 pp., $13.99.
Falk, John H., Robert L. Pruitt II, Kristi S. Rosenberg, and Tali A. Katz. *Bubble Monster and Other Science Fun*. Chicago: Chicago Review Press, 1996; 172 pp., $17.95.
Falwell, Cathryn. *Turtle Splash! Countdown at the Pond*. New York: Greenwillow, 2001; 32 pp., $15.89.
Famini, Karen, Karen Large, Bickey Shiotsu, and Rozanne Lanczak Williams. *Perfect Kids' Parties*. New York: Sterling, 2000; 128 pp., $14.95.
Fanilkner, Keith. *Pop! Went Another Balloon!* New York: Dutton, 2002; 32 pp., $10.99.
Farber, Norma. *Return of the Shadows*. New York: HarperCollins, 1992; 32 pp., $15.00.
Farmer, Nancy. *Runnery Granary*. New York: Greenwillow, 1996; 32 pp., $14.93.
Farrell, Sue. *To the Post Office with Mama*. Carlsbad, CA: Annick, 1994; 24 pp., $14.95.
Farris, Diane. *In Dolphin Time*. New York: Four Winds, 1994; 32 pp., $14.95.
Faulkner, William J. *Brer Tiger and the Big Wind*. New York: Morrow, 1995; 32 pp., $15.00.
Fearnley, Jan. *Mr. Wolf's Pancakes*. Wilton, WI: Little Tiger, 2001; 32 pp., $14.99.
Fearnley, Jan. *Mr. Wolf and the Three Bears*. San Diego: Harcourt, 2001; 32 pp., $16.00.
Fearnley, Jan. *Watch out!* Cambridge, MA: Candlewick, 2004; 32 pp., $15.99.
Feder, Paula. *Where Does the Teacher Live?* New York: Dutton, 1996; 48 pp., $12.95.
Feierabend, John M. *The Book of Fingerplays and Action Songs*. Chicago: GIA Publications, 2003; 84 pp., $11.95.
Feiffer, Jules. *I Lost My Bear*. New York: Morrow, 1998; 32 pp., $16.00.
Feldman, Jean. *Transition Tips and Tricks for Teachers*. Beltsville, MD: Gryphon, 2000; 216 pp., $19.95.
Fiarotta, Phyllis and Noel. *Cups and Cans and Paper Plate Fans*. New York: Sterling, 1992; 192 pp., $19.95.
Fiarotta, Phyllis and Noel. *Music Crafts for Kids*. New York: Sterling, 1993; 160 pp., $19.95.
Fine, Anne. *Poor Monty*. Boston: Clarion, 1991; 32 pp., $14.95.
Finn, Isobel, and Jack Tickle. *The Very Lazy Ladybug*. Wilton, CT: Tiger Tales, 1999; 32 pp., $14.95
Fischer, Carolyn. *A Twisted Tale*. New York: Knopf, 2002; 32 pp., $16.00.
Fisher, Leonard Everett. *Sailboat Lost*. New York: Macmillan, 1991; 32 pp., $15.95.
Fisher, Leonard Everett. *William Tell*. New York: Farrar, Straus & Giroux, 1996; 32 pp., $16.00.

Flanagan, Alice K. *Officer Brown Keeps Neighborhoods Safe*. New York: Children's Press, 1998; 32 pp., $19.50.
Flanagan, Alice K. *Dr. Kranner, Dentist with a Smile*. New York: Children's Press, 1997; 32 pp., $19.00.
Fleming, Denise. *Lunch*. New York: Henry, Holt, 1992; 32 pp., $15.95.
Fleming, Denise. *Where Once There Was a Wood*. New York: Henry, Holt, 1996; 32 pp., $15.95.
Flood, Bo. *I'll Go to School If*. . . . Minneapolis, MN: Fairview, 1997; 32 pp., $14.95.
Florian, Douglas. *At the Zoo*. New York: Greenwillow, 1992; 32 pp., $13.93.
Florian, Douglas. *A Beach Day*. New York: Greenwillow, 1990; 32 pp., $12.95.
Florian, Douglas. *A Chef: How We Work*. New York: Greenwillow, 1992; 32 pp., $13.93.
Florian, Douglas. *A Painter: How We Work*. New York: Greenwillow, 1993; 32 pp., $14.00.
Florie, Christine. *Lara Ladybug*. New York: Children's Press, 2005; 32 pp., $17.00.
Fluet, Connie. *A Day in the Life of a Nurse*. Mankato, MN: Capstone, 2005; 32 pp., $15.95.
Fontes, Justine. *The Littlest Leprechaun*. New York: Little Simon, 2003; 20 pp., $4.99.
Ford, Juwanda G. *K is for Kwanzaa*. New York: Scholastic, 1997; 32 pp., $10.95.
Ford, Miela. *SunFlower*. New York: Greenwillow, 1995; 32 pp., $15.93.
Ford, Miela. *What Color Was the Sky Today?* New York: Greenwillow, 1997; 24 pp., $15.00.
Foreman, George, and Fran Manushkin. *George Foreman: Let George Do It!* New York: Simon & Schuster, 2005; 32 pp., $15.95.
Fowler, Allan. *Feeling Things*. New York: Children's Press, 1991; 32 pp., $17.30.
Fowler, Allan. *Hearing Things*. New York: Children's Press, 1991; 32 pp., $18.00.
Fowler, Allan. *Seeing Things*. New York: Children's Press, 1991; 32 pp., $18.00.
Fowler, Allan. *Smelling Things*. New York: Children's Press, 1991; 32 pp., $18.00.
Fowler, Allan. *Tasting Things*. New York: Children's Press, 1991; 32 pp., $18.00.
Fowler, Susi L. *Fog*. New York: Greenwillow, 1992; 32 pp., $13.95.
Fowler, Susi L. *When Joel Comes Home*. New York: Greenwillow, 1993; 24 pp., $13.95.
Fox, Christyan and Diane. *Astronaut Piggy Wiggy*. Brooklyn, NY: Handprint, 2001; 32 pp., $9.95.
Fox, Christyan and Diane. *What Shape Is that, Piggy Wiggy?* Brooklyn, NY: Handprint, 2002; 10 pp., $5.95.
Fox, Dan. *Songs of the Wild West*. New York: Simon & Schuster, 1991; 128 pp., $19.95.
Fox, Mem. *Boo to a Goose*. New York: Dial, 1998; 32 pp., $14.99.
Fox, Mem. *The Magic Hat*. San Diego: Harcourt, 2002; 32 pp., $16.00.
Fox, Mem. *Tough Boris*. San Diego: Harcourt, 1994; 32 pp., $15.00.
Fox, Mem. *Zoo-Looking*. New York: Mondo, 1996; 32 pp., $14.95.
Frazer, Mary Ann. *I. Q. Goes to School*. New York: Walker, 2002; 32 pp., $16.85.
Fraser, Mary Ann. *I.Q. It's Time*. New York: Walker, 2005; 32 pp., $16.85.
Freedman, Claire. *Where's Your Smile, Crocodile?* Atlanta, GA: Peachtree, 2001; 32 pp., $16.95.
Freeman, Don. *Gregory's Shadow*. New York: Viking, 2000; 32 pp., $15.99.
Freeman, Dorothy Thoses, and Dianne M. MacMillan. *Kwanzaa*. Berkeley Heights, NJ: Enslow, 1992; 48 pp., $18.95.

French, Fiona. *King of Another Country*. New York: Scholastic, 1992; 32 pp., $14.95.
French, Simon, and Donna Rawlins. *Guess the Baby*. Boston: Clarion, 2002; 32 pp., $14.00.
French, Vivian. *A Christmas Star Called Hannah*. Cambridge, MA: Candlewick, 1997; 22 pp., $9.99.
French, Vivian. *Growing Frogs*. Cambridge, MA: Candlewick, 2000; 32 pp., $15.99.
French, Vivian. *Oliver's Fruit Salad*. New York: Orchard, 1998; 32 pp., $14.95.
French, Vivian. *Red Hen and Sly Fox*. New York: Simon & Schuster, 1994; 32 pp., $15.00.
French, Vivian. *T-Rex*. Cambridge, MA: Candlewick, 2004; 32 pp., $15.99.
Freymann, Saxton. *Food for Thought: The Complete Book of Concepts for Growing Minds*. New York: Scholastic, 2005; 32 pp., $14.95.
Friedman, Arthur. *Hanukkah: Festival of Lights*. Honesdale, PA: Boyds Mills, 2000; 64 pp., $7.95.
Friedman, Mel, and Ellen Weiss. *Kitten Castle*. New York: Kane, 2001; 32 pp., $4.95.
Friedrich, Molly. *You're Not My REAL Mother!* New York: Little, Brown, 2004; 32 pp., $15.99.
Friend, David. *Baseball, Football, Daddy and Me*. New York: Viking, 1990; 32 pp., $12.95.
Funke, Cornelia. *The Princess Knight*. New York: Chicken House, 2001; 32 pp., $15.99.
Fyke, Nancy, Lynn Nejam, and Vicki Overstreet. *Great Parties for Kids*. Charlotte, VT: Williamson, 1994; 128 pp., $10.95.
Gaffney, Timothy R. *Grandpa Takes Me to the Moon*. New York: Tambourine, 1996; 32 pp, $16.00.
Gag, Wanda. *The Funny Thing*. New York: Putnam, 1999; 32 pp., $9.98.
Gag, Wanda. *Millions of Cats*. New York: Putnam, 1996; 32 pp., $12.99.
Galdone, Paul. *The Three Little Pigs*. Boston.: Houghton Mifflin, 1998; 32 pp., $9.95.
Galef, David. *Tracks*. New York: Morrow, 1996; 32 pp., $16.00.
Gantos, Jack, and Nicole Rubel. *Back to School for Rotten Ralph*. New York: HarperCollins, 1998; 32 pp., $14.95.
Gardella, Tricia. *Casey's New Hat*. Boston: Houghton Mifflin, 1997; 32 pp., $14.95.
Garelli, Cristina. *Forest Friends! Five Senses*. New York: Knopf, 2001; 32 pp., $16.99.
Garland, Michael. *The Great Easter Egg Hunt*. New York: Dutton, 2005; 32 pp., $15.99.
Garland, Michael. *Miss Smith's Incredible Storybook*. New York: Dutton, 2003; 32 pp., $16.99.
Gauch, Patricia Lee. *Christina Katerina and the Great Bear Train*. New York: Putnam, 1990; 32 pp., $14.95.
Geisel, Theodor. *The 500 Hats of Bartholomew Cubbins*. New York: Vanguard, 1990; 44 pp., $14.00.
Geoghegan, Adrienne. *Dog's Don't Wear Glasses*. New York: Crocodile, 1996; 32 pp., $14.95.
George, Jean Craighead. *Dear Rebecca, Winter is Here*. New York: HarperCollins, 1993; 32 pp., $15.00.
George, Kristine O'Connell. *Book!* Boston: Clarion, 2001; 32 pp., $9.95.
George, Kristine O'Connell. *One Mitten*. Boston: Clarion, 2004; 32 pp., $15.00.
Geraghty, Paul. *Slobcat*. New York: Macmillan, 1991; 32 pp., $13.95.

Geraghty, Paul. *Solo*. New York: Crown, 1995; 32 pp., $18.99.
Gerard, Valerie J. *Summer: Signs of the Season Around North America*. Minneapolis, MN: Picture Window, 2003; 32 pp., $16.95.
Gerber, Carole. *Leaf Jumpers*. Watertown, MA: Charlesbridge, 2004; 32 pp., $15.95.
Gershator, Phillis. *Zzzng! Zzzng! Zzzng!: A Yoruba Tale*. New York: Orchard, 1998; 32 pp., $15.95.
Gerson, Mary Joan. *People of Corn*. New York: Little, Brown, 1995; 32 pp., $15.95.
Gerstein, Mordicai. *Carolinda Clatter!* New York: Roaring Brook, 2005; 32 pp., $16.95.
Gerstein, Mordicai. *The Story of May*. New York: HarperCollins, 1993; 48 pp., $15.89.
Giannini, Enzo. *Zorina Ballerina*. New York: Simon & Schuster, 1993; 32 pp., $14.00.
Gibala-Broxholm, Janice. *Let Me Do It!* New York: Bradbury, 1994; 32 pp, $14.95.
Gibbons, Gail. *Giant Pandas*. New York: Holiday House, 2002; 32 pp., $16.95.
Gibbons, Gail. *The Honey Makers*. New York: Morrow, 1997; 32 pp., $15.95.
Gibbons, Gail. *Penguins!* New York: Holiday House, 1998; 32 pp., $16.95.
Gibbons, Gail. *Pirates: Robbers of the High Seas*. New York: Little, Brown, 1993; 32 pp., $15.95.
Gibbons, Gail. *St. Patrick's Day*. New York: Holiday House, 1994; 32 pp., $15.95.
Gibbons, Gail. *Thanksgiving Is . . .* New York: Holiday House, 2004; 32 pp., $16.95.
Gibbons, Gail. *Yippee-Yay!: A Book about Cowboys and Cowgirls*. New York: Little, Brown, 1998; 32 pp., $14.95.
Gibbs, Dorothy L. *Let's Create: Paper*. Milwaukee, WI: Gareth Stevens, 2004; 32 pp., $23.33.
Giffard, Hannah. *Red Fox on the Move*. New York: Dial, 1992; 28 pp., $14.00.
Gikow, Louise A. *The Big Game*. New York: Children's Press, 2004; 32 pp., $18.50.
Gilpin, Rebecca. *Valentine Things to Make and Do*. Tulsa, OK: EDC Publishing, 2005; 32 pp., $8.95.
Ginolfi, Arthur. *The Tiny Snowflake*. Nashville, TN: Tommy Nelson, 2003; 32 pp., $7.99.
Girl Scouts of U.S. Of America. *Games for Girl Scouts*. New York: Girl Scouts of the USA, 1990; 128 pp., $6.50.
Givens, Terryl. *Dragon Scales and Willow Leaves*. New York: Putnam, 1997; 32 pp., $12.95.
Glaser, Linda. *The Borrowed Hanukkah Latkes*. Morton Grove, IL: Albert Whitman, 1997; 32 pp., $15.95.
Glaser, Linda. *It's Fall!* Minneapolis, MN: Millbrook, 2001; 32 pp., $16.43.
Glaser, Linda. *It's Spring!* Minneapolis, MN: Millbrook, 2002; 32 pp., $16.43.
Glaser, Linda. *It's Summer!* Minneapolis, MN: Millbrook, 2003; 32 pp., $7.95.
Glass, Andrew. *Charles Tarzan McBiddle*. New York: Doubleday, 1993; 32 pp., $15.00.
Glass, Beth Raisner, and Susan Lubner. *Noises at Night*. New York: Abrams, 2005; 32 pp., $15.95.
Glennon, Karen M. *Miss Eva and the Red Balloon*. New York: Simon & Schuster, 1990; 32 pp., $13.95.
Gliori, Debi. *Mr. Bear Babysits*. New York: Western, 1994; 32 pp., $13.95.
Gliori, Debi. *Penguin Post*. San Diego: Harcourt, 2002; 32 pp., $16.00.
Gliori, Debi. *Where Did that Baby Come From?* San Diego: Harcourt, 2004; 32 pp., $16.00

Goennel, Heidi. *The Circus.* New York: Tambourine, 1992; 32 pp., $15.00.
Goffe, Toni. *Joe Giant's Missing Boot: A Mothergooseville Story.* New York: Lothrop, Lee and Shepard, 1990; 32 pp., $12.95.
Goins, Barbara Lyerly; Karen J. Goldfluss; Doris J. Guerette; Ina Massler Levin; and Patricia Miriani Sima. *Arts, Crafts and More.* Westminster, CA: Teacher Created Materials, 1999; 160 pp., $12.99.
Goldin, Barbara Diamond. *Cakes and Miracles: A Purim Tale.* New York: Viking, 1991; 32 pp., $13.95.
Goldin, David. *Go-Go-Go!* New York: Abrams, 2000; 32 pp., $16.95.
Goldsmith, Howard. *Sleepy Little Owl.* New York: Learning Triangle, 1997; 32 pp., $12.95.
Goldstone, Bruce. *The Beastly Feast.* New York: Henry, Holt, 1998; 32 pp., $15.95.
Gomez, Rebecca. *It's St. Patrick's Day.* New York: Scholastic, 2003; 32 pp., $3.99.
Good, Elaine W. *Fall is Here! I Love it!* Intercourse, PA: Good Books, 1990; 32 pp., $12.95.
Goode, Diane. *Monkey Mo Goes to Sea.* New York: Blue Sky, 2002; 32 pp., $15.95.
Goodman, Joan Elizabeth. *Bernard's Bath.* Honesdale, Pa.: Boyds Mills, 1996; 32 pp., $14.95.
Gorbachev, Valeeri. *Big Little Elephant.* San Diego: Gulliver, 2005; 32 pp., $16.00.
Gorbachev, Valeri. *Ms. Turtle the Babysitter.* New York: HarperCollins, 2005; 32 pp., $16.89.
Goren, Ada, Mackie Rhodes, and Jan Trautman, editors. *The Mailbox October Arts and Crafts: Preschool–Kindergarten.* Greensboro, NC: Education Center, 2000; 32 pp., $6.95.
Goren, Ada, and Allison E. Ward. *Songs, Poems, and Fingerplays: Preschool/Kindergarten.* Greensboro, NC: Education Center, 1998; 192 pp., $22.95.
Goss, Linda. *The Frog Who Wanted to Be a Singer.* New York: Orchard, 1996; 40 pp., $15.95.
Gould, Roberta. *Making Cool Crafts and Awesome Art.* Charlotte, VT: Williamson, 1998; 158 pp., $12.95.
Grambling, Lois G. *Shoo! Scat!* Tarrytown, NY: Marshall Cavendish, 2004; 32 pp., $16.95.
Gravois, Jeanne M. *Quickly, Quigley.* New York: Tambourine, 1993; 32 pp., $14.00.
Gray, Kes. *Billy's Bucket.* Cambridge, MA: Candlewick, 2003; 32 pp., $15.99.
Gray, Kes. *Cluck O'Clock.* New York: Holiday House, 2003; 32 pp., $16.95.
Gray, Libba Moore. *Is There Room on the Feather Bed?* New York: Orchard, 32 pp., $16.95.
Gray, Libba Moore. *Small Green Snake.* New York: Orchard, 1994; 32 pp., $14.95.
Gray, Rita. *Nonna's Porch.* New York: Hyperion, 2004; 32 pp., $15.99.
Greco, Francesca. *Cyril the Mandrill.* Long Island City, NY: Star Bright, 2005; 32 pp., $16.95.
Green, Jen. *Why Throw It Away? Making Crazy Animals.* New York: Gloucester, 1992; 32 pp., $20.00.
Greenberg, David T. *Snakes!* New York: Little, Brown, 2004; 32 pp., $15.95.
Greenblat, Rodney A. *Aunt Ippy's Museum of Junk.* New York: HarperCollins, 1991; 32 pp., $14.90.

Greene, Carol. *Cat and Bear*. New York: Hyperion, 1998; 32 pp., $14.49.
Greene, Carol. *Police Officers Protect People*. New York: Child's World, 1997; 32 pp., $21.36.
Greene, Rhonda Gowler. *Firebears: The Rescue Team*. New York: Henry Holt, 2005; 32 pp., $15.95.
Greene, Rhonda Gowler. *This is the Teacher*. New York: Dutton, 2004; 32 pp., $15.99.
Greene, Rhonda Gowler. *When a Line Bends . . . Shape Begins*. Boston: Houghton Mifflin, 1997; 32 pp., $16.00.
Greenstein, Elaine. *As Big as You*. New York: Knopf, 2002; 32 pp., $6.99.
Greenstein, Elaine. *Mrs. Rose's Garden*. New York: Simon & Schuster, 1996; 28 pp., $15.00.
Greenstein, Elaine. *Emily and the Crows*. Boston: Picture Book Studios USA, 1992; 32 pp., $14.95.
Gregory, Valiska. *Babysitting for Benjamin*. New York: Little, Brown, 1993; 32 pp., $13.95.
Gregory, Valiska. *Kate's Giants*. Cambridge, MA: Candlewick, 1995; 40 pp., $14.95.
Greydanus, Rose. *Animals at the Zoo*. New York: Troll Associates, 1997; 32 pp., $2.50.
Grier, Ella. *Seven Days of Kwanzaa*. New York: Viking, 1997; 32 pp., $10.99.
Griffin, Kitty, and Kathy Combs. *Cowboy Sam and Those Confounded Secrets*. Boston: Clarion, 2001; 32 pp., $15.00.
Grindley, Sally. *Don't Rock the Boat!* New York: DK Publishing, 2001; 32 pp., $14.10.
Grindley, Sally. *Where Are My Chicks?* New York: Penguin Putnam, 2002; 32 pp., $9.99.
Grossman, Bill. *My Ltitle Sister Ate One Hare*. New York: Crown, 1996; 24 pp., $17.99.
Guest, Elissa Haden. *Iris and Walter: Lost and Found*. San Diego: Gulliver, 2004; 32 pp., $15.00.
Gugler, Laurel Dee. *There's a Billy Goat in the Garden*. Cambridge, MA: Barefoot, 2003; 32 pp., $14.99.
Guiberson, Brenda Z. *The Emperor Lays an Egg*. New York: Henry Holt, 2001; 32 pp., $16.95.
Gunson, Christopher. *Over on the Farm*. New York: Scholastic, 1995; 32 pp., $15.95.
Gurney, John Steven. *Dinosaur Train*. New York: HarperCollins, 2002; 32 pp., $14.99.
Guthrie, Woody. *New Baby Train*. New York: Little, Brown, 1999; 32 pp., $15.99.
Guthrie, Woody, and Marjorie Mazia Gunthrie. *Woody's 20 Grow Big Songs*. New York: HarperCollins, 1992; 48 pp., $16.00.
Guy, Rose. *Mother Crocodile*. New York: Delacorte, 1996; 32 pp., $6.50.
Haas, Jessie. *Mowing*. New York: Greenwillow, 1994; 32 pp., $14.00.
Hadithi, Mwenye. *Lazy Lion*. New York: Little, Brown, 1990; 32 pp., $14.95.
Hadithi, Mwenye, and Adrienne Kennaway. *Hungry Hyena*. New York: Little, Brown, 1994; 32 pp., $15.95.
Hague, Michael. *The Perfect Present*. New York: Morrow, 1996; 32 pp., $16.00.
Hall, Zoe. *The Apple Pie Tree*. New York: Blue Sky, 1996; 32 pp., $13.95.
Hall, Zoe. *Fall Leaves Fall!* New York: Scholastic, 2000; 32 pp., $15.95.
Hall, Zoe. *The Surprise Garden*. New York: Blue Sky, 1998; 32 pp., $15.95.
Hall, Donald. *Lucy's Summer*. San Diego: Browndeer, 1995; 40 pp., $15.00.
Halpern, Shari. *Moving from One to Ten*. New York: Macmillan, 1993; 32 pp., $13.95.

Hallworth, Grace. *Sing Me a Story: Song-and-Dance Tales from the Caribbean.* Little Rock, AR: August House Little Folk, 2002; 32 pp., $19.95.
Hamm, Diane Johnston. *Rock-a-Bye Farm.* New York: Simon & Schuster, 1992; 40 pp., $15.00.
Hamsa, Bobbie. *Your Pet Penguin.* New York: Children's Press, 1994; 32 pp., $17.60.
Hamilton, Kersten. *Firefighters to the Rescue!* New York: Viking, 2005; 32 pp., $15.99.
Hancock, David; Jill Hancock; Anna Murray; Lyn Orton; Cheryl Owen; and Lynda Watts. *The Grolier Kids Crafts Papercraft Book.* New York: Grolier, 1997; 48 pp., $15.00.
Harell, Beatrice Orcutt. *How Thunder and Lightning Came to Be.* New York: Dial, 1995; 32 pp., $14.89.
Hariton, Anca. *Butterfly Story.* New York: Dutton, 1995; 32 pp., $14.99.
Harper, Dan. *Telling Time with Big Mama Cat.* San Diego: Harcourt, 1998; 32 pp., $15.00.
Harper, Piers. *Little Owl.* New York: Scholastic, 2004; 32 pp., $15.95.
Harper, Wilhelmina. *The Gunniwolf.* New York: Dutton, 2003; 32 pp., $15.99.
Harrison, David L. *When Cows Come Home.* Honesdale, PA: Boyds Mills, 1994; 32 pp., $15.95.
Harry, Cindy Groom, and staff. *One-Hour Holiday Crafts for Kids.* Lincolnwood, IL: Publications International, 1994; 64 pp., $4.95.
Hartley, Karen, and Christ Macro. *Ladybug.* Barrington, IL: Heinemann, 1998; 32 pp., $14.95.
Harvey, Amanda. *Stormy Weather.* New York: Lothrop, Lee and Shepard, 1991; 32 pp., $13.95.
Hasbrouck, Ellen K. *Library Storyhour from A to Z.* New York: Center for Applied Research in Education, 1998; 269 pp., $28.95.
Hassett, John and Ann. *We Got My Brother at the Zoo.* Boston: Houghton Mifflin, 1993; 32 pp., $14.95.
Haugen, Brenda. *St. Patrick's Day.* Minneapolis, MN: Picture Window, 2004; 32 pp., $16.95.
Hauser, Jill Frankel. *Easy Art Fun! Do-it-yourself Crafts for Beginning Readers.* Charlotte, VT: Williamson, 2002; 112 pp., $12.95.
Hauser, Jill Frankel. *Little Hands Celebrate America!* Charlotte, VT: Williamson, 2004; 128 pp., $12.95.
Hauser, Jill Frankel. *Wow! I'm Reading!* Charlotte, VT: Williamson, 2000; 141 pp., $12.95.
Hautzig, Deborah. *Little Witch Learns to Read.* New York: Random House, 2003; 32 pp., $11.99.
Havill, Juanita. *Jamaica's Blue Marker.* Boston: Houghton Mifflin, 1995; 28 pp., $15.00.
Hawkes, Kevin. *His Royal Buckliness.* New York: Lothrop, Lee and Shepard, 1992; 32 pp., $14.93.
Hawkins, Colin and Jacqui. *Fairytale News.* Cambridge, MA: Candlewick, 2004; 32 pp., $15.99.
Hayes, Sarah. *Mary, Mary.* New York: Margaret K. McElderry, 1990; 32 pp., $13.95.
Hayes, Sarah. *The Grumpalump.* Boston: Clarion, 1990; 32 pp., $14.95.
Hayes, Sarah. *This Is the Bear and the Bad Little Girl.* Cambridge, MA: Candlewick, 1995; 26 pp., $12.95.

Hayles, Marsha. *Beach Play*. New York: Henry Holt, 1998; 32 pp., $14.95.
Hayles, Marsha. *The Feathered Crown*. New York: Henry Holt, 2002; 32 pp., $16.95.
Hayles, Karen, and Charles Fuge. *Whale Is Stuck*. New York: Simon & Schuster, 1992; 32 pp., $14.00.
Haynes, Max. *Dinosaur Island*. New York: Lothrop, Lee and Shepard, 1991; 32 pp., $13.95.
Haynes, Max. *In the Driver's Seat*. New York: Bantam Doubleday Dell, 1997; 26 pp., $12.95.
Hazelaar, Cor. *Zoo Dreams*. New York: Frances Foster, 1997; 32 pp., $14.00.
Hazen, Barbara Shook. *Mommy's Office*. New York: Atheneum, 1992; 32 pp., $13.95.
Healton, Sarah H. *Look What I Made!* New York: TAB Books, 1993; 110 pp., $16.95.
Heap, Sue. *Cowboy Baby*. Cambridge, MA: Candlewick, 1998; 32 pp., $15.99.
Hearn, Diane Dawson. *Dad's Dinosaur Day*. New York: Macmillan, 1993; 32 pp., $16.00.
Hebert, Holly. *60 Super Simple Crafts*. Los Angeles: Lowell House, 1996; 80 pp., $6.95.
Heidbreder, Robert. *Drumheller Dinosaur Dance*. Tonawanda, NY: Kids Can, 2004; 32 pp., $15.95.
Heide, Florence Parry, and Sylvia VanClief. *That's What Friends Are For*. Cambridge, MA: Candlewick, 2003; 32 pp., $15.99.
Heinz, Brian J. *The Monsters' Test*. Minneapolis, MN: Millbrook, 1996; 32 pp., $14.95.
Hellander, Lori. *Halloween Parties*. New York: Stewart, Tabori and Chang, 2004; 80 pp., $14.95.
Hellard, Susan. *Eleanor and the Babysitter*. New York: Little, Brown, 1991; 32 pp., $13.95.
Heller, Lora. *Sign Language for Kids*. New York: Sterling, 2004; 32 pp., $14.95.
Heller, Nicholas. *The Giant*. New York: Greenwillow, 1997; 24 pp., $14.93.
Heller, Nicholas. *Goblins in Green*. New York: Greenwillow, 1995; 32 pp., $16.00.
Henderson, Roxanne. *The Picture Rulebook of Kids' Games*. Chicago: Contemporary, 1996; 240 pp., $14.95.
Hendra, Sue. *Oliver's Wood*. Cambridge, MA: Candlewick, 1996; 32 pp., $15.99.
Henkes, Kevin. *Chrysanthemum*. New York: Greenwillow, 1991; 32 pp., $16.00.
Henkes, Kevin. *Good-bye, Curtis*. New York: Greenwillow, 1995; 24 pp., $14.93.
Henkes, Kevin. *Owen's Marshmallow Chick*. New York: Greenwillow, 2002; 32 pp., $6.95.
Hennessy, B. G. *Because of You*. Cambridge, MA: Candlewick, 2005; 32 pp., $15.99.
Hennessy, B.G. *Olympics!* New York: Viking, 1996; 32 pp., $14.99.
Hennessy, B.G. *Road Builders*. New York: Viking, 1994; 32 pp., $14.99.
Hennessy, B.G. *School Days*. New York: Viking, 1990; 32 pp., $13.95.
Henri, Adrian, and Simon Henwood. *The Postman's Palace*. New York: Atheneum, 1990; 32 pp., $13.95.
Henry, Sandi. *Cut-paper Play!* Charlotte, VT: Williamson, 1997; 60 pp., $12.95.
Herr, Judy, and Yvonne Libby Larson. *Creative Resources for the Early Childhood Classroom, 4th edition*. New York: Delmar Learning, 2004; 708 pp., $47.95.
Hest, Amy. *Baby Duck and the Bad Eyeglasses*. Cambridge, MA: Candlewick, 1996; 32 pp., $16.99.
Hest, Amy. *Don't You Feel Well, Sam?* Cambridge, MA: Candlewick, 2002; 32 pp., $15.99.

Hest, Amy. *Rosie's Fishing Trip*. Cambridge, MA: Candlewick, 1994; 32 pp., $13.95.
Hest, Amy. *Ruby's Storm*. New York: Four Winds, 1994; 32 pp., $14.95.
Hest, Amy. *You Can Do It, Sam*. Cambridge, MA: Candlewick, 2003; 32 pp., $15.99.
Hetzer, Linda. *50 Fabulous Parties for Kids*. New York: Crown, 1994; 176 pp., $10.00.
Hiatt, Fred. *If I Were Queen of the World*. New York: Margaret K. McElderry, 1997; 32 pp., $16.00.
Hill, Lee Sullivan. *Libraries Take Us Far*. Minneapolis, MN: Carolrhoda, 1998; 32 pp., $19.95.
Hill, Susan. *Stuart Little: Stuart at the Library*. New York: HarperCollins, 2001; 32 pp., $14.95.
Hill, Susanna Leonard. *Punxsutawney Phyllis*. New York: Holiday House, 2005; 32 pp., $16.95.
Hillenbrand, Will. *Fiddle-I-Fee*. San Diego: Gulliver, 2002; 32 pp., $16.00.
Hilton, Nette. *Andrew Jessup*. New York: Ticknor and Fields, 1993; 32 pp., $13.95.
Himmelman, John. *A Ladybug's Life*. New York: Children's Press, 1998; 32 pp., $17.25.
Himmelman, John. *Light's Out!* New York: Bridgewater, 1995; 32 pp., $13.95.
Himmelman, John. *Mouse in a Meadow*. Watertown, MA: Charlesbridge, 2005; 32 pp., $15.95.
Hindley, Judy. *Does a Cow Say Boo?* Cambridge, MA: Candlewick, 2002; 32 pp., $15.99.
Hindley, Judy. *Do Like a Duck Does!* Cambridge, MA: Candlewick, 2002; 32 pp., $14.99.
Hindley, Judy. *Eyes, Nose, Fingers, and Toes*. Cambridge, MA: Candlewick, 1999; 32 pp., $15.99.
Hindley, Judy. *Uncle Harold and the Green Hat*. New York: Farrar, Straus & Giroux, 1991; 26 pp., $13.95.
Hines, Anna Grossnickle. *Big Help!* Boston: Clarion, 1995; 32 pp., $13.95.
Hines, Anna Grossnickle. *Even if I Spill My Milk?* Boston: Clarion, 1994; 32 pp., $13.95.
Hines, Anna Grossnickle. *My Own Big Bed*. New York: Greenwillow, 1998; 24 pp., $20.75.
Hines, Anna Grossnickle. *When the Goblins Came Knocking*. New York: Greenwillow, 1995; 26 pp., $14.93.
Hinkes, Enid. *Police Cat*. Morton Grove, IL: Albert Whitman, 2005; 32 pp., $15.95.
Hinton, S. E. *Big David, Little David*. New York: Doubleday, 1995; 34 pp., $15.95.
Hirschi, Ron. *Summer*. New York: Cobblehill, 1991; 32 pp., $15.99.
Hiskey, Iris. *Cassandra Who?* New York: Simon & Schuster, 1992; 32 pp., $14.00.
Hissey, Jane. *Hoot*. New York: Random House, 1997; 32 pp., $18.00.
Hissey, Jane. *Jolly Snow*. New York: Philomel, 1991; 32 pp., $14.95.
Hoban, Lillian. *Arthur's Honey Bear*. New York: Harper and Row, 2000; 64 pp., $14.95.
Hoban, Lillian. *Silly Tilly's Thanksgiving Dinner*. New York: Harper and Row, 1990; 64 pp., $15.89.
Hoban, Tana. *Construction Zone*. New York: Greenwillow, 1997; 32 pp., $15.00.
Hoban, Tana. *So Many Circles, So Many Squares*. New York: Greenwillow, 1998; 32 pp., $15.00.
Hobbie, Holly. *Toot and Puddle*. New York: Little, Brown, 1997; 32 pp., $12.95.

Hobbie, Holly. *Toot and Puddle: Wish You Were Here.* New York: Little, Brown, 2005; 32 pp., $16.99.
Hobbie, Nathaniel. *Priscilla and the Pink Planet.* New York: Little, Brown, 2004; 32 pp., $15.99.
Hoberman, Mary Ann. *It's Simple, Said Simon.* New York: Knopf. 2001; 32 pp., $15.95.
Hoberman, Mary Ann. *Miss Mary Mack.* New York: Little, Brown, 1998; 32 pp., $14.95.
Hoberman, Mary Ann. *One of Each.* New York: Little, Brown, 1997; 32 pp., $15.95.
Hodges, Margaret. *The Boy Who Drew Cats.* New York: Holiday House, 2002; 32 pp., $16.95.
Hoena, B. A. *A Visit to the Library.* Mankato, MN: Capstone, 2004; 32 pp., $17.26.
Hoff, Syd. *Duncan the Dancing Duck.* Boston: Clarion, 1994; 32 pp., $13.95.
Hoffman, Mary. *Amazing Grace.* New York: Dial, 1991; 32 pp., $15.99.
Hoffman, Mary. *Henry's Baby.* New York: Dorling Kindersley, 1993; 32 pp., $13.95.
Hofmeyr, Dianne. *Do the Whales Still Sing?* New York: Dial, 1995; 28 pp., $14.89.
Hol, Coby. *Henrietta Saves the Show.* New York: North-South, 1991; 28 pp., $14.95.
Holabird, Katharine. *Alexander and the Magic Boat.* New York: Clarkson N. Potter, 1990; 32 pp., $11.95.
Holley, Cynthia, and Jane Walkup. *First Time, Circle Time.* Logan, Iowa: Fearon Teachers Aids, 1993; 287 pp., $20.99.
Holub, Joan. *Fourth of July, Sparkly Sky.* New York: Little Simon, 2003; 10 pp., $4.99.
Holwitz, Peter. *The Big Blue Spot.* New York: Philomel, 2003; 32 pp., $13.99.
Honey, Elizabeth. *The Moon in the Man.* Crows Nest, Australia: Allen and Unwin, 2002; 32 pp., $15.00.
Hood, Susan. *Caterpillar Spring, Butterfly Summer.* New York: Reader's Digest, 2003; 32 pp., $12.99.
Hook, Jason. *Where's the Dragons?* New York: Sterling, 2003; 32 pp., $14.95.
Hooker, Ruth. *Matthew the Cowboy.* Morton Grove, IL: Albert Whitman, 1990; 32 pp., $14.95.
Hooks, William H. *Rough Tough Rowdy.* New York: Viking, 1992; 32 pp., $12.50.
Horack, Petr. *A New House for Mouse.* Cambridge, MA: Candlewick, 2004; 32 pp., $12.99.
Horacek, Peter. *Silly Suzy Goose.* Cambridge, MA: Candlewick, 2006; 32 pp., $14.99.
Horowitz, Dave. *The Ugly Pumpkin.* New York: Putnam, 2005; 32 pp., $15.99.
Horse, Harry. *Little Rabbit Goes to School.* Atlanta, GA: Peachtree, 2004; 32 pp., $15.95.
Hossell, Karen Price. *Sign Language.* Barrington, IL: Heinemann, 2003; 32 pp., $17.95.
Houck, Jr., Eric L. *Rabbit Surprise.* New York: Crown, 1993; 28 pp.; $15.00.
Houghton, Eric. *The Backwards Watch.* New York: Orchard, 1991; 30 pp., $13.95.
Howard, Arthur. *Serious Trouble.* San Diego: Harcourt, 2003; 32 pp., $16.00.
Howard, Ellen. *The Big Seed.* New York: Simon & Schuster, 1993; 32 pp., $14.00.
Howard, Kim. *In Wintertime.* New York: Lothrop, Lee and Shepard, 1994; 30 pp., $15.95.
Howe, James. *Creepy-Crawly Birthday.* New York.: Morrow, 1991; 48 pp., $13.95.
Howe, James. *Hot Fudge.* New York: Morrow, 1990; 48 pp., $13.88.

Howe, James. *There's a Dragon in My Sleeping Bag*. New York: Atheneum, 1994; 40 pp., $14.95.
Howland, Naomi. *ABC Drive!* Boston: Clarion, 1994; 30 pp., $13.95.
Hoyt-Goldsmith, Diane. *Celebrating Kwanzaa*. New York: Holiday House, 1993; 32 pp., $15.95.
Hubbell, Patricia. *Hurray for Spring!* Minnetonka, MN: Northword, 2005; 32 pp., $15.95.
Huff, Mary Jo. *Fall Frolic*. Ashland, OH: Monday Morning, 2003; 64 pp., $15.00.
Hughes, Shirley. *Alfie's ABC*. New York: Lothrop, Lee and Shepard, 1998; 32 pp., $16.00.
Hulme, Joy N. *Bubble Trouble*. New York: Children's Press, 1999; 32 pp., $12.95.
Huneck, Stephen. *Sally Goes to the Beach*. New York: Abrams, 2000; 32 pp., $17.95.
Hunter, Anne. *Possum and the Peeper*. Boston: Houghton Mifflin, 1998; 32 pp., $15.00.
Hunter, Anne. *Possum's Harvest Moon*. Boston: Houghton Mifflin, 1996; 32 pp., $14.95.
Hurd, Thatcher. *Art Dog*. New York: Harper and Row, 1996; 32 pp., $14.95.
Hurd, Thatcher. *Little Mouse's Big Valentine*. New York: Harper and Row, 1992; 32 pp., $9.90.
Hutchings, Amy and Richard. *Firehouse Dog*. New York: Scholastic, 1993; 32 pp., $2.99.
Hutchins, Pat. *Happy Birthday, Sam*. New York: Greenwillow, 1992; 32 pp., $15.95.
Hutchins, Pat. *My Best Friend*. New York: Greenwillow, 1993; 32 pp., $15.93.
Hutchins, Pat. *Shrinking Mouse*. New York: Greenwillow, 1997; 32 pp., $15.00.
Hutchins, Pat. *Three-Star Billy*. New York: Greenwillow, 1994; 32 pp., $14.93.
Hutchins, Pat. *Tidy Titch*. New York: Greenwillow, 1991; 32 pp., $16.50.
Hutchins, Pat. *What Game Shall We Play?* New York: Greenwillow, 1990; 32 pp., $10.15.
Ichikawa, Satomi. *Bravo, Tanya*. New York: Philomel, 1992; 30 pp., $14.95.
Inkpen, Mick. *Billy's Beetle*. San Diego: Harcourt, 1991; 30 pp., $13.95.
Inkpen, Mick. *Nothing*. New York: Orchard, 1995; 32 pp., $14.95.
Inns, Christopher. *Nest! Please*. Berkeley: Tricycle, 2001; 32 pp., $14.95.
Intrater, Roberta Grobel. *Two Eyes, a Nose and a Mouth*. New York: Scholastic, 1995; 32 pp., $12.95.
Irvin, Christine M. *Craft Stick Mania*. New York: Children's Press, 2002; 32 pp., $23.50.
Isadora, Rachel. *On Your Toes: A Ballet ABC*. New York: Greenwillow, 2003; 32 pp., $17.89.
Isadora, Rachel. *A South African Night*. New York: Greenwillow, 1998; 24 pp., $15.00.
Jakob, Donna. *Tiny Toes*. New York: Hyperion, 1995; 32 pp., $14.49.
James, Betsy. *Mary Ann*. New York: Dutton, 1994; 32 pp., $14.99.
James, Betsy. *Tadpoles*. New York: Dutton, 1999; 32 pp., $14.99.
James, Simon. *Jake and the Babysitter*. Cambridge, MA: Candlewick, 1991; 20 pp., $4.99.
James, Simon. *Sally and the Limpet*. New York: Margaret K. McElderry, 1991; 32 pp., $13.95.
Janovitz, Marilyn. *Can I Help?* New York: North-South, 1996; 32 pp., $13.95.

Janovitz, Marilyn. *What Could Be Keeping Santa?* New York: North-South, 1997; 32 pp., $15.90.

Jaques, Florence Page. *There Once Was a Puffin*. New York: North-South, 2003; 32 pp., $16.50.

Jaramillo, Nelly Palacio. *Grandmother's Nursery Rhymes*. New York: Henry Holt, 1994; 32 pp., $14.95.

Jarman, Julia. *Big Red Tub*. New York: Orchard, 2004; 32 pp., $14.95.

Jarman, Julia, and Adriano Gan. *The Magic Backpack*. New York: Crabtree, 2001; 32 pp., $14.97.

Jasmine, Grace. *Quick and Fun Games for Toddlers*. Westminster, CA: Teacher Created Materials, 1999; 158 pp., $9.99.

Jeffers, Oliver. *Lost and Found*. New York: Philomel, 2005; 32 pp., $15.99.

Jenkins, Jessica. *Thinking about Colors*. New York: Dutton, 1992; 32 pp., $14.00.

Jenkins, Priscilla Belz. *A Safe Home for Manatees*. New York: HarperCollins, 1997; 32 pp., $14.90.

Jenkins, Steve. *Big and Little*. Boston: Houghton Mifflin, 1996; 32 pp., $14.95.

Jenkins, Steve, and Robin Page. *I See a Kookaburra!* Boston: Houghton Mifflin, 2005; 32 pp., $16.00.

Jenkins, Steve, and Robin Page. *What Do You Do with a Tail Like This?* Boston: Houghton Mifflin, 2003; 32 pp., $15.00.

Jennings, Linda. *The Brave Little Bunny*. New York: Dutton, 1995; 32 pp., $13.99.

Jennings, Linda. *Easy Peasy!* New York: Farrar, Straus & Giroux, 1997; 28 pp., $14.00.

Jenny, Gerri, and Sherrie Gould. *Rainy Day Projects for Children*. Nazareth, Pa.: Murdock, 1990; 121 pp., $10.95.

Jeschke, Susan. *Perfect the Pig*. San Diego: Holt, Rinehart & Winston, 1998; 32 pp., $11.15.

Johnson, Amy Crane. *Mason Moves Away*. Green Bay, WI: Raven Tree, 2004; 32 pp., $16.95.

Johnson, Angela. *The Leaving Morning*. New York: Orchard, 1992; 28 pp., $14.95.

Johnson, Angela. *When I am Old with You*. New York: Orchard, 1990; 32 pp., $16.99.

Johnson, D.B. *Eddie's Kingdom*. Boston: Houghton Mifflin, 2005; 32 pp., $16.00.

Johnson, Dolores. *What Kind of Baby-sitter is this?* New York: Macmillan, 1991; 32 pp., $13.95.

Johnson, Dolores. *What Will Mommy Do When I'm at School?* New York: Macmillan, 1990; 32 pp., $12.95.

Johnson, Doug. *Never Babysit the Hippopotamuses!* New York: Henry Holt, 1993; 32 pp., $14.95.

Johnson, Doug. *Never Ride Your Elephant to School*. New York: Henry Holt, 1995; 30 pp., $15.95.

Johnson, G. Francis. *Has Anybody Lost a Glove?* Honesdale, PA: Boyds Mills, 2004; 32 pp., $15.95.

Johnson, Pamela. *A Mouse's Tale*. San Diego: Harcourt, 1991; 32 pp., $11.95.

Johnson, Paul Brett. *The Cow Who Wouldn't Come Down*. New York: Orchard, 1993; 32 pp., $14.95.

Johnson, Paul Brett. *Little Bunny Foo Foo*. New York: Scholastic, 2004; 32 pp., $15.95.

Johnson, Paul Brett. *A Perfect Pork Stew*. New York: Orchard, 1998; 32 pp., $16.99.

Johnson, Rebecca. *The Kangaroos' Great Escape*. Milwaukee, WI: Gareth Stevens, 2006; 32 pp., $21.27.
Johnson, Rebecca. *Little Dolphin's Big Leap*. Milwaukee, WI: Gareth Stevens, 2006; 32 pp., $18.60.
Johnston, Marianne. *Let's Talk about Being Shy*. New York: Powerkids, 1996; 24 pp., $16.95.
Johnston, Tony. *The Badger and the Magic Fan*. New York: Putnam, 1990; 32 pp., $13.95.
Johnston, Tony. *The Barn Owls*. Watertown, MA: Talewinds, 2000; 32 pp., $16.95.
Johnston, Tony. *The Cowboy and the Black-Eyed Pea*. New York: Putnam, 1992; 32 pp., $15.95.
Johnston, Tony. *The Last Snow of Winter*. New York: Tambourine, 1993; 32 pp., $13.95.
Johnston, Tony. *Little Rabbit Goes to Sleep*. New York: HarperCollins, 1995; 32 pp., $10.15.
Johnston, Tony, and Bruce Degen. *Goblin Walk*. New York: Putnam, 1991; 32 pp., $14.95.
Jonas, Ann. *The 13th Clue*. New York: Greenwillow, 1992; 32 pp., $14.00.
Jonas, Ann. *Where Can It Be?* New York: Greenwillow, 1996; 32 pp., $11.75.
Jones, Christianne C. *The Babysitter*. Minneapolis, MN: Picture Window, 2006; 32 pp., $13.95.
Jones, Rebecca C. *Great Aunt Martha*. New York: Dutton, 1995; 32 pp., $13.99.
Joos, Francoise and Frederic. *The Golden Snowflake*. New York: Little, Brown, 1991; 32 pp., $14.95.
Joose, Barbara M. *Bad Dog School*. Boston: Clarion, 2004; 32 pp., $15.00.
Joose, Barbara M. *Papa, Do You Love Me?* San Franciso: Chronicle, 2005; 32 pp., $15.95.
Joose, Barbara M. *Snow Day!* Boston: Clarion, 1995; 32 pp., $14.95.
Jorgensen, Gail. *Gotcha!* New York: Scholastic, 1995; 32 pp., $15.95.
Joyce, William. *The Leaf Men*. New York: HarperCollins, 1996; 40pp., $15.95.
Juan, Ana. *The Night Eater*. New York: Arthur A. Levine, 2004; 32 pp., $16.95.
Jung, Minna. *William's Ninth Life*. New York: Orchard, 1993; 32 pp., $12.95.
Kadish, Sharona. *Discovering Friendship*. Milwaukee, WI: Steck-Vaughn, 1994; 32 pp., $11.95.
Kalan, Robert. *Jump, Frog, Jump*. New York: Greenwillow, 1996; 32 pp., $18.95.
Kalan, Robert. *Moving Day*. New York: Greenwillow, 1996; 28 pp., $15.00.
Karlin, Nurit. *Little Big Mouse*. New York.: HarperCollins, 1991; 32 pp., $13.95.
Kastner, Jill. *Barnyard Big Top*. New York: Simon & Schuster, 1997; 32 pp., $16.00.
Kastner, Jill. *Snake Hunt*. New York: Four Winds, 1993; 32 pp., $14.95.
Kasza, Keiko. *Grandpa Toad's Secrets*. New York: Putnam, 1995; 32 pp., $15.99.
Kasza, Keiko. *The Mightiest*. New York: Putnam, 2001; 32 pp., $15.99.
Kasza, Keiko. *A Mother for Choco*. New York: Putnam, 1992; 32 pp., $15.95.
Kasza, Keiko. *The Rat and the Tiger*. New York: Putnam, 1993; 32 pp., $14.95.
Kasza, Keiko. *When the Elephant Walks*. New York: Putnam, 1990, 32 pp., $11.95.
Katz, Karen. *Twelve Hats for Lena: A Book of Months*. New York: Margaret K. McElderry, 2002; 32 pp., $16.95.
Keats, Ezra Jack. *Goggles!* New York: Macmillan, 1998; 32 pp., $15.99.

Keats, Ezra Jack. *Kitten for a Day*. New York: Harper and Row, 1993; 32 pp., $10.15.
Keats, Ezra Jack. *My Dog is Lost!* New York: Thomas Y. Crowell, 1999; 39 pp., $5.99.
Keenan, Sheila. *Lizzy's Dizzy Day*. New York: Scholastic, 2001; 10 pp., $3.99.
Keller, Holly. *Brave Horace*. New York: Greenwillow, 1998; 32 pp., $15.00.
Keller, Holly. *Furry*. New York: Greenwillow, 1992; 24 pp., $14.00.
Keller, Holly. *Geraldine's Baby Brother*. New York: Greenwillow, 1994; 24 pp., $15.00.
Keller, Holly. *Grandfather's Dream*. New York: Greenwillow, 1994; 32 pp., $15.00.
Keller, Holly. *Harry and Tuck*. New York: Greenwillow, 1993; 24 pp., $14.00.
Keller, Holly. *Henry's Happy Birthday*. New York: Greenwillow, 1990; 32 pp., $12.88.
Keller, Holly. *Horace*. New York: Greenwillow, 1991; 32 pp., $13.88.
Keller, Holly. *Merry Christmas, Geraldine*. New York: Greenwillow, 1997; 32 pp., $15.00.
Keller, Holly. *What a Hat!* New York: Greenwillow, 2003; 32 pp., $15.99.
Keller, Holly. *What Alvin Wanted*. New York: Greenwillow, 1990; 32 pp., $12.95.
Kelley, Marty. *Winter Woes*. Madison, WI: Zino, 2003; 32 pp., $12.95.
Kellogg, Steven. *Pecos Bill*. New York: Morrow, 1995; 48 pp., $15.00.
Kellogg, Steven. *A Penguin Pup for Pinkerton*. New York: Dial, 2001; 32 pp., $15.99.
Kennaway, Adrienne. *Little Elephant's Walk*. New York: Willa Perlman, 1991; 32 pp., $13.89.
Kennedy, Kim. *Mr. Bumble*. New York: Hyperion, 1997; 32 pp., $15.95.
Keown, Elizabeth. *Emily's Snowball: The World's Biggest*. New York: Atheneum, 1992; 32 pp., $13.95.
Kepes, Charles. *Run, Little Monkeys, Run, Run, Run*. New York: Harper and Row, 1996; 64 pp., $14.89.
Kern, Noris. *I Love You with All My Heart*. San Francisco: Chronicle, 1998; 32 pp., $14.95.
Kessler, Leonard. *Kick, Pass and Run*. New York: Harper and Row, 1996; 64 pp., $14.89.
Kevi. *Don't Talk to Strangers*. New York: Scholastic, 2003; 32 pp., $13.95.
Ketteman, Helen. *Heatwave*. New York: Walker, 1998; 32 pp., $15.95.
Kezzeiz, Ediba. *Ramadan Adventure of Fafoose Mouse*. Plainfield, IN: American Trust Publications, 1991; 32 pp., $3.00.
Khdir, Kate, and Sue Nash. *Little Ghost*. Hauppauge, NY: Barron's Educational Series, 1991; 32 pp., $12.95.
Kilby, Janice Eaton, and Terry Taylor. *The Book of Wizard Parties*. New York: Lark, 2002; 144 pp., $19.95.
Kimmel, Eric A. *I Took My Frog to the Library*. New York: Viking, 1992; 32 pp., $10.20.
Kimmelman, Leslie. *Hanukkah Lights, Hanukkah Nights*. New York: HarperCollins, 1992; 32 pp., $11.15.
Kimmelman, Leslie. *Happy 4th of July, Jenny Sweeney!* Morton Grove, IL: Albert Whitman, 2003; 32 pp., $16.95.
Kimpton, Diana. *Edison's Fantastic Phonograph*. London: Frances Lincoln, 2003; 32 pp., $7.95.
King, Bob. *Sitting on the Farm*. New York: Orchard, 1991; 32 pp., $13.96.
King, Penny, and Clare Roundhill. *Making Pictures: Secrets of the Sea*. Milwaukee, WI: Rigby Interactive Library, 1997; 29 pp., $21.36.
King, Penny, and Clare Roundhill. *Making Pictures: Spooky Things*. Milwaukee, WI: Rigby Interactive Library, 1997; 29 pp., $21.36.

King-Smith, Dick. *The Spotty Pig*. New York: Farrar, Straus & Giroux, 1997; 32 pp., $14.00.
Kinney, Maxine. *Paper Plate Kinney*. Grand Rapids, MI: T.S. Denison, 1993; 80 pp., $8.95.
Kinsey-Warnock, Natalie. *When Spring Comes*. New York: Dutton, 1993; 32 pp., $14.95.
Kinsey-Warnock, Natalie, and Helen Kinsey. *The Bear that Heard Crying*. New York: Cobblehill, 1993; 32 pp., $14.99.
Kipling, Rudyard. *The Sing-song of Old Man Kangaroo*. New York: Peter Bedrick, 1991; 32 pp., $14.95.
Kirk, Daniel. *Bigger*. New York: Putnam, 1998; 32 pp., $15.99.
Kirk, Daniel. *Lunchroom Lizard*. New York: Putnam, 2004; 32 pp., $15.99.
Kirk, Daniel. *Trash Trucks!* New York: Putnam, 1997; 32 pp., $15.95.
Kirk, David. *Miss Spider's New Car*. New York: Scholastic, 1997; 32 pp., $16.95.
Kirk, David. *Miss Spider's Tea Party*. New York: Scholastic, 1994; 32 pp., $15.95.
Kittinger, Jo S. *When I Grow Up*. New York: Children's Press, 2003; 32 pp., $19.50.
Kladder, Jeri. *Story Hour: 55 Preschool Programs for Public Libraries*. Jefferson, N.C.: McFarland, 1995; 219 pp., $38.50.
Klettenheimer, Ingrid. *Great Paper Craft Projects*. New York.: Sterling, 1992; 80 pp., $13.16.
Knutson, Kimberley. *Ska-tat!* New York: Macmillan, 1993; 32 pp., $14.95.
Kobe, Liz Cromwell, Dixie Hibner and John R. Faitel. *Finger Frolics 2*. Beltsville, MD: Gryphon House, 1996; 134 pp., $12.95.
Koehler, Rhoebe. *The Day We Met You*. New York: Bradbury, 1990; 40 pp., $15.00.
Kohl., MaryAnn R. *First Art: Art Experiences for Toddlers and Twos*. Beltsville, MD: Gryphon House, 2002; 154 pp., $14.95.
Kohl, MaryAnn R. *Making Make-Believe*. Beltsville, MD: Gryphon House, 1999; 191 pp., $14.95.
Kohl, MaryAnn. *Preschool Art*. Beltsville, MD: Gryphon House, 1994; 260 pp., $19.95.
Kohl, MaryAnn F., and Cindy Gainer. *Good Earth Art*. Bellingham, Wash.: Bright Ring, 1991; 224 pp., $16.95.
Kohl, MaryAnn R., and Jean Potter. *Storybook Art*. Bellingham, Wash.: Bright Ring, 2003; 144 pp., $14.95.
Koller, Jackie French. *No Such Thing*. Honesdale, PA: Boyds Mills, 1997; 32 pp., $14.95.
Komoda, Beverly. *The Winter Day*. New York: HarperCollins, 1991; 32 pp., $13.90.
Koren, Edward. *Very Hairy Harry*. New York: HarperCollins, 2003; 32 pp., $15.99.
Konigsburg, E.L. *Samuel Todd's Book of Great Colors*. New York: Atheneum, 1990; 32 pp., $13.95.
Kordon, Klaus. *The Big Fish*. New York: Macmillan, 1992; 32 pp., $13.95.
Koscielniak, Bruce. *Geoffrey Groundhog Predicts the Weather*. New York: Houghton Mifflin, 1995; 32 pp., $13.95.
Kovalski, MaryAnn. *Pizza for Breakfast*. New York: Morrow, 1990; 32 pp., $13.90.
Kovalski, MaryAnn. *Take Me Out to the Ball Game*. Allston, MA: Fitzhenry and Whiteside, 2004; 32 pp., $19.95.
Kowalski, Kathiann M. *The Everything Kids' Nature Book*. Avon, MA: Adams Media, 2000; 132 pp., $9.99.

Krasilovsky, Phyllis. *The Man Who Was Too Lazy to Fix Things.* New York: Tambourine, 1992; 32 pp., $14.95.
Krasilovsky, Phyllis. *The Woman Who Saved Things.* New York: Tambourine, 1993; 32 pp., $14.95.
Kraus, Robert. *Fables Aesop Never Wrote.* New York: Viking, 1994; 32 pp., $14.99.
Kraus, Robert. *Little Louie the Baby Bloomer.* New York: HarperCollins, 1998; 32 pp., $15.95.
Kraus, Robert. *Musical Max.* New York: Simon & Schuster, 1990; 32 pp., $13.95.
Krensky, Stephen. *Bubble Trouble.* New York: Aladdin, 2004; 32 pp., $15.00.
Krensky, Stephen. *How Santa Got His Job.* New York: Simon & Schuster, 1998; 32 pp., $15.00.
Kroll, Steven. *The Candy Witch.* New York: Holiday House, 1996; 32 pp., $7.70.
Kroll, Steven. *It's Groundhog Day!* New York: Holiday House, 1991; 32 pp., $2.99.
Kroll, Steven. *Mary McLean and the St. Patrick's Day Parade.* New York: Scholastic, 1991; 32 pp., $15.95.
Kroll, Steven. *The Squirrel's Thanksgiving.* New York: Holiday House, 1991; 32 pp., $14.95.
Kroll, Steven. *Will You Be My Valentine?* New York: Holiday House, 1993; 32 pp., $14.95.
Kroll, Virginia. *A Carp for Kimiko.* Watertown, MA: Charlesbridge, 1993; 32 pp., $15.00.
Kroll, Virginia L. *Hands!* Honesdale, PA: Boyds Mills, 1997; 30 pp., $7.95.
Kroll, Virginia L. *Masai and I.* New York: Four Winds, 1992; 32 pp., $16.00.
Kroninger, Stephen. *If I Crossed the Road.* New York: Atheneum, 1997; 32 pp., $16.00.
Kropf, Latifa Berry. *It's Hanukkah Time!* Minneapolis, MN: Kar-Ben Publishing, 2004; 32 pp., $12.95.
Krosoczka, Jarrett J. *Bubble Bath Pirates!* New York: Viking, 2003; 32 pp., $15.99.
Krudop, Walter Lyon. *Something Is Growing.* New York: Atheneum, 1995; 32 pp., $15.00.
Krull, Kathleen. *Gonna Sing My Head Off!* New York: Knopf, 1992; 147 pp., $12.00.
Krull, Kathleen. *It's My Earth, Too.* New York: Bantam Doubleday Dell, 1992; 32 pp., $13.50.
Kubler, Annie. *My First Signs.* New York: Child's Play, 2004; 32 pp., $6.99.
Kuffner, Trish. *Picture Book Activities.* Minnetonka, MN: Meadowbrook, 2001; 244 pp., $12.00.
Kuffner, Trish. *The Preschooler's Busy Book.* Minnetonka, MN: Meadowbrook, 1998; 395 pp., $9.99.
Kuklin, Susan. *All Aboard! A True Train Story.* New York: Orchard, 2005; 32 pp., $16.95.
Kuklin, Susan. *Fighting Fires.* New York: Bradbury, 1993; 32 pp., $15.00.
Kunhardt, Edith. *Red Day, Green Day.* New York: Greenwillow, 1992; 32 pp., $14.00.
Kurtz, Jane. *Rain Romp.* New York: Greenwillow, 2002, 32 pp., $17.89.
Kurtz, Jane and Christopher. *Water Hole Waiting.* New York: Greenwillow, 2002; 32 pp., $15.95.
Kuskin, Karla. *So What's It Like to Be a Cat?* New York: Atheneum, 2005; 32 pp., $15.95.
Kuskin, Karla. *Under My Hood I Have a Hat.* New York: Laura Geringer, 2004; 32 pp., $14.99.

Kutner, Merrily. *Down on the Farm*. New York: Holiday House, 2004; 32 pp., $16.95.
Kvasnosky, Laura. *Mr. Chips*. New York: Farrar, Straus & Giroux, 1996; 32 pp., $15.00.
Kwitz, Mary DeBall. *Little Chick's Friend, Duckling*. New York: HarperCollins, 1992; 28 pp., $11.80.
Lachner, Dorothea. *Meredith, the Witch Who Wasn't*. New York: North-South, 1997; 32 pp., $15.95.
Lacoe, Addie. *Just Not the Same*. Boston: Houghton Mifflin, 1992; 32 pp., $14.95.
Lacome, Julie. *I'm a Jolly Farmer*. Cambridge, MA: Candlewick, 1994; 24 pp., $13.95.
Ladd, Frances Ann. *Tough Tracks: The Crane*. New York: Scholastic, 2003; 32 pp., $13.96.
Laden, Nina. *Grow Up!* San Francisco: Chronicle, 2003; 10 pp., $6.95.
Lainez, Rene Colato. *I am Rene, the Boy*. Houston, TX: Piñata Books, 2005; 32 pp., $14.95.
Laird, Elizabeth. *The Day Veronica Was Nosy*. New York: Tambourine, 1990; 32 pp., $11.90.
Lakin, Patricia. *Aware and Alert*. Milwaukee, WI: Steck-Vaughn, 1995; 32 pp., $19.97.
Lakin, Patricia. *Clarence the Copy Cat*. New York: Random House, 2002; 32 pp., $15.95.
Lakin, Pat. *Dad and Me in the Morning*. Morton Grove, IL: Albert Whitman, 1994; 32 pp., $14.95.
Lamont, Priscilla. *Playtime Rhymes*. New York: DK Publishing, 1998; 32 pp., $12.95.
Lane, Adam J. B. *Monsters Party All Night Long*. San Francisco: Chronicle, 2004; 32 pp., $15.95.
Langham, Tony. *Creepy Crawly Calypso*. Cambridge, MA: Barefoot, 2004; 32 pp., $16.99.
Lanton, Sandy. *Lots of Latkes: A Hanukkah Story*. Minneapolis, MN: Kar-Ben, 2003; 32 pp., $14.95.
Larranago, Ana Martin. *Woo! The Not-so-scary Ghost*. New York: Scholastic, 2000; 32 pp., $15.95.
Lasky, Kathryn. *Fourth of July Bear*. New York: Morrow, 1991; 32 pp., $13.95.
Lasky, Kathryn. *Lunch Bunnies*. New York: Little, Brown, 1996; 32 pp., $14.95.
Latimer, Jim. *Fox Under First Base*. New York: Scribner's, 1991; 32 pp., $13.95.
Lattimore, Deborah Nourse. *CinderHazel: The Cinderella of Halloween*. New York: Blue Sky, 1997; 32 pp., $15.95.
Lauber, Patricia. *Be a Friend to Trees*. New York: HarperCollins, 1994; 32 pp., $14.89.
Law, Felicia. *Bamboo and Friends: The Rainy Day*. Minneapolis, MN: Picture Window, 2004; 32 pp., $18.99.
Law, Felicia. *The Tree*. Minneapolis, Minn.: Picture Window, 2004; 32 pp., $16.95.
Leaney, Cindy. *Field Trip: A Story About Sharing*. Vero Beach, FL: Rourke, 2004; 32 pp., $19.95.
Leaney, Cindy. *It's Your Turn Now: A Story about Politeness*. Vero Beach, FL: Rourke, 2004; 32 pp., $19.95.
Lears, Laurie. *Ian's Walk: A Story about Autism*. Morton Grove, IL: Albert Whitman, 1998; 32 pp., $15.95.
Lee, Jeanne M. *Silent Lotus*. New York: Farrar, Straus & Giroux, 1991; 32 pp., $14.95.

Leedy, Loreen. *Follow the Money*. New York: Holiday House, 2002; 32 pp., $16.95.
Leedy, Loreen. *The Great Trash Bash*. New York: Holiday House, 1991; 32 pp., $15.95.
Leeson, Christine. *Molly and the Storm*. Wilton, CT: Tiger Tales, 2003; 32 pp., $16.95.
Lee Vaughan, Richard. *Eagle Boy*. Seattle, WA: Sasquatch, 2000; 32 pp., $16.95.
Lehan, Daniel. *Wipe Your Feet!* New York: Dutton, 1992; 26 pp., $14.00.
Lehn, Barbara. *What Is an Artist?* Minneapolis, MN: Millbrook, 2002; 32 pp., $21.90.
Lehne, Judith Logan. *The Never-Be-bored Book*. New York: Sterling, 1992; 128 pp., $17.95.
Lember, Barbara Hirsch. *A Book of Fruit*. New York: Ticknor and Fields, 1994; 32 pp., $14.95.
Lemieux, Michele. *The Pied Piper of Hamelin*. New York: Morrow, 1993; 32 pp., $14.95.
Lenssen, Ann. *A Rainbow Balloon*. New York: Cobblehill, 1992; 32 pp., $13.50.
Lerner, Harriet, and Susan Goldhor. *What's So Terrible about Swallowing an Appleseed?* New York: HarperCollins, 1996; 40 pp., $14.95.
Lester, Alison. *Magic Beach*. New York: Little, Brown, 1990; 32 pp., $13.95.
Lester, Helen. *Tacky and the Winter Games*. Boston: Houghton Mifflin, 2005; 32 pp., $16.00.
Lester, Helen. *Tacky Locks and the Three Bears*. Boston: Houghton Mifflin, 2002; 32 pp., $15.00.
Lester, Julius. *John Henry*. New York: Dial, 1994; 48 pp., $16.89.
Lester, Julius. *Princess Penelope's Parrot*. Boston: Houghton Mifflin, 1996; 32 pp., $14.95.
Leuck, Laura. *Goodnight, Baby Monster*. New York: HarperCollins, 2002; 32 pp., $16.89.
Leuck, Laura. *Teeny, Tiny Mouse: A Book about Colors*. New York: Bridgewater, 1998; 32 pp., $15.95.
Levine, Abby. *Gretchen Groundhog, It's Your Day!* Morton Grove, IL: Albert Whitman, 1998; 32 pp., $15.95.
Levine, Abby. *This Is the Pumpkin*. Morton Grove, IL: Albert Whitman, 1997; 32 pp., $11.50.
Levinson, Nancy Smiler. *Snowshoe Thompson*. New York: HarperCollins, 1992; 64 pp., $15.89.
Lewin, Betsy. *Animal Snackers*. New York: Henry Holt, 2004; 32 pp., $15.95.
Lewin, Betsy. *Chubbo's Pool*. Boston: Clarion, 1996; 32 pp., $14.95.
Lewis, Amanda. *The Jumbo Book of Paper Crafts*. Tonawanda, NY: Kids Can, 2002; 160 pp., $14.95.
Lewis, Paeony. *No More Cookies!* New York: Chicken House, 2005; 32 pp., $16.95.
Lewis, Paul Owen. *Storm Boy*. Hillsboro, OR: Beyond Words, 1995; 32 pp., $14.95.
Lewis, Rob. *Henrietta's First Winter*. New York: Farrar, Straus & Giroux, 1990; 32 pp., $11.95.
Lewis, Shari. *Shari Lewis Presents 101 Games and Songs for Kids to Play and Sing*. New York: Random House, 1993; 90 pp., $9.99.
Lewison, Wendy Cheyette. *The Rooster Who Lost His Crow*. New York: Dial, 1995; 32 pp., $14.99.
Lichtenheld, Tom. *What Are You So Grumpy About?* New York: Little, Brown, 2003; 32 pp., $13.95.

Liebman, Dan. *I Want to Be a Police Officer*. Buffalo, NY: Firefly, 2000; 32 pp., $14.95.
Lies, Brian. *Hamlet and the Enormous Chinese Dragon Kite*. Boston: Houghton Mifflin, 1994; 32 pp., $14.95.
Lieurance, Suzanne. *Pennies*. New York: Children's Press, 2002; 32 pp., $14.25.
Lillegard, Dee. *My Yellow Ball*. New York: Dutton, 1993; 32 pp., $12.99.
Lillegard, Dee. *Tiger, Tiger*. New York: Putnam, 2002; 32 pp., $18.95.
Lillegard, Dee. *Tortoise Brings the Mail*. New York: Dutton, 1997; 32 pp., $14.99.
Lillegard, Dee. *The Wild Bunch*. New York: Putnam, 1997; 32 pp., $15.95.
Lillie, Patricia. *When the Rooster Crowed*. New York: Greenwillow, 1991; 32 pp., $13.88.
Lillie, Patricia. *When This Box Is Full*. New York: Greenwillow, 1993; 24 pp., $14.00.
Lilly, Melinda. *Eye Spy a Ladybug!* New York: Price Stern Sloan, 1997; 10 pp., $6.95.
Lin, Grace. *Fortune Cookie Fortunes*. New York: Knopf, 2004; 32 pp., $15.95.
Lin, Grace. *Robert's Snow*. New York: Viking, 2004; 32 pp., $15.99.
Lindbergh, Reeve. *There's a Cow in the Road*. New York: Dial, 1993; 32 pp., $13.99.
Lindeen, Carol K. *Fire Trucks*. Mankato, MN: Capstone, 2005; 32 pp., $14.95.
Lindgren, Astrid. *I Want a Brother or Sister*. New York: Farrar, Straus & Giroux, 1988; 32 pp., $10.95.
Lionni, Leo. *A Busy Year*. New York: Knopf, 1992; 32 pp., $10.99.
Lionni, Leo. *An Extraordinary Egg*. New York: Knopf, 1994; 40 pp., $16.00.
Lionni, Leo. *Let's Play*. New York: Knopf, 1993; 10 pp., $6.99.
Lionni, Leo. *Matthew's Dream*. New York: Random House, 1995; 32 pp., $5.99.
Lissy, Jessica. *A Blue's Clue's Chanukah*. New York: Simon Spotlight, 2003; 32 pp., $3.99.
Littlefield, Cindy A. *Awesome Ocean Science!* Charlotte, VT: Williamson, 2003; 120 pp., $12.95.
Livingston, Irene. *Finklehopper Frog*. Berkeley, CA: Tricycle, 2003; 32 pp., $14.95.
Llewellyn, Claire. *Ladybugs*. Danbury, CT: Franklin Watts, 2000; 32 pp., $15.75.
Loewen, Nancy. *Fire Safety*. New York: Child's World, 1997; 24 pp., $12.95.
Loewen, Nancy. *Save, Spend, or Divide?* Minneapolis, MN: Picture Window, 2005; 32 pp., $16.95.
Loewen, Nancy. *Spotted Beetles: Ladybugs in Your Backyard*. Minneapolis, MN: Picture Window, 2004; 32 pp., $16.95.
Loewen, Nancy. *Traffic Safety*. New York: Child's World, 1997; 24 pp., $18.50.
Lofgren, Ulf. *Alvin the Pirate*. Minneapolis, MN: Carolrhoda, 1990; 32 pp., $13.95.
Lonborg, Rosemary. *Helpin' Bugs*. Scituate, MA: Little Friend, 1995; 32 pp., $14.95.
London, Jonathan. *Condor's Egg*. San Francisco: Chronicle, 1994; 32 pp., $13.95.
London, Jonathan. *Do Your ABC's, Little Brown Bear*. New York: Dutton, 2005; 32 pp., $15.99.
London, Jonathan. *Froggy's Day with Dad*. New York.: Viking, 2004; 32 pp., $15.99.
London, Jonathan. *Froggy's First Kiss*. New York: Viking Penguin, 1998; 32 pp., $14.99.
London, Jonathan. *Giving Thanks*. Cambridge, MA: Candlewick, 2003; 32 pp., $16.99.
London, Jonathan. *Hurricane!* New York: Lothrop, Lee and Shepard, 1998; 32 pp., $16.00.

London, Jonathan. *A Koala for Katie: An Adoption Story*. Morton Grove, IL: Albert Whitman, 1993; 24 pp., $13.95.

London, Jonathan. *Let's Go, Froggy*. New York: Viking, 1994; 30 pp., $14.99.

London, Jonathan. *The Owl Who Became the Moon*. New York: Dutton, 1993; 32 pp., $15.99.

London, Jonathan. *Puddles*. New York: Viking Penguin, 1997; 32 pp., $15.99.

London, Jonathan. *Sled Dogs Run*. New York: Walker, 2005; 32 pp., $16.95.

London, Jonathan. *What Newt Could Do for Turtle*. Cambridge, MA: Candlewick, 1996; 32 pp., $16.99.

London, Sara. *The Good Luck Glasses*. New York: Scholastic, 2000; 10 pp., $3.99.

Long, Jan Freeman. *The Bee and the Dream*. New York: Dutton, 1996; 40 pp., $15.99.

Long, Melinda. *How I Became a Pirate*. San Diego: Harcourt, 2003; 32 pp., $16.00.

Long, Teddy Cameron. *Fantastic Paper Holiday Decorations*. New York: Sterling, 1994; 96 pp., $19.98.

Loomans, Diana, and Karen Kolberg. *The Laughing Classroom*. Novato, CA: New World Library, 1993; 226 pp., $15.95.

Loomis, Christine. *Cowboy Bunnies*. New York: Putnam, 1997; 30 pp., $15.95.

Loomis, Christine. *The Hippo Hop*. Boston: Houghton Mifflin, 1995; 32 pp., $14.95.

Lopez, Loretta. *The Birthday Swap*. New York: Lee and Low, 1997; 32 pp., $15.95.

Low, William. *Chinatown*. New York: Henry Holt, 1997; 32 pp., $15.95.

Lowenstein, Felicia. *What Does a Doctor Do?* Berkeley Heights, NJ: Enslow, 2005; 32 pp., $15.95.

Ludwig, Warren. *Old Noah's Elephants*. New York: Putnam, 1991; 32 pp., $14.95.

Luenn, Nancy. *Mother Earth*. New York: Atheneum, 1992; 32 pp., $15.00.

Lund, Deb. *Dinosailors*. San Diego: Harcourt, 2003; 32 pp., $16.00.

Lundgren, Mary Beth. *Seven Scary Monsters*. Boston: Clarion, 2003; 32 pp., $15.00.

Luthardt, Kevin. *Hats*. Morton Grove, IL: Albert Whitman, 2004; 32 pp., $15.95.

Luthardt, Kevin. *Larabee*. Atlanta, GA: Peachtree, 2004; 32 pp., $15.95.

Luttrell, Ida. *Milo's Toothache*. New York: Dial, 1992; 40 pp., $10.89.

Luttrell, Ida. *Three Good Blankets*. New York: Atheneum, 1990; 32 pp., $13.95.

Luvmour, Josette and Ba. *Winn-Winn Games for All Ages*. Gabriola Island, Canada: New Society Publishers, 2002; 130 pp., $13.95.

Lyon, George Ella. *Counting on the Woods*. New York: DK Publishing, 1998; 32 pp., $15.95.

Lyon, George Ella. *Mama is a Miner*. New York: Orchard, 1994; 32 pp., $15.95.

Maass, Robert. *When Spring Comes*. New York: Henry Holt, 1994; 32 pp., $14.95.

Maass, Robert. *When Summer Comes*. New York: Henry Holt, 1993; 32 pp., $14.95.

Maccarone, Grace. *Peter Rabbit's Happy Easter*. New York: Scholastic, 2006; 32 pp., $5.99.

Maccarone, Grace. *The Silly Story of Goldie Locks and the Three Squares*. New York: Scholastic, 1996; 32 pp., $3.50.

MacDonald, Elizabeth. *Mike's Kite*. New York: Orchard, 1990; 32 pp., $19.25.

MacDonald, Maryann. *Little Hippo Gets Glasses*. New York: Dial, 1991; 28 pp., $11.00.

MacDonald, Maryann. *The Pink Party*. New York: Hyperion, 1994; 40 pp., $11.49.

MacDonald, Maryann. *Rabbit's Birthday Kite*. New York: Bantam, 1991; 32 pp., $9.99.

MacDonald, Maryann. *Rosie and the Poor Rabbits*. New York: Atheneum, 1994; 32 pp., $13.95.
MacDonald, Maryann. *Sam's Worries*. New York: Hyperion, 1990; 28 pp., $13.95.
MacDonald, Suse. *Peck, Slither, and Slide*. San Diego: Gulliver, 1997; 48 pp., $15.00.
MacGill-Callahan, Sheila. *And Still the Turtle Watched*. New York: Dial, 1991; 32 pp., $14.90.
MacGill-Callahan, Sheila. *To Capture the Wind*. New York: Dial, 1997; 32 pp., $14.99.
MacLean, Christine Kole. *Even Firefighters Hug Their Moms*. New York: Dutton, 2002; 32 pp., $15.99.
Maddisan, Beth. *The Big Book of Stories, Songs and Sing-Alongs*. Westport, CT: Libraries Unlimited, 2003; 281 pp., $35.00.
Maestro, Betsy. *Why Do Leaves Change Color?* New York: HarperCollins, 1994; 32 pp., $14.89.
Maestro, Betsy and Giulio. *Bike Trip*. New York: HarperCollins, 1992; 32 pp., $15.89.
Maestro, Betsy and Giulio. *Delivery Van*. Boston: Clarion, 1990; 32 pp., $14.95.
Maguire, Jack. *Hopscotch, Hangman, Hot Potato and Ha, Ha, Ha*. Paramus, NJ: Prentice Hall, 1990; 304 pp., $13.95.
Mahoney, Daniel J. *A Really Good Snowman*. Boston: Clarion, 2005; 32 pp., $15.00.
Mahy, Margaret. *Beaten by a Balloon*. New York: Viking, 1997; 32 pp., $15.99.
Mahy, Margaret. *A Busy Day for a Good Grandmother*. New York: Margaret McElderry, 1993; 26 pp., $14.95.
Mahy, Margaret. *The Pumpkin Man and the Crafty Creeper*. New York: Lothrop, Lee and Shepard, 1990; 28 pp., $14.88.
Mahy, Margaret. *The Queen's Goat*. New York: Dial, 1991; 32 pp., $12.95.
Mahy, Margaret. *A Summer Saturday Morning*. New York: Viking, 1998; 32 pp., $15.99.
Mainland, Pauline. *A Yoga Parade of Animals*. Boston: Element, 1998; 32 pp., $15.95.
Maloney, Peter, and Felicia Zekauskas. *Bronto Eats Meat*. New York: Dial, 2003; 32 pp., $16.99.
Mandel, Peter. *Boats on the River*. New York: Scholastic, 2004; 32 pp., $6.99.
Marciano, John Bemelmans. *There's a Dolphin in the Grand Canal*. New York: Viking, 2005; 32 pp., $15.99.
Marino, Jane. *Mother Goose Time*. Bronx, NY: H. W. Wilson, 1992; 172 pp., $30.00.
Markes, Julie. *Shhhhh! Everybody's Sleeping*. New York: HarperCollins, 2005; 32 pp., $15.89.
Markes, Julie. *Thanks for Thanksgiving*. New York: HarperCollins, 2004; 32 pp., $12.99.
Markle, Sandra. *A Mother's Journey*. Watertown, MA: Charlesbridge, 2005; 32 pp., $15.95.
Markun, Patricia M. *The Little Painter of Sabana Grande*. New York: Simon & Schuster, 1993; 32 pp., $14.95.
Marlow, Layn. *The Witch with a Twitch*. Wilton, CT: Tiger Tales, 2005; 32 pp., $15.95.
Marshak, Samuel. *Hail to Mail*. New York: Henry Holt, 1990; 32 pp., $9.50.
Marston, Hope Irvin. *Fire Trucks*. New York: Cobblehill, 1996; 48 pp., $14.99.
Martin, Ann. *Rachel Parker, Kindergarten Show-Off*. New York: Holiday House, 1992; 40 pp., $15.95.

Martin, Antoinette Truglio. *Famous Seaweed Soup*. Morton Grove, IL: Albert Whitman, 1993; 32 pp., $14.95.

Martin, Jr., Bill. *Little Granny Quarterback!* Honesdale, PA: Boyds Mill, 2001; 32 pp., $15.95.

Martin, Jr., Bill. *Polar Bear, Polar Bear, What Do You Hear?* New York: Henry Holt, 1991; 32 pp., $15.95.

Martin, Jr., Bill, and Michael Sampson. *Swish!* New York: Henry Holt, 1997; 32 pp., $14.95.

Martin, David. *Five Little Piggies*. Cambridge, MA: Candlewick, 1998; 40 pp., $16.99.

Martin, David. *Piggy and Dad Go Fishing*. Cambridge, MA: Candlewick, 2005; 32 pp., $14.99.

Martin, David. *We've All Got Bellybuttons!* Cambridge, MA: Candlewick, 2005; 32 pp., $15.99.

Martin, Laura. *Nature's Art Box*. North Adams, MA: Storey Kids, 2003; 215 pp., $23.95.

Martin, Mary Jane. *From Anne to Zach*. Honesdale, PA: Boyds Mills, 1996; 40 pp., $14.95.

Martin, Rafe. *The Brave Little Parrot*. New York: Putnam, 1998; 32 pp., $15.99.

Marzollo, Jean. *Snow Angel*. New York.: Scholastic, 1995; 34 pp., $14.95.

Marzollo, Jean. *Ten Cats Have Hats*. New York: Scholastic, 1994; 24 pp., $6.95.

Massey, Jeanne. *The Littlest Witch*. New York: Knopf, 1959; unpaged, $5.00

Massie, Diane Redfield. *The Baby Beebee Bird*. New York: HarperCollins, 2000; 32 pp., $16.99.

Mastas, Margaret A. *Mommy's Best Kisses*. New York: HarperCollins, 2003; 32 pp., $16.99.

Masurel, Claire. *Ten Dogs in the Window*. New York: North-South, 1997; 32 pp., $15.95.

Mather, Karen Trella. *Silas the Bookstore Cat*. Camden, ME: Down East Books, 1994; 32 pp., $14.95.

Mathews, Judith, and Fay Robinson. *Nathaniel Willy, Scared Silly*. New York: Bradbury, 1994; 32 pp., $15.00.

May, Jim. *The Boo Baby Girl Meets the Ghost of Mable's Gable*. Elgin, IL: Brotherstone, 1992; 32 pp., $14.95.

Mayer, Mercer. *Liverwurst Is Missing*. New York: Macmillan, 1990; 32 pp., $16.00.

Mayer, Pamela. *The Scariest Monster in the Whole Wide World*. New York: Putnam, 2001; 32 pp., $15.99.

Mayhew, James. *Who Wants a Dragon?* New York: Orchard, 2004; 32 pp., $15.95.

Maynard, Christ. *Science Fun at Home*. New York: DK Publishing, 2006; 93 pp., $9.99.

Mazer, Anne. *The Salamander Room*. New York: Knopf, 1991; 32 pp., $17.99.

McAllister, Angela. *Matepo*. New York: Dial, 1991; 32 pp., $12.95.

McBratney, Sam. *The Caterpillow Fight*. Cambridge, MA: Candlewick, 1996; 24 pp., $9.99.

McBratney, Sam. *The Dark at the Top of the Stairs*. Cambridge, MA: Candlewick, 1996; 28 pp., $15.99.

McBratney, Sam. *Guess How Much I Love You*. Cambridge, MA: Candlewick, 1994; 32 pp., $15.95.

McBratney, Sam. *Just You and Me.* Cambridge, MA: Candlewick, 1998; 28 pp., $15.99.
McCain, Becky Ray. *Grandmother's Dreamcatcher.* Morton Grove, IL: Albert Whitman, 1998; 32 pp., $15.95.
McCarthy, Bobette. *See You Later, Alligator.* New York: Macmillan, 1995; 32 pp., $15.00.
McCaughrean, Geraldine. *Unicorns! Unicorns!* New York: Holiday House, 1997; 32 pp., $15.95.
McClintock, Barbara. *Molly and the Magic Wishbone.* New York: Frances Foster, 2001; 32 pp., $16.00.
McCourt, Lisa. *The Best Night Out with Dad.* Deerfield Beach, FL: Health Communications, Inc., 1997; 32 pp., $14.95.
McCourt, Lisa. *I Love You, Stinky Face.* New York: Bridgewater, 1997; 32 pp., $15.95.
McCully, Emily Arnold. *Beautiful Warrior: The Legend of the Nun's Kung Fu.* New York: Scholastic, 1998; 32 pp., $16.95.
McCuly, Emily Arnold. *My Real Family.* San Diego: Browndeer, 1994; 32 pp., $14.00.
McCutcheon, John. *Happy Adoption Day.* New York: Little, Brown, 1996; 32pp., $15.95.
McDermott, Gerald. *Anansi the Spider.* New York: Harper and Row, 1995; 40 pp., $15.95.
McDermott, Gerard. *Tim O'Toole and the Wee Folk.* New York: Viking, 1990; 32 pp., $5.99.
McDermott, Gerald. *Zomo the Rabbit.* San Diego: Harcourt, 1992; 32 pp., $14.95.
McDonald, Megan. *Insects Are My Life.* New York: Orchard, 1995; 32 pp., $16.99.
McDonald, Megan. *Penguin and Little Blue.* New York: Atheneum, 2003; 32 pp., $15.95.
McDonald, Megan. *Whoo-oo is it?* New York: Orchard, 1992; 32 pp., $16.99.
McDonnell, Flora. *I Love Boats.* Cambridge, MA: Candlewick, 1995; 32 pp., $16.99.
McDonnell, Janet. *Celebrating Earth Day.* New York: Children's Press, 1994; 31 pp., $17.50.
McDonnell, Janet. *Fourth of July.* New York: Children's Press, 1994; 32 pp., $17.50.
McDonnell, Janet. *Kangaroo's Adventure in Alphabet Town.* New York: Children's Press, Inc.,1992; 32 pp., $18.20.
McFarland, Lyn Rossiter. *Widget and the Puppy.* New York: Farrar, Straus & Giroux, 2004; 32 pp., $16.00.
McGeorge, Constance W. *Boomer Goes to School.* San Francisco: Chronicle, 1996; 26 pp., $13.95.
McGhee, Alison. *Countdown to Kindergarten.* San Diego: Silver Whistle, 2002; 32 pp., $16.00.
McGovern, Ann. *The Lady in the Box.* New York: Group West, 1997; 32 pp., $14.95.
McGovern, Ann. *Too Much Noise!* Boston: Houghton Mifflin, 1967; 45 pp., $16.00.
McGowan, Diane, and Mark Schrooten. *Math Play!: 80 Ways to Count and Learn.* Charlotte, Vt.: Williamson, 1997; 144 pp., $12.95.
McGrath, Barbara Barbieri. *The Little Green Witch.* Watertown, MA: Charlesbridge, 2005; 32 pp., $14.95.

McGraw, Phillip C., and Vincent Douglas. *Paper and Paint: Hands-On Crafts for Everyday Fun*. New York: Waterbird, 2003; 48 pp., $12.95.
McGrory, Anik. *Kidogo*. New York: Bloomsbury, 2005; 32 pp., $15.95.
McGuire, Richard. *The Orange Book*. New York: Children's Universe, 1995; 40 pp., $4.99.
McGuire-Turcotte, Casey A. *How Honu the Turtle Got His Shell*. Milwaukee, WI: Steck-Vaughn Co., 1991; 30 pp., $22.83.
McKay, Hilary. *There's a Dragon Downstairs*. New York: Margaret K. McElderry, 2003; 32 pp., $16.95.
McKean,Thomas. *Hooray for Grandma Jo!* New York: Crown, 1994; 32 pp., $14.00.
McKee, David. *Elmer and the Kangaroo*. New York: HarperCollins, 2000; 32 pp., $14.95.
McKinlay, Penny. *Bumposaurus*. New York: Phyllis Fogelman, 2003; 32 pp., $15.99.
McKissack, Patricia and Frederick. *Messy Bessey's School Desk*. New York: Children's Press, 1998; 31 pp., $16.00.
McLerran, Alice. *I Want to Go Home*. New York: Tambourine, 1992; 32 pp, $15.00.
McMahan, Patricia. *Listen for the Bus: David's Story*. Honesdale, PA: Boyds Mills, 1995; 48 pp., $15.95.
McMillan, Bruce. *Going on a Whale Watch*. New York: Scholastic, 1992; 40 pp., $14.95.
McMillan, Bruce. *Jelly Bean for Sale*. New York: Scholastic, 1996; 32 pp., $15.95.
McMillan, Bruce. *Sense Surprise: A Guessing Game for the Five Senses*. New York: Scholastic, 1994; 32 pp., $15.95.
McMullan, Kate. *Pearl and Wagner: Three Secrets*. New York: Dial, 2004; 32 pp., $14.99.
McMullan, Kate and Jim. *I'm Mighty!* New York: HarperCollins, 2003; 32 pp., $16.89.
McNamara, Margaret. *The Playground Problem*. New York: Aladdin, 2004; 32 pp., $15.00.
McNaughton, Colin. *Autumn*. New York: Dial, 1984; 24 pp., $4.95.
McPhail, David. *Edward and the Pirates*. New York: Little, Brown, 1997; 32 pp., $15.95.
McPhail, David. *Moony B. Finch, the Fastest Draw in the West*. New York: Western, 1994; 32 pp., $12.95.
McPhail, David. *Pigs Ahoy!* New York: Dutton, 1995; 32 pp., $14.99.
McPhail, David. *Pigs Aplenty, Pigs Galore!* New York: Dutton, 1993; 32 pp., $14.99.
McPhail, David. *The Puddle*. New York: Farrar, Straus & Giroux, 1998; 32 pp., $15.00.
McPhail, David. *Tinker and Tom and the Star Baby*. New York: Little, Brown, 1998; 32 pp., $14.95.
Meddaugh, Susan. *Cinderella's Rat*. Boston: Houghton Mifflin, 1997; 32 pp., $15.00.
Meddaugh, Susan. *Hog-Eye*. Boston: Houghton Mifflin, 1995; 32 pp., $14.95.
Meddaugh, Susan. *Martha Walks the Dog*. Boston: Houghton Mifflin, 1998; 32 pp., $15.00.
Meddaugh, Susan. *Perfectly Martha*. Boston: Houghton Mifflin, 2004; 32 pp., $15.00.
Meddaugh, Susan. *Tree of Birds*. Boston: Houghton Mifflin, 1990; 32 pp., $16.00.
Meddaugh, Susan. *The Witches' Supermarket*. Boston: Houghton Mifflin, 1991; 32 pp., $13.95.
Meddaugh, Susan. *The Witch's Walking Stick*. Boston: Houghton Mifflin, 2005; 32 pp., $16.00.

Medearis, Angela Shelf. *The Biggest Snowball Fight.* New York: Scholastic, 2001; 10 pp., $3.99.
Medearis, Angela Shelf. *Dancing with the Indians.* New York: Holiday House, 1991; 32 pp., $15.95.
Medearis, Angela Shelf. *Lucy's Quiet Book.* San Diego: Harcourt, 2000; 32 pp., $12.95.
Medearis, Angela Shelf. *The Zebra-Riding Cowboy.* New York: Henry Holt, Inc., 1992; 32 pp., $14.95.
Meiners, Cheri J. *Be Polite and Kind.* Minneapolis, MN: Free Spirit, 2004; 32 pp., $10.95.
Meister, Cari. *Luther's Halloween.* New York: Viking, 2004; 32 pp., $15.99.
Melling, David. *The Kiss that Missed.* Hauppauge, NY: Barron's Educational Series, 2002; 32 pp., $14.95.
Melmed, Laura Krauss. *Fright Night Flight.* New York: HarperCollins, 2002; 32 pp., $17.89.
Merriam, Eve. *Bam, Bam, Bam.* New York: Henry Holt, 1994; 32 pp., $14.95.
Michel, Margaret. *The Best of the Mailbox, Book 1: Preschool/Kindergarten edition.* Greensboro, N.C.: Education Center, 1993; 192 pp., $22.95.
Michel, Margaret. *The Best of the Mailbox, Book 2: Preschool/Kindergarten edition.* Greensboro, N.C.: Education Center, 1996; 192 pp., $22.95.
Milgrim, David. *Cows Can't Fly.* New York: Viking, 1998; 32 pp., $15.99.
Miller, Edna. *Mousekin's Lost Woodland.* New York: Simon & Schuster, 1992; 32 pp., $13.00.
Miller, Heather. *What Does a Dentist Do?* Berkeley Heights, NJ: Enslow, 2006; 32 pp., $21.26.
Miller, Kathryn Ann. *Did My First Mother Love Me?: A Story for an Adopted Child.* Buena Park, Calif.: Morning Glory, 1994; 48 pp., $12.95.
Miller, Margaret. *Big and Little.* New York: Greenwillow, 1998; 32 pp., $15.00.
Miller, Margaret. *My Five Senses.* New York: Simon & Schuster, 1994; 24 pp., $16.00.
Miller, Margaret. *Now I'm Big.* New York: Greenwillow, 1996; 32 pp., $15.00.
Miller, Ned. *Emmett's Snowball.* New York: Henry Holt, 1990; 32 pp., $14.95.
Miller, Virginia. *Be Gentle!* Cambridge, MA: Candlewick, 1997; 32 pp., $15.99.
Millman, Isaac. *Moses Goes to a Concert.* New York: Farrar, Straus & Giroux, 1998; 32 pp., $16.00.
Millman, Isaac. *Moses Goes to the Circus.* New York: Frances Foster, 2003; 32 pp., $16.00.
Millman, Isaac. *Moses Sees a Play.* New York: Frances Foster, 2004; 32 pp., $16.00.
Mills, Claudia. *Phoebe's Parade.* New York: Macmillan, 1994; 32 pp., $14.95.
Mills, Claudia. *Ziggy's Blue Ribbon Day.* New York: Farrar, Straus & Giroux, 2005; 32 pp., $16.00.
Milton, Tony. *Riddledy Piggledy: A Book of Rhymes and Riddles.* New York: Random House, 2003; 32 pp., $16.95.
Minarik, Else Holmelund. *The Little Girl and the Dragon.* New York: Greenwillow, 1991; 24 pp., $20.00.
Miranda, Anne. *Baby-sit.* New York: Little, Brown, 1990; 14 pp., $9.95.
Miranda, Anne. *To Market, To Market.* San Diego: Harcourt, 1997; 32 pp., $16.00.

Mitchell, Rhonda. *The Talking Cloth.* New York: Orchard, 1997; 32 pp., $15.95.
Modesitt, Jeanne. *Mama, If You Had a Wish.* New York: Green Tiger, 1993; 40 pp., $15.00.
Mogensen, Jan. *The Tiger's Breakfast.* New York: Crocodile, 1991; 28 pp., $14.95.
Molk, Laurel. *Good Job, Oliver!* New York: Crown, 1999; 32 pp., $18.99.
Mollel, Tololwa M. *Ananse's Feast: An Ashanti Tale.* Boston: Clarion, 1997; 32 pp., $14.95.
Monks, Lydia. *Aaaarrgghh! Spider!* Boston: Houghton Mifflin, 2004; 32 pp., $16.00.
Monson, A.M. *Wanted: Best Friend.* New York: Dial, 1997; 32 pp., $14.99.
Montague-Smith, Ann. *First Shape Book.* New York: Kingfisher, 2002; 32 pp., $12.95.
Montijo, Rhode. *Cloud Boy.* New York: Simon & Schuster, 2006; 32 pp., $12.95.
Moon, Nicola. *Lucy's Picture.* New York: Dial, 1994; 32 pp., $15.99.
Moon, Nicola. *Mouse Tells the Time.* London: Pavilion, 2002; 32 pp., $18.00.
Moon, Nicola. *Something Special.* Atlanta, GA: Peachtree, 1995; 32 pp., $14.95.
Moon, Nicola. *Tick-Tock, Drip-Drop!* New York: Bloomsbury, 2004; 32 pp., $16.95.
Moore, Inga. *Fifty Red Night-Caps.* San Francisco: Chronicle, 1998; 32 pp., $12.95.
Moore, Inga. *Little Dog Lost.* New York: Macmillan, 1991; 28 pp., $14.95.
Mora, Pat. *Tomas and the Library Lady.* New York: Knopf, 1997; 32 pp., $17.00.
Morales, Yuyi. *Just a Minute.* San Francisco: Chronicle, 2003; 32 pp., $15.95.
Moran, Alex. *Popcorn.* San Diego: Green Light Readers, 1999; 32 pp., $10.95.
Morgan, Michaela. *Helpful Betty to the Rescue.* Minneapolis, MN: Carolrhoda, 1993; 32 pp., $18.60.
Morninghouse, Sundaira. *Habari Gani? What's the News?* New York: Open Hand, 1992; 32 pp., $14.95.
Morris, Ann. *The Baby Book.* Parsippany, NJ: Silver, 1996; 32 pp., $13.95.
Morris, Ann. *On the Go.* New York: Lothrop, Lee and Shepard, 1990, 28 pp., $15.93.
Morrow, Priscella. *Totally Tubeys!* Fort Atkinson, WI: Upstart, 2003; 80 pp., $16.95.
Moss, Jeffrey. *The Sesame Street ABC Storybook.* New York: Random House, 1974; 72 pp., $5.99.
Moss, Marissa. *After School Monster.* New York: Lothrop, Lee and Shepard, 1991; 32 pp., $4.99.
Moss, Marissa. *Amelia Lends a Hand.* Middleton, WI: Pleasant, 2002; 32 pp., $14.95.
Moss, Marissa. *But Not Kate.* New York: Lothrop, Lee and Shepard, 1992; 32 pp., $14.00.
Moss, Marissa. *Regina's Big Mistake.* Boston: Houghton Mifflin, 1990; 28 pp., $16.00.
Moss, Marissa. *The Ugly Menorah.* New York: Farrar, Straus & Giroux, 1996; 32 pp, $14.00.
Most, Bernard. *Cock-a-Doodle-Moo!* San Diego: Harcourt, 1996; 32 pp., $12.00.
Most, Bernard. *The Cow That Went Oink.* San Diego: Harcourt, 1990; 36 pp., $13.00.
Most, Bernard. *Dinosaur Questions.* San Diego: Harcourt, 1995; 36 pp., $15.00.
Most, Bernard. *Four and Twenty Dinosaurs.* New York: Harper and Row, 1990; 32 pp., $8.95.
Most, Bernard. *Zoodles.* San Diego: Harcourt, 1992; 32 pp., $13.95.
Mueller, Stephanie R., and Ann E. Wheeler. *101 Great Gifts from Kids.* Beltsville, MD: Gryphon House, 2002; 174 pp., $14.95.

Munsch, Robert. *Alligator Baby*. New York: Scholastic, 1997; 32 pp., $10.95.
Murphy, Jill. *All for One*. Cambridge, MA: Candlewick, 2002; 32 pp., $15.99.
Murphy, Jill. *Five Minutes' Peace*. New York: Putnam, 1995; 32 pp., $16.95.
Murphy, Mary. *How Kind!* Cambridge, MA: Candlewick, 2002; 32 pp., $14.99.
Murphy, Mary. *Little Owl and the Star: A Christmas Story*. Cambridge, MA: Candlewick, 2003; 32 pp., $12.99.
Murphy, Pat. *Pigasus*. New York: Dial, 1996; 32 pp., $14.99.
Murphy, Stuart J. *The Best Vacation Ever*. New York: HarperCollins, 1997; 40 pp., $14.90.
Murphy, Stuart J. *Game Time*. New York: HarperCollins, 2000; 32 pp., $15.89.
Murphy, Stuart J. *Get Up and Go!* New York: HarperCollins, 1996; 40 pp, $14.89.
Murphy, Stuart J. *It's About Time!* New York: HarperCollins, 2005; 32 pp., $15.99.
Murphy, Stuart J. *The Penny Pot*. New York: HarperCollins, 1998; 32 pp., $14.95.
Murphy, Stuart J. *Three Little Firefighters*. New York: HarperCollins, 2003; 32 pp., $15.99.
Murphy, Stuart J. *Too Many Kangaroo Things to Do!* New York: HarperCollins, 1996; 40 pp., $14.89.
Murray, Andrew. *The Very Sleepy Sloth*. Wilton, CT: Little Tiger, 2003; 32 pp., $15.95.
Murray, Marjorie Dennis. *Don't Wake Up the Bear!* Tarrytown, NY: Marshall Cavendish, 2003; 32 pp., $14.95.
Myers, Lynne Born. *Turnip Soup*. New York: Hyperion, 1994; 32 pp., $13.90.
Myers, Walter Dean. *How Mr. Monkey Saw the Whole World*. New York: Doubleday, 1996; 32 pp., $14.95.
Namm, Diane. *Pick a Pet*. New York: Children's Press. 2004; 32 pp., $18.50.
Napoli, Donna Jo. *Pink Magic*. Boston: Clarion, 2005; 32 pp., $15.00.
Nash, Ogden. *The Tale of Custard the Dragon*. New York: Little, Brown, 1995; 32 pp., $14.95.
Naylor, Phyllis Reynolds. *Ducks Disappearing*. New York: Atheneum, 1999; 32 pp., $13.00.
Naylor, Phyllis Reynolds. *Jennifer Jean, the Cross-Eyed Queen*. Minneapolis, MN: Carolrhoda, 1994; 32 pp., $5.99.
Neeham, Bobbe. *Ecology Crafts for Kids*. New York: Sterling, 1998; 144 pp., $24.95.
Neitzel, Shirley. *The House I'll Build for the Wrens*. New York: Greenwillow, 1997; 32 pp., $15.00
Neitzel, Shirley. *We're Making Breakfast for Mother*. New York: Greenwillow, 1997; 32 pp., $15.00.
Nelson, S.D. *The Star People: A Lakota Story*. New York: Abrams, 2003; 32 pp., $14.95.
Nerlove, Miriam. *Valentine's Day*. Morton Grove, IL: Albert Whitman, 1992; 32 pp., $13.95.
Neubecker, Robert. *Beasty Bath*. New York: Orchard, 2004; 32 pp., $14.99.
Newcome, Zita. *Head, Shoulders, Knees, and Toes and Other Action Rhymes*. Cambridge, MA: Candlewick, 1999; 32 pp., $15.99.
Newcome, Zita. *Toddlerobics*. Cambridge, MA: Candlewick, 1996; 32 pp., $14.99.
Newcome, Zita. *Toddlerobics: Animal Fun*. Cambridge, MA: Candlewick, 1999; 32 pp., $15.99.
Newman, Leslea. *The Eight Nights of Chanukah*. New York: Abrams, 2005; 32 pp., $12.95.

Newman, Leslea. *A Fire Engine for Ruthie.* Boston: Clarion, 2004; 32 pp, $16.00.
Newman, Leslea. *Remember That.* Boston: Clarion, 1993; 32 pp., $14.95.
Newman, Leslea. *Runaway Dreidel!* New York: Henry Holt, 2002; 32 pp., $17.95.
Newman, Leslea. *Where Is Bear?* San Diego: Gulliver, 2004; 32 pp., $16.00.
Newman, Marjorie. *Mole and the Baby Bird.* New York: Bloomsbury, 2002; 32 pp., $16.95.
Newman, Nanette. *There's a Bear in the Bath!* San Diego: Harcourt, 1994; 32 pp., $13.95.
Nicholls, Judith. *Billywise.* New York: Bloomsbury, 2002; 32 pp., $16.95.
Nichols, Judy. *Storytimes for Two-Year-Olds, 2nd edition.* Chicago: ALA, 1998; 249 pp., $28.00.
Nielsen, Laura F. *Jeremy's Muffler.* New York: Atheneum, 1995; 32 pp., $15.00.
Nightingale, Sandy. *Cider Apples.* San Diego: Harcourt, 1996; 28 pp., $15.00.
Nikola, Lisa, W. *1, 2, 3 Thanksgiving!* Morton Grove, IL: Albert Whitman, 1991; 32 pp., $24.50.
Noble, Sheilagh. *Let's Look at Eyes.* Chicago: Zero to Ten, 2003; 32 pp., $9.95.
Noble, Trinka Hakes. *Jimmy's Boa and the Bungee Jump Slam Dunk.* New York: Dial, 2003; 32 pp., $16.99.
Nobleman, Marc Tyler. *Independence Day.* Minneapolis, MN: Compass Point, 2005; 32 pp., $14.95.
Nobleman, Marc Tyler. *Summer Activities.* New York: Kaplan, 2006; 240 pp., $12.00.
Nolan, Lucy. *A Fairy in a Dairy.* Tarrytown, NY: Marshall Cavendish, 2003; 32 pp., $16.95.
Nolen, Jerdine. *Raising Dragons.* San Diego: Harcourt, 1998; 32 pp., $16.00.
Noll, Sally. *I Have a Loose Tooth.* New York: Greenwillow, 1992; 32 pp., $14.00.
Norac, Carl. *I Love You So Much.* New York: Doubleday, 1998; 26 pp., $9.95.
Norac, Carol. *My Daddy Is a Giant.* Boston: Clarion, 2004; 32 pp., $16.00.
Novak, Matt. *Too Many Bunnies.* New York: Roaring Brook, 2005; 32 pp., $7.95.
Numeroff, Laura. *The Best Mouse's Cookie.* New York: HarperCollins, 1999; 12 pp., $6.99.
Numeroff, Laura. *Chimps Don't Wear Glasses.* New York: Simon & Schuster, 1995; 32 pp., $14.00.
Numeroff, Laura. *If You Give a Pig a Pancake.* New York: HarperCollins, 1998; 32 pp., $14.95.
Numeroff, Laura. *If You Give a Pig a Party.* New York: HarperCollins, 2005; 32 pp., $16.89.
Numeroff, Laura. *What Mommies Do Best/What Daddies Do Best.* New York: Simon & Schuster, 1998; 36 pp., $13.00.
Numeroff, Laura, and Nate Evans. *Sherman Crunchley.* New York: Dutton, 2003; 32 pp., $15.99.
Nunes, Susan Miho. *The Last Dragon.* Boston: Clarion, 1995; 32 pp., $14.95.
Nurik, Cindy Bunin. *Fun with Mommy & Me.* New York: Dutton, 2001; 306 pp., $20.00.
Oberman, Sheldon. *By the Hanukkah Light.* Honesdale, PA: Boyds Mills, 1997; 32 pp., $15.95.
O'Brien, John. *The Farmer in the Dell.* Honesdale, PA: Boyds Mills, 2000; 32 pp., $14.95.

O'Brien, John. *Poof!* Honesdale, PA: Boyds Mills, 1999; 32 pp., $14.95.
O'Bryan, Sharon. *Old Fashioned Children's Games.* Jefferson, NC: McFarland, 1999; 143 pp., $29.95.
O'Connell, Jennifer. *Ten Timid Ghosts.* New York: Scholastic, 2000; 32 pp., $3.25.
O'Connor, Jane. *Fancy Nancy.* New York: HarperCollins, 2006; 32 pp., $15.99.
O'Donnell, Elizabeth Lee. *Patrick's Day.* New York: Morrow, 1994; 32 pp., $15.00.
O'Donnell, Elizabeth Lee. *The Twelve Days of Summer.* New York: Morrow, 1991; 32 pp., $13.95.
Offen, Hilda. *As Quiet as a Mouse.* New York: Dutton, 1994; 32 pp., $12.99.
Offen, Hilda. *A Fox Got My Socks.* New York: Dutton, 1992; 28 pp., $10.00.
Ogburn, Jacqueline K. *The Noise Lullaby.* New York: Lothrop, Lee and Shepard, 1995; 32 pp., $15.00.
O'Malley, Kevin. *Carl Caught a Flying Fish.* New York: Simon & Schuster, 1996; 32 pp., $13.00.
O'Malley, Kevin. *Straight to the Pole.* New York: Walker, 2003; 32 pp., $15.95.
Oppenheim, Joanne. *Rooter Remembers.* New York: Viking, 1991; 32 pp., $11.95.
Oram, Hiawyn. *Baba Yaga and the Wise Doll.* New York: Dutton, 1997; 32 pp., $15.99.
Oram, Hiawyn. *Badger's Bring Something Party.* New York: Lothrop, Lee and Shepard, 1995; 32 pp., $15.00.
Orgel, Doris. *The Spaghetti Party.* New York: Bantam, 1995; 32 pp., $12.95.
Orgel, Doris, and Ellen Schecter. *The Flower of Sheba.* New York: Bantam, 1994; 48 pp., $18.60.
Orloff, Karen Kaufman. *I Wanna Iguana.* New York: Putnam, 2004; 32 pp., $15.99.
Ormerod, Jan. *Ms. MacDonald Has a Class.* Boston: Clarion, 1996; 32 pp., $15.95.
Ormerod, Jan. *When an Elephant Comes to School.* New York: Orchard, 2005; 32 pp., $16.95.
Orr, Katherine. *Story of a Dolphin.* Minneapolis, MN: Carolrhoda, 1993; 32 pp., $19.95.
Orton, Lyn. *The Grolier Kids Crafts Puppet Book.* New York: Grolier, 1997; 48 pp., $15.00.
Osofsky, Audrey. *Dreamcatcher.* New York: Orchard, 1992; 32 pp., $16.99.
Osofsky, Audrey. *My Buddy.* New York: Henry Holt, 1992; 32pp., $15.95.
Ostheeren, Ingrid. *Coriander's Easter Adventure.* New York: North-South, 1992; 32 pp., $14.95.
Ostheeren, Ingrid. *Martin and the Pumpkin Ghost.* New York: North-South, 1994; 32 pp., $14.90.
Ostrow, Vivian. *My Brother is from Outer Space (The Book of Proof).* Morton Grove, IL: Albert Whitman, 1996; 32 pp., $14.95.
Otten, Charlotte F. *January Rides the Wind: A Book of Months.* New York: Lothrop, Lee and Shepard, 1997; 32 pp., $16.00.
Otto, Carolyn. *I Can Tell by Touching.* New York: HarperCollins, 1994; 32 pp., $14.89.
Otto, Carolyn. *That Sky, That Rain.* New York: Thomas Y. Crowell, 1990; 32 pp., $12.95.
Owen, Ann. *Delivering Your Mail.* Minneapolis, MN: Picture Window, 2004; 32 pp., $16.95.
Owen, Ann. *Keeping You Healthy: A Book About Doctors.* Minneapolis, MN: Picture Windows, 2004; 32 pp., $16.95.

Owen, Ann. *Keeping You Safe: A Book About Police Officers.* Minneapolis, MN: Picture Window, 2004; 32 pp., $16.95.
Owen, Ann. *Protecting Your Home.* Minneapolis, MN: Picture Window, 2004; 32 pp., $16.95.
Owen, Cheryl, and Anna Murray. *The Grolier Kids Crafts Craft Book.* New York: Grolier, 1997; 48 pp., $15.00.
Owen, Cheryl, and Anna Murray. *Pack-O-Fun Magazine.* Des Plaines, IL: Clapper, April, 2005; $4.99.
Owen, Cheryl, and Anna Murray. *Pack-O-Fun Magazine.* Des Plaines, IL: Clapper, February, 2006, $4.99.
Packard, Mary. *Don't Make a Sound.* Milwaukee, WI: Gareth Stevens, 2004; 32 pp., $14.50.
Packard, Mary. *The Kite.* New York: Children's Press, 1990; 28 pp., $3.95.
Palatini, Margie. *Elf Help: http://www.falala.com.* New York: Hyperion, 1997; 32 pp., $14.95.
Palatini, Margie. *Goldie Is Mad.* New York: Hyperion, 2003; 32 pp., $14.99.
Palatini, Margie. *Moo Who?* New York: HarperCollins, 2004; 32 pp., $16.89.
Palatini, Margie. *The Perfect Pet.* New York: HarperCollins, 2003; 32 pp., $16.89.
Palatini, Margie. *Piggie Pie!* Boston: Clarion, 1995; 32 pp., $13.95.
Palatini, Margie. *The Three Silly Billies.* New York: Simon & Schuster, 2005; 32 pp., $15.95.
Pancella, Peggy. *Stranger Danger.* Barrington, IL: Heinemann, 2005; 32 pp., $18.00.
Paraskevas, Betty. *Cecil Bunions and the Midnight Train.* San Diego: Harcourt, 1996; 32 pp., $16.00.
Parish, Peggy. *Mind Your Manners.* New York: Greenwillow, 1994; 56 pp., $10.15.
Parker, Marjorie Blain. *Hello, Fire Truck!* New York: Scholastic, 2004; 32 pp., $3.99.
Parker, Mary Jessie. *City Storm.* New York: Scholastic, 1990; 32 pp., $12.95.
Parker, Vic, and Emily Bolam. *Bearobics: A Hip-Hop Counting Story.* New York: Viking, 1997; 26 pp., $14.99.
Parr, Todd. *Reading Makes You Feel Good.* New York: Little, Brown, 2005; 32 pp., $15.99.
Paschen, Elise. *Poetry Speaks to Children.* Naperville, IL: Sourcebooks Media Fusion, 2005; 32 pp., $19.95.
Passen, Lisa. *The Incredible Shrinking Teacher.* New York: Henry Holt, 2002; 32 pp., $15.95.
Patz, Nancy. *To Annabella Pelican from Thomas Hippotamus.* New York: Four Winds, 1991; 32 pp., $13.95.
Paul, Ann Whitford. *Hello Toes! Hello Feet!* New York: DK Publishing, 1998; 32 pp., $15.95.
Paul, Ann Whitford. *Little Monkey Says Good Night.* New York: Farrar, Straus & Giroux, 2003; 32 pp., $16.00.
Paul, Ann Whitford. *Shadows Are About.* New York: Scholastic, 1992; 32 pp., $13.95.
Paulson, Tim. *Jack and the Beanstalk and the Beanstalk Incident.* New York: Carol Publishing Group, 1996; 32 pp., $12.95.
Paxton, Tom. *Engelbert Joins the Circus.* New York: Morrow, 1997; 32 pp., $15.00.
Paxton, Tom. *Engelbert the Elephant.* New York: Morrow, 1990; 32 pp., $14.95.
Paye, Won-Ldy, and Margaret H. Lippert. *Mrs. Chicken and the Hungry Crocodile.* New York: Henry Holt, 2003; 32 pp., $16.95.

Payne, Tony and Jan. *The Hippo-not-amus.* New York: Orchard, 2003; 32 pp., $15.95.
Pearson, Susan. *Who Swallowed Harold?* Tarrytown, NY: Marshall Cavendish, 2005; 32 pp., $16.95.
Pearson, Tracey Campbell. *The Purple Hat.* New York: Farrar, Straus & Giroux, 1997; 32 pp., $16.00.
Peat, Ann. *Shapes.* Barrington, IL: Heinemann, 2005; 32 pp., $20.64.
Pellegrini, Nina. *Families Are Different.* New York: Holiday House, 1991; 30 pp., $14.95.
Pendziwol, Jean. *No Dragons for Tea.* Tonawanda, NY: Kids Can, 1999; 32 pp., $14.95.
Pendziwol, Jean E. *A Treasure at Sea for Dragon and Me.* Tonawanda, NY: Kids Can, 2005; 32 pp., $14.95.
Penn, Malka. *The Miracle of the Potato Latkes.* New York: Holiday House, 1994; 32 pp., $15.95.
Perez, Eulalia. *101 Best Games.* Hauppauge, NY: Barron's Educational Series, 2000; 127 pp., $12.95.
Perlman, Janet. *The Emperor Penguin's New Clothes.* New York: Viking, 1994; 32 pp., $14.99.
Peteraf, Nancy J. *A Plant Called Spot.* New York: Delacorte, 1994; 32 pp., $13.95.
Peters, Lisa Westberg. *October Smiled Back.* New York: Henry Holt, 1996; 32 pp., $14.95.
Peters, Lisa Westberg. *When the Fly Flew in . . .* New York: Dial, 1994; 32 pp., $15.99.
Peterson, Carolyn Sue, and Brenny Hall. *Story Programs: A Source Book of Materials.* Lanham, Md.: Scarecrow, 1999; 294 pp., $29.50.
Peterson, Julienne. *Caterina: The Clever Farm Girl.* New York: Dial, 1996; 32 pp., $14.99.
Pfanner, Louise. *Louise Builds a Boat.* New York: Orchard, 2000; 32 pp., $10.95.
Pfeffer, Wendy. *What's It Like to Be a Fish?* New York: HarperCollins, 1996; 32 pp., $14.89.
Pfiffner, George. *Earth-Friendly Wearables.* Hoboken, NJ: John Wiley, 1994; 128 pp., $12.95.
Pfister, Marcus. *Hopper's Treetop Adventure.* New York: North-South, 1997; 32 pp., $15.95.
Pfister, Marcus. *How Leo Learned to Be King.* New York: North-South, 1998; 32 pp., $15.95.
Pfister, Marcus. *Milo and the Magical Stones.* New York: North-South, 1997; 32 pp., $18.95.
Pfister, Marcus. *The Rainbow Fish.* New York: North-South, 1992; 32 pp., $18.95.
Pfister, Marcus. *Rainbow Fish and the Big Blue Whale.* New York: North-South, 1998; 32 pp., $18.95.
Pfister, Marcus. *Rainbow Fish and the Sea Monsters' Cave.* New York: North South, 2001; 32 pp., $18.88.
Phelps, Joan Hilyer. *Finger Tales.* Fort Atkinson, WI: Upstart, 2002; 87 pp., $15.95.
Phillips, Sally Kahler. *Nonsense.* New York: Random House, 2006; 32 pp., $14.95.
Pilegard, Virginia Walton. *The Warlord's Kites.* Gretna, LA: Pelican, 2004; 32 pp., $15.95.
Pilkey, Dav. *'Twas the Night Before Thanksgiving.* New York: Orchard, 1990; 32 pp., $16.99.

Pinkney, Andrea Davis. *Seven Candles for Kwanzaa*. New York: Dial, 1993; 32 pp., $14.89.

Pinkwater, Daniel. *Author's Day*. New York: Macmillan, 1993; 32 pp., $14.00.

Pinkwater, Daniel. *The Big Orange Splot*. Norwalk, CT: Hastings House, 1992; 31 pp., $12.95.

Pinkwater, Daniel. *Doodle Flute*. New York: Macmillan, 1991; 32 pp., $12.95.

Pinnington, Andrea. *Rainy Day Activity Book*. New York: St. Martin's, 2004; unpaged, $21.99.

Pirotta, Savior. *Turtle Bay*. New York: Farrar, Straus & Giroux, 1997; 32 pp., $15.00

Pitcher, Caroline. *The Snow Whale*. San Francisco: Sierra Club, 1996; 24 pp., $15.95.

Pitre, Felix. *Paco and the Witch*. New York: Lodestar, 1995; 32 pp., $13.99.

Plourde, Lynn. *Dad, Aren't You Glad?* New York: Dutton, 2005; 32 pp., $12.99.

Plourde, Lynn. *Mother, May I?* New York: Dutton, 2004; 32 pp., $12.99.

Polacco, Patricia. *Aunt Chip and the Great Triple Creek Dam Affair*. New York: Philomel, 1996; 32 pp., $15.95.

Polacco, Patricia. *Babushka's Mother Goose*. New York: Philomel, 1995; 64 pp., $17.95.

Polacco, Patricia. *The Bee Tree*. New York: Philomel, 1993; 32 pp., $14.95.

Polacco, Patricia. *Emma Kate*. New York: Philomel, 2005; 32 pp., $16.99.

Polacco, Patricia. *Some Birthday!* New York: Simon & Schuster, 1991; 32 pp., $15.00.

Polacco, Patricia. *The Trees of the Dancing Goats*. New York: Simon & Schuster, 1996; 32 pp., $16.00.

Pollak, Barbara. *Our Community Garden*. Hillsboro, OR: Beyond Words, 2005; 32 pp., $15.95.

Pomerantz, Charlotte. *You're Not My Best Friend Anymore*. New York: Dial, 1998; 32 pp., $15.89.

Poole, Amy Lowry. *The Pea Blossom*. New York: Holiday House, 2005; 32 pp., $16.95.

Porter, A.P. *Kwanzaa*. Minneapolis, MN: Carolrhoda, 1991; 56 pp., $18.60.

Posada, Mia. *Ladybugs: Red, Fiery and Bright*. Minneapolis, MN: Carolrhoda, 2002; 32 pp., $15.95.

Potter, Beatrix. *Peter Rabbit's Rainbow Shapes and Colors*. New York: Penguin, 2006; 10 pp., $5.99.

Powell, Consie. *The First Day of Winter*. Morton Grove, IL: Albert Whitman, 2005; 32 pp., $15.95.

Powell, Jillian. *The Lazy Scarecrow*. Minneapolis, MN: Picture Window, 2001; 32 pp., $13.95.

Poydar, Nancy. *Bunny Business*. New York: Holiday House, 2003; 32 pp., $16.95.

Prater, John. *Again!* Hauppauge, NY: Barron's Educational Series, 2000; 32 pp., $12.95.

Prater, John. *The Greatest Show on Earth*. Cambridge, MA: Candlewick, 1995; 32 pp., $14.95.

Prater, John. *Once Upon a Time*. Cambridge, MA: Candlewick, 1993; 32 pp., $14.95.

Prelutsky, Jack. *The Frogs Wore Red Suspenders*. New York: Greenwillow, 2002; 64 pp., $16.95.

Press, Judy. *All Around Town: Exploring Your Community through Craft Fun*. Charlotte, VT: Williamson, 2002; 128 pp., $12.95.

Press, Judy. *Alphabet Art*. Charlotte, VT: Williamson, 1998; 144 pp., $12.95.

Press, Judy. *Animal Habitats!* Charlotte, VT: Williamson, 2005; 128 pp., $12.95.

Press, Judy. *Around the World Art and Activities.* Charlotte, VT: Williamson, 2001; 128 pp., $12.95.
Press, Judy. *Art Starts for Little Hands.* Charlotte, VT: Williamson, 2000; 120 pp., $12.95.
Press, Judy. *At the Zoo!: Explore the Animal World with Craft Fun.* Charlotte, VT: Williamson, 2002; 128 pp., $12.95.
Press, Judy. *Creative Fun for 2-to-6-Year-Olds: The Little Hands Big Fun Craft Book.* Charlotte, VT: Williamson, 1996; 144 pp., $12.95.
Press, Judy. *Vroom! Vroom!: Making 'Dozers, 'Copters, Trucks and More.* Charlotte, VT: Williamson, 1997; 160 pp., $12.95.
Priceman, Marjorie. *Hot Air: The (Mostly) True Story of the First Hot-Air Balloon Ride.* New York: Atheneum, 2005; 32 pp., $16.95.
Priddy, Roger. *Baby's Book of the Body.* New York: DK Publishing, 1996; 18 pp., $9.95.
Primavera, Elise. *Plantpet.* New York: Putnam, 1994; 32 pp., $15.95.
Primavera, Elise. *Ralph's Frozen Tale.* New York: Putnam, 1991; 32 pp., $14.95.
Pringle, Laurence. *Octopus Hug.* Honesdale, PA: Boyds Mills, 1996; 32 pp., $6.95.
Propp, Jim. *Tuscanini.* New York: Bradbury, 1992; 32 pp., $7.95.
Provencher, Rose-Marie. *Slithery Jake.* New York: HarperCollins, 2004; 32 pp., $15.99.
Pryor, Bonnie. *Birthday Blizzard.* New York: Morrow, 1993; 32 pp., $12.95.
Pulver, Robin. *Axle Annie and the Speed Grump.* New York: Dial, 2005; 32 pp., $16.99.
Pulver, Robin. *Mrs. Toggle's Beautiful Blue Shoe.* New York: Four Winds, 1994; 32 pp., $13.95.
Rabe, Tish. *Fine Feathered Friends.* New York: Random House, 1998; 32 pp., $7.99.
Radcliffe, Theresa. *Bashi, Elephant Baby.* New York: Viking, 1997; 32 pp., $13.99.
Radcliffe, Theresa. *Cimru the Seal.* New York: Viking, 1996; 32 pp., $12.99.
Rader, Laura (illustrator). *Mother Hubbard's Cupboard: A Mother Goose Surprise Book.* New York: Tambourine, 1993; 45 pp., $12.95.
Raney, Ken. *It's Probably Good Dinosaurs Are Extinct.* New York: Green Tiger, 1993; 32 pp., $14.00.
Rankin, Joan. *Wow!: It's Great Being a Duck.* New York: Margaret K. McElderry, 1997; 32 pp., $16.00.
Rankin, Kim. *Cut and Create! Holidays.* Carthage, IL: Teaching and Learning, 1997; 80 pp., $12.43.
Ransom, Candice. *Shooting Star Summer.* Honesdale, PA: Caroline House/Boyds Mills, 1992; 32 pp., $14.95.
Raschka, Chris. *Elizabeth Imagined an Iceberg.* New York: Orchard, 1994; 32 pp., $15.99.
Rassmus, Jens. *Farmer Enno and His Cow.* New York: Orchard, 1997; 32 pp., $14.95.
Rathmann, Peggy. *Goodnight, Gorilla.* New York: Putnam, 1994; 40 pp., $14.99.
Rathmann, Peggy. *Officer Buckle and Gloria.* New York: Putnam, 1995; 37 pp., $15.95.
Rau, Dana Meachen. *The Secret Code.* New York: Children's Press, 1998; 31 pp., $17.00.
Ready, Dee. *Doctors.* Mankato, MN: Bridgestone, 1997; 24 pp., $14.00.
Reay, Joanne, and Adriano Gon. *Bumpus Rumpus and the Rainy Day.* Boston: Houghton Mifflin, 1995; 32 pp., $14.95.
Reed, Neil. *The Midnight Unicorn.* New York: Sterling, 2006; 32 pp., $14.95.
Reeves, Rhonda. *Fun Around the World for Preschoolers.* Birmingham, AL: New Hope, 2004; 93 pp., $7.99.

Reid, Barbara. *The Subway Mouse*. New York: Scholastic, 2003; 32 pp., $15.95.
Reiser, Lynn. *Any Kind of Dog*. New York: Greenwillow, 1992; 24 pp., $14.00.
Reiser, Lynn. *The Surprise Family*. New York: Greenwillow, 1994; 32 pp., $15.93.
Reiser, Lynn. *Two Dogs Swimming*. New York: Greenwillow, 2005; 32 pp., $16.89.
Relf, Adam. *Fox Makes Friends*. New York: Sterling, 2005; 32 pp., $14.95.
Renberg, Dalia Hardof. *King Solomon and the Bee*. New York.: HarperCollins, 1994; 32 pp., $14.90.
Reneaux, J.J. *Why Alligator Hates Dog: A Cajun Folktale*. Little Rock, AR: August House, 1995; 32 pp., $15.95.
Repchuk, Caroline. *The Glitter Dragon*. New York: Marlowe, 1995; 32 pp., $14.95.
Rey, Margaret. *Curious George Flies a Kite*. Boston: Houghton Mifflin, 1997; 80 pp., $8.95.
Reynolds, Aaron. *Chicks and Salsa*. New York: Bloomsbury, 2005, 32 pp., $15.95.
Reynolds, Peter H. *Sydney's Star*. New York: Simon & Schuster, 2001; 32 pp., $14.00.
Rhatigan, Joe. *The Kids' Guide to Nature Adventures*. New York: Lark, 2003; 128 pp., $17.95.
Rhatigan, Joe, and Rain Newcomb. *Run, Jump, Hide, Slide, Splash: The 200 Best Outdoor Games Ever*. New York: Lark, 2004; 128 pp., $19.95.
Rhiannon, Ann. *Bear with Me*. New York: Random House, 2003; 10 pp., $3.99.
Rhodes, Mackie, and Jan Trautman, editors. *November Arts and Crafts: Preschool–Kindergarten*. Greensboro, NC: Education Center, 2000; 32 pp., $6.95.
Rice, James. *Cowboy Rodeo*. Gretna, LA: Pelican, 1992; 32 pp., $14.95.
Richardson, Jean. *Thomas's Sitter*. New York: Four Winds, 1991; 32 pp., $13.95.
Richardson, Judith Benet. *The Way Home*. New York: Macmillan, 1991; 32 pp., $13.95.
Richmond, Margie Hayes. *Look What You Can Make with Paper Plates*. Honesdale, PA: Boyds Mills, 1997; 41 pp., $5.95.
Riddell, Edwina. *My First Day at Preschool*. Hauppauge, NY: Barron's Educational Series, 1992; 32 pp., $9.95.
Rieheckly, Janet. *Kwanzaa*. New York: Children's Press, 1993; 31 pp., $17.50.
Riggers, Maxine. *Amazing Alligators and Other Story Hour Friends*. Ashland, OH: Monday Morning, 1990; 208 pp., $12.95.
Riley, Linnea. *Mouse Mess*. New York: Blue Sky, 1997; 32 pp., $15.95.
Ripple, Wilhelminia. *Christmas Parties: What Do I Do?* Littleton, CO: Oakbrook, 2000; 192 pp., $19.95.
Ritter, Darlene. *Literature-Based Art Activities*. Huntington Beach, CA: Creative Teaching, 1991; 104 pp., $9.98.
Robert, François and Jean. *Find a Face*. San Francisco: Chronicle, 2004; 32 pp., $14.95.
Roberts, Bethany. *Cat Skidoo*. New York: Henry Holt, 2004; 32 pp., $16.95.
Roberts, Bethany. *Fourth of July Mice!* Boston: Clarion, 2004; 32 pp., $13.00.
Roberts, Bethany. *Halloween Mice!* Boston: Clarion,1995; 32 pp., $12.95.
Roberts, Bethany. *Monster Manners*. Boston: Clarion, 1996; 32 pp., $15.00.
Roberts, Bethany. *The Two O'Clock Secret*. Morton Grove, IL: Albert Whitman, 1993; 32 pp., $13.95.
Roberts, Bethany. *Valentine Mice!* Boston: Clarion, 1997; 32 pp., $13.00.
Robertson, M. P. *The Dragon Snatcher*. New York: Dial, 2005; 32 pp., $16.99.

Robertson, M. P. *The Sandcastle*. Flagstaff, AZ: Rising Moon, 2001; 32 pp., $15.95.
Robins, Deri; Meg Sanders; and Kate Crocker. *The Kids' Can Do It Book*. New York: Kingfisher, 1993; 80 pp., $9.95.
Roca, Nuria. *The Seasons: Fall*. Hauppage, NY: Barron's Educational Series, 2004; 32 pp., $6.95.
Roche, Denis. *Loo-Loo, Boo, and Art You Can Do*. Boston: Houghton Mifflin, 1996; 32 pp., $14.95.
Rockwell, Anne. *Boats*. New York: Dutton, 1993; 32 pp., $4.99.
Rockwell, Anne. *Honey in a Hive*. New York: HarperCollins, 2005; 32 pp., $15.99.
Rockwell, Anne. *I Fly*. New York: Crown, 1997; 36 pp., $17.99.
Rockwell, Anne. *The Storm*. New York: Hyperion, 1994; 32 pp., $15.95.
Rodger, Ellen (editor). *Arty Facts: Animals and Art Activities*. New York: Crabtree, 2002; 48 pp., $23.92.
Roehe, Stephanie. *"That's Not Fair!"* New York: Penguin, 2004; 32 pp., $14.99.
Roemer, Heidi B. *Come to My Party and Other Shape Poems*. New York: Henry Holt, 2004; 32 pp., $17.95.
Rogers, Fred. *Let's Talk about It: Adoption*. New York: Putnam, 1994; 32 pp., $15.95.
Rogers, Fred. *Mister Rogers' Playtime*. Philadelphia: Running Press, 2001; 127 pp., $12.95.
Rogers, Paul. *The Shapes Game*. New York: Henry Holt, 1995; 32 pp., $12.95.
Rogers, Paul and Emma. *Quacky Duck*. New York.: Little, Brown, 1995; 26 pp., $14.95.
Rogers, Sally. *Earthsong*. New York: Dutton, 1998; 32 pp., $15.99.
Roop, Peter and Connie. *Let's Celebrate Halloween*. Minneapolis, MN: Millbrook, 1997; 36 pp., $19.90.
Roop, Peter and Connie. *Let's Celebrate St. Patrick's Day*. Minneapolis, MN: Millbrook, 2003; 32 pp., $22.90.
Roosa, Karen. *Beach Day*. Boston: Clarion, 2001; 32 pp., $15.00.
Root, Phyllis. *Contrary Bear*. New York: Laura Geringer, 1996; 32 pp., $13.95.
Root, Phyllis. *Meow Monday*. Cambridge, MA: Candlewick, 2000; 32 pp., $10.99.
Root, Phyllis. *Mrs. Potter's Pig*. Cambridge, MA: Candlewick, 1996; 32 pp., $5.99.
Root, Phyllis. *One Duck Stuck*. Cambridge, MA: Candlewick, 1998; 40 pp., $15.99.
Root, Phyllis. *Soggy Saturday*. Cambridge, MA: Candlewick, 2001; 32 pp., $10.99.
Rose, Deborah Lee. *Meredith's Mother Takes the Train*. Morton Grove, IL: Albert Whitman, 1991; 24 pp., $10.95.
Rose, Deborah Lee. *The Twelve Days of Kindergarten*. New York: Abrams, 2003; 32 pp., $14.95.
Rosen, Michael. *This is Our House*. Cambridge, MA: Candlewick, 1996; 32 pp., $15.99.
Rosenberg, Dan (editor). *Better Homes and Gardens Big Book of Kids' Crafts*. Des Moines, IA: Meredith, 2004; 304 pp., $19.95.
Rosenberg, Liz. *Mama Goose: A New Mother Goose*. New York: Philomel, 1994; 32 pp., $15.95.
Rosenberg, Liz, and Susan Gaber. *Eli and Uncle Dawn*. San Diego: Harcourt, 1997; 32 pp., $15.00.
Rosenberry, Vera. *The Growing Up Tree*. New York: Holiday House, 2003; 32 pp., $16.95.

Rosenberry, Vera. *Vera's Baby Sister*. New York: Henry Holt, 2005; 32 pp., $16.95.
Rosenberry, Vera. *Vera Goes to the Dentist*. New York: Henry Holt, 2002; 32 pp., $16.95.
Rosenberry, Vera. *Vera Rides a Bike*. New York: Henry Holt, 2004; 32 pp., $16.95.
Ross, Dave. *Making UFOs*. Danbury, CT: Franklin Watts, 1980; 32 pp., $7.90.
Ross, Diana. *The Story of the Little Red Engine*. Albuquerque, NM: Transatlantic Arts, 32 pp., $11.95.
Ross, Kathy. *All New Crafts for Earth Day*. Minneapolis, MN: Millbrook, 2006; 48 pp., $25.26.
Ross, Kathy. *The Best Birthday Parties Ever!* Minneapolis, MN: Millbrook, 1999; 80 pp., $24.90.
Ross, Kathy. *The Big Book of Christian Crafts*. Minneapolis, MN: Millbrook, 2002; 176 pp., $19.95.
Ross, Kathy. *Christmas Ornaments Kids Can Make*. Minneapolis, MN: Millbrook, 1998; 64 pp., $23.40.
Ross, Kathy. *Crafts for Easter*. Minneapolis, MN: Millbrook, 1995; 48 pp., $21.90.
Ross, Kathy. *Crafts for Hanukkah*. Minneapolis, MN: Millbrook, 1996; 48 pp., $21.90.
Ross, Kathy. *Crafts for Kids Who are Wild about Dinosaurs*. Minneapolis, MN: Millbrook, 1997; 48 pp., $22.40.
Ross, Kathy. *Crafts for Kids Who are Wild about Insects*. Minneapolis, MN: Millbrook, 1997; 48 pp., $22.40.
Ross, Kathy. *Crafts for Kids Who are Wild about Rainforests*. Minneapolis, MN: Millbrook, 1997; 48 pp., $22.40.
Ross, Kathy. *Crafts for Kwanzaa*. Minneapolis, MN: Millbrook, 1994; 48 pp., $21.00.
Ross, Kathy. *Crafts for St. Patrick's Day*. Minneapolis, MN: Millbrook, 1999; 48 pp., $26.00.
Ross, Kathy. *Crafts for Valentine's Day*. Minneapolis, MN: Millbrook, 2002, 48 pp., $21.90.
Ross, Kathy. *Crafts from Your Favorite Fairy Tales*. Minneapolis, MN: Millbrook, 1997, 48 pp., $22.40.
Ross, Kathy. *Crafts to Celebrate God's Creation*. Minneapolis, MN: Millbrook, 2001; 64 pp., $26.00.
Ross, Kathy. *Crafts to Make in the Fall*. Minneapolis, MN: Millbrook, 1998, 64 pp., $23.40.
Ross, Kathy. *Crafts to Make in the Summer*. Minneapolis, MN: Millbrook, 1999; 64 pp., $22.40.
Ross, Kathy. *Crafts to Make in the Winter*. Minneapolis, MN: Millbrook, 1999; 64 pp., $22.40.
Ross, Kathy. *Every Day Is Earth Day*. Minneapolis, MN: Millbrook, 1995, 48 pp., $21.90.
Ross, Kathy. *The Jewish Holiday Craft Book*. Minneapolis, MN: Millbrook, 1997, 96 pp., $25.90.
Ross, Kathy. *Learning is Fun! Kathy Ross Crafts*. Minneapolis, MN: Millbrook, 2002; 64 pp., $25.26.
Ross, Kathy. *Letter Shapes*. Minneapolis, MN: Millbrook, 2002; 64 pp., $25.26.

Ross, Kathy. *Look What You Can Make with Dozens of Household Items!* Honesdale, Pa.: Boyds Mills, 1998; 48 pp., $24.99.
Ross, Kathy. *Make Yourself a Monster! A Book of Creepy Crafts.* Minneapolis, MN: Millbrook, 1999; 32 pp., $24.90.
Ross, Kathy. *Play-Doh: Fun and Games.* Minneapolis, MN: Millbrook, 2003; 48 pp., $25.26.
Ross, Kathy. *Star Spangled Crafts.* Minneapolis, MN: Millbrook, 2003; 48 pp., $23.90.
Ross, Kathy. *The Storytime Craft Book.* Minneapolis, MN: Millbrook, 2003; 176 pp., $19.95.
Ross, Kathy. *Triangles, Rectangles, Circles and Squares.* Minneapolis, MN: Millbrook, 2002; 48 pp., $23.90.
Roth, Susan L. *Hanukkah, oh Hanukkah.* New York: Dial, 2004; 32 pp., $15.99.
Roth, Susan L. *My Love for You All Year Round.* New York: Dial, 2003; 32 pp., $14.99.
Rothenberg, Joan. *Inside-Out Grandma: A Hanukkah Story.* New York: Hyperion, 1995; 32 pp., $14.95.
Rotner, Shelley, and Sheila M. Kelly. *Lots of Dads.* New York: Dial, 1997; 24 pp., $12.99.
Rounds, Glen. *Cowboys.* New York: Holiday House, 1991; 32 pp., $15.95.
Rowe, John A. *Tommy DoLittle.* New York: North-South, 2002; 32 pp., $16.95.
Royston, Angela. *Big Machines.* New York: Little, Brown, 1994; 32 pp., $12.95.
Royston, Angela. *What's it Like?: Deafness.* Barrington, IL: Heinemann, 2005; 32 pp., $25.36.
Rubel, Nicole. *The Ghost Family Meets Its Match.* New York: Dial, 1992; 32 pp., $13.89.
Rubin, C.M. *Eleanor, Ellatony, Ellencake, and Me.* New York: Gingham Dog, 2003; 32 pp., $14.95.
Ruelle, Karen Gray. *Easter Egg Disaster.* New York: Holiday House, 2004; 32 pp., $14.95.
Ruffin, Frances E. *Police Dogs.* New York: Bearport, 2005; 32 pp., $23.96.
Rush, Ken. *Friday's Journey.* New York: Orchard, 1994; 30 pp., $15.99.
Russell, Joan Plummer. *Aero and Officer Mike: Police Partners.* Honesdale, PA: Boyds Mills, 2001; 32 pp., $15.95.
Russo, Marisabina. *Alex is my Friend.* New York: Greenwillow, 1992; 30 pp., $13.95.
Russo, Marisabina. *When Mama Gets Home.* New York: Greenwillow, 1998; 32 pp., $15.00.
Ryden, Hope. *Joey: The Story of a Baby Kangaroo.* New York: Tambourine, 1994; 40 pp., $14.93.
Ryder, Joanne. *A House by the Sea.* New York: Morrow, 1994; 32 pp., $15.00.
Ryder, Joanne. *Jaguar in the Rainforest.* New York: Morrow, 1996; 32pp., $15.93.
Rylant, Cynthia. *The Bookshop Dog.* New York: Blue Sky, 1996; 40 pp., $14.95.
Rylant, Cynthia. *Henry and Mudge and the Great Grandpas.* New York: Simon & Schuster, 2005; 32 pp., $14.95.
Rylant, Cynthia. *The High-Rise Private Eyes: The Case of the Baffled Bear.* New York: Greenwillow, 2004; 32 pp., $15.89.
Rylant, Cynthia. *The High-Rise Private Eyes: The Case of the Troublesome Turtle.* New York: Greenwillow, 2001; 32 pp., $14.95.

Rylant, Cynthia. *If You'll Be My Valentine*. New York: HarperCollins, 2005; 32 pp., $14.99.

Rylant, Cynthia. *Long Night Moon*. New York: Simon & Schuster, 2004; 32 pp., $16.95.

Rylant, Cynthia. *Mr. Putter and Tabby Pick the Pears*. San Diego: Harcourt, 1995; 44 pp., $12.00.

Rylant, Cynthia. *The Old Woman Who Named Things*. San Diego: Harcourt, 1996; 32 pp., $15.00.

Rylant, Cynthia. *Poppleton in Spring*. New York: Blue Sky, 1999; 32 pp., $15.95.

Rylant, Cynthia. *The Whales*. New York: Blue Sky, 1996; 40 pp., $14.95.

Sadler, Judy Ann. *The Kids Can Press Jumbo Book of Easy Crafts*. Tonawanda, NY: Kids Can, 2001; 208 pp., $14.95.

Sadler, Marilyn. *Alistair and the Alien Invasion*. New York: Simon & Schuster, 1994; 48 pp., $15.00.

Saint-James, Synthia. *The Gifts of Kwanzaa*. Morton Grove, IL: Albert Whitman, 1994; 32 pp., $14.95.

Saltzberg, Barney. *I Love Cats*. Cambridge, MA: Candlewick, 2005; 32 pp., $8.99.

Saltzberg, Barney. *Star of the Week*. Cambridge, MA: Candlewick, 2006; 32 pp., $15.99.

Samton, Sheila White. *Tilly and the Rhinoceros*. New York: Philomel, 1993; 32 pp., $14.95.

Samuels, Barbara. *Happy Valentine's Day, Dolores*. New York: Farrar, Straus & Giroux, 2006; 32 pp., $16.00.

Samuels, Jenny. *A Nose Like a Hose*. New York: Scholastic, 2003; 32 pp., $12.95.

Sanders, Nancy I. *A Kids' Guide to African American History*. Chicago: Chicago Review Press, 2000; 242 pp., $14.95.

Sanfield, Steve, and Susan Gaber. *Bit by Bit*. New York: Philome, 1995; 32 pp., $15.95.

San Souci, Daniel. *Space Stations Mars*. Berkeley, CA: Tricycle, 2005; 32 pp., $15.95.

Sasser, Shari. *Grand Activities*. Franklin Lakes, N.J.: Career, 1999; 167 pp., $12.95.

Sathre, Vivian. *Three Kind Mice*. San Diego: Harcourt, 1997; 32 pp., $13.00.

Savadier, Elvira. *No Haircut Today!* New York: Roaring Brook, 2005; 32 pp., $15.95.

Say, Allen. *Allison*. Boston: Houghton Mifflin, 1997; 32 pp., $17.00.

Say, Allen. *Stranger in the Mirror*. Boston: Houghton Mifflin, 1995; 32 pp., $16.95.

Say, Allen. *Tree of Cranes*. Boston: Houghton Mifflin, 1991; 32 pp., $17.95.

Sayre, April Pulley. *The Bumblebee Queen*. Watertown, MA: Charlesbridge, 2005; 32 pp., $14.95.

Sayre, April Pulley. *Crocodile Listens*. New York: Greenwillow, 2001; 32 pp., $15.89.

Sayre, April Pulley. *Shadows*. New York: Henry Holt, 2002; 32 pp., $16.95.

Sayre, April Pulley. *Turtle, Turtle, Watch Out!* New York: Orchard, 2000; 32 pp., $17.99.

Scamell, Ragnhild. *The Wish Come True Cat*. Hauppauge, NY: Barron's Educational Series, 2001; 32 pp., $14.00.

Schachner, Judith Byron. *The Grannyman*. New York: Dutton, 1999; 32 pp., $15.99.

Schaefer, Lola M. *Loose Tooth*. New York: HarperCollins, 2004; 10 pp., $3.99.

Schaefer, Lola M. *Some Kids are Deaf*. Mankato, MN: Capstone, 2001; 32 pp., $11.95.

Scheffler, Axel. *Room on the Broom*. New York: Dial, 2001; 32 pp., $15.99.

Schick, Eleanor. *My Navajo Sister*. New York: Simon & Schuster, 1996; 32 pp., $16.00.

Schiller, Pam. *School Days*. Beltsville, MD: Gryphon House, 2006; 128 pp., $19.95.
Schiller, Pam. *The Complete Resource Book for Toddlers and Twos*. Beltsville, MD: Gryphon House, 2003; 640 pp., $34.95.
Schiller, Pam, and Jackie Silberg. *The Complete Book of Activities, Games, Stories, Props, Recipes and Dances for Young Children*. Beltsville, MD: Gryphon House, 2003; 640 pp., $29.95.
Schiller, Pam, and Joan Rossano. *The Instant Curriculum*. Beltsville, MD: Gryphon House, 2005; 376 pp., $29.95.
Schlein, Miriam. *Big Talk*. New York: Bradbury, 1990; 32 pp., $12.95.
Schlein, Miriam. *More Than One*. New York: Greenwillow, 1996; 24 pp., $15.00.
Schlein, Miriam. *The Way Mothers Are*. Morton Grove, IL: Albert Whitman, 1993; 32 pp., $14.95.
Schneider, Howie. *Uncle Lester's Hat*. New York: Putnam, 1993; 32 pp., $13.95.
Schnitter, Jane T. *William Is My Brother*. Boys Town, NE: Perspectives, 1991; 32 pp., $10.95.
Schoener, John. *Bear*. New York: Philomel, 1991; 32 pp., $14.95.
Schotter, Roni. *A Fruit and Vegetable Man*. New York: Little, Brown, 1993; 32 pp., $15.95.
Schubert, Ingrid and Dicter. *Wild Will*. Minneapolis, MN: Carolrhoda, 1992; 32 pp., $19.95.
Schuette, Sarah L. *Purple: Seeing Purple Around Us*. Mankato, MN: Capstone, 2003; 32 pp., $16.95.
Schuh, Mari C. *St. Patrick's Day*. Mankato, MN: Capstone, 2003; 32 pp., $11.95.
Schulman, Janet. *A Bunny for All Seasons*. New York: Knopf, 2003; 32 pp., $9.95.
Schulman, Janet. *10 Trick-or-Treaters*. New York: Knopf, 2005; 32 pp., $8.95.
Schulz, Kathy. *Always Be Safe*. New York: Children's Press, 2003; 32 pp., $19.50.
Schwartz, David M. *Supergrandpa*. New York: Lothrop, Lee and Shepard, 1991; 32 pp., $16.93.
Schwartz, Henry. *Albert Goes Hollywood*. New York: Orchard, 1992; 32 pp., $15.95.
Schwartz, Linda. *Likeable Recyclables*. Santa Barbara, CA: Learning Works, 1992; 128 pp., $9.95.
Schwartz, Roslyn. *Rose and Dorothy*. New York: Orchard, 1990; 32 pp., $4.95.
Schweninger, Ann. *Autumn Days*. New York: Viking, 1993; 32 pp., $12.95.
Schweninger, Ann. *Let's Look at the Seasons: Springtime*. New York: Viking, 1993; 32 pp., $13.50.
Scieszka, Jon. *The Frog Prince Continued*. New York: Viking, 1991; 32 pp., $14.95.
Scott, Ann Herbert. *Hi*. New York: Philomel, 1994; 32 pp., $14.95.
Seaman, Rosie. *Focus on Spring*. Logan, IA: Fearon Teacher Aids, 1992; 79 pp., $10.99.
Seaman, Rosie. *Focus on Winter*. Logan, IA: Fearon Teacher Aids, 1992; 79 pp., $10.99.
Sebastian, John. *J.B.'s Harmonica*. San Diego: Harcourt, 1993; 32 pp., $13.95.
Seeger, Laura Vaccaro. *Lemons Are Not Red*. New York: Roaring Brook, 2004; 32 pp., $14.95.
Seeley, Laura L. *McSpot's Hidden Spots*. Atlanta, GA: Peachtree, 1994; 32 pp., $16.95.
Selby, Jennifer. *Beach Bunny*. San Diego: Harcourt, 1995; 32 pp., $14.00.
Sendak, Maurice. *Maurice Sendak's Really Rosie Starring the Nutshell Kids*. New York: Harper and Row, 1975; 64 pp., $16.95.

Senisi, Ellen B. *Secrets.* New York: Dutton, 1995; 32 pp., $13.99.
Serfozo, Mary. *Benjamin Bigfoot.* New York: Margaret McEldery, 1993; 32 pp., $14.95.
Serfozo, Mary. *Plumply, Dumply Pumpkin.* New York: Margaret K. McElderry, 2001; 32 pp., $12.95.
Serfozo, Mary. *There's a Square.* New York: Scholastic, 1996; 32 pp., $6.95.
Seuss, Dr. *Dr. Seuss's All Aboard the Circus McGurkus!* New York: Random House, 2004; 10 pp., $6.99.
Seymour, Tres. *Hunting the White Cow.* New York: Orchard, 1993; 32 pp., $17.95.
Shannon, David. *Alice the Fairy.* New York: Blue Sky, 2004; 32 pp., $15.95.
Shannon, David. *Duck on a Bike.* New York: Blue Sky, 2002; 32 pp., $15.95.
Shannon, George. *Heart to Heart.* Boston: Houghton Mifflin, 1995; 32 pp., $13.95.
Shannon, George. *Lizard's Guest.* New York: Greenwillow, 2003; 32 pp., $16.89.
Shannon, George. *Seeds.* Boston: Houghton Mifflin, 1994; 28 pp., $13.95.
Shannon, George. *Tomorrow's Alphabet.* New York: Greenwillow, 1996; 52 pp., $15.93.
Shannon, Margaret. *Elvira.* New York: Ticknor and Fields, 1991; 32 pp., $13.95.
Sharmat, Marjorie. *Mitchell Is Moving.* New York: Simon & Schuster, 1996; 47 pp., $15.00.
Sharmat, Marjorie. *Tiffany Dino Works Out.* New York: Simon & Schuster, 1995; 32 pp., $15.00.
Sharratt, Nick. *My Mom and Dad Make Me Laugh.* Cambridge, Mass.: Candlewick, 1994; 26 pp., $12.95.
Shaw, Nancy. *Sheep Out to Eat.* Boston: Houghton Mifflin, 1992; 32 pp., $14.00.
Shaw, Nancy. *Sheep Trick or Treat.* Boston: Houghton Mifflin, 1997; 32 pp., $14.00.
Shelby, Anne. *The Someday House.* New York: Orchard, 1996; 32 pp., $14.95.
Shelby, Anne. *What to Do about Pollution . . . .* New York: Orchard, 1993; 32 pp., $13.95.
Sheldon, Dyan, and Neil Reed. *Unicorn Dreams.* New York: Dial, 1997; 32 pp., $14.99.
Shepherd, Nellie. *My Party Art Class.* New York: DK Publishing, 2004; 48 pp., $12.99.
Sher, Barbara. *Smart Play.* Hoboken, NJ: John Wiley, 2004; 178 pp., $14.95.
Sherman, Josepha. *Splish! Splash!: A Book About Rain.* Minneapolis, MN: Picture Window, 2004; 32 pp., $16.95.
Shields, Carol Diggory. *The Bugliest Bug.* Cambridge, MA: Candlewick, 2002; 32 pp., $15.99.
Shields, Carol Digory. *Day by Day a Week Goes Round.* New York: Dutton, 1998; 32 pp., $7.99.
Shields, Carol Diggory. *I Wish My Brother Was a Dog.* New York: Dutton, 1997; 32 pp., $14.99.
Shields, Carol Diggory. *Lucky Pennies and Hot Chocolate.* New York: Dutton, 2000; 32 pp., $13.99.
Shipton, Jonathan. *No Biting, Horrible Crocodile!* New York: Western, 1995; 32 pp., $12.95.
Shireman, Samantha and Bill. *If the World Ran Out of Bs.* Hillsboro, OR: Beyond Words, 2002; 32 pp., $15.95.
Shively, Julie D. *Baby Elephant.* Nashville: Candy Cane, 2005; 32 pp., $10.00.
Shore, Diane Z., and Jessica Alexander. *Look Both Ways: A Cautionary Tale.* New York: Bloomsbury, 2005; 32 pp., $15.95.

Shorto, Russell. *Cinderella and Cinderella: The Untold Story*. New York: Carol Publishing, 1997; 32 pp., $12.95.
Showers, Paul. *Ears are for Hearing*. New York: Thomas Y. Crowell, 1990; 32 pp., $12.89.
Showers, Paul. *The Listening Walk*. New York: HarperCollins, 1991; 32 pp., $14.90.
Showers, Paul. *Where Does the Garbage Go?* New York: HarperCollins, 1994; 32 pp., $12.89.
Shub, Elizabeth. *Seeing Is Believing*. New York: Greenwillow, 1994; 64 pp., $14.00.
Shulevitz, Uri. *Snow*. New York: Farrar, Straus & Giroux, 1998; 32 pp., $16.00.
Shulevitz, Uri. *Toddle Creek Post Office*. New York: Farrar, Straus & Giroux, 1990; 32 pp., $14.95.
Shute, Linda. *Halloween Party*. New York: Lothrop, Lee and Shepard, 1994; 32 pp., $15.00.
Shute, Linda. *How I Named the Baby*. Morton Grove, IL: Albert Whitman, 1993; 32 pp., $14.95.
Siebert, Diane. *Train Song*. New York: Thomas Y. Crowell, 1990; 32pp., $15.89.
Siegenthaler, Rolf. *Never Fear, Snake My Dear!* New York: North-South, 1999; 32 pp., $15.95.
Sierra, Judy. *Counting Crocodiles*. San Diego: Gulliver, 1997; 32 pp., $15.00.
Sierra, Judy, and Robert Kaminski. *Children's Traditional Games*. Phoenix, AZ: Oryx, 1995; 232 pp., $26.50.
Sierra, Judy. *Good Night, Dinosaurs*. Boston: Clarion, 1996; 31 pp., $15.00.
Sierra, Judy. *The House That Drac Built*. San Diego: Gulliver, 1995; 34 pp., $14.00.
Sierra, Judy. *Wild About Books*. New York: Knopf, 2004; 32 pp., $16.95.
Sierra, Judy. *Schoolyard Rhymes*. New York: Knopf, 2005; 32 pp., $17.99.
Silberg, Jackie. *Games to Play with Toddlers*. Beltsville, MD: Gryphon House, 1993; 285 pp., $14.95.
Silberg, Jackie. *300 Three Minute Games*. Beltsville, MD: Gryphon House, 1997; 191 pp., $12.95.
Silberg, Jackie, and Pam Schiller. *The Complete Book of Rhymes, Songs, Poems, Fingerplays and Chants*. Beltsville, Md.: Gryphon House, 2002; 512 pp., $29.95.
Silverman, Erica. *Don't Fidget a Feather!* New York: Macmillan, 1994; 32 pp., $16.00.
Silverman, Erica. *The Halloween House*. New York: Farrar, Straus & Giroux, 1997; 32 pp., $15.00.
Silverman, Erica. *Mrs. Peachtree's Bicycle*. New York: Simon & Schuster, 1996; 32 pp., $15.00.
Simonds, Nina; Leslie Swartz; and The Children's Museum. *Moonbeams, Dumplings and Dragon Boats*. San Diego, Calif.: Gulliver, 2002; 75 pp., $20.00.
Simmons, Jane. *Come Along, Daisy!* New York: Little, Brown, 1997; 32 pp., $12.95.
Simmons, Jane. *Little Fern's First Winter*. New York: Little, Brown, 2001; 32 pp., $13.95.
Simon, Norma. *Firefighters*. New York: Simon & Schuster, 1995; 32 pp., $13.00.
Singer, Marilyn. *Block Party Today!* New York: Knopf, 2004; 32 pp., $18.99.
Singer, Marilyn. *Quiet Night*. Boston: Clarion, 2002; 32 pp., $15.00.
Sirett, Dawn. *My First Paint Book*. New York: Dorling Kindersley, 1994; 48 pp., $12.95.

Sitarz, Paula Gaj. *More Picture Book Story Hours: From Parties to Pets.* Westport, CT: Libraries Unlimited, 1990; 166 pp., $20.00.

Skalak, Barbara Anne. *Waddle, Waddle, Quack, Quack, Quack.* San Francisco: Chronicle, 2005; 32 pp., $14.95.

Skarmeas, Nancy J. *The Story of Thanksgiving.* New York: Candy Cane, 1999; 10 pp., $6.95.

Sklansky, Amy E. *Zoom Fun with Friends.* New York: Little, Brown, 1999; 62 pp., $7.95.

Skofield, James. *Round and Around.* New York: HarperCollins, 1993; 32 pp., $14.89.

Skurzynski, Gloria. *Here Comes the Mail.* New York: Bradbury, 1992; 38 pp., $13.95.

Skutch, Robert. *Albie's Trip to the Jumble Jungle.* Berkeley, CA: Tricycle, 2002; 32 pp., $14.95.

Slate, Joseph. *Miss Bindergarten Celebrates the 100th Day of Kindergarten.* New York: Dutton, 1998; 32 pp., $14.99.

Slate, Joseph. *Miss Bindergarten Has a Wild Day in Kindergarten.* New York: Dutton, 2005; 32 pp., $16.99.

Slater, Teddy. *Pigs in Love.* New York: Sterling, 2005; 32 pp., $6.95.

Slegers, Liesbet. *Kevin Goes to the Hospital.* New York: Kane/Miller, 2002; 32 pp., $7.95.

Slepian, Jan. *Emily Just in Time.* New York: Philomel, 1998; 32 pp., $15.99.

Slepian, Jan, and Ann Seidler. *The Hungry Thing Returns.* New York: Scholastic, 1990; 32 pp., $11.95.

Slingsby, Janet. *Hush-a-bye Babies.* Hauppauge, NY: Barron's Educational Series, 2001; 32 pp., $14.95.

Sloat, Teri. *Berry Magic.* Portland, OR: Alaska Northwest, 2004; 32 pp., $15.95.

Sloat, Teri. *Sody Sallyratus.* New York: Dutton, 1997; 32 pp., $15.99.

Slobodkina, Esphyr. *Circus Caps for Sale.* New York: HarperCollins, 2002; 32 pp., $5.39.

Sloss, Lesley. *Anthony and the Aardvark.* New York: Lothrop, Lee and Shepard, 1991; 25 pp., $13.95.

Smalls, Irene. *Beginning School.* Parsippany, NJ: Silver, 1997; 32 pp., $11.95.

Smee, Nicola. *Freddie Visits the Dentist.* Hauppauge, NY: Barron's Educational Series, 2000; 10 pp., $4.95

Smith, Allistar. *The Ultimate Book of Games and Puzzles.* Tulsa, OK: EDC Publishing, 1994; 40 pp., $12.95.

Smith, Dana Kessimakis. *A Brave Spaceboy.* New York: Hyperion, 2005; 32 pp., $15.99.

Smith, Dana Kessimakis, and Laura Freeman. *A Wild Cowboy.* New York: Jump at the Sun, 2004; 32 pp., $14.99.

Smith, Debbie. *Holidays and Festivals Activities Fun!* New York: Crabtree, 1994; 63 pp., NA.

Smith, Janice Lee. *Jess and the Stinky Cowboys.* New York: Dial, 2004; 32 pp., $14.99.

Smith, Jos A. *Circus Train.* New York: Abrams, 2001; 32 pp., $17.95.

Smith, Lane. *Glasses, Who Needs 'Em?* New York: Viking, 1991; 32 pp., $15.99.

Smith, Linda. *There Was an Old Woman Who Lived in a Boot.* New York: HarperCollins, 2003; 32 pp., $16.89.

Smith, Linda, and Karen Patkau. *Sir Cassie to the Rescue.* Custer, WA: Orca, 2003; 32 pp., $16.95.

Smith, Maggie. *Argo, You Lucky Dog*. New York: Lothrop, Lee and Shepard, 1994; 32 pp., $15.00.
Smith, Maggie. *Dear Daisy, Get Well Soon*. New York: Crown, 2000; 32 pp., $14.95.
Smith, Maggie. *Paisley*. New York: Knopf, 2004; 32 pp., $15.95.
Smythe, Theresa. *Snowbear's Christmas Countdown*. New York: Henry Holt, 2004; 32 pp., $14.95.
Snape, Juliet and Charles. *Frog Odyssey*. New York: Simon & Schuster, 1991; 28 pp., $14.00.
Snyder, Carol. *One Up, One Down*. New York: Atheneum, 1995; 32 pp., $15.00.
So, Meilo. *The Emperor and the Nightingale*. New York: Bradbury, 1992; 26 pp., $13.95.
Sockabasin, Allen. *Thanks to the Animals*. Gardiner, ME: Tilbury House, 2005; 32 pp., $16.95.
Solga, Kim. *Make Gifts!* Danbury, Conn.: Grolier Educational, 1991; 48 pp., $11.99.
Sommer, Carl. *The Sly Fox and the Chicks*. Houston, TX: Advance, 2000; 32 pp., $14.95.
Spanyol, Jessica. *Carlo and the Really Nice Librarian*. Cambridge, MA: Candlewick, 2004; 32 pp., $15.99.
Speechley, Greta. *Crafts for Kids: Myths and Tales Book*. New York: Grolier, 2002; 32 pp., $18.00.
Spelman, Cornelia. *Your Body Belongs to You*. Morton Grove, IL: Albert Whitman, 1997; 32 pp., $12.95.
Spinelli, Eileen. *Do You Have a Hat?* New York: Simon & Schuster, 2004; 32 pp., $16.95.
Spinelli, Eileen. *I Know It's Autumn*. New York: HarperCollins, 2004; 32 pp., $16.89.
Spinelli, Eileen. *Night Shift Daddy*. New York: Hyperion, 2000; 32 pp., $14.74.
Spinelli, Eileen. *Now It Is Winter*. Grand Rapids, MI: Eerdmans, 2004; 32 pp., $16.00.
Spinelli, Eileen. *Somebody Loves You, Mr. Hatch*. New York: Bradbury, 1991; 32 pp., $15.00.
Spirn, Michele Sobel. *I Am the Turkey*. New York: HarperCollins, 2004; 32 pp., $16.89.
Spurr, Elizabeth. *Halloween Sky Ride*. New York: Holiday House, 2005; 32 pp., $16.95.
Stadler, Alexander. *Beverly Billingsly Borrows a Book*. San Diego: Harcourt, 2002; 32 pp., $16.00.
Stadler, John. *The Cats of Mrs. Calamari*. New York: Orchard, 1997; 32 pp., $15.95.
Stamper, Judith. *Halloween Holiday Grab Bag*. New York: Troll Associates, 1993; 48 pp., $11.89.
Stanley, Diane. *The Giant and the Beanstalk*. New York: HarperCollins, 2004; 32 pp., $15.99.
Stanley, Diane. *Rumpelstiltskin's Daughter*. New York: Morrow, 1997; 32 pp., $14.93.
Stanley, Sanna. *The Rains Are Coming*. New York: Greenwillow, 1993; 32 pp., $13.93.
Steer, Dugald. *Snappy Little Farmyard*. San Diego: Silver Dolphin, 2005; 32 pp., $12.95.
Steig, William. *Dr. DeSoto Goes to Africa*. New York: HarperCollins, 1994; 32 pp., $5.95.
Steig, William. *Pete's a Pizza*. New York.: HarperCollins, 1998; 32 pp., $13.95.
Steig, William. *The Toy Brother*. New York: HarperCollins, 1996; 32 pp., $14.89.

Stetson, Emily, and Vicky Congdon. *Little Hands Fingerplays and Action Songs.* Charlotte, VT: Williamson, 2002; 128 pp., $12.95.

Stevens, Janet, and Susan Stevens Crummel. *The Great Fuzz Frenzy.* San Diego: Harcourt, 2005; 32 pp., $17.00.

Stevens, Kathleen. *Aunt Skilly and the Stranger.* New York: Ticknor and Fields, 1994; 32 pp., $14.95.

Stevenson, James. *The Oldest Elf.* New York: Greenwillow, 1996; 32 pp., $14.93.

Stevenson, James. *Sam the Zamboni Man.* New York: Greenwillow, 1998; 32 pp., $15.00.

Stevenson, Robert Louis. *My Shadow.* New York: Putnam, 1990; 32 pp., $4.95.

Stewart, Amber. *Rabbit Ears.* New York: Bloomsbury, 2006; 32 pp., $16.95.

Stock, Catherine. *Easter Surprise.* New York: Bradbury, 1991; 32 pp., $13.00.

Stoeke, Janet Morgan. *Minerva Louise at School.* New York: Dutton, 1996; 32 pp., $13.95.

Stojic, Manya. *Rain.* New York: Crown, 2000; 32 pp., $15.95.

Stojic, Manya. *Snow.* New York: Knopf, 2002; 32 pp., $15.95.

Stops, Sue. *Dulcie Dando, Soccer Star.* New York: Henry Holt, 1992; 30 pp., $14.95.

Stot, Dorothy. *The Big Book of Games.* New York: Dutton, 1998; 64 pp., $17.99.

Stow, Jenny. *Growing Pains.* New York: Bridgewater, 1995; 32 pp., $13.95.

Strete, Craig Kee, and Michelle Netten Chacon. *How the Indians Bought the Farm.* New York: Greenwillow, 1996; 32 pp., $15.00.

Strete, Craig Kee. *The Rattlesnake Who Went to School.* New York: Putnam, 2004; 32 pp., $15.99.

Strete, Craig Kee. *They Thought They Saw Him.* New York: Greenwillow, 1996; 32 pp, $15.00.

Stull, Kathie. *20-Minute Crafts.* New York: Sterling, 2001; 128 pp., $12.95.

Sturges, Philemon. *I Love Bugs!* New York: HarpersCollins, 2005; 32 pp., $12.99.

Sturges, Philemon. *I Love Trains!* New York: Scholastic, 2001; 32 pp., $12.95.

Sturges, Philemon. *Ten Flashing Fireflies.* New York: North-South, 1995; 32 pp., $15.88.

Sturges, Philemon. *Waggers.* New York: Dutton, 2005; 32 pp., $16.99.

Sturges, Philemon. *What's That Sound, Woolly Bear?* New York: Little, Brown, 1996; 32 pp., $14.95.

Stutson, Caroline. *Cowpokes.* New York: Lothrop, Lee and Shepard, 1999; 32 pp., $14.89.

Suen, Anastasia. *Man on the Moon.* New York: Viking, 1997; 32 pp., $15.99.

Suen, Anastasia. *Window Music.* New York: Viking, 1998; 32 pp., $15.99.

Sun, Chyng Feng. *Mama Bear.* Boston: Houghton Mifflin, 1994; 32 pp., $14.95.

Swallow, Pamela Curtis. *Groundhog Gets a Say.* New York: Putnam, 2005; 32 pp., $15.99.

Swamp, Chief Jake. *Giving Thanks: A Native American Good Morning Message.* New York: Lee and Low, 1995; 24 pp., $14.95.

Sweat, Lynn, and Louis Phillips. *The Smallest Stegosaurus.* New York: Viking, 1995; 32 pp., $4.99.

Sweeney, Joan. *Once Upon a Lily Pad.* San Francisco: Chronicle, 1995; 32 pp., $9.95.

Szekeres, Cyndy. *The Deep Blue Sky Twinkles with Stars.* New York: Scholastic, 1998; 30 pp., $12.95.

Taback, Simms. *Joseph Had a Little Overcoat*. New York: Viking, 1999; 32 pp., $15.99.
Tafuri, Nancy. *I Love You, Little One*. New York: Scholastic, 1998; 32 pp., $15.95.
Tafuri, Nancy. *This is the Farmer*. New York: Greenwillow, 1994; 24 pp.,$14.00.
Tafuri, Nancy. *Where Did Bunny Go?* New York: Scholastic, 2001; 32 pp., $3.86.
Tagger, Sam, and Susan Williamson. *Great Games*. Charlotte, VT: Williamson, 2004; 128 pp., $12.95.
Talkington, Bruce. *Pooh's Wishing Star*. New York: Disney, 1997; 32 pp., $12.95.
Tanis, Joel E., and Jeff Grooters. *The Dragon Pack Snack Attack*. New York: Four Winds, 1993; 32 pp., $14.95.
Tarpley, Natasha Anastasia. *I Love My Hair!* New York: Little, Brown, 1998; 32 pp., $14.95.
Tarsky, Sue. *The Busy Building Book*. New York: Putnam, 1997; 32 pp., $15.95.
Tavares, Matt. *Mudball*. Cambridge, MA: Candlewick, 2005; 32 pp., $15.99.
Taylor, Alastair. *Mr. Blewitt's Nose*. Boston: Houghton Mifflin, 2005; 32 pp., $16.00.
Taylor, Alastair. *Swollobog*. Boston: Houghton Mifflin, 2001; 32 pp., $15.00.
Taylor, Thomas. *The Loudest Roar*. New York: Arthur A. Levine, 2002; 32 pp., $15.95.
Teague, Mark. *Baby Tamer*. New York: Scholastic, 1997; 32 pp., $15.95.
Teague, Mark. *Detective LaRue: Letters from the Investigation*. New York: Scholastic, 2004; 32 pp., $15.95.
Teague, Mark. *The Lost and Found*. New York: Scholastic, 1998; 32 pp., $15.95.
Teague, Mark. *Pigsty*. New York: Scholastic, 1994; 32 pp., $13.95.
Tegen, Katherine. *The Story of the Easter Bunny*. New York: HarperCollins, 2005; 32 pp., $13.89.
Tekavec, Heather. *What's That Awful Smell?* New York: Dial, 2004; 32 pp., $15.99.
Temko, Florence. *Traditional Crafts from China*. Minneapolis, MN: Lerner, 2001; 64 pp., $23.93.
Tews, Susan. *Lizard Sees the World*. Boston: Clarion, 1997; 32 pp., $15.00.
Teyssedre, Fabienne. *Joseph Wants to Read*. New York: Dutton, 2001; 32 pp., $10.99.
———. *The Ultimate Show-me-how Activity Book*. New York: Smithmark, 1997; 256 pp., $14.98.
Thaler, Mike. *The Librarian from the Black Lagoon*. New York: Scholastic, 1997; 32 pp., $2.99.
Thayer, Ernest Lawrence. *Casey at the Bat*. New York: Atheneum, 1994; 32 pp., $15.00.
Thiessen, Brad. *Orso, the Troll Who Couldn't Scare*. New York: Cds Books, 2005; 32 pp., $16.95.
Thomas, Frances. *One Day, Daddy*. New York: Hyperion, 2001; 32 pp., $15.99.
Thomas, Pat. *I Can Be Safe: A First Look at Safety*. Hauppauge, NY: Barron's Educational Series, 2003; 32 pp., $5.95.
Thomassie, Tynia. *Feliciana Meets d'Loop Garou*. New York: Little, Brown, 1998; 32 pp., $15.95.
Tomczyk, Mary. *Shapes, Sizes and More Surprises!* Charlotte, VT: Williamson, 1996; 141 pp., $12.95.
Thompson, Helen Davis. *Let's Celebrate Kwanzaa: An Activity Book for Young Readers*. New York: Gumbs & Thomas, 1992; 28 pp., $5.95.
Thompson, Lauren. *Little Quack's Bedtime*. New York: Simon & Schuster, 2005; 32 pp., $14.95.

Thompson, Lauren. *Little Quack's Hide and Seek.* New York: Simon & Schuster, 2004; 32 pp., $14.95.

Thompson, Lauren. *Mouse's First Spring.* New York: Simon & Schuster, 2005; 32 pp., $12.95.

Thompson, Lauren. *Polar Bear Night.* New York: Scholastic, 2004; 32 pp., $15.95.

Thompson, Mary. *Gran's Bees.* Minneapolis, MN: Millbrook, 1996; 32 pp., $21.90.

Thomson, Pat. *Beware of the Aunts!* New York: Margaret McElderry, 1992; 28 pp., $14.95.

Thomson, Sarah L. *Tigers.* New York: HarperCollins, 2004; 32 pp., $16.89.

Thong, Roseanne. *Round is a Mooncake.* San Francisco: Chronicle, 2000; 32 pp., $13.95.

Thornhill, Jan. *Wild in the City.* San Francisco: Sierra Club, 1995; 32 pp., $16.95.

Titherington, Jeanne. *Baby's Boat.* New York: Greenwillow, 1992; 24 pp., $16.95.

Titus, Eve. *Anatole and the Piano.* New York: McGraw-Hill, 1966; 32 pp., $6.95.

Titus, Eve. *Anatole Over Paris.* New York: McGraw-Hill, 1991; 32 pp., $7.89.

Tolhurst, Marilyn. *Somebody and the Three Blairs.* New York: Orchard, 1990; 30 pp., $15.95.

Tomczyk, Mary. *Early Learning Skill Builders: Colors, Shapes, Numbers and Letters.* Charlotte, Vt.: Williamson, 2003; 128 pp., $12.95.

Tomecek, Steve. *Dirt.* Washington, D.C.: National Geographic, 2002; 32 pp., $16.95.

Tomlinson, Jill. *The Owl Who Was Afraid of the Dark.* Cambridge, MA: Candlewick, 2000; 32 pp., $15.99.

Torres, Laura. *Best Friends Forever!* New York: Workman, 2004; 148 pp., $13.95.

Torres, Laura. *Disney's Ten-Minute Crafts for Preschoolers.* New York: Disney, 2000; 64 pp., $14.99.

Totline Staff. *1001 Rhymes and Fingerplays.* Grand Rapids, MI: Warren, 1994; 312 pp., $29.98.

Totten, Kathryn. *Storytime Crafts.* Fort Atkinson, WI: Alleyside, 1998; 101 pp., $23.54.

Townsend, Laura. *Let's Get Ready for Kindergarten.* New York: Rigby, 2002; 175 pp., $15.95.

Trapani, Iza. *How Much Is that Doggie in the Window?* Watertown, MA: Whispering Coyote, 1997; 32 pp., $15.95.

Trapani, Iza. *Oh Where, Oh Where Has My Little Dog Gone?*. Watertown, MA: Whispering Coyote, 1996; 32 pp., $18.60.

Trapani, Iza. *Twinkle, Twinkle, Little Star.* Watertown, MA: Whispering Coyote, 1994; 32 pp., $15.95.

Treinen, Sara Jane. *Incredibly Awesome Crafts for Kids.* Des Moines, IA: Better Homes and Gardens, 1992; 168 pp., $11.95.

Tresselt, Alvin. *Rain Drop Splash.* New York: Lothrop, Lee and Shepard, 1990; 26 pp., $4.95.

Trivizas, Eugene. *The Three Little Wolves and the Big Bad Pig.* New York: Margaret K. McElderry, 1993; 32 pp., $17.00.

Trumbauer, Lisa. *What Does a Mail Carrier Do?* Berkeley Heights, NJ: Enslow, 2005; 32 pp., $21.26.

Tryon, Leslie. *Albert's Field Trip.* New York: Atheneum, 1993; 32 pp., $16.00.

Tryon, Leslie. *Albert's Halloween: The Case of the Stolen Pumpkins.* New York: Atheneum, 1998; 32 pp., $16.00.

Tucker, Kathy. *Do Cowboys Ride Bikes?* Morton Grove, IL: Albert Whitman, 1997; 32 pp., $15.95.
Tucker, Kathy. *Do Pirates Take Baths?* Morton Grove, IL: Albert Whitman, 1994; 32 pp., $15.95.
Tucker, Kathy. *The Leprechaun in the Basement.* Morton Grove, IL: Albert Whitman, 1998; 32 pp., $15.95.
Turner, Ann. *Rainflowers.* New York: HarperCollins, 1992; 32 pp., $14.00.
Turner, Ann. *Through Moon and Stars and Night Skies.* New York: Harper and Row, 1990; 32 pp., $14.89.
Turner, Charles. *The Turtle and the Moon.* New York: Dutton, 1991; 30 pp., $14.99.
Turner, Gwenda. *Shapes.* New York: Viking, 1991; 32 pp., $9.95.
Turner, Priscilla. *The War Between the Vowels and Consonants.* New York: Farrar, Straus & Giroux, 1996; 32 pp., $15.00.
Twinem, Nancy. *Baby Snakes' Shapes/Las formas de Bebe Serpiente.* Flagstaff, AZ: Luna Rising, 2004; 12 pp., $5.95.
Tyler, Anne. *Tumble Tower.* New York: Orchard, 1993; 32 pp., $15.95.
Tyler, Michael. *The Skin You Live In.* Chicago: Chicago Children's Museum, 2005; 32 pp., $14.95.
Udry, Janice May. *Is Susan Here?* New York: HarperCollins, 1993; 32 pp., $14.00.
Uhlberg, Myron. *The Printer.* Atlanta, Ga.: Peachtree, 2003; 32 pp., $16.95.
Ulmer, Wendy. *A Campfire for Cowboy Billy.* Flagstaff, AZ: Rising Moon, 1997; 32 pp., $15.95.
Umnik, Sharon Dunn. *175 Easy-to-Do Halloween Crafts.* Honesdale, PA: Boyds Mills, 1995; 63 pp., $6.95.
Umnik, Sharon Dunn. *175 Easy-to-Do Everyday Crafts.* Honesdale, PA: Boyds Mills, 1995; 63 pp., $6.95.
Umnik, Sharon Dunn. *175 Easy-to-Do Thanksgiving Crafts.* Honesdale, PA: Boyds Mills, 1996; 63 pp., $6.95.
Ungar, Richard. *Rachel's Library.* Toronto, Ontario: Tundra, 2004; 32 pp., $22.99.
Vagin, Vladimir. *The Enormous Carrot.* New York: Scholastic, 1998; 32 pp., $15.95.
Van Hise, Carol L. *Seasonal Activities for 3 Year Olds.* Greensboro, NC: Carson-Dellosa, 1997; 64 pp., $8.95.
Van Laan, Nancy. *A Tree for Me.* New York: Knopf, 2000; 32 pp., $15.30.
Van Laan, Nancy. *Little Fish, Lost.* New York: Atheneum, 1998; 32 pp., $15.00.
Van Laan, Nancy. *This Is the Hat.* New York: Little, Brown, 1992; 30 pp., $14.95.
Van Leeuwen, Jean. *Amanda Pig, Schoolgirl.* New York: Dial, 1997; 48 pp., $13.99.
Van Leeuwen, Jean. *A Fourth of July on the Plains.* New York: Dial, 1997; 32 pp., $14.89.
Van Leeuwen, Jean. *Going West.* New York: Dial, 1992; 48 pp., $14.89.
Van Rossum, Heleen. *Will You Carry Me?* New York: Kane/Miller, 2005; 32 pp., $15.95.
Van Rynbach, Iris. *Five Little Pumpkins.* Honesdale, PA: Boyds Mills, 1995; 34 pp., $7.95.
VanCleave, Janice. *Play and Find Out About Math.* Hoboken, NJ: John Wiley, 1998; 122 pp., $12.95.
Vangsgard, Amy. *Hit of the Party.* Sarasota, FL: Cool Hand Communications, 1994; 385 pp., $10.00.

Vaughan, Marcia. *Kapoc the Killer Croc.* Columbus, OH: Silver Burdett, 1995; 32 pp., $10.95.
Vaughan, Marcia. *Snap!* New York: Scholastic, 1994; 32 pp., $14.95.
Vaughan, Marcia, and Patricia Mullins. *The Sea-Breeze Hotel.* New York: Willa Perlman, 1992; 32 pp., $13.89.
Vecchione, Glen. *Sidewalk Games.* New York: Sterling, 2003; 80 pp., $17.95.
Vecchione, Glen. *World's Best Outdoor Games.* New York: Sterling, 1993; 128 pp., $5.95.
Vecere, Joel. *A Story of Courage.* Milwaukee, WI: Raintree Steck, 1992; 32 pp., NA.
Velthuijs, Max. *Crocodile's Masterpiece.* New York: Farrar, Straus & Giroux, 1991; 32 pp., $14.00.
Verboven, Agnes. *Ducks Like to Swim.* New York: Orchard, 1996; 26 pp., $13.95.
Vesey, Amanda. *Duncan's Tree House.* Minneapolis, MN: Carolrhoda, 1993; 32 pp., $11.13.
Voake, Charlotte. *Here Comes the Train.* Cambridge, MA: Candlewick, 1998; 32 pp., $15.99.
Vogel, Elizabeth. *Let's Exercise.* New York: Rosen, 2001; 32 pp., $10.95.
Vrombaut, An. *Clarabella's Teeth.* Boston: Clarion, 2003; 32 pp., $14.00.
Vulliamy, Clara. *Ellen and Penguin.* Cambridge, MA: Candlewick, 1993; 26 pp., $13.95.
Vulliamy, Clara. *Ellen and Penguin and the New Baby.* Cambridge, MA: Candlewick, 1996; 32 pp., $5.99.
Vyner, Sue. *Arctic Spring.* New York: Viking, 1992; 32 pp., $13.99.
Waber, Benard. *I Was All Thumbs.* Boston: Houghton Mifflin, 1990; 48 pp, $4.95.
Waber, Benard. *A Lion Named Shirley Williamson.* Boston: Houghton Mifflin, 1996; 40 pp., $15.95.
Waber, Benard. *Lyle at Christmas.* Boston: Houghton Mifflin, 1998; 32 pp., $16.00.
Waddell, Martin. *Farmer Duck.* Cambridge, MA: Candlewick, 1991; 32 pp., $16.99.
Waddell, Martin. *Good Job, Little Bear.* Cambridge, MA: Candlewick, 1999; 32 pp., $15.99.
Waddell, Martin. *Hi, Harry!* Cambridge, MA: Candlewick, 2003; 32 pp., $14.99.
Waddell, Martin. *It's Quacking Time!* Cambridge, MA: Candlewick, 2005; 32 pp., $15.99.
Waddell, Martin. *Let's Go Home, Little Bear.* Cambridge, MA: Candlewick, 1991; 32 pp., $14.95.
Waddell, Martin. *Little Mo.* Cambridge, MA: Candlewick, 1993; 32 pp., $14.95.
Waddell, Martin. *Once There Were Giants.* New York: Delacorte, 1995; 30 pp., $15.99.
Waddell, Martin. *Owl Babies.* Cambridge, MA: Candlewick, 1992; 32 pp., $15.99.
Waddell, Martin. *Sleep Tight, Little Bear.* Cambridge, MA: Candlewick, 2005; 32 pp., $15.99.
Waddell, Martin. *Small Bear Lost.* Cambridge, MA: Candlewick, 1996; 32 pp., $15.99.
Waddell, Martin. *The Toymaker.* Cambridge, MA: Candlewick, 1991; 32 pp., $13.95.
Waddell, Martin. *You and Me, Little Bear.* Cambridge, MA: Candlewick, 1996; 32 pp., $15.99.
Waggoner, Karen. *The Lemonade Babysitter.* New York: Little, Brown, 1992; 32 pp., $14.95.

Wajtowycz, David. *Can You Moo?* New York: Cartwheel, 2001; 32 pp., $12.95.
Waldman, Neil. *The Never-Ending Greenness.* New York: Morrow, 1997; 32 pp., $16.00.
Wallace, Ian. *A Winter's Tale.* Ontario: Groundwood, 1997; 32 pp., $15.95.
Wallace, Mary. *I Can Make Art So Easy to Make!* Toronto, Ontario: Greeyde Pencier, 1997; 32 pp., $17.95.
Wallace, Mary. *I Can Make That!: Fantastic Crafts for Kids.* Toronto, Ontario, Canada: Maple Tree Press, 2002; 160 pp., $19.95.
Wallace, Mary. *I Can Make Toys.* Toronto, Ontario: Greeyde Pencier, 1994; 32 pp., $17.95.
Wallace, Nancy Elizabeth. *Leaves! Leaves! Leaves!* Tarrytown, NY: Marshall Cavendish, 2003; 32 pp., $16.95.
Wallace, Nancy Elizabeth. *Seeds! Seeds! Seeds!* Tarrytown, NY: Marshall Cavendish, 2004; 32 pp., $16.95.
Wallace, Nancy Elizabeth. *The Valentine Express.* Tarrytown, NY: Marshall Cavendish, 2004; 32 pp., $16.95.
Wallwork, Amanda. *No DoDos: A Counting Book of Endangered Animals.* New York: Scholastic, 1993; 26 pp., $14.95.
Walsh, Ellen Stoll. *Dot and Jabber and the Mystery of the Missing Stream.* San Diego: Harcourt, 2002; 32 pp., $15.00.
Walsh, Ellen Stoll. *Pip's Magic.* San Diego: Harcourt, 1994; 32 pp., $13.95.
Walsh, Jill Paton. *Connie Came to Play.* New York: Penguin, 1995; 32 pp., $12.99.
Walsh, Melanie. *Do Monkeys Tweet?* Boston: Houghton Mifflin, 1997; 32 pp., $15.00.
Walt, Fiona. *That's Not My Train . . .* Oklahoma: EDC Publishing, 2000; 32 pp., $7.95.
Walter, F. Virginia. *Fun with Paper Bags and Cardboard Tubes.* New York: Sterling, 1992; 80 pp., $19.95.
Walter, F. Virginia. *Great Newspaper Crafts.* New York: Sterling/Hyperion, 1991; 80 pp., $17.95.
Walters, Donna Gadling; Dr. Lottie Riekehof; and Pastor Daniel M. Pokorny. *Lift up Your Hands: Popular Songs in Sign Language.* Washington, D.C.: The National Grange, 1992; 62 pp., $20.00.
Walton, Rick. *How Many, How Many, How Many.* Cambridge, MA: Candlewick, 1993; 32 pp., $14.95.
Ward, Jennifer. *The Seed and the Giant Saguaro.* Flagstaff, AZ: Rising Moon, 2003; 32 pp., $15.95.
Ward, Michael. *Mike and the Bike.* Greensboro, NC: Carson-Dellosa, Inc., 2005; 32 pp., $16.99.
Warner, Penny. *Kids' Holiday Fun.* Minnetonka, MN: Meadowbrook, 1994; 214 pp., $12.00.
Warner, Penny. *Kids' Outdoor Parties.* Minnetonka, MN: Meadowbrook, 1999; 112 pp., $8.00.
Warner, Sunny. *The Magic Sewing Machine.* Boston: Houghton Mifflin, 1997; 32 pp., $16.00.
Warnes, Tim. *Mommy Mine.* New York: HarperCollins, 2005; 32 pp., $15.99.
Warren, Celia. *Lenny's Lost Spots.* Irvine, CA: QEB Publishing, 2004; 32 pp., $15.95.
Warren, Jean. *Crafts: Early Learning Activities.* Ashland, OH: Monday Morning, 1996; 80 pp., $7.95.

Warren, Jean. *Theme-a-saurus II*. Grand Rapids, MI: Warren, 1990; 278 pp., $21.95.
Warshaw, Hallie, and Mark Shulman. *Zany Rainy Days: Indoor Ideas for Active Kids*. New York: Sterling, 2000; 126 pp., $19.95.
Washington, Donna L. *The Story of Kwanzaa*. New York: HarperCollins, 1996; 40 pp., $15.95.
Waterman, Pamela. *The Absolute Best Play Days: From Airplanes to Zoos (and Everything in Between!)* Naperville, IL: Sourcebooks, 1999; 264 pp., $34.37.
Watkins, Sherrin. *Green Snake Ceremony*. Tulsa, OK: Council Oak, 1995; 32 pp., $17.95.
Watson, Wendy. *Happy Easter Day!* Boston: Clarion, 1993; 32 pp., $14.95.
Watson, Wendy. *Hurray for the Fourth of July*. Boston: Clarion, 1992; 32 pp., $14.95.
Watts, Irene N. *Great Theme Parties for Children*. New York: Sterling, 1991; 128 pp., $13.95.
Weitzman, Jacqueline Preiss. *You Can't Take a Balloon into the Museum of Fine Arts*. New York: Dial, 2002; 32 pp., $18.99.
Weitzman, Jacqueline Preiss, and Robin Preiss Glasser. *You Can't Take a Balloon into the Metropolitan Museum*. New York: Dial, 1998; 32 pp., $16.99.
Welch, Willy. *Playing Right Field*. New York: Scholastic, 1995; 32 pp., $13.95.
Weller, Frances Ward. *I Wonder if I'll See a Whale*. New York: Philomel, 1991; 32 pp., $11.15.
Welling, Peter J. *Shawn O'Hisser, the Last Snake in Ireland*. Gretna, LA: Pelican. 2002; 32 pp., $15.95.
Wellington, Monica. *Apple Farmer Annie*. New York: Dutton, 2001; 32 pp., $14.99.
Wellington, Monica. *The Sheep Follow*. New York: Dutton, 1992; 32 pp., $13.00.
Wells, Rosemary. *Bunny Money*. New York: Dial, 1997; 32 pp., $14.99.
Wells, Rosemary. *Fritz and the Mess Fairy*. New York: Dial, 1991; 32 pp., $13.89.
Wells, Rosemary. *The Little Lame Prince*. New York: Dial, 1990; 32 pp., $12.95.
Wells, Rosemary. *Max and Ruby's First Greek Myth: Pandora's Box*. New York: Dial, 1993; 32 pp., $11.99.
Wells, Rosemary. *Max's New Suit*. New York: Dial, 1998; unpaged, $5.99.
Wells, Rosemary. *McDuff and the Baby*. New York: Hyperion, 1997; 26 pp., $12.95.
Wells, Rosemary. *McDuff Comes Home*. New York: Hyperion, 1997; 24 pp., $12.95.
Wells, Rosemary. *McDuff's Wild Romp*. New York: Hyperion, 2005; 32 pp., $9.99.
Wells, Rosemary. *Read to Your Bunny*. New York: Scholastic, 1997; 28 pp., $7.95.
Weninger, Brigitte. *Davy, Help! It's a Ghost!* New York: North-South, 2002; 32 pp., $16.50.
West, Colin. *"Buss, Buzz, Buzz," went Bumblebee*. Cambridge, MA: Candlewick, 1996; 24pp., $9.99.
Westcott, Nadine Bernard. *There's a Hole in the Bucket*. New York: Harper and Row, 1990; 26 pp., $12.89.
Weston, Anne. *My Brother Needs a Boa*. Long Island City, NY: Star Bright, 2005; 32 pp., $15.95.
Weston, Martha. *Bea's 4 Bears*. Boston: Clarion, 1992; 32 pp., $9.95.
Weston, Martha. *Tuck in the Pool*. Boston: Clarion, 1995; 32 pp., $12.95.
West, Robin. *My Very Own Thanksgiving: A Book of Cooking and Crafts*. Minneapolis, MN: Carolrhoda, 1993; 64 pp., $21.27.

Wheeler, Cindy. *More Simple Signs*. New York: Viking, 1998; 32 pp., $14.99.
Wheeler, Lisa. *Farmer Dale's Red Pickup Truck*. San Diego: Harcourt, 2004; 32 pp., $16.00.
Whishaw, Iona. *Henry and the Cow Problem*. Carlsbad, CA: Annick, 1995; 24 pp., $15.95.
Whitcher, Susan. *Moonfall*. New York: Farrar, Straus & Giroux, 1993; 32 pp., $14.00.
White, Kathryn. *The Nutty Nut Chase*. Intercourse, PA: Good Books, 2004; 32 pp., $16.00.
Whitehead, Kathy. *Looking for Uncle Louie on the Fourth of July*. Honesdale, PA: Boyds Mills, 2005; 32 pp., $15.95.
Whitney, Brooks. *Super Slumber Parties*. Middleton, WI: Pleasant, 1997; 64 pp., $7.95.
Whybrow, Ian. *Harry and the Dinosaurs Say "Raahh!"* New York: Random House, 2001; 32 pp., $14.95.
Wiesner, David. *Hurricane*. Boston: Clarion, 1990; 32 pp., $16.00.
Wiesner, David. *Tuesday*. Boston: Clarion, 1991; 32 pp., $15.95.
Wild, Margaret. *All the Better to See You With!* Morton Grove, IL: Albert Whitman, 1992; 32 pp., $14.95.
Wild, Margaret. *The Queen's Holiday*. New York: Orchard, 1992; 32 pp., $13.99.
Wilde, Oscar. *The Selfish Giant*. New York: Putnam, 1995; 32 pp., $14.99.
Wildsmith, Brian and Rebecca. *Jack and the Meanstalk*. New York: Knopf, 1994; 26 pp., $15.99.
Wilhelm, Hans. *A Cool Kid—Like Me!* New York: Crown, 1990; 32 pp., $3.99.
Willans, Tom. *Wait! I Want to Tell You a Story*. New York: Simon & Schuster, 2004; 32 pp., $15.95.
Wilkes, Angela. *Child Magazine's Book of Children's Parties*. New York: DK Publishing, 1996; 80 pp., $18.95.
Willard, Nancy. *The Mouse, the Cat and Grandmother's Hat*. New York: Little, Brown, 2003; 32 pp., $14.95.
Willard, Nancy. *The Well Mannered Balloon*. San Diego: Harcourt, 1991; 28 pp., $3.95.
Willey, Margaret. *Thanksgiving with Me*. New York: Laura Geringer, 1998; 32 pp., $14.95.
Williams, Barbara. *Albert's Impossible Toothache*. Cambridge, MA: Candlewick, 2003; 32 pp., $15.99.
Williams, Karen Lynn. *When Africa Was Home*. New York: Orchard, 1991; 32 pp., $16.99.
Williams, Nancy. *A Kwanzaa Celebration*. New York: Simon & Schuster, 1995; 14 pp., $11.95.
Williams, Vera B. *Lucky Song*. New York: Greenwillow, 1997; 24 pp., $15.00.
Williamson, Sarah. *Stop, Look and Listen*. Charlotte, VT: Williamson, 1996; 144 pp., $12.95.
Williamson, Susan. *Summer Fun!: 60 Activities for a Kid-Perfect Summer*. Charlotte, VT: Williamson, 1999; 138 pp., $12.95.
Willis, Jeanne. *Don't Let Go!* New York: Putnam, 2002; 32 pp., $16.99.
Willis, Jeanne, and Tony Ross. *Misery Moo*. New York: Henry Holt, 2005; 32 pp., $16.95.

Willis, Jeanne, and Tony Ross. *Shhh!* New York: Hyperion, 2004; 32 pp., $15.99.
Willis, Val. *The Mystery in the Bottle.* New York: Farrar, Straus & Giroux, 1991; 32 pp., $14.95.
Willis, Val. *The Surprise in the Wardrobe.* New York: Farrar, Straus & Giroux, 1990; 32 pp., $15.00.
Wilmes, Liz and Dick. *Felt Board Fingerplays.* Elgin, IL: Building Blocks, 1997; 80 pp., $18.00.
Wilson, Etta. *Music in the Night.* New York: Cobblehill, 1993; 32 pp., $12.99.
Wilson, Karma. *Bear's New Friend.* New York: Margaret K. McElderry, 2006; 32 pp., $16.95.
Wilson, Karma. *Bear Wants More.* New York: Margaret K. McElderry, 2003; 32 pp., $16.95.
Wilson, Karma, and Joan Rankin. *A Frog in the Bog.* New York: Margaret K. McElderry, 2003; 32 pp., $16.95.
Wilson, Karma. *Mama Always Comes Home.* New York: HarperCollins, 2005; 32 pp, $16.89.
Winch, John. *The Old Woman Who Loved to Read.* New York: Holiday House, 1996; 32 pp., $15.95.
Winkleman, Katherine K. *Police Patrol.* New York: Walker, 1996; 32 pp., $15.95.
Winstead, Rosie. *Ruby and Bubbles.* New York: Dial, 2006, 32 pp., $15.99.
Winters, Kay. *The Teeny Tiny Ghost.* New York: HarperCollins, 1997; 32 pp., $14.95.
Winters, Kay. *The Teeny Tiny Ghost and the Monster.* New York: HarperCollins, 2004; 32 pp., $15.89.
Winthrop, Elizabeth. *Dancing Granny.* Tarrytown, NY: Marshall Cavendish, 2003; 32 pp., $16.95.
Wise, Debra. *Great Big Book of Children's Games.* New York: McGraw-Hill, 2003; 318 pp., $12.95.
Wiswell, Phil. *Kids' Games.* New York: Doubleday, 1987; 169 pp., $12.95.
Witte, Anna. *The Parrot Tico Tango.* Cambridge, MA: Barefoot, 2004; 32 pp., $15.99.
Wolf, Erica. *Brave Little Raccoon.* New York: Henry Holt, 2005; 32 pp., $16.95.
Wolf, Jake. *Daddy, Could I Have an Elephant.* New York: Greenwillow, 1996; 32 pp., $15.00.
Wojciechowski, Susan. *The Best Halloween of All.* Cambridge, MA: Candlewick, 1998; 32 pp., $9.99.
Wolff, Ferida. *The Emperor's Garden.* New York: Tambourine, 1994; 32 pp., $14.95.
Wong, Janet S. *Apple Pie 4th of July.* San Diego: Harcourt, 2002; 32 pp., $16.00.
Wong, Janet S. *Buzz.* San Diego: Harcourt, 2000; 32 pp., $15.00.
Wood, A.J. *The Little Penguin.* New York: Dutton, 2001; 32 pp., $15.99.
Wood, Audrey. *Jubal's Wish.* New York: Blue Sky, 2000; 32 pp., $16.95.
Wood, Audrey. *Rude Giants.* San Diego: Harcourt, 1993; 32 pp., $13.95.
Wood, Audrey. *Sweet Dream Pie.* New York: Blue Sky, 1998; 32 pp., $15.95.
Wood, Audrey. *Ten Little Fish.* New York: Blue Sky, 2004; 32 pp., $15.95.
Wood, Douglas. *What Teachers Can't Do.* New York: Simon & Schuster, 2002; 32 pp., $14.95.
Woodruff, Elvira. *Show-and-Tell.* New York: Holiday House, 32 pp., $14.95.
Woodruff, Elvira. *Tubtime.* New York: Holiday House, 1990; 32 pp., $14.95.

Woodworth, Viki. *Daisy the Firecow.* Honesdale, Pa.: Boyds Mills, 2001; 32 pp., $15.95.
Wormell, Christopher. *Blue Rabbit and the Runaway Wheel.* New York: Penguin Putnam, 2001; 32 pp., $15.99.
Wormell, Mary. *Hilda Hen's Happy Birthday.* San Diego, Calif.: Harcourt, 1995; 32 pp., $14.00.
Woychuk, Denis. *Mimi and Gustav in Pirates!* New York: Lothrop, Lee and Shepard, 1992; 32 pp., $13.95.
Wright, Rachel. *Look and Make: Presents.* North Mankato, MN: Sea-to-Sea, 2005; 32 pp., $27.10.
Wyllie, Stephen. *A Flea in the Ear.* New York: Dutton, 1995; 32 pp., $14.99.
Yaccarino, Dan. *An Octopus Followed Me Home.* New York: Viking, 1997; 32 pp., $15.99.
Yee, Paul. *Roses Sing on New Snow: A Delicious Tale.* New York: Macmillan, 1991; 32 pp., $13.95.
Yee, Wong Herbert. *Big Black Bear.* Boston: Houghton Mifflin, 1993; 32 pp., $14.95.
Yee, Wong Herbert. *Fireman Small.* Boston: Houghton Mifflin, 1994; 32 pp., $13.95.
Yee, Wong Herbert. *Fireman Small: Fire Down Below!* Boston: Houghton Mifflin, 2001; 32 pp., $15.00.
Yee, Wong Herbert. *Mrs. Brown Went to Town.* Boston: Houghton Mifflin, 1996; 32 pp., $14.95.
Yeoman, John, and Quentin Blake. *Old Mother Hubbard's Dog Needs a Doctor.* Boston: Houghton Mifflin, 1990; 32 pp., $6.95.
Yolen, Jane. *Beneath the Ghost Moon.* New York: Little, Brown, 1994; 32 pp., $14.95.
Yolen, Jane. *The Emperor and the Kite.* New York: Putnam, 1998; 27 pp., $5.99.
Yolen, Jane. *Jane Yolen's Old MacDonald Songbook.* Honesdale, PA: Boyds Mills, 1994; 96 pp., $16.95.
Yolen, Jane. *Welcome to the Greenhouse.* New York: Putnam, 1997; 32 pp., $5.95.
Yorinks, Arthur. *Happy Bees!* New York: Abrams, 2005; 32 pp., $15.95.
Yorinks, Arthur. *Ugh.* New York: Farrar, Straus & Giroux, 1990; 32 pp., $13.95.
Yorke, Jane. *My First Look at Touch.* New York: Random House, 1990; 18 pp., $6.95.
Yoshida, Toshi. *Rhinoceros Mother.* New York: Philomel, 1991; 32 pp., $14.95.
Young, Ed. *Seven Blind Mice.* New York: Philomel, 1992; 40 pp., $17.99.
Young, Ruth. *Daisy's Taxi.* New York: Smithmark, 1991; 32 pp., $4.95.
Young, Ruth. *A Trip to Mars.* New York: Orchard, 1990; 32 pp., $14.95.
Zidrou. *Ms. Blanche, the Spotless Cow.* New York: Henry Holt, 1992; 32 pp., $14.95.
Ziefert, Harriet. *40 Uses for a Grandpa.* Maplewood, NJ: Blue Apple, 2005; 32 pp., $12.95.
Ziefert, Harriet. *Bigger Than a Baby.* New York HarperCollins, 1991; 32 pp., $13.95.
Ziefert, Harriet. *Circus Parade.* Maplewood, NJ: Blue Apple, 2005; 32 pp., $15.95.
Ziefert, Harriet. *Hats Off for the Fourth of July!* New York: Viking, 2000; 32 pp., $15.99.
Ziefert, Harriet. *I'm Going to New York to Visit the Lions.* New York: Sterling, 2005; 32 pp., $11.95.
Ziefert, Harriet. *My Friend Grandpa.* Maplewood, NJ: Blue Apple, 2004; 32 pp., $15.95.

Ziefert, Harriet. *Oh, What a Noisy Farm!* New York: Tambourine, 1995; 32 pp., $15.00.

Ziefert, Harriet. *What Is Hanukkah?* New York: Harper Festival, 1994; 32 pp., $5.95.

Ziefert, Harriet. *You Can't Buy a Dinosaur with a Dime.* Maplewood, NJ: Blue Apple, 2003; 32 pp., $15.95.

Ziefert, Harriet, and Simms Taback. *Zoo Parade.* Maplewood, NJ: Blue Apple, 2003; 32 pp., $8.95.

Ziegler, Sandra. *The Child's World of Manners.* New York: Child's World, 1998; 23 pp., $18.50.

Zimelman, Nathan. *Treed by a Pride of Irate Lions.* New York: Little, Brown, 1990; 30 pp., $14.95.

Zimmermann, H. Werner. *A Circle Is Not a Valentine.* Don Mills, Ontario: Oxford University Press, 1990; 32 pp., $3.95.

Zion, Gene. *Harry and the Lady Next Door.* New York: Harper and Row, 1996; 32 pp., $14.89.

Zolotow, Charlotte. *The Bunny Who Found Easter.* Boston: Houghton Mifflin, 1998; 32 pp., $15.00.

Zweibel, Alan. *Our Tree Named Steve.* New York: Putnam, 2005; 32 pp., $14.99.

3 Recommended Videos and DVDs

NOTE: Numbers at the end of each entry are program numbers.

Abel's Island. 30 min., Italtoons Corporation, 14
Adventures of Scamper the Penguin. 85 min., Library Video Company, 31
Adventures of Two Piggy Bands: Learning to Save. 30 min., Library Video Company, 102
Alejandro's Gift. 8 min., Charles Clark Co., Inc., 40, 110
Alexander and the Terrible, Horrible, No Good, Very Bad Day. 14 min., Charles Clark Co., Inc., 60
Alexander and the Wind-up Mouse. 24 min., Mulberry Park, Inc., 1, 14, 136
Alexander, Who Used to be Rich Last Sunday. 14 min., Charles Clark Co., Inc., 102
Alexandria's Clean-up, Fix-up Parade. EOHSI-Resource Center of Rutgers University, 15 min. 38, 39, 56
Alphabet Zoo. 25 min., Kimbo Educational, 3
Alligators All Around. 2 min., Weston Woods, 3, 118
Alphabet Dragon, The. 16 min., Phoenix Films, Inc., 3, 26
Amazing Bone, The. 11 min., Weston Woods, 16, 99
American Tall Tale Heroes. 15 min., Phoenix Films, Inc., 64
Anansi and the Talking Melon. 23 min., Live Oak Media, 71
And the Dish Ran Away with the Spoon. 24 min. Spoken Arts, 59
Andy and the Lion. 10 min., Weston Woods, 13, 40
Angus and the Ducks. 12 min., Charles Clark Co., Inc., 29
Angus Lost. 11 min., Phoenix Films, Inc., 9
Annie Oakley. 30 min., Weston Woods, 64
Ant and the Dove, The. 8 min., Coronet Films, 92
Ant and the Grasshopper, The. 11 min., Charles Clark Co., Inc., 41
Antarctic Antics. 19 min., Weston Woods, 31
Apt. 3. 19 min., Charles Clark Co., Inc., 77, 131
Arbor Day. 30 min., Schlessinger Video Productions, 140
Are You My Mother? 30 min., Charles Clark Co., Inc., 61
Art Dog. 11 min., Charles Clark Co., Inc., 18, 117, 129
Arthur Babysits. 11 min., Charles Clark Co., Inc., 20
Arthur's Baby. 15 min., Random House/Miller-Brody Productions, 19
Arthur's Christmas Cookies. 40 min., Random House/Miller-Brody Productions, 79
Arthur's Eyes. 30 min., Sony Music Distribution, 75
Arthur's Halloween. 40 min., Random House/Miller-Brody Productions, 83
Arthur's Lost Library Book. 30 min., Library Video Co., 97
Arthur's Pet Business. 30 min., Sony Music Distribution, 112
Aunt Ippy's Museum of Junk. 26 min., Sony Music Distribution, 56

Barney's Best Manners. 30 min., Lyons Group, 100
Beady Bear. 8 min. Live Oak Media, 6

Cinder-Elly. 12 min., Charles Clark Co., Inc., 68
Circus Baby. 5 min., Weston Woods, 11, 42, 100
Clean Your Room, Harvey Moon. 6 min., Charles Clark Co., Inc., 38
Clifford's Fun with Shapes. 30 min., Schoolmasters, 47
Cloudy with a Chance of Meatballs. 15 min., Random House/Miller-Brody Productions, 110, 141, 143
Cold Blooded Penguin, The. 10 min., Western Publishing Co., Inc., 31
Come on, Rain. 12 min., Weston Woods, 141
Company's Coming. 9.5 min., Spoken Arts, 60, 133
Corduroy. 16 min., Weston Woods, 44, 136
Cornelius. 30 min., Charles Clark Co., Inc., 118
Cow Who Fell in the Canal, The. 9 min., Weston Woods, 8
Curious George. 83 min., Baker and Taylor Video, 15, 35
Curious George at the Mini Marathon. 20 min., Sony Music Distribution, 58
Curious George Goes to the Hospital. 15 min., Charles Clark Co., Inc., 88
Curious George Goes to the Library. 30 min., Sony Music Distribution, 97
Curious George Rides a Bike. 10 min., Weston Woods, 27, 42, 139

D. W. Rides Again. 30 min., Sony Music Distribution, 122
Dancing with the Indians. 8 min., Live Oak Media, 57
Danny and the Dinosaurs. 9 min., Weston Woods, 51
Day Jimmy's Boa Ate the Wash, The. 5 min., Weston Woods, 90, 119
Dazzle the Dinosaur. 30 min., Sony Music Distribution, 51
Disney Presents Mickey Loves Minnie. 25 min., Disney Educational Productions, 54
Do it Yourself. 25 min., Buena Vista Home Video, 130
Don't Eat Too Much Turkey! 7.5 min., Spoken Arts, 87
Dora: Saves the Day! 98 min., Library Video Co., 10
Dora: Super Silly Fiesta. 90 min., Kimbo Educational, 111
Dorothy and the Clock. 10 min., Phoenix Films, Inc., 43
Dorothy and the Kite. 8 min., Phoenix Films, Inc., 96
Dorothy and the Ostrich. 9 min., Phoenix Films, Inc., 28
Dot the Fire Dog. 9 min., Weston Woods, 35
Dragon and the Unicorn, The. 16.5 min., Spoken Arts, 106
Dragon Tales: Let's Work Together, 42 min., Sony Music Distribution, 39
Dr. DeSoto. 10 min., Weston Woods, 34
Dr. Seuss's ABC. 30 min., Fox Video Inc., 26
Dr. Seuss's My Many Colored Days. 45 min., Weston Woods, 22
Dr. Seuss's Sleep Book. 30 min., Charles Clark Co., Inc., 21
Draghetto. 12 min., Phoenix Films, Inc., 35, 52
Dragon Stew. 13 min., Phoenix Films, Inc., 52, 65
Drummer Hoff. 5 min., Weston Woods, 98
Duck for President. 16 min., Weston Woods, 29
Dumbo. 63 min., Baker and Taylor Video, 11

Easter Bunny, The. 4.5 min., Spoken Arts, 80
Elephant's Child. 30 min., Mulberry Park, Inc., 11
Elmocize. 30 min., Sesame Street, 58

Elves and the Shoemaker, The. 6 min., Troll Associates, 39, 79, 106
Emily's First 100 Days of School. 36 min., Weston Woods, 123
Emperor's New Clothes, The. 10 min., Phoenix Films, Inc., 44, 90, 91, 121
Empty Pot, The. 7 min., A. W. Peller and Associates, Inc., 114
Everybody Knows That. 15 min., Charles Clark Co., Inc., 95

Fire Safety for Kids. 23 min., Library Video Co., 122
Firehouse Dog. 11 min., Phoenix Films, Inc., 35
First Easter Rabbit, The. 25 min., Coronet Films, 80
Fish Is Fish. 30 min, Listening Library, 63
Fisherman and his Wife, The. 20 min., Weston Woods, 26, 63
Fitness Fun with Goofy. 19 min., Disney Educational Productions, 58
Five Chinese Brothers, The. 10 min., Weston Woods, 67
Foot Book, The. 15 min., A. W. Peller and Associates, Inc., 4
Franklin and the Secret Club. 25 min., PolyGram Video, 129
Franklin Is Messy. 25 min., PolyGram Video, 38, 120
Frederick. 24 min., Mulberry Park, Inc., 14
Freight Train. 6 min., Charles Clark Co., Inc., 46, 138, 139
Frog Goes to Dinner. 12 min., Phoenix Films, Inc., 65, 112
Frog and Toad are Friends: Spring. 60 min., Random House/Miller-Brody Productions, 126
Frog and Toad are Friends: A Swim. 60 min., Random House/Miller-Brody Productions, 127, 134
Frog and Toad are Friends: The Story. 60 min., Random House/Miller-Brody Productions, 69, 70
Frog and Toad Together: Dragons and Giants. 60 min., Random House/Miller-Brody Productions, 52, 74
Frog and Toad Together: The Garden. 60 min., Random House/Miller-Brody Productions, 114
Frog Prince, The. 6 min., Mulberry Park, Inc., 70
Frog Princess, The. 6 min., Coronet Films, 70
Frog Went A-Courtin'. 12 min., Weston Woods, 70, 105
Frosty the Snowman. 30 min., Library Video Inc., 142
Fruit: Close Up and Very Personal. 30 min., Stage Fright Productions, 71
Funny Little Bunnies. 7 min., Disney Educational Productions, 80

Garbage Day! 25 min., Library Video Co., 53
George Washington's Teeth. 30 min., Spoken Arts, 34
George Washington's Mother. 20 min., Library video Co., 61
Georgie. 6 min., Weston Woods, 73, 83
Ghost with the Halloween Hiccups. 7 min, Coronet Films, 73, 83
Giant Devil-Dingo, The. 10 min., Weston Woods, 74
Giggle, Gaggle, Quack. 57 min., Kimbo Educational, 5
Gingerbread Boy, The. 8 min., Troll Associates, 59
Giving Thanks. 8 min., Weston Woods, 53, 56, 57, 87
Giving Tree, The. 10 min., Weston Woods, 22, 140
Goggles. 11 min., Phoenix Films, Inc., 75

Goodnight, Gorilla! 10 min., Weston Woods, 108, 146
Goofy Look at Valentine's Day, A. 10 min., Disney Educational Productions, 86
Goofy over Dental Health. 13 min., Library Video Co., 34
Grandfather's Mitten. 10 min., Phoenix Films, Inc., 23, 25
Grandpa. 27 min., Weston Woods, 76
Grasshopper and the Ants, The. 11 min., Coronet Films, 92
Great Kapok Tree, The. 10 min., Weston Woods, 140
Green Eggs and Ham. 51 min., Listening Library, 65
Grey Lady and the Strawberry Snatcher. 10 min., Charles Clark Co., Inc., 71

Halloween. 6.5 min., Live Oak Media, 83
Hansen and Gretel. 14 min., Random House/Miller-Brody Productions, 145
Hanukkah. 12 min., Encyclopedia Britannica Educational Corp., 78
Happy Birthday, Moon. 7 min., Weston Woods, 32
Happy Lion. 8 min., Weston Woods, 69
Happy Lion's Treasure. 9 min., Encyclopedia Britannica Educational Corp., 13, 146
Happy Owls, The. 7 min., Weston Woods, 30
Harold and His Amazing Green Plants. 13 min., Disney Educational Productions, 114
Harold and the Purple Crayon. 8 min., Weston Woods, 18, 46, 90, 91
Harold's Fairy Tale. 8 min., Weston Woods., 59
Harry the Dirty Dog. 10 min., Weston Woods, 9, 38
Hat, The. 6 min., Weston Woods, 44, 45
Have You Seen My Duckling? 6 min., Charles Clark Co., Inc., 117, 130
Helpful Little Fireman. 11 min., Coronet Films, 35
Henny Penny. 6 min., Troll Associates, 5, 59, 62
Hercules. 11 min., Weston Woods, 35
Hiawatha. 12 min., Weston Woods, 57
Holidays for Children: Kwanzaa. 25 min., Library Video Co., 84
Holidays for Children: St. Patrick's Day. 25 min., Library Video Co., 85
Horton Hatches an Egg. 30 min., Charles Clark Co., Inc., 11, 28, 39, 40, 41
Hospital, The. 10 min., Disney Educational Productions, 88
Hot Air Henry. 12 min., Charles Clark Co., Inc., 116, 136
Hot Hippo. 5 min., Weston Woods, 6, 55
How Do Dinosaurs Get Well Soon? 8 min., Weston Woods, 51
How Much is a Million? 9 min., Weston Woods, 49
How the Rhinoceros Got His Skin. 30 min., Library Video Co., 55
How the Trollusk Got His Hat. 30 min., Mulberry Park, Inc., 45
How the Whale Got His Throat. 25 min., Listening Library, 10
How to Exercise. 11 min., Disney Educational Productions, 58
Hush the Baby. 5 min., Weston Woods, 19

I Can Read with My Eyes Shut. 30 min., Random House/Miller-Brody Productions, 1
If You Made a Million. 17 min., Weston Woods, 102
I'm Safe on Wheels. 10 min., Library Video Co., 27
I Stink! 9 min., Weston Woods, 38
I Wanna be an Astronaut. 30 min., Better Book Co., 133
I Wanna be a Cowboy. 30 min., Better Book Co., 144

Ouch! 14 min., Live Oak Media, 121
Over in the Meadow. 9 min., Weston Woods, 49
Owen. 9 min., Weston Woods, 22, 54
Owl and the Pussycat, The. 7 min., Phoenix Films, Inc., 7, 30, 115
Owl Moon. 8 min., Charles Clark Co., Inc., 30, 108

Paddington Helps Out: Paddington Dines Out. 50 min., Coronet Films, 6
Patrick's Dinosaurs. 28 min., Media Basics Video, 51
Pebble and the Penguin. 24 min., Library Video Co., 31
Pecos Bill. 30 min., Rabbit Ears Production Inc., 64, 144
Pegasus. 17 min., Charles Clark Co., Inc., 106
Penny Lee and Her TV. 8 min., Spoken Arts, 1
Pete's a Pizza. 6 min., Weston Woods, 65
Pet Show! 45 min., Children's Circle, 112
Peter Rabbit. 30 min, Charles Clark Co., Inc., 17, 24
Peter's Chair. 6 min., Weston Woods, 19, 22, 60, 69
Pete's Dragon. 105 min., Brodart Company, 52
Petunia. 10 min., Weston Woods, 1, 69
Picnic. 13 min., Weston Woods, 23
Picture for Harold's Room, A. 6 min., Weston Woods, 18, 91
Pierre: A Cautionary Tale. 50 min., Coronet Films, 6, 24
Pig's Picnic, The. 5 min., Charles Clark Co., Inc., 16, 101
Pig's Wedding, The. 7 min., Charles Clark Co., Inc., 16
Pilgrims of Plimoth, The. 26 min., Weston Woods, 87
Pirate Adventure, The. 30 min., Library Video Co., 113
Pirate Island. 30 min., Library Video Co., 113
Planting a Rainbow. 7 min., Weston Woods, 46
Play, The. 9 min., Disney Educational Productions, 77
Players in Pigtails. 12 min., Weston Woods, 134
Pocket for Corduroy, A. 20 min., Phoenix Films, Inc., 44, 136
Pokey Little Puppy, The. 30 min., Mulberry Park, Inc., 9
Police Station, The. 11 min., Disney Educational Productions, 37
Postman Pat. 30 min., Good Time Home Videos, 36
Prince Cinders. 26 min., First Run Features, 68
Princess Scargo and the Birthday Pumpkin. 30 min., Weston Woods, 32, 57
Puff the Magic Dragon. 45 min., Listening Library, 52
Pumpkin Who Couldn't Smile. 23 min., Mulberry Park, Inc., 83
Puss in Boots. 14 min., Charles Clark Co., Inc., 7

Rain. 10 min., Charles Clark Co., Inc., 141
Rainbow Fish, The. 30 min., Sony Music Distribution, 25
Rainbow of My Own, A. 5 min., Live Oak Media, 141
Reading to Your Bunny. 9 min., Weston Woods, 1
Really Rosie. 26 min., Weston Woods, 49, 50, 105
Recess Queen, The. 7 min., Spoken Ats, 24, 121
Recycle Rex. 10 min., Disney Educational Productions, 53
Regina's Big Mistake. 30 min., Plains National Instructional Television, 18, 130

4 Classic "Not to Be Missed" Picture Book Titles

125 of Still My Favorite Titles from the Original *Storytime Sourcebook!*

Alistair in Outer Space, Marilyn Sadler
Alistair's Elephant, Marilyn Sadler
And to Think I Saw it on Mulberry Street, Dr. Seuss
Androcles and the Lion, Janet Stevens
Andy and the Wild Ducks, Mayo Short
Animals Should Definitely Not Wear Clothing, Judy Barrett
Apple Pigs, Ruth Orbach
Arnold of the Ducks, Mordicai Gerstein
Around the Clock with Harriet, Betsy and Giulio Maestro
Arthur's Eyes, Marc Brown
Arthur's Loose Tooth, Lillian Hoban
Ask Mr. Bear, Marjorie Flack

Babar and the Ghost, Laurent deBrunhoff
Baby Rattlesnake, Te Ala
Baby Sitter for Frances, A, Russell Hoban
Bargain for Frances, A, Russell Hoban
Berenstain Bears Visit the Dentist, The, Stan Berenstain and Jan Berenstain
Big Anthony and the Magic Ring, Thomas dePaola
Blind Man and the Elephant, The, Lillian Quigley
Blue Balloon, The, Mick Inkpen
Blueberries for Sal, Robert McCloskey

Caps for Sale, Esphyr Slobodkina
Caterpillar and the Polliwog, The, Jack Kent
Chalk Box Story, The, Don Freeman
Circus Baby, The, Maud Petersham
Clifford's Good Deeds, Norman Bridwell
Clifford's Puppy Days, Norman Bridwell
Cloudy with a Chance of Meatballs, Judy Barrett
Crocus, Roger Duvoisin
Curious George Goes to School, Margret Rey and Alan J. Shalleck
Curious George Goes to the Dentist, Margaret Rey
Curious George Rides a Bike, Hans Rey
Curious George Visits a Police Station, Margaret and H.A. Rey

Day the Teacher went Bananas, The, James Howe
Devin's New Bed, Sally Freedman
Don't Ever Wish for a 7 Ft. Bear, Robert Benton

Elmer, David McKee

Fat Cat, The, Jack Kent
Fish Out of Water, A, Helen Palmer
Follow Me, Cried Bee, Jan Wahl
Frances, Face-maker, William Cole
Frederick's Fables, Leo Lionni

Georgie and the Magician, Nathaniel Benchley
Geraldine, the Music Mouse, Leo Lionni
Going to the Dentist, Fred Rogers
Goodnight, Moon, Margaret Brown

Happy Lion, The, Louise Fatio
Harriet Goes to the Circus, Betsy Maestro
Harry by the Sea, Gene Zion
Harry the Dirty Dog, Gene Zion
Have You Seen My Duckling? Nancy Tafuri
Hector Penguin, Louise Fatio
Henry's Wrong Turn, Harriet Ziefert

Horse with the Easter Bonnet, The, Catherine Wooley
Horton Hatches an Egg, Dr. Seuss
Hot Air Henry, Mary Calhoun
Hunt for Rabbit's Galosh, The Ann Schweninger

I Unpacked My Grandmother's Trunk, Susan Hoguet
I Was a Second Grade Werewolf, Daniel Pinkwater
If the Dinosaurs Came Back, Jean Polhamus
If You Give a Mouse a Cookie, Laura Numeroff
In a Dark, Dark, Room and other Scary Stories, Alvin Schwartz
It Looked Like Spilt Milk, Charles Shaw

Jeanne-Marie Counts Her Sheep, Francoise Seignobosc
Jennie's Hat, Ezra Jack Keats
Jimmy's Boa Bounces Back, Trinka Noble
Joey, Jack Kent
Johnny Lion's Book, Edith Hurd

Katy and the Big Snow, Virginia Burton
Katy No-Pocket, Emmy Payne

Lady with the Alligator Purse, The, Nadine Bernard Westcott
Laughing Latkes, M.B. Goffstein
Legend of Bluebonnet, The, Tomie dePaola
Little Blue and Little Yellow, Leo Lionni
Little Red Hen, The, Paul Galdone
Littlest Leaguer, The Sydney Hoff
Long Red Scarf, The, Nette Hilton
Loose Tooth, Steven Kroll

Madeline's Rescue, Ludwig Bemelmans
Magic Porridge Pot, The, Paul Galdone
Make a Face, Lynn Yudell
Max's Chocolate Chicken, Rosemary Wells
Miss Nelson Has a Field Day, Harry Allard
Miss Nelson is Back, Harry Allard
Missing Piece, The, Shel Silverstein
Mitten, The, Jan Brett
Moon Bear, Frank Asch
Mother, Mother I Want Another, Maria Polushkin
Mouse Paint, Ellen Walsh
Mufaro's Beautiful Daughter, John Steptoe
Mysterious Tadpole, The, Steven Kellogg

Once-Upon-a-Time Dragon, The, Jack Kent
Owl Moon, Jane Yolen
Owly, Mike Thaler

Peony's Rainbow, Martha Weston
Pig's Picnic, The, Keiko Kasza
Plant Sitter, The, Gene Zion
Popcorn, Frank Asch
Potato Pancakes All Around, Marilyn Hirsh
Principal's New Clothes, The, Stephanie Calmenson
Put Me in the Zoo, Robert Lopshire

Quiet on Account of Dinosaurs, Catherine Wooley
Quiet! There's a Canary in the Library, Don Freeman

Rabbit Goes to Night School, Judy Delton
Rain Makes Applesauce, Julian Scheer
Really Rosie, Maurice Sendak

Seven Froggies Went to School, Kate Duke
Story of Jumping Mouse, The, John Steptoe
Sylvester and the Magic Pebble, William Steig

Tacky the Penguin, Helen Lester
Tale of Georgie Grub, The, Jeanne Willis
Ten Black Dots, Donald Crews
There's No Such Thing as a Dragon, Jack Kent
Too Many Books!, Caroline Bauer
Treeful of Pigs, A, Arnold Lobel

True Story of the Three Little Pigs, The, Jon Scieszka
Turnip, The, Janina Domanska
Turtle Tale, Frank Asch

Veronica and the Birthday Present, Roger Duvoisin

Very Hungry Caterpillar, The, Eric Carle

Walter's Magic Wand, Eric Houghton
Whistle for Willie, Ezra Jack Keats
Who Took the Farmer's Hat?, Joan Lexau
Whose Hat?, Margaret Miller
Witch Bazooza, Dennis Nolan

Part II:

Directories Storytellers Can Use Every Day

1 Directory of Publishers of Recommended Books

ALA
50 East Huron Street
Chicago, IL 60611
800-545-2433
ala.org

Abingdon
Division of United Methodist Publishers House
201 Eighth Avenue South
P.O. Box 801
Nashville, TN 37202
800-251-3320
abingdonpress.com

Abrams
See Harry N. Abrams Inc.

Adams Media Corporation
57 Littlefield Street
Avon, MA 02322
800-872-5627
adamsmedia.com

Advance Publishing, Incorporated
6950 Fulton Street
Houston, TX 77022
800-917-9630
advancepublishing.com

Aladdin Paperbacks
Imprint of Simon & Schuster Children's Publishing Division

Allen and Unwin
83 Alexander Street
Crows Nest NSW 2065 Australia
612-425-0100
allenandunwin.com

Alaska Northwest Books
Imprint of Graphic Arts Center Publishing Company
P.O. Box 10306
Portland, OR 97296
503-226-2402
gacpc.com

Albert Whitman & Co.
6340 Oakton Street
Morton Grove, IL 60053
800-255-7675
albertwhitman.com

Alfred A. Knopf, Incorporated
Subsidiary of Random House, Inc.

Alleyside Press
Division of Highsmith Press

American Trust Publications
Distributed by Islamic Book Service
2622 East Main Street
Plainfield, IN 46168
317-839-8150

Annick Press Ltd.
Distributed by Dominie Press Inc.
1949 Kellog Avenue
Carlsbad, CA 92008
800-232-4570
dominie.com

Arthur A. Levine Books
Imprint of Scholastic Press

Atheneum Books for Young Readers
Imprint of Simon & Schuster

August House Little Folk
P.O. Box 3223
Little Rock, AR 72203
501-372-5450
augusthouse.com

Backpack Books
122 Fifth Avenue
New York, NY 10011

Bantam Books, Inc.
Division of Bantam Doubleday Dell Publishing Group
1540 Broadway
New York, NY 10036
800-223-6834
randomhouse.com

Barefoot Books
2067 Massachusetts Avenue
Cambridge, MA 02140
617-349-1610
barefoot-books.com

Barnesyard Books
P.O. Box 254
Sergeantsville, NJ 08557
609-397-6600
barnesyardbooks.com

Barron's Educational Series, Inc.
250 Wireless Boulevard
Hauppauge, NY 11788
800-645-3476
baronsedu.com

Bearport Publishing
101 Fifth Avenue, Suite 6R
New York, NY 10003
877-337-8577
bearportpublishing.com

Better Homes & Gardens
Division of Meredith Corporation

Beyond Words Publishing, Inc.
20827 NW Cornell Road, Suite 500
Hillsboro, OR 97124
800-284-9673
beyondword.com

Bloomsbury Children's Books
175 Fifth Avenue
New York, NY 10010
bloomsbury.com

Blue Apple Books
515 Valley Street
Maplewood, NJ 07040
973-763-8191
blueapplebooks.com

Blue Sky Press
Imprint of Scholastic, Inc.

Boyds Mills Press
815 Church Street
Honesdale, PA 18431
800-949-7777
boydsmillspress.com

Bradbury Press
Affiliate of Macmillan, Inc.
866 Third Avenue
New York, NY 10022

Bridgestone Books
Imprint of Capstone Press Incorporated

Bridgewater Books
Imprint of Troll Associates, Inc.

Bright Ring Publishing, Inc.
P.O. Box 31338
Bellingham, WA 98228-3338
800-480-4278
brightring.com

Browndeer Press
Division of Harcourt, Inc.

Bungalo Books
Distributed by Firefly Books Ltd.
bungalobooks.com

Camden House Publications
Distributed by Firefly Books Ltd.

Candlewick Press
2067 Massachusetts Avenue
Cambridge, MA 02140
800-526-0275
candlewick.com

Candy Cane Press
Imprint of Ideals Publications
535 Metroplex Drive, Suite 250
Nashville, TN 37211
615-333-0478
idealspublications.com

Capstone
151 Good Counsel Drive
P.O. Box 669
Mankato, MN 56002
800-747-4992
capstonepress.com

Career Press
3 Tice Road
P.O. Box 687
Franklin Lakes, NJ 07417
201-848-0310
careerpress.com

Carol Publishing Company
120 Enterprise Avenue
Secaucus, NJ 07094
201-866-0490

Carolrhoda Books, Inc.
Division of Lerner Publishing Group

Carson-Dellosa Publishing Co., Inc.
7027 Albert Pick Road
Greensboro, NC 27409
336-632-0084
CarsonDellosa.com

Cartwheel Books
Division of Scholastic, Inc.

Cds Books
425 Madison Avenue
New York, NY 10017
(212) 223-2969
cdsbooks.com

Charlesbridge Publishing
85 Main Street
Watertown, MA 02172
617-926-0329
charlesbridge.com

Charles Scribner's and Sons
Imprint of McGraw-Hill Educational

Chicago Children's Museum
700 East Grand Avenue
Chicago, IL 60611
(312) 527-1000
ChiChildrensMuseum.org

Chicago Review Press
814 North Franklin Street
Chicago, IL 60610
312-337-0747
ipqbook.com

Chicken House
Division of Scholastic, Inc.

Child and Family Press
410 First Street
NW, Third Floor
Washington, DC 20001

Children's Press
Division of Scholastic, Inc.

Children's Television Workshop
Division of Random House, Inc.

Children's Universe
Imprint of Universe Publishing
Distributed by St. Martin's Press

Chronicle Books
85 Second Street
San Francisco, CA 94103
800-722-6657
chroniclebooks.com

Clapper Publishing Company, Inc.
2400 Devon, Suite 375
Des Plaines, IL 60018-4618
847-635-5800

Clarion Books
Division of Houghton Mifflin Co.

Clarkson N. Potter, Inc.
Distributed by Crown Publications, Inc.

Cobblehill Books
Imprint of Dutton's Children's Books

Compass Point Books
3109 West 50th Street, #115
Minneapolis, MN 55410
1-817-371-1536
compasspointbooks.com

Cool Hand Communications Inc.
Imprint of Book World Press Inc.
1933 Whittfield Park Loop
Sarasota, FL 34243
800-444-2524
bookworld.com

Council Oak Books
2105 E. 15th Street, Suite B
Tulsa, OK 74104
800-247-8850
counciloakbooks.com

Coward
Division of Putnam Publishers Co.

Crabtree Publishing Company
PMB 16A, 350 Fifth Avenue, Suite 3308
New York, NY 10118
800-355-7166
crabtreebooks.com

Crocodile Books USA
Distributed by Kane/Miller Book Publishers

Crown Publications, Inc.
Distributed by Random House Inc.

DK Publishers, Inc.
95 Madison Avenue
New York, NY 10016
212-213-4800
dk.com

Delacorte Press
Division of Dell Publishing

Dell Publishing
1540 Broadway
New York, NY 10036
800-223-6834
bdd.com

Delmar Learning
Division of Thomson Learning Inc.

T.S. Denison & Co., Inc.
P.O. Box 1650
Grand Rapids, MI 49501-5431
800-253-5469
instructionalfair.com

Dial Books for Young Readers
Division of Penguin Putnam

Disney Press
114 Fifth Avenue
New York, NY 10011-5690
212-633-4400
disneybooks.com

Doubleday and Co., Inc.
Division of Random House, Inc.

Down East Books
Box 679
Camden, ME 04843
800-766-1670

Dutton Children's Books
Division of Penguin Putnam Books for Young Readers

EDC Publishing
10302 East 55th Place
Tulsa, OK 74146
800-475-4588
edcpub.com

Education Center, Inc.
P.O. Box 9753
Greensboro, NC 27429
800-334-0298
themailbox.com

Educators Press
5333 NW Jackson Street.
Camas, WA 98607
360-834-3049
educatorspress.com

Eerdmans Books for Young Readers
255 Jefferson South East
Grand Rapids, MI 49503
800-253-7521
eerdmans.com

Element Books, Inc.
160 North Washington Street, 4th Floor
Boston, MA 02114
617-915-9400
element@cove.com

Enslow Publications Incorporated
40 Industrial Road
Box 398
Berkeley, Heights, NJ 07922
enslow.com

Fairview Press
2450 Riverside Avenue South
Minneapolis, MN 55454
800-544-8207
fairviewpress.org

Farrar, Straus & Giroux, Inc.
19 Union Square West
New York, NY 10035
888-330-8477
fsgbooks.com

Fearon Teachers Aids
Imprint of K-12 Publishing Group
Distributed by The Perfection Learning Corp.
1000 North Second Avenue
P.O. Box 500
Logan, IA 51546
800-831-4190
plconline.com

Firefly Books, Ltd.
P.O. Box 1338
Ellicott Station
Buffalo, NY 14205
800-387-5085
fireflybooks.com

Fitzhenry and Whiteside
121 Harvard Avenue, Suite 2
Allston, MA 02134
800-387-9776
fitzhenry.ca

Four Winds Publishing
Imprint of Sterling House Publications

Frances Foster Books
Imprint of Farrar, Straus & Giroux

Frances Lincoln Limited
4 Torriano Mews
Torriano Avenue
London, NW52RZ

Franklin Watts, Inc.
Subsidiary of Grolier Inc.

Free Spirit Publishing, Inc.
217 Fifth Avenue North,
Suite 200
Minneapolis, MN 55401
612-338-2068
freespirit.com

Fulcrum Publishing
16100 Table Mountain Parkway
Suite 300
Golden, CO 80403
800-922-2908
fulcrum-resources.com

Gareth Stevens Publishing
330 West Olive Street, Suite 100
Milwaukee, WI 53212
800-542-2595

Garlic Press
605 Powers Street
Eugene, OR 97402
541-345-0063
garlicpress.com

GIA Publications, Incorporated
7404 South Mason Avenue
Chicago, IL 60638

Gibbs Smith, Publishers
P.O. Box 667
Layton, UT 84041
800-748-5439
gibbs-smith.com

Gingham Dog Press
Imprint of McGraw-Hill Children's Publishing

Girl Scouts of the USA
420 Fifth Avenue
New York, NY 10018
800-478-7248
gsusa.org

Gloucester Press (Inactive)

Good Books
P.O. Box 419
Intercourse, PA 17534
800-762-7171
goodbks.com

Green Light Readers
Division of Harcourt, Inc.

Green Tiger Press
Distributed by Simon & Schuster

Greenwillow Books
Division of William Morrow & Co.

Grolier, Inc.
90 Sherman Turnpike
Danbury, CT 06816
203-797-3500
publishing.grolier.com

Grosset and Dunlap
345 Hudson Street
New York, NY 10014

Gryphon House, Inc.
P.O. Box 207
Beltsville, MD 20704-0207
800-638-0928
gryphonhouse.com

Gulliver Books
Division of Harcourt, Inc.

Gumbs & Thomas Publishers, Inc.
Distributed by Bookpeople
bookpeople.com

Handprint Books
413 Sixth Avenue
Brooklyn, NY 11215
800-722-6657
handprintbooks.com

Harcourt, Inc.
525 B Street
San Diego, CA 92101
www.harcourt.com

Harper and Row Junior Books
Imprint of McGraw-Hill Educational

Harper Festival
Division of HarperCollins Publishers

HarperCollins Publishers
10 East 53rd Street
New York, NY 10022
212-207-7000
harpercollins.com

Harry N. Abrams Inc.
115 West 18th Street
New York, NY 10011
212-206-7715
abramsbooks.com

Hastings House Publishers
Imprint of United Publishers Group
50 Washington Street
7th Floor
Norwalk, CT 06854
203-838-4083
upub.com

Heinemann Library
1000 Hart Road, 3rd Floor
Barrington, IL 60010
888-454-2279
heinemannlibrary.com

Henry Holt & Co.
115 West 18th Street
New York, NY 10011
800-488-5233
henryholt.com

Highsmith Press
W5527 Highway 106
P.O. Box 800
Fort Atkinson, WI 53538
800-558-2110
hpress.highsmith.com

Holiday House, Inc.
425 Madison Avenue
New York, NY 10017
212-688-0085
holidayhouse.com

Holt, Rinehart & Winston
Division of Harcourt, Inc.

Houghton Mifflin Co.
222 Berkeley Street
Boston, MA 02116
800-225-3362
houghtonmifflinbooks.com

Hunter House Publishers, Inc.
P.O. Box 2914
Alameda, CA 94501
800-266-5592
hunterhouse.com

Hyperion Books for Children
114 Fifth Avenue
New York, NY 10011
800-343-9204
hyperionchildrensbooks.com

Instructional Fair
Division of T.S. Denison

Joanna Cotler Books
Imprint of HarperCollins Publishers

John Wiley and Sons, Inc.
111 River Street
Hoboken, NJ 07030
201-748-6011
wiley.com

Jump at the Sun
Imprint of Hyperion Books for Children

Kane Press
240 West 35th Street
Suite 300
New York, NY 10001
212-268-1435
kanepress.com

Kaplan Publishing
Division of Simon & Schuster, Inc.

Kar-Ben Publishing, Inc.
Division of Lerner Publishing Group
Karben.com

Katherine Tegen Books
Imprint of HarperCollins Publishers

Kids Can Press, Ltd.
2250 Military Road
Tonawanda, NY 14150
866-481-5827

Kingfisher
Imprint of Larousse Kingfisher Chambers, Inc.
80 Maiden Lane
New York, NY 10038
kingfisherpub.com

Knopf
See Alfred A. Knopf Inc.

Lark Books
Division of Sterling Publishing Co.

Laura Geringer Books
Imprint of HarperCollins Publishers

Learning Triangle Press
Distributed by McGraw-Hill School Division
mhschool.com

Learning Works, Inc.
P.O. Box 6187
Santa Barbara, CA 93160
800-235-5767
thelearningworks.com

Lee and Low Books, Inc.
95 Madison Avenue
New York, NY 10016
212-779-4400
leeandlow.com

Lerner Publishing Group
241 First Avenue North
Minneapolis, MN 55401
800-328-4929
lernerbooks.com

Libraries Unlimited
88 Post Road West
Westport, CT 06881
203-226-3571
lu.com

Linnet Books
Imprint of Shoe String Press, Inc.

J.B. Lippincott Co.
Subsidiary of Harper and Row Publishers, Inc.

Little, Brown & Co.
Division of Time, Incorporated
1271 Avenue of the Americas
New York, NY 10020
800-759-0190
lb-kids.com

Little Friend Press
28 New Driftway
Scituate, MA 02066
800-617-3734

Little Simon
Imprint of Simon & Schuster

Little Tiger Press
202 Old Ridgefield Road
Wilton, CT 06897
littletigerpress.com

Lodestar Books
See Dutton

Lothrop, Lee and Shepard Books
Division of William Morrow

Lowell House Juvenile
2020 Avenue of the Americas
Suite 300
Los Angeles, CA 90067
310-552-7555
lowellh.com

Luna Rising
P.O. Box 1389
Flagstaff, AZ 86002
lunarisingbooks.com

Macmillan Publishing Co., Inc.
Division of Simon & Schuster, Inc.

Maple Tree Press, Inc.
51 Front Street East
Suite 200
Toronto, Ontario M5E 1B3

McFarland & Company, Inc.
Box 611
Jefferson, NC 28640
800-253-2187
mcfarlandpub.com

McGraw-Hill Companies
Two Penn Plaza
New York, NY 10121
books.mcgraw-hill.com

Margaret K. McElderry Books
Imprint of Simon & Schuster Children's Publishing Division

Marlowe and Co.
245 West 17th Street, 11th Floor
New York, NY 10011
212-614-7880
marlowepub.com

Marshall Cavendish
99 White Plains Road
Tarrytown, NY 10591
914-332-8888
marshallcavendish.com

Meadowbrook Press
5451 Smetana Drive
Minnetonka, MN 55343
800-338-2232
meadowbrook.com

Melanie Kroupa Books
Imprint of Farrar, Straus & Giroux

Meredith Corporation
1716 Locust Street
Des Moines, IA 50309
515-284-2363
bhgstore.com

Michael Neugebauer Book
Division of North-South Books

Milk and Cookies Press
24 West 25th Street
11th Floor
New York, NY 10010

Millbrook Press, Inc.
Division of Lerner Publishing Group

Monday Morning Books, Inc.
Box 388
Ashland, OH 4495
800-255-6049
mondaymorningbooks.com

Mondo Publishing
980 Avenue of the Americas
New York, NY 10018
mondopub.com

Monjeu Press
P.O. Box 64353
Tucson, AZ 85728
520-293-4908
ozstarnet.com/~many

Morning Glory Press, Inc.
6595 San Haroldo Way
Buena Park, CA 90620
1-888-612-8254
morninggloryp ress.com

Morrow
See William Morrow & Co.

Murdoch Books Incorporated
P.O. Box 390
Nazareth, PA 18064

NADJA Publishing
P.O. Box 326
Lake Forest, CA 92630
714-459-9750

National Geographic
1145 17th Street, NW
Washington, DC 20036
800-647-5463
nationalgeographic.com

Neal Porter Books
Division of Roaring Brook Press

New Hope Publishers
P.O. Box 12065
Birmingham, AL 35202
205-991-4078
newhopepubl.com

New Society Publishers
P.O. Box 189
Gabriola Island, BCVOR
1XO, Canada
800-567-6772

New World Library
14 Pamaron Way
Novato, CA
415-884-2100
newworldlibrary.com

North-South Books
845 Sixth Avenue
Suite 1901
New York, NY 10001
212-706-4545
northsouth.com

Northword
11571 K-Tel Drive
Minnetonka, MN 55343
tnkidsbooks.com

Oakbrook Publishing House
P.O. Box 2463
Littleton, CO 80161
303-730-1733
whatdoidobooks.com

Orca Book Publishers
P.O. Box 468
Custer, WA
800-210-5277
orcabook.com

Orchard Books
Imprint of Scholastic, Inc.

Oryx Press
4041 North Central at Indian School Road
Phoenix, AZ 85012
800-279-6799
oryxpress.com

Oxford University Press
198 Madison Avenue
New York, NY 10016
212-726-6000
oup-usa.org

Parents Magazine Press
Division of Penguin Putnam

Pavilion Children's Books
Imprint of Chrysalis Books
64 Brewery Road
London, N7 9 NT

PAWS IV
Published by Sasquatch Books

Peachtree Publishing Ltd.
1700 Chattahoochee Avenue
Atlanta, GA 30318
800-241-0113
peachtree-online.com

Pebble Books
Imprint of Capstone Press

Pelican Publishing Company Inc.
1000 Burmaster Street
Gretna, LA 70054
800-843-1724
pelicanpub.com

Penguin Putnam Books for Young Readers
345 Hudson St.
New York, NY 10014
212-366-2000
penguinputnam.com

Perspectives Press
Distributed by Boys Town Press
14100 Crawford Street
Boys Town, NE 68010
800-282-6657
ffbh.boystown.org

Peter Bedrick Books
Distributed by Harper and Row

Philomel Books
Imprint of Penguin Putnam

Phyllis Fogelman Books
Imprint of Penguin Putnam

Picture Book Studios USA
2 Conter Plaza
Boston, MA 02108

Picture Window Books
5115 Excelsior Boulevard, Suite 232
Minneapolis, MN 55416
877-845-8392
picturewindowbooks.com

Piñata Books
452 Cullen Performance Hall
Houston, TX 77204

Pleasant Company Publications
8400 Fairway Place
Middleton, WI 53562
800-233-0264
pleasantcopublications.com

Powerkids Press
Division of Rosen Publishers Group, Inc.

Prentice Hall Press
240 Frisch Court
Paramus, NJ 07652
800-947-7700
phdirect.com

Price Stern Sloan Inc.
Division of Penguin Putnam Inc.

Prima Publishing
3000 Lava Ridge Court
Roseville, CA 95661
800-632-8676
primalifestyles.com

Publications International Ltd.
7373 North Cicero Avenue
Lincolnwood, IL 60646
800-595-8484
pubint.com

Putnam
See Penguin Putnam

Putnam and Grosset
Division of Penguin Putnam

QEB Publishing Inc.
23062 La Cadena Drive
Laguna Hills
Irvine, CA 92653
qeb-publishing.com

R & S Books
Distributed by Farrar, Straus & Giroux

Raintree Steck-Vaughn Company
310 West Wisconsin Avenue
Milwaukee, WI 53203
800-531-5015
steck-vaughn.com

Random House, Inc.
1745 Broadway
New York, NY 10019
800-200-3552
randomhouse.com/kids

Raven Tree Press
200 South Washington Street
Suite 306
Green Bay, WI 54301
877-256-0579
raventreepress.com

Rayve Productions Inc.
Box 726
Windsor, CA 95492
707-838-6200
rayve.com

Reader's Digest Children's Books
Readers Digest Road
Pleasantville, NY 10570
914-244-4800
readersdigestkids.com

Reunion Research
3145 Geary Boulevard #14
San Francisco, CA 94118
209-855-2101
reuniontips.com

Rigby Interactive Library
Division of Raintree Steck-Vaughn

Rising Moon
2900 North Fort Valley Road
Flagstaff, AZ 86001
800-346-3257
northlandpub.com

Roaring Brook Press
Division of Henry, Holt, Inc.

Rosen Publishing Group, Inc.
29 East 21st Street
New York, NY 10010
800-237-9932

Rourke Publishing Group
Box 3328
Vero Beach, FL 32964
772-234-6001
rourkepublishing.com

Running Press
125 South 22nd Street
Philadelphia, PA 19103
212-567-5080
runningpress.com

Sasquatch Books
615 Second Avenue
Seattle, WA 98104
206-467-4300
SasquatchBooks.com

Scarecrow Press Inc.
4501 Forbes Boulevard, Suite 200
Lanham, MD 20706
800-459-3366
scarecrowpress.com

Scholastic, Inc.
557 Broadway
New York, NY 10012
800-SCHOLASTIC
scholastic.com

Scribner's
See Charles Scribner's and Sons

Sea Star Books
Division of North-South Books, Incorporated

Sea-to-Sea
2140 Howard Road., West
North Mankato, MN 56003

Shoe String Press Incorporated
2 Linsley Street
North Haven, CT 06473
203-239-2702
shoestringpress.com

Sierra Club Books for Children
85 Second Street
San Francisco, CA 94105
415-977-5500
sierraclub.org/books

Silver Burdett Press
4350 Equity Drive
Columbus, OH 43228
800-321-3106
sselem.com

Silver Dolphin Books
Imprint of Advantage Publishers Group
5880 Oberlin Drive
San Diego, CA 92121
dolphinbooks.com

Silver Whistle
Division of Harcourt, Inc.

Simon Spotlight
Imprint of Simon & Schuster

Simon & Schuster
Children's Book Division
1230 Avenue of the Americas
New York, NY 10020
212-698-7200
simonsayskids.com

Sleeping Bear Press
310 North Main Street
P.O. Box 20
Chelsea, MI 48118
800-487-2323
sleepingbearpress.com

Sourcebooks Media Fusion
Imprint of Sourcebooks, Inc.
P.O. Box 4410
Naperville, IL 60567
630-961-3900
sourcebooks.com

Star Bright Books
42-26 28th Street
Suite 2C
Long Island City, NY 11101
800-788-4439
starbrightbooks.com

Steck-Vaughn Company
310 West Wisconsin Avenue
Milwaukee, WI 53203
800-531-5015
steck-vaughn.com

Sterling Publishing Co., Inc.
The Sterling Building
387 Park Avenue South
New York, NY 10016
212-532-7160
sterlingpub.com

Stewart, Tabori and Chang
115 West 18th Street
New York, NY 10011

Storey Kids
210 Mass MoCA Way
North Adams, MA 01247
800-793-9396
storeykids.com

St. Martin's Press
175 Fifth Avenue
New York, NY 10010
stmartins.com

TAB Books
Division of McGraw-Hill

Talewinds
Imprint of Charlesbridge

Tambourine Books
Imprint of William Morrow & Co.,

Teacher Created Materials, Inc.
6421 Industry Way
Westminster, CA 92683
800-662-4321
teachercreated.com

Teaching & Learning Co.
1204 Buchanan Street
P.O. Box 10
Carthage, IL 62321
217-357-2591
http://teachinglearning.com

Thameside Press
Distributed by Smart Apple Media
1980 Lookout Drive
North Mankato, MN 56003

Thomas Y. Crowell
Division of Harper and Row

Thomson Learning, Inc.
5 Maxwell Drive
Clifton Park, NY 12065

Three Rivers Press
Division of Crown Publishing Group

Ticknor and Fields
Division of Houghton Mifflin

Tiger Tales
Imprint of ME Media, LLC
202 Old Ridgefield Road
Wilton, CT 06897
203-834-0005
tigertalesbooks.com

Tilbury House Publishers
2 Mechanic Street
Gardiner, ME 04345
800-582-1899
tilburyhouse.com

Tommy Nelson
Division of Thomas Nelson, Inc.
501 Nelson Place
Nashville, TN 37214
800-251-4000
tommynelson.com

Totline Publications
Imprint of McGraw Hill Children's Publishing

Transatlantic Arts, Inc.
Box 6086
Albuquerque, NM 87197
505-898-2289
transatlantic.com/direct

Tricycle Press
Division of Ten Speed Press
P.O. Box 7123
Berkeley, CA 04707
800-841-2665
tenspeed.com

Troll Associates
Division of Scholastic, Inc.

Tundra Books
481 University Avenue
Toronto, Ontario
Canada, M5G 2E9
800-785-1074
tundrabooks.com

Upstart Books
Division of Highsmith Press

Vanguard Press, Inc.
(Inactive)

Viking Penguin, Inc.
345 Hudson St.
New York, NY 10014
800-331-4624

Walker & Company
104 Fifth Avenue
NY, NY 10011
212-727-8300
walkeryoungreaders.com

Warren Publishing House, Inc.
Division of Frank Schaffer Publications
P.O. Box 141487
Grand Rapids, MI 49514
800-417-3261
frankschaffer.com

Waterbird Books
Imprint of McGraw-Hil

Weekly Reader Early Learning
Imprint of Gareth Stevens, Inc.

Western Publishing Co., Inc.
Division of Random House, Inc.

Whispering Coyote Press
85 Main Street
Watertown, MA 02472
Imprint of Charlesbridge

Willa Perlman Books
Division of HarperCollins Publishers

William Morrow & Co., Inc.
1350 Avenue of the Americas
New York, NY 10019
800-843-9389
williammorrow.com

Williamson Publishing Company
P.O. Box 185
Charlotte, VT 05445
800-234-8791
williamsbooks.com

H. W. Wilson
950 University Avenue
Bronx, NY 10452
800-367-6770
hwwilson.com

Workman Publishing Co., Inc.
708 Broadway
New York, NY 10003
212-254-5900
workman.com

Zino Press Children's Books
P.O. Box 52
Madison, WI
800-618-1570
zinopress.com

Zoo to Ten Limited
814 North Franklin Street
Chicago, IL 60610

2 Directory of Distributors for Recommended Videos and DVDs

Ambrose Video Publishers, Incorporated
145 West 45th Street
Suite 1115
New York, NY 11036
800-526-4663
ambrosevideo.com

A.W. Peller & Associates Inc.
Subsidiary of Educational Impressions
116 Washington Avenue
Hawthorne, NJ 07507
800-451-7450
awpeller.com

Baker & Taylor Video
Corporate Headquarters
8140 North Lehigh Avenue
Morton Grove, IL 60053
800-775-2600
btent.com

Brodart Company
500 Arch Street
Williamsport, PA 17701
800-474-9802
brodart.com

Buena Vista Home Video
350 South Buena Vista Street
MailCode 7912
Burbank, CA 91521
818-295-5768
bvhe.com/au

Charles Clark Co., Inc.
4540 Preslyn Drive
Raleigh, NC 27616
800-247-7009

Children's Circle
Division of Weston Woods

Coronet Films/MTI
Division of Phoenix Learning Group

Disney Educational Productions
105 Terry Drive
Suite 120
Newtown, PA 18940
800-295-5010
disney.com/EducationalProduction

Encyclopedia Britannica Educational Corp. (EBEC)
331 North LaSalle Street
Chicago, IL 60610
800-621-3900
eb.com

First Run Features
630 Ninth Avenue
Suite 1213
New York, NY 10036
212-243-0600
firstrunfeatures.com

Golden Book Videos
(see Western Publishing Co.)

Good Times Home Videos
16 East 40th Street
New York, NY 10016
212-951-3000
goodtimes.com

Italtoons Corporation
32 West 40th Street
New York, NY 10018
212-730-0280

Kimbo Educational
P.O. Box 477
Long Branch, NJ 07740
800-631-2187
kimboed.com

Library Video Co.
P.O. Box 580
Wynnewood, PA 19096
800-843-3620
libraryvideo.com

Listening Library
Division of Random House, Inc.

Live Oak Media
2630 Exposition Boulevard
Suite 203
Austin, TX 78703
512-472-5000
liveoak.com

The Lyon Group
See Lyrick Studios

Lyrick Studios
2435 North Central Expressway
Suite 1600
Richardson, TX 75080
972-390-6000
lyrickstudios.com

MCA Family Entertainment Inc.
Universal Home Video
70 Universal City Plaza, North 435
Universal City, CA 91608
818-733-0226
mca.com/index.html

Media Basics Video
16781 Chagrin Boulevard
Box130
Shaker Heights, OH 44120
800-542-2505
mediabasicsvideo.com

Mulberry Park, Inc.
Distributed by William Morrow & Co.
1350 Avenue of the Americas
New York, NY 10019
800-843-9389
williammorrow.com

Paramount Pictures
5555 Melrose Avenue
Hollywood, CA 90038
323-956-5000
paramount.com

Phoenix Learning Group
2349 Chaffee Drive
Saint Louis, MO 63146
800-221-1274
phoenixlearninggroup.com

Plains National Instructional Television
(Inactive)

PolyGram Video
Division of Polygram Records Inc.
825 Eighth Avenue
New York, NY 10019
212-333-8000
polygram.com/polygram

Rabbit Ears Production Inc.
One Turkey Hill Road South
Westport, CT. 06880
rabbitears.com

Random House, Inc.
400 Hahn Road
Westminster, MD 21157
800-659-2436
library.booksontape.com

Schlessinger Video Productions
Division of Library Video Co.

Schoolmasters
745 State Circle
P. O. Box 1941
Ann Arbor, MI 48106
800-521-2832
school-tech.com

Sesame Street
c/o Children's Television Workshop
Division of Random House, Inc.

Society for Visual Education, Inc.
Clearvue & SVE
6465 North Avondal Avenue
Chicago, IL 60631
800-444-9855
clearvue.com

Sony Music Distribution
Sony Music Entertainment Inc.
550 Madison Avenue
RM 2341
New York, NY 10022
212-833-4548

Spoken Arts
195 South White Rock Road
Holmes, NY 12531
800-326-4090
spokenartsmedia.com

Stage Fright Productions
P.O. Box 373
Geneva, IL 60134
800-979-6800
stagefrightproductions.com

Troll Associates
School and Library Division
100 Corporate Drive
Mahwah, NJ 07430
800-654-3037
trollcarnival.com

Western Publishing Co., Inc.
Division of Random House, Inc.
randomhouse.com/golden

Weston Woods Productions
143 Main Street
Norwalk, CT 06851
800-243-5020
scholastic.com/westonwoods

3 Directory of Distributors for Recommended Music and CDs

Appleseed Production
1025 Locust Avenue
Charlottesville, VA 22901
800-977-6321
folkmusic.com

Arista Records, Inc.
6 West 57th Street
New York, NY 10019
212-489-7400

Baby Boom Music, Inc.
19000 Maple Lane
Excelsior, MN 55331
952-470-1667

Bear Paw Recordings
P.O. Box 1345
Brattleboro, VT 05302
802-254-5270

Buena Vista Records
(see Walt Disney Records)

Columbia
See Sony Music Entertainment, Inc.

CTP/ Youngheart
P.O. Box 6017
Cypress, CA 90630
800-444-4287

David S. Polansky
P.O. Box 5061
Cochituale, MA 01778
508-655-5046
davidpolansky.com

Disneyland Records
See Walt Disney Records

Drive Entertainment Incorporated
10351 Monica Boulevard, Suite 404
Los Angeles, CA 90025
310-553-3490

Educational Activities, Incorporated
P.O. Box 87
Baldwin, NY 11510
800-645-3739
edact.com

Educational Graphics Press
See Shadow Play Records

Elephant Records
365 Bloor Street, East
Suite 1610
Toronto, Ontario M4W 3L4
416-921-9214
casablancakids.com

GMR Records
Box 651
Brattleboro, VT 05302
802-257-9566

Good Moo's Productions
Distributed by Educational Record Center
3233 Burnt Mill Drive, Suite 100
Wilmington, NC 28403
888-372-4543
erc-inc.com

G-Spot
P.O. Box 11575
Berkeley, CA 94712
gunnarmadsen.com

Guitar Bob
Oak Ridge, NJ
201-208-9435

Hap-Pal Music, Incorporated
P.O. Box 8343
Northridge, CA 91324
818-885-0200
happalmer.com

Homeland Publishing
Division of Troubadour Records

Hug Bug Music
Box 58067, Station "L"
Vancouver, B.C., Canada V6P 6C5
604-274-8216

Kids Rhino
Division of Rhino Records Inc.
2225 Colorado Avenue
Santa Monica, CA 90404
800-432-0020
rhino.com

Kidsongs
30765 Pacific Coast Highway #286
Malibu, CA 90265
866-221-4459
kidsongs.com

Kidzup Productions, Inc.
555 VT RTE 78
Suite 146, Box 717
Swanton, VT 05488
888-321-KIDS
kidzup.com

Kimbo Educational
P.O. Box 477, Dept. S
Long Branch, NJ 07740
800-631-2187
kimboed.com

Koch Entertainment
740 Broadway
New York, NY 10003
kochentertainment.com/kids

Kurtoons
425 Washington Terrace
Leonia, NJ 97605
201-585-9823

Laserlight Digital
Delta Entertainment
Los Angeles, CA 90025
deltaentertainment.com

Laurie
Distributed by Two Tomatoes
P.O. Box 250774
Columbia University Station
New York, NY 10025
212-222-6834
twotomatoes.com

Lightyear Entertainment
434 Avenue of the Americas, 6th Floor
New York, NY 10011
212-353-5084
lightyear.com

Lizard's Rock Music
Distributed by Baker & Taylor Books
1120 Route 22 East
Bridgewater, NJ 08807
800-775-1500
baker-taylor.com

Madacy Entertainment Group, Inc.
3333 Graham Boulevard, Suite 102
Montreal, Quebec, Canada H34 3L5
514-341-5600

Marlboro Records, Incorporated
845 Marlboro Spring Road
Kennett Square, PA 19348

Music for Little People
P.O. Box 1460
Redway, CA 95560
800-409-2457
mflp.com

Peanutbutterjam (PBJ)
Box 2687
Hartford, CT 06146

Price Stern Sloan
Division of Penguin Young Readers Group
345 Hudson Street
New York, NY 10014

Rainbow Planet Tapes
Rainbow Planet, Inc.
5110 Cromwell Drive
Gig Harbor, WA 98335
253-265-3785
rainbowplanet.com

Re-Bop Records
858 Brook Rd.
Marshfield, VT 05658
800-657-3267
reboprecords.com

Rounder Records Corporation
One Camp Street
Cambridge, MA 02140
800-768-6337
rounder.com

Sesame Street Records
c/o Children's Television Workshop
1 Lincoln Plaza
New York, NY 10023
212-595-3456
ctw.org

Shadow Play Records
Educational Graphics Press, Incorporated
P.O. Box 180476
Austin, TX 78718
800-274-8804
hellojoe.com

Shoreline Records
Division of Troubadour
Distributed by Rounder Records

Singing Toad Productions
P.O. Box 359
Mineral Point, WI 53565

Sony Kids' Music
Sony Music Entertainment, Inc.
550 Madison Avenue
New York, NY 10022
212-833-4548
sony.com

St. Clair Entertainment Group
P.O. Box 34512
Place Vertu, Montreal
QC H4R 2P4

Sundance Music
100 Cedar Street, Suite B19
Dobbs Ferry, NY 10522
914-674-0247
tomchapin.com

Ta-Dum Productions, Incorporated
6552 Via Barona
Carlsbad, CA 92009
619-438-6552

Tickle Tune Typhoon
P.O. Box 96
Mount Vernon, WA 98273
206-632-9466
tickletyphoon.com

Troubadour Records, Limited
See Rounder Records Corporation

Ujima Publishing
P.O. Box 11055
Baltimore, MD 21212
410-435-3936

Viacom International Inc.
Division of Rhino Entertainment Company
10635 Santa Monica Boulevard
Los Angeles, CA 90025
rhino.com

Walt Disney Records
500 South Buena Vista Street
Burbank, CA 91520
800-295-5010
disney.com

Warner Brothers Records
3300 Warner Ave.
Burbank, CA 91510
800-274-9700
wbr.com

Western Publishing Co., Inc.
Subsidiary of Western Publishing Group Inc.
850 Third Avenue
7th Floor
New York, NY 10022
800-558-5972

Wonder Workshop, Inc.
Distributed By Madacy Entertainment Group, Inc.

Part III:

Recommended A–Z Themed Programs

1 Activities: Reading

Topical Calendar Tie-in:

March 2

"Read Across America Day"—This is a day set aside for all children and adults to read together in celebration of the birth of one our most beloved authors, Dr. Seuss. Invite local celebrities and government officials to join you in setting aside time to read with children.

Videos:

Alexander and the Wind-Up Mouse (Leo Lionni's Caldecotts)
Beverly Billngsly Borrows a Book
I Can Read with My Eyes Shut (Dr. Seuss's ABC video)
Penny Lee and Her TV
Petunia
Reading to Your Bunny
Wild About Books

Picture Books:

The Bee Tree, Patricia Polacco
The Bird, the Frog and the Light, Avi
Book!, Kristine O'Connell George
But Excuse Me That Is My Book, Lauren Child
Don't Tease the Guppies, Pat Lowery Collins
Hog-Eye, Susan Meddaugh
Joseph Wants to Read, Fabienne Teyssedre
Little Witch Learns to Read, Deborah Hautzig
Miss Smith's Incredible Storybook, Michael Garland
More Than Anything Else, Marie Bradby
The Old Woman Who Loved to Read, John Winch
Reading Makes You Feel Good, Todd Parr
Read to Your Bunny, Rosemary Wells
Secret Code, Dana Meachen Rau
Silas the Bookstore Cat, Karen Trella Mather
Storyhour—Starring Megan!, Julie Brillhart
Wild About Books, Judy Sierra

Music/Movement:

"Story Circle"
Sung to: "Here We Go Around the Mulberry Bush"
Source: *Fall Frolic*, Mary Jo Huff

Crafts:

"Touch-Me Books"
Many children get their early experience with reading by using books that allow them to touch various textures mentioned in the story. Try making your own "Touch-Me" book. Prepare a small three-page book with one large illustration and word per page. (Suggestion: Use a duck, a rabbit, and a cat.) At the program, allow time to color the illustrations, then provide the appropriate textures to glue to the pictures (feathers,

cottonballs for a rabbit's tail, and pieces of fur). Children have a feeling of accomplishment by creating a book of their own for identifying textures as well as animals.

"Triangle Page Markers"
Here's a simple quick bookmark to design using old envelopes. You may either use colorfully designed envelopes to begin with, or plain envelopes that can be decorated with markers and trim later. To recycle old envelopes, simply cut the corner from the bottom of an envelope about 4 inches across. This forms a little triangle pocket that may be placed on the corner of a page in your book.

Source: *Triangles, Rectangles, Circles and Squares,* Kathy Ross

Activities:

"Word Matching"
Using large flashcards with simple words (for example, cat or ball) and illustrations on them, discuss the pictures and words with the children. Next pass out cards with only the words on them, then see how many children can match these to the flashcards. The level of the words will depend on the age level of your group.

"The Elephant Story"
Develop a story about an elephant who carries peanuts. Have the children pretend to be an elephant and use a spoon to carry peanuts from one location, past various obstacles, and to the kitchen at the end of the room. As the storyteller tells the story of the elephant named (child's name), she will indicate the path the elephant must take to get to the kitchen. Suggested verses are listed in this source. Try peanut butter and cracker snacks to end the game.

Source: *300 Three Minute Games,* Jackie Silberg

Songs:

(Audio) "A Book is a Wonderful Friend"

Source: *Peanutbutterjam Incredibly Spreadable*

2 Adoption: Orphans

Topical Calendar Tie-in:

October

"Adopt a Shelter Dog Month"—People are not the only ones that get adopted. The ASPCA uses the message "Make pet adoption your first option" to encourage people to adopt shelter animals. Let children learn about this other form of adoption.

Videos:

"Let's Get a Pup!" said Kate
Madeline
The Three Robbers

Picture Books:

Allison, Allen Say
The Day We Met You, Phoebe Koehler
Did My First Mother Love Me?: A Story for an Adopted Child, Kathryn Ann Miller
A Family for Jamie: An Adoption Story, Suzanne Bloom
A Family Forever, Roslyn Bauish
Families are Different, Nina Pellegrini
Happy Adoption Day, John McCutcheon
Horace, Holly Keller
How I Was Adopted, Joanna Cole
A Koala for Katie: An Adoption Story, Jonathan London
Let's Talk About It: Adoption, Fred Rogers
My Real Family, Emily Arnold McCully
Through Moon and Stars and Night Skies, Ann Turner
When Joel Comes Home, Susi Gregg Fowler
William is My Brother, Jane T. Schnitter
You're Not My REAL Mother!, by Molly Friedrich

Music/Movement:

"You're Special"
Source: *Songs, Poems, and Fingerplays: Preschool/Kindergarten*, Ada Green and Allison E. Ward (editors)

Crafts:

"The Me Board"
The "Me Board" is a craft that is unique to each child in your group. It will allow them to illustrate what is special about them and allow their family, or adopted family, to add to the artwork to show what they feel is special about the child in their family. Simple instructions are supplied to this book to design a pin-up board. Poster board can be used to trace the body. Add features and then paste on pictures illustrating the child's hobbies, interests, etc. It can be hung up in the classroom or the child can take it home to hang on their bedroom door for a very unique display.
Source: *Crafts from Recyclables*, Colleen Van Blaricom (editor)

"Picture Magnet"
Adopted children need to know that they are an important part of their new family—just as all children do. Picture magnets depicting each important member of the family will help with this goal. Collect jar lids of all different types. Let the children decorate them with construction paper or paints. Place a magnet on the exterior of the lid and a picture of the child on the interior. Do one for each member of the family so they can be placed in a prominent place in the home.

Source: *Rainy Day Projects for Children*,
Gerri Jenny and Sherrie Gould

Activities:

"Who Loves You?"
Children need to know that their family loves them. Adopted children are often confused about the loss of their original family and insecure about the love of their new family. Encourage them through this activity of "Who Loves You?" to list all who love them, and then turn it into a wonderful decoration for their house as a reminder of that special love.

Source: *The Preschooler's Busy Book*, Trish Kuffner

"Three-Legged Race"
Children who are adopted are usually told that they were specially chosen by their adoptive parents so that they could share their love with this child. Here is a game that requires one classmate to look around and specially choose the friend they want to share their game with (and their leg). Once the pairs have been chosen, have each group tie their closest legs together with scarves and let the races begin.

Songs:

(Audio) "Happy Adoption Day"
Source: *Celebration of Family*,
Raffi, John Lennon, Faith Hill and others

3 Alphabet

Topical Calendar Tie-in:

October 16th

"Dictionary Day"—Along with children learning the alphabet, let them celebrate the birthday of Noah Webster. Encourage each child to own his or her own dictionary.

Videos:

Alligators All Around
The Alphabet Dragon
Chica Chicka Boom Boom
Dr. Seuss's ABC
The Shout it Out Alphabet Film
The Z was Zapped
Alphabet Zoo

Picture Books:

A-B-C Discovery, Izhar Cohen
ABC Drive!, Naomi Howland
ABC I Like Me!, Nancy Carlson
Alfie's ABC, Shirley Hughes
The A to Z Beastly Jamboree, Robert Bender
Do Your ABCs, Little Brown Bear, Jonathan London
From Anne to Zach, Mary Jane Martin
Goblins in Green, Nicholas Heller
Harold's ABC, Crockett Johnson
The Hollabaloo ABC, Beverly Cleary
If the World Ran Out of B's, Samantha and Bill Shireman
Joseph Wants to Read, Fabienne Teyssedre
Mrs. McTats and Her Houseful of Cats, Alyssa Satin Capucilli
On Your Toes: A Ballet ABC, Rachel Isadora
Tomorrow's Alphabet, George Shannon
The War Between the Vowels and Consonants, Priscilla Turner

Music/Movement:

"Letters, Letters Everywhere"
Sung to: "Alphabet Song"
(Suggestion: Make a flannel board for a child named Sean and add the letters of his name to the board as you sing the song. Later have the children make their own name letters for the board.)

ABCDEFG
Where are the letters that are me?
S is the leader.
E follows behind.
A jumps into the row and
N gets in line.
Letters letters everywhere,
I found these and made them mine.

Crafts:

"Pick-A-Letter"
Display all the letters of the alphabet somewhere in the room. Some children may know them all, while others may recognize only a few. Have each child choose one letter that he or she knows and tell the group what it is. Next have each child take construction paper and in one corner trace the letter with glue and sprinkle with glitter. Design a cover for the new booklet, "My Alphabet Book," to which the child can add letters later as he or she learns them.

"Letter Shapes"
Kathy Ross has done it again, creating an outstanding craft book to use with your alphabet programs, and if you own an Ellison machine with the alphabet to cut out, life will be even easier for you. This book demonstrates a single craft for each letter of the alphabet. Letter B has two letter Bs back to back, glued together with a Popsicle stick in the center. Put on some antennae to decorate the Bs and you have a butterfly. The letter H is folded in half and formed into a horse. Finally, in the last pages of the book you will find two pages of wonderful ideas for decorating your alphabet for display on the wall. Kindergarten and preschool teachers will find this book invaluable.

Source: *Letter Shapes*, Kathy Ross

Activities:

"Letter Hopscotch"
Bring back the old fashioned game of Hopscotch with a twist. I don't think many of today's children have ever played this game, so it will be something new to them. Instead of numbers, construct the hopscotch board using the alphabet instead of numbers. Children will learn letter recognition and such physical activities as hopping and motor planning in moving from location to location. *Smart Play* also offers variations on this game that includes broad jumping, sequential patterns, and more letter recognition patterns for your hopscotch boards. Resurrect this game for a new generation and have loads of fun at the same time.

Source : *Smart Play*, Barbara Sher

"Lively Letters"
These lively letters will be found giggling, stretching, and having a great old time today. Play this guessing game with a group of children indoors or out where they can spread out on the ground, forming letters of the alphabet or words with multiple bodies. Follow further recommendations for this game and a large collection of physical activities offered in this book.

Source: *Hey Mom, I'm Bored!*, Story Evans and Lise O'Haire

Song:

(Audio) "Bean Bag Alphabet Rag"

Source: *Can a Cherry Pie Wave Goodbye?*

4 Anatomy: Body Parts

Topical Calendar Tie-in:

April

"Foot Health Awareness Month"—This is a month for respecting the health of our feet. Discuss with children how to keep their feet healthy, and using team relay races, celebrate the importance of our feet in daily fun.

Videos:

The Foot Book
Imogene's Antlers
Mop Top
Magic School Bus: Human Body

Picture Books:

Baby's Book of the Body, Roger Priddy
Eyes, Nose, Fingers, and Toes, Judy Hinkley
Find a Face, François and Jean Robert
Hands!, Virginia L. Kroll
Happy Birthday, Sam, Patricia Hutchins
Hello Toes! Hello Feet!, Ann Whitford Paul
I Love My Hair!, Natasha Anastasia Tarpley
I've Got Your Nose!, Nancy Bentley
Eyes, Nose, Fingers, Toes, Ruth Krauss
Let's Look at Eyes, Sheilagh Noble
More Parts, Tedd Arnold
Mr. Blewitt's Nose, Alastair Taylor
My Hands, Aliki
No Haircut Today!, Elvira Savadier
The Skin You Live In, Michael Tyler
Tiny Toes, Donna Jakob
Two Eyes, a Nose and a Mouth, Roberta Grobel Intrater
Very Hairy Harry, Edward Koren
We've All Got Bellybuttons!, David Martin

Music/Movement:

"What's on a Face?"
Source: *Felt Board Fingerplays*, Liz and Dick Wilmes

Crafts:

"X-Ray Vest"
Here's a unique method of teaching children the parts of their body. Visible body parts are easy enough to point out, but show them what is inside all of us. Create vests out of large brown shopping bags. Give each child eight strips of white paper to represent ribs and a paper heart, then instruct them on placing these items in the proper location.
Source: *Learning is Fun! Kathy Ross Crafts*, Kathy Ross

"Bad Hair Day Pin"
Try a discussion on how everyone's hair is not only different in color but in texture, length and style. Show a variety of hairstyles that have been used down the span of the centuries. It will bring some laughs to the children to see what their parents thought was a cool hairstyle. We all have bad hair days, so try a pin craft using plaster of paris to make a "Bad Hair Day" pin, letting your friends know that you have a sense of humor about this.

Source: *Wearable Art with Sondra*, Sondra Clark

Activities:

"Circus Seals"
Divide the children into a number of small groups and give each group a balloon. The goal of each group is to keep their balloon in the air longer than the other groups. If it touches the ground their team will be eliminated. Here's the catch. A caller leads the game by calling out how you may touch the ball. He will call out such body parts as "elbows," "noses," "hips," etc. Only when he calls "flippers" may a child use his hands like a circus seal.

Source: *Great Theme Parties for Children*, Irene N. Watts

"Body Talk"
"Say what?" Body language can communicate more to a person than the words they are using. Help the children play this guessing game, in which they use the various parts of the body to express such ideas as "Be quiet, please," "Yuck!," and more. Explain that they may not say one word or sound while trying to get their friends to say what they are thinking. Look for these and other great variations of this game, such as "What am I?" and more in this book.

Source: *The Little Hands Playtime! Book*, Regina Curtis

Songs:

(Audio "Them Bones")

Source: *My Favorite Kidsongs Collections #3*

"I'm a Pretzel"

Source: *So Big: Activities and Songs for Little Ones*

5 Animals

Topical Calendar Tie-in:

October

"National Animal Safety and Protection Month"—Take this month to learn the proper method to protect and care for your favorite family pet or learn how to keep yourself safe around wild animals. Take this time to teach children that safety around animals is important no matter how tame they seem to you.

Videos:

The Camel Who Took a Walk
Henny Penny
Sylvester and the Magic Pebble
That New Animal
The Three Little Pigs
Giggle, Giggle, Quack

Picture Books:

Can You Moo?, David Wajtowycz
Don't Wake Up the Bear!, Marjorie Dennis Murray
Ducks Like to Swim, Agnes Verboven
The Hippo-not-amus, Tony and Jan Payne
If Frogs Made Weather, Marion Dane Bauer
Lizard Sees the World, Susan Tews
Mrs. Brown Went to Town, Wong Herbert Yee
The Nutty Nut Chase, Kathryn White
Peck, Slither and Slide, Suse MacDonald
Raccoon's Last Race, Joseph and James Bruchac
The Sheep Follow, Monica Wellington
Sitting on the Farm, Bob King
Thanks to the Animals, Allen Sockabasin
Treed by a Pride of Irate Lions, Nathan Zimelman
Who Hops?, Katie Davis

Music/Movement:

"Winter Animal Friends"
Source: *101 Fingerplays, Stories and Songs to Use with Finger Puppets*, Diane Briggs

Crafts:

"Leaf-Tailed Squirrel"
Cut out a simple squirrel pattern from brown or tan construction paper or card stock. Bush up the squirrel's tail by gluing the leaves children have gathered during one of your outings. Add a Popsicle stick if you want to make a puppet out of your creations. This source offers a pattern for the squirrel and other recommendations for completing this craft.
Source: *The Mailbox: October Arts and Crafts: Preschool–Kindergarten*, Ada Goren, Mackle Rhodes, and Jan Trautman (editors)

"Monkeys in a Tree"
This peek-a-boo torn paper artwork project will be a popular project with the younger crowd. A three-dimensional tree can be constructed from torn construction paper, and some monkeys hiding beneath the tree leaves can be made from peanuts. How many are in the tree? Some you can see and some you cannot.
Source: *At the Zoo*, Better Homes and Gardens

Activities:

"Animal Ball Toss"
In this circle activity, children will need to be quick to catch the ball tossed to them. Be sure you know your animals. Do they belong to land, sea or air? Be quick or you can be eliminated.
Source: *101 Best Games*, Eulalia Perez

"Find the Animals"
Hide a number of animal pictures throughout the room. Each child is told a different animal to find. Searching for a chosen animal, the child is instructed not to tell other children the animal he or she is trying to locate or to tell which animals have already been found. This is a good time filler, and young children love little secrets.
Source: *Great Theme Parties for Children*, Irene N. Walls

Songs:

(Audio) "One More River"
Source: *Wee Sing: Sing-Alongs*

6 Animals: Bears

Topical Calendar Tie-in:

November 14th

"National American Teddy Bear Day"—Try this celebration of the creation of America's most beloved child's companion, the teddy bear, named in honor of President Theodore Roosevelt who spared the life of a bear cub while on a big game hunt. You might encourage everyone, including yourself, to bring in their favorite teddy bear for a special party.

Videos:

Beady Bear
Bear Snores On
The Bear and the Fly
Blueberries for Sal
Paddington Helps Out: Paddington Dines Out (Paddington Bear, vol. 2)
Pierre: A Cautionary Tale
Winnie the Pooh and Tigger, Too!

Picture Books:

Bear, John Schoenher
The Bear that Heard Crying, Natalie Kinsey-Warnock and Helen Kinsey
The Bear Under the Stairs, Helen Cooper
Bear Wants More, Karma Wilson
Don't Wake Up the Bear!, Marjorie Dennis Murray
Don't You Feel Well, Sam?, Amy Hest
The Grizzly Sisters, Cathy Bellows
Maggie's Whopper, Sally Hobart Alexander
Mr. Bear Babysits, Debi Gliori
Ralph's Frozen Tale, Elise Primavera
Skating with the Bears, Andrew Breakspeare
Sleep Tight, Little Bear, Martin Waddell
Sody Sallyratus, Teri Sloat
There's a Bear in the Bath!, Nanette Newman
Touch the Sky, My Little Bear, David Bedford
Where is Bear?, Leslea Newman

Music/Movement:

"Baby Bear"
Baby bear, Baby Bear, come on home.
The snow is coming and you shouldn't roam.
Baby bear, baby bear, don't be late.
It's time for every bear to hibernate.
(lie down and go to sleep)

Crafts:

"Teddy Bear—Fuzzy Friend"
Let's make a teddy bear character with a soft, furry texture. Begin by cutting a basic bear form from cardboard or poster board. Add decorative texture by cutting short lengths of brown yarn and gluing it to the bear

form. Finish your fuzzy friend by adding nose, eyes, and the pads of the paws with construction paper or felt.

Source: *The Fun-to-Make Book*, Colette Lamargue

"Bear Containers"

You will find an attractive container craft in this source, which provides a bear template that can be photocopied and enlarged to hold the size of the tube container you have selected. Have the child decorate the wide tube and glue it to the bear's lap, then simply fold the bear up around the tube where shown. These containers can be used for storing just about anything (party snacks, paper clips, string, pencils, etc.).

Source: *Great Paper Craft Projects*, Ingrid Klettenheimer

Activities:

"Warming Up"

Many people believe polar bears are white when they are actually cream-colored or light yellow. Each hair on a polar bear is transparent and hollow, and the skin of the bear is black. Polar bears really wouldn't stay warm if their fur was white. This fun science experiment will help children understand a little bit about the polar bear's anatomy and lifestyle and also the sun's warmth. Through the use of simple everyday items, children will see how white reflects the sun's energy but clear plastic lets the sun's energy through. The transparent fur of the polar bear helps the bear stay warmer.

Source: *The Everything Kids' Nature Book*, Kathiann M. Kowalski

"Hibernating Bears"

This game is similar to Simon Says. Discuss with the children a bear's experiences with the changes of the seasons. Let the children lie on the floor pretending to be bears hibernating. Continue by calling out various instructions, such as "Mother Nature says the bears are stretching." Remember, don't fool with Mother Nature. If she doesn't tell you what to do, then just sleep.

Source: *Kids and Seasons*, Kathy Darling

Songs:

(Audio) "The Bear Went over the Mountain"

Source: *Children's Favorite Songs, vol. 2*, Walt Disney

7 Animals: Cats

Topical Calendar Tie-in:

January 2

"Happy New Year for Cats Day"—After celebrating the New Year with your family it's time to sit down and celebrate the "mew" year with your cat. Showing their independent attitude, cats have their own day to celebrate. So, let's party and howl!

Videos:

The Cat in the Hat (Dr. Seuss Showcase II)
Let's Give Kitty a Bath!
Millions of Cats
Owl and the Pussycat
The Story of Puss in Boots

Picture Books:

Cat Among the Cabbages, Alison Bartlett
Cat and Bear, Carol Greene
Cat Skidoo, Bethany Roberts
The Cats of Mrs. Calamari, John Stadler
Clarence the Copy Cat, Patricia Lakin
Easy Peasy!, Linda Jennings
Feathers for Lunch, Lois Ehlert
Have You Seen My Cat?, Eric Carle
I Love Cats, Barney Saltzberg
Kate, the Cat and the Moon, David Almond and Stephen Lambert
Kitten for a Day, Ezra Jack Keats
Meow!, Katya Arnold
Michael and the Cats, Barbara Abercrombie
Millions of Cats, Wanda Gag
So What's It like to be a Cat?, Karla Kuskin
Wanted: Best Friends, A.M. Monson

Music/Movement:

"Mrs. Kitty"
Source: *The Big Book of Stories, Songs and Sing-Alongs*, Beth Maddigan

Crafts:

"Cat Animal Clips"
Break out those leftover clothespins to make your own animal clips. This book offers a variety of animal patterns for you to reproduce, including a cat made out of poster board, glue, and a pom-pom for a nose. You might even use pipe cleaners for whiskers and add a magnet to the back of your clothespin to be able to use it as a magnet or a clip. It's a simple craft that can become a nice gift.
Source: *Rainy Day Activity Book*, Andrea Pinnington

"Terrific Tiger"
Explain to children that when they talk about cats, it doesn't just mean the cute little kittens that they have at home. There is a larger family of cats that includes tigers, lions, and many more. At the end of the lesson on the cat family, prepare to turn your class into cats with masks. This book gives uncomplicated instructions on making tiger masks from paper plates, orange and black paints, and pipe cleaners. The lower portion of the plate is cut off to allow for more comfort. Let masked children prowl the classroom in search of other cats like themselves.
Source: *Little Hands Paper Plate Crafts*, Laura Check

Activities:

"Copy Cats"
Try a form of the familiar game Simon Says, but with a feline theme. Tell the children we are all going to become our favorite cat. They should describe what kind of cat they are (color, long or short tail, eye color, house cat, outdoor cat, etc.). Talk about the many things cats do, including cleaning themselves, using litter boxes, types of play, and more. Pick a leader to pretend to be the lead cat and explain to them that at the sound of the first "meow" they are now cats and must try and follow the actions of the lead cat. Have the lead cat speed up his actions to see who can keep up. Be sure that each child gets a chance to be lead cat throughout the activity.

"Cat and Mouse"
Catch me if you can is the goal of this cat-and-mouse game. Can the cat who is blindfolded locate the mice in his house? Let the fun begin as the little "squeakers" give clues to their location. See more on this game and others that young children will enjoy in this useful source.
Source: *Hey Mom, I'm Bored!*, Story Evans and Lise O'Haire

Songs:

(Audio) "What Kind of Cat are You"
Source: *Totally Zany*

8 Animal: Cows

Topical Calendar Tie-in:

July 15

"Cow Appreciation Day"—Vermont residents celebrate the contributions of the cow to our daily dairy production with a party consisting of ice cream, butter, cheese products, and more. So remember the cow the next time you drink that favorite milkshake!

Videos:

Click Clack Moo: Cows That Type
The Cow Who Fell in the Canal
The Silver Cow
Moo Cow Kaboom

Picture Books:

Calico Cows, Arlene Dubanevich
Cock-a-Doodle-Moo!, Bernard Most
The Cow That Went Oink, Bernard Most
The Cow Who Wouldn't Come Down, Paul Brett Johnson
Cows Can't Fly, Milgrim
The Day Veronica was Nosy, Elizabeth Laird
Emily and the Cows, Elaine Greenstein
Henry and the Cow Problem, Iona Whishaw
Hunting the White Cow, Tres Seymour
Moo Who?, Margie Palatini
Moonstruck: The True Story of the Cow Who Jumped Over the Moon, Gennifer Choldenko
Ms. Blanche, the Spotless Cow, Zidrou
Rude Giants, Audrey Wood
There's a Cow in the Road, Reeve Lindbergh
When Cows Come Home, David L. Harrison

Music/Movement:

"Slow, Slow Cow"
Source: *Storytime Crafts*, Kathryn Totten

Crafts:

"Cowbell"
On a farm cows are set out into the pasture to graze; in Austria they are sent out on the mountainsides. When it's time to locate these animals for milking, some farms send out a dog. Bells are placed on the cows so that they can be easily located. Make your own cow bells with small flowerpots and other materials suggested in this book. Send some of your cows (children in the class) out in the schoolyard with their bells. Can you locate them with your eyes closed?
Source: *International Crafts and Games*, Cynthia G. Adams

"Over the Moon"

Help the cow jump over the moon with this easy paper plate craft. Make a cow from poster board and let the children add the features with markers. Design the moon from a paper plate, then attach the cow with a strip of poster board and paper fasteners. Just move the cow across the top of the plate as the children recite the rhyme.

Source: *175 Easy-to-Do Everyday Crafts*, Sharon Dunn Umnik (editor)

Activities:

"Let's Make Butter"

Following an extensive lesson on dairy farms and perhaps a field trip to a local dairy if one is nearby, have the children participate in the process themselves. Collect some baby food jars that can be partially filled with whipping cream. Children will need to take turns shaking these jars to produce their butter and will realize how much time their ancestors took to make even a small portion. Be sure to follow health precautions and other directions set out in this source.

Source: *Creative Resources for the Early Childhood Classroom, 4th edition*, Judy Herr and Yvonne Libby Larson

"Musical Cowpies"

Before starting this game you might have to explain to children what a "cowpie" or "cow patty" is and the legend that "stepping on cowpies brings good luck," even if it is messy. This farmyard version of musical chairs is made by making brown cowpies out of construction paper. Have a picture of a cow on the back of every cowpie except one. Throw them out across the floor randomly and put on some farm music. As the children move from one cowpie to the next, they hope they will land on one with a cow on the back when the music stops. They will never know who will be eliminated until the music stops and they turn over their cowpies. The one without a cow on it is eliminated, while the others are lucky enough to remain. Remove one with a cow on it and toss them out again to continue the game.

Songs:

(Audio) "Moo-Moo"

Source: *Dance and Sing! The Best of Nick Jr.*

9 Animals: Dogs

Topical Calendar Tie-in:

August 26

"National Dog Day"—On this special day, it's time to honor man's best friend for his love, loyalty, and life-saving skills. Learn more about a dog's life as a seeing-eye companion, a sled dog, a pet, and much more.

Videos:

Angus Lost
A Boy, a Dog, and a Frog
Harry the Dirty Dog
The Pokey Little Puppy (Best Loved Golden Books)
Whistle for Willie

Picture Books:

Bad Dog School, Barbara M. Joose
Be Brown!, Barbara Bottner
The Bookshop Dog, Cynthia Rylant
A Flea in the Ear, Stephen Wyllie
McDuff Comes Home, Rosemary Wells
McSpot's Hidden Spots, Laura L. Seeley
Martha Walks the Dog, Susan Meddaugh
Oh Where, Oh Where Has My Little Dog Gone, Iza Trapani
Perfectly Martha, Susan Meddaugh
Sled Dogs Run, Jonathan London
Some Dogs Do, Jez Alborough
Two Dogs Swimming, Lynn Reiser
Waggers, Philemon Sturges
Walter's Tail, Lisa Campbell Ernst
Widget and the Puppy, Lyn Rossiter McFarland

Music/Movement:

"All Around My Backyard"
Sung to: "I'm a Little Teapot"
Source: *It's Great to be Three: The Encyclopedia of Activities for Three-Year-Olds*, Kathy Charmer and Maureen Murphy (editors)

Crafts:

"Paper Bag Dog"

Paper bag creations are one of the easiest and least expensive of crafts. They are also great fun for children. Try making a paper bag dog mask. Use a brown grocery bag and cut a hole on one side the size of the child's face.

Discuss with the children the parts of a dog's face. You can use construction paper to put long, floppy ears on the side. Get some clown makeup to color the child's nose black.

"Dog Bone Parcel"

Man's best friend needs our love and gifts too. How about showing your dog how much you love him by giving him a gift of doggie treats in a very special parcel? Fashion and decorate a bone-shaped board and place little pockets over it where you can store his favorite treats. Hang it where you can reach it for your best friend at all times.

Source: *Fantastic Paper Holiday Decorations*, Teddy Cameron Long

Activities:

"Good Dog"

Children who have no pets have no idea what it takes to train a pet to behave in your household. Parents would welcome the chance to bring their child to a program where members of a pet obedience school staff appear. Let the staff bring in some dogs and cats and talk to the children about the various methods they use to train their pets and what they would have to do at home to prepare a pet for living in their house. Parents who have children insisting they will take care of the dog may thank you when their child's eyes are opened to the work involved. As an extension of this program, you might invite in people who train dogs to be future seeing-eye dogs or dogs that help with various handicaps.

"In the Doghouse" Math

Gather small individual milk cartons and Popsicle sticks for this special game. The cartons can be decorated as doghouses with special numbers and mathematical symbols on the door. The craft sticks can be decorated as dogs with numbers on them and placed in the doghouses. As dogs are drawn, children will have to do the math suggested. This book also gives suggestions for adapting this game to introduce nouns, verbs, and more.

Source: *Arts, Crafts and More*, Barbara Lyerty Goins, Karen J. Goldfluss, Doris J. Guerette, Ina Massler Levin, and Patricia Miriani Sima

Songs:

(Audio) "Rags"

Source: *Great Big Hits!*, Sharon, Lois and Bram

10 Animals: Dolphins, Whales

Topical Calendar Tie-in:

May 13

"Mother Ocean Day"—This day is celebrated annually on the day before Mother's Day. Discover the vastness of the ocean and the creatures it nurtures, such as the dolphin and the great whale, along with the multitude of smaller creatures and plants.

Videos:

Burt Dow: Deep-Water Man
How the Whale Got his Throat (Rudyard Kipling classics)
Willie, the Operatic Whale
Whales
Dora: Save the Day!

Picture Books:

Big Blue Whale, Nicola Davies
Cimru the Seal, Theresa Radcliffe
D is for Dolphin, Cami Berg
Do the Whales Still Sing?, Dianne Hofmeyr
In Dolphin Time, Diane Farris
I Wonder if I'll See a Whale, Frances Ward Weller
Little Dolphin's Big Leap, Rebecca Johnson
Rainbow Fish and the Big Blue Whale, Marcus Pfister
The Snow Whale, Caroline Pitcher
Story of a Dolphin, Katherine Orr
There's a Dolphin in the Grand Canal, John Bemelmans Marciano
Whale, Judy Allen
Whale Is Stuck, Karen Hayles and Charles Fuge
The Whales, Cynthia Rylant
Whale Snow, Debby Dahl Edwardson

Music/Movement:

"Whale"
Source: *Once Upon a Childhood: Fingerplays, Action Rhymes and Fun Times for the Very Young*, Dolores Chupela

Crafts:

"Nutshell Families"
Here's a fun craft that children may create after discussing various types of animal families. Collect many intact walnut shell halves. If you would like to make a whale family that includes a mother, father, and one baby, you will need two walnut shells and one pistachio shell. Paint them gray, add wiggly eyes, and add a spout using gray or white paper. Connect them together with a long string and the child can pull them across the table.
Source: *Crafts from Recyclables*, Colleen Van Blaricom

"A Whale of a Time"
Create a whale of a sea scene with the use of bubbles. Mix blue paint and dish soap with a little water in a bowl. Using a straw, blow bubbles to fill the bowl, then lay a sheet of white paper gently across the top. The bubbles create a beautiful water scene. Frame it with a green seaweed border and add sea creatures of your choice.

Source: *Making Pictures: Secrets of the Sea*, Penny King and Clare Roundhill

Activities:

"Pin the Spout on the Whale"
Pin the tail on the donkey goes out to sea with this game. Talk about what whales use their spout for in daily life. Also talk about how each whale has unique markings on their tails that identify them. With that, create a game played the same as the donkey game but with water spouts to be pinned onto the whale. Also, have the children try to locate the correct spot for those tails.

"Save the Dolphins"
This is a variation of an ancient game called "Glue." Indicate that the entire play area is the ocean and all the children are now dolphins, except one who is a fisherman. Unfortunately this fisherman fishes with a net. Scatter throughout the room the fisherman's net constructed out of paper streamers but leave the children paths to get around them. The fisherman gets to chase the dolphins through the room to catch (tag) them. If a dolphin steps in a net he is caught until another dolphin who is still free can get to him and tag him to set him free. Any dolphin tagged by the fisherman must go to a net until freed. A great stepping off game for discussing safe fishing and caring for animals.

Songs:

(Audio) "Baby Beluga"

Source: *Raffi in Concert with the Rise and Shine Band*

11 Animals: Elephants

Topical Calender Tie-in:

September 21

"Elephant Appreciation Day"—Here's a day to celebrate the largest and most endangered land animal. Learn about its life in the wild, in the circus, and some of children's literature's favorite elephants, such as Dumbo and Horton.

Videos:

Circus Baby
Dumbo
The Elephant's Child
Horton Hatches an Egg
The Saggy Baggy Elephant (Golden Jungle Animal Tales)
Uncle Elephant

Picture Books:

A Nose Like a Hose, Jenny Samuels
Baashi, the Elephant Baby, Theresa Radcliffe
Baby Elephant, Julie D. Shively
Big Little Elephant, Valeri Gorbachev
Emma Kate, Patricia Polacco
Engelbert the Elephant, Tom Paxton
Kidogo, Anik McGrory
Little Elephant's Walk, Adrienne Kennaway
The Mightiest, Keiko Kasza
Old Noah's Elephants, Warren Ludwig
Rose and Dorothy, Roslyn Schwartz
Tabu and the Dancing Elephants, Rene Deetlefs
That's What Friends Are For, Florence Parry Heide and Sylvia Van Clief
The Way Home, Judith Benet Richardson
When the Elephant Walks, Keiko Kasza

Music/Movement:

"The Elephant Goes"
Source: *The Complete Book of Rhymes, Songs, Poems, Fingerplays and Chants*, Jackie Silberg and Pam Schiller

Crafts:

"Easy Elephant"
Break out your basic supplies and fashion a comical elephant mask that children can use in an elephant march. This source uses staple craft products of paper plates and paper strips to turn children into elephants with large ears and a long nose. Here's a simple craft with a world of fun embedded in it.
Source: *Arts Starts for Little Hands*, Judy Press

"Baked Elephant Ears"

"How do you eat an elephant? One bite at a time!" Here is a really BIG treat for children. It will require some adult supervision in the final stages for making the elephant ears, but the fun of making the treat is worth it. Be inspired by the special recipe offered here and serve them by drawing your own elephant plate, and serve them by placing them on the sides of the elephant's head.

Source: *At the Zoo*, Better Homes and Gardens

Activities:

"One Elephant"

Children love to pretend to be various animals, and elephants are very familiar to them from zoos and circuses. In this event, the children sit in a circle while a single child uses his arm for a trunk and walks around the circle pretending to be an elephant as the group recites the rhyme provided in the following source. At the appropriate point in the rhyme, the child selects another to be an elephant. The first child will put her remaining arm through his legs to hold hands with the second child's elephant trunk arm and continue around the circle while the verse is repeated. How many elephants can you string together before the children giggle and fall to the floor?

Source: *The Complete Book of Activities, Games, Stories, Props, Recipes, and Dances for Young Children*, Pam Schiller and Jackie Silberg

"Animal Blind Man's Bluff"

After reading the story of *The Blind Men and the Elephant*, this animal rendering of "Blind Man's Bluff" will have more meaning. This game has the blind man blindfolded and standing in the center of a group of animals. Talk about different types of animals and what sounds they make. In this game, the blind man will have to identify the animal by sound rather than by feel. Your blind man can stand with his pointer stick in the center blindfolded as the animals move around. He will need to identify who he has selected by a variety of animal clues offered. See this book for engaging clues to the different animals.

Source: *Fun and Games for Family Gatherings*, Adrienne Anderson

Songs:

(Audio) "The Elephant"

Source: *Early Childhood Classics*, Hap Palmer

12 Animals: Kangaroos

Topical Calendar Tie-in:

January 26
"Australia Day"—Celebrate the foundation day of the homeland of the kangaroo. Australia was originally established as a prison colony but the beautiful land is home to a delight of animal friends, including the kangaroo.

Videos:

Joey Runs Away
Katy No-Pocket

Picture Books:

Big Talk, Miriam Schlein
Boing!, Nick Bruel
Elmer and the Kangaroo, David McKee
Grumble Rumble!, Siobhan Dodds
I Love You, Blue Kangaroo, Emma Chichester Clark
Joey: The Story of a Baby Kangaroo, Hope Ryden
Kangaroo's Adventure in Alphabet Town, Janet McDonnell
McGillycuddy Could!, Pamela Duncan Edwards
Moonbear's Dream, Frank Asch
The Perfect Present, Michael Hague
The Sing-Song of Old Man Kangaroo, Rudyard Kipling
Too Many Kangaroo Things to Do!, Stuart J. Murphy
What Shall We Do, Blue Kangaroo?, Emma Chichester Clark
Will You Take Care of Me?, Margaret Park Bridges

Music/Movement:

"Six Down Under"
Source: *Ready, Set, Go!: Children's Programming for Bookmobiles and Other Small Spaces*, Dolores Chupela

Crafts:

"Katherine, the Kangaroo"
This is a very easy paper plate craft that can be related to *Katy No-Pocket* by Emmy Payne or any of the other kangaroo stories suggested here. All that is required is two paper plates, brown markers, tape and scissors. The children can make a mother kangaroo with a pocket holding her baby kangaroo. The children can even use this craft for their desks, where you can leave their papers when returning them or hold handy supplies.
Source: *Alphabet Art*, Judy Press

"Jumping Joey"
Assemble your own Jumping Joey toy for each child. This is an excellent craft when talking about Australia and the creatures living there. A simple pattern is supplied so you may trace and cut out a kangaroo out of posterboard. Punch a hole at the top, attach a long rubber band and a button to the other end. Now the children can bounce these little creatures all over

the room while repeating the verse "Jump, Jump, Kangaroo, Jump," also provided here.

Source: *Storytime Crafts*, Kathryn Totten

Activities:

"Kangaroo Tag"

Teach the children the proper way to jump like a kangaroo, then select one child to be the mother kangaroo. The mother is searching for her little joeys by jumping around and tagging them. As one is tagged she becomes the next mother kangaroo. Stress that kangaroos jump but do not run. Variations of this game are also offered in the source cited here.

Source: *The Giant Encyclopedia of Theme Activities for Children 2 to 5*, Kathy Charner

"Kangaroo Hop"

Line up your players of each team one behind the other. Each child should pass the ball over their heads to the back of the line. The last player places the ball between his knees and hops to the beginning of the line. Continue in this manner until your team is as it originally began.

Source: *Making Children's Parties Click*, Virginia W. Husselman

Songs:

(Audio) "Five Little Joeys"

Source: *Dance Party*, The Wiggles

13 Animals: Lions and Tigers

Topical Calendar Tie-in:

October 19

"Birthday of Winnie the Pooh's Friend Tigger"—The creation day of children's lovable character Tigger is believed to be in October 1928, which is the year *The House at Pooh Corner* was first published. Celebrate this creation with a bouncing good time, since "Bouncing is what Tiggers do best!"

Videos:

Andy and the Lion
Happy Lion's Treasure
Leo on Vacation
The Lion and the Mouse (Mr. Know it Owl's Video Tales: Aesop's Fables Vol. 1)
Tawny Scrawny Lion (Golden Jungle Animal Tales)

Picture Books:

Brer Tiger and the Big Wind, William J. Faulkner
Ella and the Naughty Lion, Anne Cottringer
I'm Going to New York to Visit the Lions, Harriet Ziefert
It's Simple, Said Simon, Mary Ann Hoberman
Little Lions, Jim Arnosky
Little Louie the Baby Bloomer, Robert Kraus
Loudest Roar, Thomas Taylor
Nobody Laughs at a Lion!, Paul Bright
The Rat and the Tiger, Keiko Kasza
Roar!: A Noisy Counting Book, Pamela Duncan Edwards
The Tiger's Breakfast, Jan Mogensen
Tigers, Sarah L. Thomson
Tiger, Tiger, Dee Lillegard
Wait! I Want to Tell You a Story, Tom Willans
Who is the Beast?, Keith Baker

Music/Movement:

"Lion Hunt"
Source: *52 Programs for Preschoolers*, Diane Briggs

Crafts:

"Lion Face"
Using markers, have the children draw the eyes, nose, and mouth of a lion on a paper plate. Cut strips of yellow construction paper to be glued all the way around the perimeter of the plate to form the lion's mane. You may curl each strip using scissors.

If you want to turn this into a mask, simply add string to the sides, or better yet, put it on a stick to be held in the child's hand.

"Larry the Lion"

Directions are supplied in this source for children to make their own lion sculpture. A cardboard paper tube is used for the body. This body can be covered with brown construction paper, with features such as the tail, feet, and face added at the end. Uncomplicated assembly instructions are provided with illustrations. This simple sculpture can easily be adapted for making a tiger, if needed.

Source: *Alphabet Art*, Judy Press

Activities:

"Tiger Trap"

Let's go on a tiger hunt. This is a two team event with the tigers on one side and the tiger trap on the other. It will require a playing field or room where the children can fan out to try to escape the tiger trap trying to envelope them in the net. After five minutes, the groups can switch positions to try the other part of the game.

Source: *Fun and Games for Family Gatherings*, Adrienne Anderson

"Red Lion"

Red Rover takes a totally different turn in this game, which requires the running and dodging that children love and burns up some of their extra energy. Keep that lion in his den unless you are brave enough to challenge him. Chant and tease that lion and he will come after you. If you get caught, you can still save yourself and return to the game. Find out how to stay safe from the lion's den in this source.

Source: *Kids' Games*, Phil Wiswell

Songs:

(Audio) "The Lion Sleeps Tonight"

Source: *Jack in the Box 2*, Jack Grunsky

14 Animals: Mice

Topical Calendar Tie-in:

JULY 22, 1376

"Pied Piper of Hamelin: Anniversary—Maybe"—This day has been set aside to recognize the Pied Piper of Hamelin who, according to legend, contracted to lead the rats that were infesting the town out by using his pipe music.

Videos:

Abel's Island
Alexander and the Wind-Up Mouse
Frederick (Leo Lionni's Caldecotts)
Mickey Mouse, The Brave Little Tailor (Cartoon Classics Collection, Vol. 6)
Norman the Doorman

Picture Books:

The Best Mouse Cookie, Laura Numeroff
The Dark at the Top of the Stairs, Sam McBratney
Do You See Mouse?, Marion Crume
Ella's Games, David Bedford and Peter Kavanagh
Milo and the Magical Stones, Marcus Pfister
Never Fear, Snake My Dear!, Rolf Siegenthaler
Seven Blind Mice, Ed Young
Stuart Little: Stuart at the Library, Susan Hill
The Subway Mouse, Barbara Reid
Three Blind Mice, Lorinda Bryan Cauley
Tom's Tail, Arlene Dubanevich
Three Kind Mice, Vivian Sathre
Two Tiny Mice, Alan Baker
Watch Out!, Jan Fearnley
Watch Out! Big Bro's Coming!, Jez Alborough

Music/Movement:

"Where Are the Baby Mice?"
Source: *Storytimes for Two-Year-Olds, second edition*, Judy Nichols

Crafts:

"Photo Mouse"
This photograph holder will delight little children because it's easy to make but also because it gives the appearance of something difficult accomplished. It is constructed from paper, with a three-dimensional mouse head. Add whiskers, a curling tail, and a photo of the child on the mouse's stomach, and any parent will be proud to display this on their refrigerator.
Source: *175 Easy-to-Do Thanksgiving Crafts*, Sharon Dunn Umnik

"Shamrock Mouse Magnet"
Try a different twist on crafts normally used around St. Patrick's Day with this shamrock mouse magnet. Cut a small shamrock from green felt or

craft foam. The stem of the shamrock will be placed at the top and become your mouse's tail. Glue two pink hearts in the upper portions of your shamrock for ears and add eyes, nose, and whiskers to the lower third of the shamrock. Add a magnet to the back or a pin if you would rather wear your mouse. This is an inexpensive and fun craft for any group.

Source: *Crafts for St. Patrick's Day*, Kathy Ross

Activities:

"Mousetrap 1"

This game can be played with any number of children. Let one child be the cat, another the mouse and the remainder of the group will be the trap. The children form the trap by holding hands in a circle. The cat stands outside facing away. While the mouse goes in and out of the circle the children hold their hands up until the cat yells "trap." If the mouse is outside the trap he can become the next cat. Other interesting modifications are also offered in this source. Keyed to the size and ages of the group.

Source: *The Picture Rulebook of Kids' Games*, Roxanne Henderson

"Mousetrap 2"

Here's a board game version of mousetrap. Follow the instructions offered to create mice for each player out of corks, string, and some artwork. A circular playing board is constructed as well as a spinner. One player gets to be the trapper with a bucket trying to snare as many mice as he can. Spinners determine when he can make his attempt. Hope your reflexes are quick. Can you get away fast?

Source: *The Ultimate Book of Games and Puzzles*, Allistar Smith

Songs:

(Audio) "The Mice go Marching"

Source: *Rhythms on Parade*, Hap Palmer

15 Animals: Monkeys

Topical Calendar Tie-in:

April 3, 1934

"Birth of Jane Goodall"—Celebrate the life and work of the world's foremost authority on chimpanzees. Jane lived with the chimps and gained their confidence. Learn more about chimpanzee and other ape behaviors. Also learn about the famous signing gorilla, Koko, on her own Web site www.koko.org.

Videos:

Caps for Sale
Curious George
Why Monkeys Live in the Trees (Magical Tales from Other Lands)

Picture Books:

The Boy Who Loved Bananas, George Elliott
Curious George Flies a Kite, Margaret Rey
Cyril the Mandrill, Francesca Greco
Don't Wake up Mama, Eileen Christelow
Fifty Red Night-Caps, Inga Moore
Five Little Monkeys Sitting in a Tree, Eileen Christelow
How Mr. Monkey Saw the Whole World, Walter Dean Myers
Matepo, Angela McAllister
Monkey Do!, Allan Ahlberg
Monkey Mo Goes to Sea, Diane Goode
Monkey Tricks, Camilla Ashforth
Naughty Little Monkeys, Jim Aylesworth
Run, Little Monkeys, Run, Run, Run, Charles Kepes
The Turtle and the Monkey, Paul Galdone
Water Hole Waiting, Jane Kurtz and Christopher Kurtz

Music/Movement:

"Monkeys"

Sung to: "Hickory, Dickory, Dock"

The monkeys climb up in the trees
(pretend to climb up tree)
To see what they can see.
A snake slithers round
(slide arm across body like a snake)
The monkeys run down
(run in place)
As fast as they can flee!

Crafts:

"Silly Salt-Box Monkey"

A salt box (circular salt container) can be made into a container for collecting prize possessions. With the youngest children, you may wish to have parts precut for this craft. This can be made into a monkey with the use of construction paper and glue. Begin with a collection of salt box animals.

Source: *Sticks and Stones and Ice Cream Cones*, Phyllis Fiarotta

"Twirling Monkey"
Monkey see, monkey do. Keep those monkeys twirling through the room with this little craft. Simply made of paper circles and limbs constructed of chenille sticks, our monkey clings desperately to a drinking straw as the children twirl him around and around.

Source: *175 Easy-to-Do Everyday Crafts*, Sharon Dunn Umnik (editor)

Activities:

"Monkey See, Monkey Do"

Monkey see, Monkey do
I can———and you can, too.

Play this game in the same fashion as Simon Says, substituting the word "monkey" for Simon.

"Monkey's Tail
Let the children pair off to find out who is the top monkey. Add a tail to each child by tying a long string with a crayon on the end around the child's waist. Give it enough length so that it almost touches the floor but not quite. The goal of this game is for the child to be the first to place the end of his monkey tail inside the jar that is located on the floor, of course without using his hands.

Source: *Child Magazine's Book of Children's Parties*, Angela Wilkes

Songs:

(Audio) "Monkey"

Source: *Animal Alphabet Songs*, David Polansky

16 Animals: Pigs

Topical Calendar Tie-in:

March 1

"National Pig Day"—This day is set aside to celebrate the pig as one of man's most useful domesticated animals. Discuss what pigs offer us and talk about the variety of pigs in children's literature, such as the three little pigs.

Videos:

The Amazing Bone
Pig's Picnic
The Pig's Wedding
The Three Little Pigs

Picture Books:

Barnyard Big Top, Jill Kastner
Bed Hogs, Kelly DiPucchio and Howard Fine
Five Little Piggies, David Martin
Hog-Eye, Susan Meddaugh
If You Give a Pig a Pancake, Laura Numeroff
Mrs. Potter's Pig, Phyllis Root
Perfect the Pig, Susan Jeschke
Piggie Pie!, Margie Palatini
Pigsty, Mark Teague
Pigs Aplenty, Pigs Galore!, David McPhail
A Pile of Pigs, Judith Ross Enderle
The Spotty Pig, Dick King-Smith
Toot and Puddle, Holly Hobbie
Tuck in the Pool, Martha Weston
Wriggly Pig, Jon Blake

Music/Movement:

"Two Mother Pigs" or "The Pigs"
Source: *52 Programs for Preschoolers: The Librarian's Year-Round Planner*, Diane Briggs

Crafts:

"Spicy Shapes"
This book offers a recipe for cinnamon dough that can be used to make spicy shapes, but is not meant to be eaten. The wonderful thing about this is that the final creations will last for years. Pigs are not the most aromatic of animals, so let's change their reputation by representing them in a pleasing way. Use pig cookie cutters to cut out your shapes. These can be hung in any area that you want to add a fragrant aroma that will be pleasing to all. Send your aromatic gift to your favorite person and spread the word that pigs are good.
Source: *Grand Activities*, Shari Sasser

"Piggy Bank"
A piggy bank with a little pizzazz will make an enjoyable activity for the children. A plastic bleach bottle or milk bottle, thoroughly cleaned, gives you the shape of the pig at the start. Thread spools make great little legs. Linda Schwartz's book gives you easy-to-follow instructions on how the children may cover the bottle with multicolored tissue paper, then add the final features including its curly tail.

Source: *Likeable Recyclables*, Linda Schwartz

Activities:

"Pigs to Market"
"To market, to market to buy a fat pig." Try this race, which requires some speed and a lot of control. With just sticks and some old plastic soda bottles, the children can try to get those pigs to market for the sale, but try not to let your pig bump into anyone else's pig or you will have to start all over again.

Source: *Sidewalk Games*, Glen Vecchione

"Pig Out, Pig Stop"
A slight change from the conventional "Red Light, Green Light" that all the children are familiar with, this little game will be a surefire hit with young children. One child faces the wall while the other children are at the opposite end of the room. As the children move closer to him, the person who is "it" calls out "Pig Out" or "Pig Stop." If he calls "Pig Out" the children must walk on all fours like a pig. If "Pig Stop" is called, everyone freezes and "it" turns around. Anyone moving must start all over again from the starting point.

Source: *The Penny Whistle Birthday Party Boo*, Meredith Brokaw and Annie Gilbar

Songs:

(Audio) "This Old Sow"

Source: *One Elephant, Deux Elephants*, Sharon, Lois and Bram

17 Animals: Rabbits

Topical Calendar Tie-in:

July 15–21
"National Rabbit Week"—Enjoy this national week of celebration honoring the rabbit as a great house pet for children and of great value as a therapy pet. Teach children the proper way to care for rabbits as pets.

Videos:

The Little Rabbit Who Wanted Red Wings
Morris' Disappearing Bag
Peter Rabbit
The Tortoise and the Hare
Who's in Rabbit's House

Picture Books:

The Brave Little Bunny, Linda Jennings
A Bunny for all Seasons, Janet Schulman
Bunny Business, Nancy Poydar
Good Job, Oliver, Laurel Molk
Hopper's Treetop Adventure, Marcus Pfister
Little Bunny Foo Foo, told by the Good Fairy
Little Rabbit Goes to Sleep, Tony Johnston
Max and Ruby's First Greek Myth: Pandora's Box, Rosemary Wells
Rabbit Ears, Amber Stewart
Rabbits and Raindrops, Jim Arnosky
Rabbit's Good News, Ruth Lercher Bornstein
Too Many Bunnies, Matt Novak
Where Did Bunny Go?, Nancy Tafuri
Zomo the Rabbit, Gerald McDermott

Music/Movement:

"Funny Bunny"
Source: *Fun with Mommy and Me*, Dr. Cindy Bunin Nurick

Crafts:

"Silly Salt Box Bunny"
A salt box can be made into a container for collecting prize possessions. With the youngest children you may wish to have parts precut for this craft. This may be made into a bunny with the use of construction paper and glue. Begin with a collection of salt box animals.

If you are using this for an Easter program, you may wish to treat the children to an Easter surprise by filling it with paper grass and a special treat.
Source: *Sticks and Stones and Ice Cream Cones*, Phyllis Fiarotta

"Necktie Bunny Puppet"
Have some old-fashioned neckties lying around? Collect these dated fashions and recycle them into puppets. A colorful bunny puppet can be

made with the widest section of the tie becoming the face of the bunny. Don't throw anything out. The narrow sections that you cut off can become the ears. Add features as desired. See this source for guidelines and other useful crafts for young children.

Source: *Crafts for Easter*, Kathy Ross

Activities:

"Rabbit Ball"

This is a group activity that develops good lower muscle strength, children will be rolling with laughter as they try not to bump into each other while trying to perform the different types of jumping skills called out by the teacher. Each child will need a soft ball that they can hold between their knees while performing the skills. While the author of this game calls it "Kangaroo Ball," it can be easily adapted for rabbits or any animal that jumps. Check the variety of skills to be performed in this source.

Source: *Smart Play*, Barbara Sher

"Hopping Down the Bunny Trail"

Here are two bunny-related activities that children can enjoy and will require little preparation. The first, "Hopping Down the Bunny Trail," involves a simple trail marked with the taped Xs throughout the room, finishing at a cardboard hutch filled with rabbit storybooks for the children to enjoy. The second is the "Rabbit Patch Pull." Design a collection of cardboard carrots with paper clips on them. Place the carrots in that same hutch and let your little rabbits hop that trail again and try to fetch the carrots by dropping strings with magnets on it into the hutch.

Source: *First Time, Circle Time*, Cynthia Holley and Jane Walkup

Songs:

(Audio) "Little Peter Rabbit"

Source: *Wee Sing: Children's Songs and Fingerplays*

18 Art

Topical Calendar Tie-in:

September 7
"Grandma Moses Day"—Time to have a party for Anna Mary (Robertson) Moses who began painting at the age of 78. Encourage children to paint with their grandparents and show them you are never too old to learn something new. You might even try a grandparent/child art event at your school or library in celebration of this great lady.

Videos:

Art Dog
Harold and the Purple Crayon
Norman the Doorman
A Picture for Harold's Room
Regina's Big Mistake
Roberto the Insect Architect

Picture Books:

Art Dog, Thacher Hurd
Badly Drawn Dog, Emma Dodson
The Boy Who Drew Cats, Margaret Hodges
Crocodile's Masterpiece, Max Velthuijs
Eddie's Kingdom, D.B. Johnson
Ernie's Little Lie, Dan Elliott
I Ain't Gonna Paint No More!, Karen Beaumont
Lucy's Picture, Nicola Moon
Matthew's Dream, Leo Lionni
Once Upon a Lily Pad, Joan Sweeney
A Painter: How We Work, Douglas Florian
Regina's Big Mistake, Marissa Moss
Sydney's Star, Peter H. Reynolds
What is an Artist?, Barbara Lehn

Music/Movement:

"Painting Fun"
Sung to: "Twinkle, Twinkle Little Star"
Source: *The Big Book of Stories, Songs and Sing-Alongs*, Beth Maddigan

Crafts:

"Potato or Ink Pad Printing"
Children are fond of working with any type of printing materials. Try potato printing. With this you can arrange any design by cutting it from a potato then using ink pads and paper to design cards, pictures, etc.

If time doesn't permit you to use potato printing, try collecting various styles of ink stamps and the children will do the rest.
Source: *The Fun-to-Make Book*, Colette Lamargue

"Newspaper Snake"
Using the simple tools of old newspaper, wallpaper paste, tape, and paint, children can make their own snake sculpture. This is a simple craft that demands minimal skills and time. It also can be used in a program encouraging recycling and the saving of the environment.

Source: *Great Newspaper Crafts*, F. Virginia Walter

Activities:

"Color Hunt"
Divide the children into small groups and designate a color for that team by hanging around each member's neck a string with a piece of colored paper attached to it.

Hide a number of objects in the room that are the same color as those selected for the groups. The number of objects selected will vary with your group sizes, but each group should have an equal number to locate.

At a given signal, allow all to hunt for the items that are the same color as their group. The first group to find them all and return them to their base wins. Repeat the game by changing group colors or mixing up the members of the groups again.

"Draw-a-Face Relay"
Create two teams supplied with markers or crayons. The simple goal is for the children to take turns adding the features of a face until it's completed. Find this and other simple games you may have forgotten in this worthwhile book.

Source: *Pin the Tail on the Donkey and other Party Games*, Joanna Cole and Stephanie Calmenson

Songs:

(Audio) "Let's Paint a Picture"

Source: *Toddlers' Next Steps: Playtime Songs*

19 Babies

Topical Calendar Tie-in:

April 1

"National Love Our Children Day"—This holiday is like Mother's and Father's Day but is now an opportunity for parents to honor their children and protect them. Parents can take this time to show how much they love their children without waiting for a birthday.

Videos:

Arthur's Baby
Hush Little Baby
Peter's Chair
Smile for Auntie
That New Animal

Picture Books:

The Baby Book, Ann Morris
Ellen and Penguin and the New Baby, Clara Vulliamy
Geraldine's Baby Brother, Holly Keller
Guess the Baby, Simon French and Donna Rawlins
How I Named the Baby, Linda Shute
I Wish My Brother Was a Dog, Carol Diggory Shields
McDuff and the Baby, Rosemary Wells
New Baby Train, Woody Guthrie
One Up, One Down, Carol Snyder
Shoe Baby, Joyce Dunbar
That Terrible Baby, Jennifer Armstrong
Twinnies, Eve Bunting
Vera's Baby Sister, Vera Rosenberry
We Got My Brother at the Zoo, John and Ann Hassett
Where Did that Baby Come From?, Debi Gliori

Music/Movement:

"The Little Baby"
Sung to: "Eensy Weensy Spider"

The little tiny baby
Lay on the floor and cried *(lie down and cry)*
In came the Mom and
Hugged her till she sighed. *(Mom hugs)*
Now came the Dad who
Played peek-a-boo til she smiled
(mime peek-a-boo)
and the little tiny baby
lay down his sleepy head. *(go to sleep)*

Crafts:

"Playing Cards Photo Frame"

Here's an inspiring use of old playing cards. Kathy Ross leads us step by step through this simple craft turning old playing cards into a four-page foldout photo holder that can fit in Dad's wallet. Fathers will be proud to show off their baby's pictures in something so unique and humorous.

Source: *All New Crafts for Earth Day*, Kathy Ross

"Baby's Homemade Bib"

Whether you are a babysitter or the older sibling of a newly born baby this personalized gift will be gratefully received by your parents. Show them how much you love your new brother or sister by making him or her a special homemade bib. Follow the simple, worry-free methods of decorating offered along with directions to other craft sources that will come in handy here.

Source: *Wearable Art with Sondra*, Sondra Clark

Activities:

"Germ Buster"

Talk to children about new babies in their family and how careful they must be about sharing any items with the baby that might contain germs. Introduce this little game of "Germ Buster" to show that big brothers and sisters want to protect the baby. This game is a combination of tag and dodgeball, including a member who is the "Germ Buster" and the rest of the class who are germs. Check out the fun in this creative book.

Source: *Hey Mom, I'm Bored!*, Story Evans and Lise O'Haire

"Caring for Babies"

When a new baby comes along toddlers need to be kept in the loop when discussion occurs about taking care of their little brother or sister. Encourage children to help out, but clearly outline how they can watch out for the child's safety. For activities that they are too small to help with, provide a small doll and let the child "practice" for when they are old enough to help. This book mentions how people from Angola wear large pieces of cloth wrapped around their bodies to carry the baby; they're called panos. Provide a suitable cloth and baby doll as shown in the illustrations to let the child carry an infant.

Source: *Fun around the World for Preschoolers*, Rhonda Reeves

Songs:

(Audio) "All the Pretty Little Horses"

Source: *Wee Sings: Children's Songs and Fingerplays*

20 Babysitters and Babysitting

Topical Calendar Tie-in:

March 4
"Babysitter Safety Day"—Take this opportunity to discuss proper safety procedures when babysitting. Don't forget to include police and firefighters in your presentations, and talk to little children about the importance of listening to their babysitters.

Videos:

Arthur Babysits
The Best Babysitter Ever
Berenstain Bears get a Babysitter

Picture Books:

Baby-sit, Anne Miranda
The Babysitter, Christianne C. Jones
Babysitting for Benjamin, Valiska Gregory
Baby Tamer, Mark Teague
Eleanor and the Babysitter, Susan Hellard
Five Little Monkeys Play Hide and Seek, Eileen Christelow
Jake and the Babysitter, Simon James
Lemonade Babysitter, Karen Waggoner
Looking After Little Ellie, Dosh and Mike Archer
Mr. Bear Babysits, Debi Gliori
Ms. Turtle the Babysitter, Valeri Gorbachov
Never Babysit the Hippopotamuses!, Doug Johnson
Thomas's Sitter, Jean Richardson
Time for Bed, the Babysitter Said, Peggy Perry Anderson
What Alvin Wanted, Holly Keller
What Kind of Baby-sitter is this?, Dolores Johnson

Music/Movement:

"The Family"
Source: *Story Programs: A Source Book of Materials*, Carolyn Sue Peterson and Brenny Hall

Crafts:

"Babysitter's Kit"
Discuss with the children about helping Mom and Dad with smaller siblings. Let the children list what they feel they would need in their special kit in order to help out (rattles, stuffed toys, etc.). Decorate a special bag for the children to store these tools of the trade.

Since most of the children you are speaking to still need babysitters themselves, have them put together babysitter kits for their own babysitters. Let the children list and collect all the items they would like to see their babysitters bring with them when they come to watch them for the day.

"Oatmeal Box Cradles"
Review with the children the many things babies need for their daily life. Collect a number of oatmeal boxes and cut a section out of them to form the shape of a baby's cradle. Pass them out to the children and supply them with an assortment of items to decorate with (lace, stickers, paint, etc.). The children can be encouraged to use their cradle to rock their dolls to sleep or give to a friend who needs one. A good babysitter should know how to rock and sing a baby to sleep when the need arises.

Source: *Look What I Made!*, Sarah H. Healton

Activities:

"The Babysitter's Lost the Baby"
The babysitter (you) has lost the baby and must go in search of him immediately. Along the way you will encounter a number of other babies that are lost (calf, duckling, puppy, etc.) along with items that belong to them (feathers, bone rattle, etc.).

The teacher has placed boxes with pictures of each baby's mother on it. As you find the baby or his belongings, return them to his mom.

Divide the class up into teams and time their search. The team to return all the babies to their moms safely along with their toys in the shortest time wins.

"Outdoor Tic-Tac-Toe"
Babysitters need to be prepared to entertain the children they have been put in charge of. Talk to the children about what types of things babysitters might take with them to entertain young children. Once you have made a list of items you will need, explain that not all entertainment need cost you money. Take your group outside and collect sticks, stones, and wood to make their own game to add to the babysitter's game collection. Here's a nice use of these items for a Tic-Tac-Toe game.

Source: *Hey Kids! Come Craft with Me*, Mary Engelbreit

Songs:

(Audio) "Da Baby Sitter"

Source: *In My Hometown*, Tom Chapin

21 Bedtime Stories

Topical Calendar Tie-in:

April 15
"Stories Day"—This day is designated to honor stories to be told at bedtime and other group gatherings. Share a story with a friend. Put on your pajamas, bring your favorite bedtime toy, and sit together for bedtime tales for everyone.

Videos:

Bear Snores On
Dr. Seuss's Sleep Book
Ira Sleeps Over
The Napping House
Sweet Dreams, Spot

Picture Books:

Bed Hogs, Kelly DiPucchio and Howard Fine
The Boy Who Wouldn't Go to Bed, Helen Cooper
The Caterpillow Fight, Sam McBratney
Cowboy Baby, Sue Heap
Don't Wake Up the Bear!, Majorie Dennis Murray
Goodnight, Baby Monster, Laura Leuck
Good Night Dinosaurs, Judy Sierra
"I'm Not Sleepy," Denys Cazet
Little Donkey Close Your Eyes, Margaret Wise Brown
No Nap for Benjamin Badger, Nancy White Carlstrom
Shadow Night, Kay Chorao
Shhhhh! Everybody's Sleeping, Julie Markes
Tick-Tock, Drip-Drop!, Nicola Moon
Under the Bed, Paul Bright and Ben Cort

Music/Movement:

"Bedtime"

Sung to: "The Farmer in the Dell"

It's time to go to bed; it's time to go to bed.
Let's get ready now
It's time to go to bed.

I brush my teeth this way; I brush my teeth this way.
Up, down and rinse it now.
I brush my teeth this way.

I put my pj's on, I put my pj's on.
Pull them, up, then over my head.
I put my pj's on.

I pull the covers up,
I lay my small head down.
I close my eyes and go to sleep
Until the morning light.

Crafts:

"Night's Nice"
After discussing what happens at night and asking the children to identify what they see in the sky at night, pass out materials for the children to make their own night sky. This is simple enough for young children. A piece of black paper, one yellow sticker dot (moon), and star stickers are all that is needed for them to enjoy themselves.

"Seven Sleepy Dwarfs"
Tuck the seven little dwarfs into their own little bed with this Kathy Ross craft. Take the bottom of an egg carton and turn it over so that the mounds face up. Cover the bottom row with various colors of cloth pieces for blankets and the top level will become the faces of the dwarfs. You will, of course, have to add one more section to the egg carton so you have 7 dwarfs. Add a headboard and footboard. Check the source book for specific instructions and illustrations to guide you in this craft.
Source: *The Storytime Craft Book*, Kathy Ross

Activities:

"The Princess and the Pea"
This adaptation of the Princess and the Pea might keep everyone up for a long night. Gather a collection of small items obviously of different shapes and sizes (toy car, pencil, flat box, etc.). Display them for all to see. Take out a group of small pillows and place them around the room. One of the pillows will have an item hidden beneath it. At the sound of the royal bell, a prince and a princess will set out to find the hidden item by laying or sitting on the pillows. Once found they must then identify the item by its feel through the pillow. If it's correctly identified he or she can then challenge another royal until there is only one prince or princess left. Change the hidden item with each round.

"Teddy's Bedtime"
This is a team event that will have the children giggling all the way through it. Supply the children with a pair of adult slippers to wear, a teddy bear to hold in one arm and an unlit candle to hold in the other hand. Now watch as they race from one end of the room to the other to put teddy to bed. Special phrases for the runner and teammates to call out during the game are also supplied in order to make it a team effort.
Source: *Giving a Children's Party*, Jane Cable-Alexander

Songs:

(Audio) "Ten in the Bed"
Source: *Playtime Favorites*

22 Behavior: Growing Up

Topical Calendar Tie-in:

1906
Commemorate the invention of the character Peter Pan originally invented by J. M. Barrie in his novel *The Little White Bird* and later developed into the play and the movie children are familiar with today. This character that never wanted to grow up will help everyone stay young. Sing "I won't grow up."

Videos:

Dr. Seuss's My Many Colored Days
The Giving Tree
Leo the Late Bloomer
Owen
Peter's Chair
Will I Have a Friend?

Picture Books:

As Big as You, Elaine Greenstein
Bigger Than a Baby, Harriet Ziefert
Cleversticks, Bernard Ashley
Emily Just in Time, Jan Slepian
Growing Pains, Jenny Stow
Grow Up!, Nina Laden
It's Going to be Perfect!, Nancy Carlson
Little Bear's Little Boat, Even Bunting
The Littlest Wolf, Larry Dane Brimner
Now I'm Big, Margaret Miller
Rabbit Ears, Amber Stewart
Someone Bigger, Jonathan Emmett
Tadpoles, Betsy James
Touch the Sky, My Little Bear, David Bedford
Will You Take Care of Me?, Margaret Park Bridges

Music/Movement:

"Growing Up"
Sung to: "Mulberry Bush"

This is the way I rocked with my mom,
Rocked with my mom, rocked with my mom.
This is the way I rocked with my mom
When I was just a baby!
(Rock baby in your arms.)

This is the way I crawled on the floor,
Crawled on the floor, crawled on the floor.
This is the way I crawled on the floor.
When I was still a baby.
(crawl across the floor)

This is the way I took my first step
Took my first step, took my first step
This is the way I took my first step
When I grew to a toddler.
(pretend wobbly walking)

This is the way I run really fast
Run really fast, run really fast
This is the way I run really fast
Now that I've grown so big again.
(run around the room)

Crafts:

"When I was Young . . ."

This is a great follow-up to Cynthia Rylant's book *When I Was Young in the Mountains.* After the story help the children to create their own book of when they were young. This is a great keepsake that the children and their family will treasure for a long time.

Source: *The Best of the Mailbox, Book 1: Preschool/Kindergarten,* Margaret Michel

"Growing Girl"

Little girls love to play with paper dolls. In this book you will find basic instructions to make your paper doll actually grow! With a little preparation beforehand, girls and boys alike can make a simple paper puppet that grows before your eyes. Check it out!

Source: *Let's Create: Paper,* Dorothy L. Gibbs (editor)

Activities:

"When I Grow Up . . ."

This is a simple mime game that even the youngest child can participate in with the group. Create a stage area at the front of the room by drawing a circle. One child at a time enters the circle, says, "When I grow up I want to be . . . ," and then mimes the occupation he is interested in at the time. The remainder of the group will attempt to guess with the member who guesses correctly getting to go next.

Source: *Great Theme Parties for Children,* Irene N. Watts

"I Can Do It"

This is a variation of the game "King of the Hill" that will help children demonstrate what they are capable of doing. It is a wonderful method of illustrating self-reliance and more while having a great deal of fun and laughter.

In a bag place a large number of papers each listing activities the children need to perform to show growth in their life (Ex: Bounce a ball, tie your shoes, put on your own shirt, etc.). These activities can be physical or verbal acts and often change depending on the age of the group playing the game.

Each child sits at the bottom of a flight of stairs. If the child is able to perform the action the leader announces from the paper drawn from the bag he moves up one step. If he is unable to do it, he simply waits for his next turn. The first to reach the top of the hill wins. This is a game children will ask for repeatedly.

Songs:

(Audio) "I Wonder if I'm Growing"

Source: *Singable Songs for the Very Young*

23 Behavior: Losing Things

Topical Calendar Tie-in:

July 17

"Wrong Way Corrigan Day"—Commemorate the anniversary of the flight of Douglas Groce Corrigan, dubbed "Wrong Way" because his flight intended to leave New York and end in California but actually ended in Dublin, Ireland, when he lost his sense of direction.

Videos:

Grandfather's Mitten
No Roses for Harry!
Old Bear: Lost and Found
Picnic
Spot's Lost Bone
The Three Little Kittens

Picture Books:

Billy's Beetle, Mick Inkpen
The Blanket, John Burningham
D.W.'s Lost Blankie, Marc Brown
Has Anybody Lost a Glove?, G. Francis Johnson
I Lost My Bear, Jules Feiffer
Iris and Walter: Lost and Found, Elissa Haden Guest
The Letters are Lost, Lisa Campbell Ernst
Lollopy, Joyce Dunbar
Losing Things at Mr. Mudd's, Carolyn Coman
The Lost and Found, Mark Teague
Small Bear Lost, Martin Waddell
T-Rex is Missing!, Tomie DePaola
When Charlie McButton Lost Power, Suzanne Collins and Mike Lester
Where Are You, Little Zack?, Judith Ross Enderle and Stephanie Gordon Tessler
Where Can It Be?, Ann Jonas
Where's Your Smile, Crocodile?, Claire Freedman

Music/Movement:

"Where Can They Be?"

Sung to: "Baa, Baa, Black Sheep"

Searching, searching, searching for my keys
Look up, look down
Where can they be?
Are they on the ceiling?
Are they on the floor?
Or are they still hanging in
The lock of the door?

Searching, searching, searching for my keys
Which door, which door
In which door can they be?

Crafts:

"The Kitten's Mittens"
Using various colors of construction paper, cut out enough mitten shapes to allow each child to have a matching pair. One method of getting the child more involved in the craft is to give each child only one mitten in the color of his choice. Place the matching mittens in the front of the room or hide them around the room, then allow the children to search for the match.

Now give the children crayons, glitter (if you don't mind the mess), and sticker dots and stars (an all-time favorite with toddlers). Allow them to decorate the mittens to their own taste. Finally, give them string to attach one to the other and hang their creations around their necks.

This can also be a nice decoration to hang on the library or classroom windows.

Source: *101 Easy Art Activities*, Trudy Aarons and Francine Koelsch

Craft and Activity:

"Tide's Out!"
If your school or library is near any seashore coastlines, take your group out to search for the number of hidden sea creatures that inhabit the tide pools in your area. Many marine animals attach themselves to the rocky areas beneath the water. Take a look at those rocky residences with special spy glasses made out of an empty can, plastic wrap, and a rubber band. Once the viewers are created, lower the plastic-wrapped end into the water and the children will have a clear and fantastic view of the creatures below the surface of the water. Everyone can search for the different types of lost items found below the water.

Source: *Awesome Ocean Science!*, Cindy A. Littlefield

Activities:

"Yoga for Children: The Tree"
Get into fitness with this fantastic book on yoga for children. It requires no special athletic skills and is perfect for stretching and warmup exercises for ages 3 and up. You will discover an entire chapter on yoga stances for developing cooperation and trust in children. This particular pose is called "Lost and Found." Have children pair off and face each other with eyes closed. Teams will bring their hands to chest level staying close to their partner's hands but not touching. Can they feel their partner's warmth? Now have them try turning around 3 times then attempt to locate their partner's hands by the sense of warmth they felt before. A variety of motions are suggested here in which the children must feel their partner's presence and energy. There is a wide variety of positions the children will enjoy creating. Lose yourself in the fun of this book.

Source: *Yoga Games for Children*, Danielle Bersma and Marjoke Visscher

Songs:

(Audio) "Where oh Where has my little dog gone?"

Source: *Storytime: 52 Favorite Lullabies, Nursery Rhymes and Whimsical Songs*

24 Behavior: Misbehavior

Topical Calendar Tie-in:

April 30

"National Honesty Day"—Offer children the Honest Abe Awards for being honest and honorable in all things they do each day. Schools and other organizations are encouraged to make honesty a subject for discussion on a regular basis.

Videos:

It's Mine
Miss Nelson is Missing
Peter Rabbit
Pierre: A Cautionary Tale
The Recess Queen
Where the Wild Things Are

Picture Books:

Big Black Bear, Wong Herbert Yee
Contrary Bear, Phyllis Root
Ella and the Naughty Lion, Anne Cottringer
The Grizzly Sisters, Cathy Bellows
How to Lose all your Friends, Nancy Carlson
The Little Green Witch, Barbara Barbieri McGrath
Little Rabbit Goes to School, Harry Horse
Loudest Roar, Thomas Taylor
McDuff's Wild Romp, Rosemary Wells
Naughty Little Monkeys, Jim Aylesworth
The Parrot Tico Tango, Anna Witte
No Biting, Horrible Crocodile!, Jonathan Shipton
Rooter Remembers, Joanne Oppenheim
Rough Tough Rowdy, William H. Hooks
That Terrible Baby, Jennifer Armstrong
This is the Bear and the Bad Little Girl, Sarah Hayes

Music/Movement:

"My Puppy"
Sung to: "My Bonnie Lies over the Ocean"

My puppy chewed up my new sneakers,
(point to sneakers)
My puppy chewed up my new pants.
(point to pants)
My puppy made a puddle in the kitchen.
(hold your nose)
Oh he tries to be good but he can't.
Oh please, oh please,
(put hands together to plead)
Help my new puppy be good, be good.
Oh please, Oh please
Help him learn clothes are not food.

Crafts:

"Monkey Business"

Most children are already familiar with Curious George the curious monkey that's always getting himself in a load of trouble. Talk about George's behavior and how he could have stayed out of trouble then follow it up by making their own swinging monkey out of paper and pipe cleaners, as suggested in this book.

Another point mentioned in this source is how monkeys are treated differently in other areas of the world. This can lead to another great discussion.

Source: *Cut-Paper Play!*, Sandi Henry

"Hit the Piñata!"

Mom says don't hit, so when is it okay? Redirect a child's extra energy into constructive use of hitting and banging. Let children build things with hammers, push stuffing into toys, and create something beautiful to dissipate their anger. Today they can learn that a game, besides baseball, where we can hit with a stick is played with a piñata. Involve the children in building their own piñata using the instructions offered in this book, which also has a wonderfully easy story of its construction that you can read to children. Now let's party!

Source: *Piñata!*, Rebecca Emberley

Activities:

"Bank Robber" or "Grab the Loot"

Here is a great party planner book with an abundance of ideas for children who want to have fun. "Bank Robber" and "Grab the Loot" are two team activities with some delicious loot to be stolen from the opposite team. "Bank Robber" will have the children holding bags of treats to be stolen while "Grab the Loot" locates the loot in the center of the room requiring numbers to be called out for team members to attempt their robbery. The great thing is you get to eat your plundered loot.

Source: *Kid's Outdoor Parties*, Penny Warner

"Because"

Explain the difference to children between lies and stories for entertainment. Be sure they understand the difference before beginning your game. Children will be describing a string of outrageous events that happened to them without explanations as to why it happened. Let the next player in the game explain and so on. Prepare to hear some outlandish stories. Look for suggestions and guidance for this activity in the source book.

Source: *The Big Book of Games*, Dorothy Stott

Songs:

(Audio) "Ants in my Pants"

Source: *Ants in My Pants*

25 Behavior: Sharing

Topical Calendar Tie-in:

March 27

"Education and Sharing Day"—Proclaimed for the last week in March or the first week in April, this day encourages everyone to share ideas. Learn from each other. Designate a time each day during this week for someone in your group to share something from their life and teach others something new.

Videos:

Grandfather's Mitten
Learning to Share (Sesame Street)
The Rainbow Fish
The Story of Jumping Mouse
There's Something in My Attic
Wilfrid Gordon McDonald Partridge

Picture Books:

Ananse's Feast: An Ashanti Tale, Totolwa M. Mollel
Bone Button Borscht, Aubrey Davis
Copy Crocs, David Bedford
Chubbo's Pool, Betsy Lewin
Connie Came to Play, Jill Paton Walsh
Doodle Flute, Daniel Pinkwater
Earthsong, Sally Rogers
Field Trip: A Story About Sharing, Cindy Leaney
Grandpa's Surprise, Rosalind Beardshaw
Just Not the Same, Addie Lacoe
Mrs. Rose's Garden, Elaine Greenstein
One of Each, Mary Ann Hoberman
The Rainbow Fish, Marcus Pfister
Rosie and the Poor Rabbits, Maryann MacDonald
"*That's Not Fair!*," Stephanie Roehe

Music/Movement:

"It's Fun to Work Together"
Source: *1001 Rhymes and Fingerplays*, Totline Staff

Crafts:

"Jigsaw Junk"
Don't throw away those pieces of puzzles. When you are finished with them turn them into a beautiful picture frame. Allow the children to share the photograph of their favorite time with a friend or family member by placing it in a frame made of various puzzle pieces. It's simple and economical, as well as a good lesson in recycling.
Source: *Incredibly Awesome Crafts for Kids*, Sara Jane Treinen (editor)

"Monkey Bank—Job Sharing Jar"
This is a piggy bank craft designed like a monkey face and constructed from a glass jar and paper. It can also be used as a job sharing jar. Stop monkeying around and share the chores with the family. Fill the jar with papers listing jobs the family feels everyone should share. Each day everyone in the family agrees to pull one slip from the jar and do that task for the family.

Activities:

"Beanbag Bop"
Here's a wonderful control mechanism when working with young children in a large group. Have the children sit in a group circling you. As you hold a bean bag toss it to any child in the group who must then respond to whatever question you present to them. This, of course, will necessitate that everyone pay attention since they never know when the bean bag will be coming their way.

Use this as a sharing session. Let the child who receives the bean bag share something of himself with the group.
Source: *The Best of the Mailbox, Book 1: Preschool/ Kindergarten edition*, Margaret Michel

"Lily Pads"
In this everyone's a winner game, children learn to share, cooperate, and have fun. This frog version of musical chairs has each child standing on their own lily pads (newspapers or large lily pads you design). While the music is playing each child hops from one lily pad to the next hoping to be standing on one when the music stops. The child left out when the music stops isn't eliminated but must share a pad with another frog and another lily pad is removed. Of course these lily pads will get very crowded, so children are told they must have at least some portion of their body touching the pad. "Success in this game is working together to get everyone on the last pad so they all can win." Check this book for additional variations to this game.
Source: *Smart Play*, Barbara Sher

Songs:

(Audio) "Share"
Source: *Babysong*, Hap Palmer

26 Behavior: Wishing

Topical Calendar Tie-in:

March 26
"Make Up Your Own Holiday Day"—This is the day you can name anything you want. Design your own holiday around something you have wished for all your life. Have your entire group make their holidays and celebrate them throughout the school year.

Videos:

The Alphabet Dragon
Dr. Seuss' Pontoffel Pock and His Magic Picnic
The Fisherman and His Wife
King Midas and the Golden Touch
Kipper: The Rainbow Puddle
The Little Rabbit Who Wanted Red Wings

Picture Books:

The Big Fish, Klaus Kordon
Emily and the Golden Acorn, Ian Beck
Jubal's Wish, Audrey Wood
The Longest Hair in the World, Lois Duncan
Mama, If You Had a Wish, Jeanne Modesitt
Molly and the Magic Wishbone, Barbara McClintock
Mordant's Wish, Valerie Coursen
Pizza for Breakfast, Maryann Kovalski
Ruby's Wish, Shirin Yim Bridges
Toot and Puddle: Wish You Were Here, Holly Hobbie
Twinkle, Twinkle, Little Star, Iza Trapani
The Wish Come True Cat, Ragnhild Scamell
A Wish for Wings that Work, Berkeley Breathed
The Wishing of Biddy Malone, Joy Cowley
The Witch's Walking Stick, Susan Meddaugh

Music/Movement:

"Sea Star Wish"
Source: *Best of Totline: Volume 2*, Gayle Bittinger

Crafts:

"The Wishing Well"
Use salt or oatmeal boxes to design a wishing well bank. Glue two popsicle sticks to the sides of the box to support a small tilted roof. Glue red paper to the exterior portion of the box, and have the children design the bricks with markers.

Use the newly made bank to save your money for other prizes you may be wishing for at that time.

"Wishing Pin"

Remember all those wishes you made on those chicken or turkey wishbones? This will take some collecting on your part or if you have contacts with parents before Thanksgiving, you can ask parents to save the wishbones to bring in to the class. As a librarian I have a great staff who are willing to collect such items from their families when I have an upcoming program. Talk to your staff. Well, how about keeping them in one piece and making them into a wishing pin that you can wish on for months to come? Here you will locate instructions for drying and polishing the wishbone, along with suggestions for decorating it to become a special wishing pin for your best friend or other loved ones.

Source: *The Never-be-Bored Book*, Judith Logan Lehne

Activities:

"The Wishing Candle"

Place a large candle in the center of a table. Each player should be blindfolded, then spun around three times near the table. The first child who can blow out the wishing candle is the winner.

This activity can precede a discussion of what each child would wish for if he or she were granted one wish. (Caution: This game must be supervised by an adult because of the open flame!)

"Twist a Pretzel"

Let's make a wish. Many people know about the assorted traditions for making wishes, such as blowing out your birthday candle, breaking the turkey wishbone, wish upon a star, or throwing a coin into a fountain and making a wish. You may not know that people used to make wishes with twisted bread, such as pretzels. You were to hook your fingers through the loops, make a silent wish, and pull. Just like the turkey bone, if you got the largest part your wish would come true. A simple recipe to make twisted pretzels is offered here and can be baked within 15 minutes. This could make a nice activity for birthday parties to help guests make their wishes come true.

Source: *Days of Knights and Damsels: An Activity Guide*, Laurie Carlson

Songs:

(Audio) "My Teacher Turned into a Fish"

Source: *Toddlers Next Steps: Silly Songs*

27 Bicycles

Topical Calendar Tie-in:

July 1–23

"Tour de France"—One of the best recreational activities for families is bicycling and one of the great sporting events is the well-known Tour de France, where cyclists compete in many stages across the countryside of France. Hold your own Tour de _______ at your school or library.

Videos:

Curious George Rides a Bike
I'm Safe on Wheels
The Remarkable Riderless Runaway Tricycle

Picture Books:

Annie Flies the Birthday Bike, Crescent Dragonwagon
A Bicycle for Rosaura, Daniel Barbot
Blue Rabbit and the Runaway Wheel, Christopher Wormell
Charles Tarzan McBiddle, Andrew Glass
Don't Let Go!, Jeanne Willis
Duck on a Bike, David Shannon
Franklin's Bicycle Helmet, Paulette Bourgeois and Brenda Clark
Franklin Rides a Bike, Paulette Bourgeois and Brenda Clark
Go-Go-Go!, David Goldin
Grandpa's Surprise, Rosalind Beardshaw
Let's Go Froggy!, Jonathan London
Mike and the Bike, Michael Ward
Mrs. Peachtree's Bicycle, Erica Silverman
Poppleton in Spring, Cynthia Rylant
Supergrandpa, David M. Schwartz
Ugh!, Arthur Yorinks
Vera Rides a Bike, Vera Rosenberry

Music/Movment:

"My Bike"
Source: *The Complete Book of Rhymes, Songs, Poems, Fingerplays and Chants*, Jackie Silberg and Pam Schille

Crafts:

"Wind Wheels"
The wheels on the bike go round and round. Sing a song about wheels with the children and try to name all the things that have wheels. You might even try going outside and rolling hoops around the parking lot. Now let's make our own wind wheels from old plastic lids and attach streamers. While outside let the children run with their wind wheels and watch the streamers fly. Talk about the direction the streamers fly and what causes that.
Source: *The Instant Curriculum*, Pam Schiller and Joan Rossano

"Bicycle Safety Signals"
Make your own personalized safety signals for your bicycle. If you are fortunate enough to own a Pampered Chef can opener this will be a simple craft for your class. Collect old can tops once they are opened. If you've used the special can opener from Pampered Chef you don't have to worry about sharp edges, if not, put tape around the outer edges. Make available to the class puffy paint and glow-in-the-dark paint to decorate their signal that will be taken home to attach to the back of their bike. The children might even wish to put it on their backpacks when walking at night.

Activities:

"Bicycle Safety Course"
With the cooperation of the local police department you might set up a small obstacle course for the children to ride their bicycles through. It should be emphasized to all that this is a safety course and not a racetrack.

You will need to close off a portion of your parking lot for this event and might even want to invite older children to attend. Chalk out a course to be followed by arrows. At various key spots in the course place a stop sign, a small ramp and, if possible, a working traffic light.

Many police departments will send a police officer to speak with the children and will also donate such items as bike reflectors for those children completing the course.

"Zooming Wheels"
Do you have a collection of brave parents? Well this is the activity for you. Gather some very large paper, some poster paints, and some old, small toy cars and trains and let the children create their own wheel painting. Let them run those wheels across the paper after dipping them in paint (or ink). Watch the children's eyes light up at this event and try not to show your dread of the mess. It's a great deal of fun. Look for variations and tips to make this a wonderful experience for all concerned.

Source: *First Art: Art Experiences for Toddlers and Twos*, MaryAnn F. Kohl

Songs:

(Audio): "Ride My Bike"
Source: *I've Got a Yo-Yo*

28 Birds

Topical Calendar Tie-in:

May 13

"International Migratory Bird Day"—This day is set aside internationally to educate people about migratory birds and the methods of preserving their habitats. List the variety of migratory birds and help the children identify them in various ways and offer helpful tips on keeping their little feathered friends safe.

Videos:

Dorothy and the Ostrich
Horton Hatches an Egg
The Little Red Hen
The Most Wonderful Egg in the World
The Ugly Duckling

Picture Books:

A Bird for You: Caring for Your Bird, Susan Blackaby
Condor's Egg, Jonathan London
Ernest and the Bit Itch, Laura T. Barnes
Feathers for Lunch, Lois Ehlert
Fine Feathered Friends, Tish Rabe
Goose, Molly Bang
The House I'll Build for the Wrens, Shirley Neitzel
How the Ostrich Got Its Long Neck, Verna Aardema
Ruby and Bubbles, Rosie Winstead
Mole and the Baby Bird, Marjorie Newman
Silly Suzy Goose, Petr Horacek
Stellaluna, Janell Cannon
The Tree, Felicia Law
Tree of Birds, Susan Meddaugh
What's the Magic Word?, Kelly DiPucchio
Where Did Bunny Go?, Nancy Tafuri

Music/Movement:

"Five Pretty Blue Birds"

Source: *101 Fingerplays, Stories and Songs to use with Finger Puppets*, Diane Briggs

Crafts:

"Winter Bird"

This is a surprisingly simple use of everyday products to create a winter bird scene. I can also see it being easily tweaked to use in the spring seasons. Cut the bottom portion off milk containers for a base (or try saving some of those deep Styrofoam trays from the supermarket). For a winter scene, cotton balls for snow can be used then cover the entire base with plastic wrap. You now have a background scene to glue on stars, a bird and a twig for a branch. Do you want a spring or summer scene? Make a change by simply substituting the cotton balls with twigs the children have collected to form a nest.

Source: *Fun to Make Crafts for Every Day*, Tom Daning (editor)

"Backyard Bird Café"
Help our bird friends keep warm during the winter by adding the fat in their diet they need through these special snacks. Gather those unsalted rice cakes that Mom can't get you to eat, along with peanuts, sunflower seeds (for birds), pumpkin seeds, birdseed, and peanut butter. Now allow the children to make some artistic dinners for their bird friends. Further instructions and other fun-filled activities can be found in this book.
Source: *Go Outside!*, Nancy Blakey

Activities:

"Inuit Clay Bird Game"
Here's a game from the frozen north played by Inuit children. When winter comes and it's too cold to go out, this game will make a delightfully simple pastime. Follow simple directions offered here to create 15 small birds out of air-drying clay. It sounds like it might be complicated but these little birds take only a little rolling and pinching of clay that even the youngest child will be able to accomplish. Now let's play the game. Children sitting in a circle will be shaking and tossing these little birds to the floor and depending on their position when they land get to pick them up again. The child with the most birds in the end will win the game.
Source: *Winter Day Play!*, Nancy F. Castaldo

"Floating Feathers"
This is perfect for playing in rooms with limited space available to you. Can you keep the feather in the air without touching it or it touching you? Find this and other simple games in this source.
Source: *My Party Book*, Marion Elliot

Songs:

(Audio) "Woodpecker"
Source: *Rhythms on Parade*

29 Birds: Ducks

Topical Calendar Tie-in:

August 26–27

"The Great American Duck Race"—Usually held the fourth weekend of August in Deming, New Mexico, this charity event raises money for the Special Olympics and the Sunnyfield Association which provides sheltered workshops for people with disabilities.

Videos:

Angus and the Ducks
Duck for President
Make Way for Ducklings
Mother Duck and the Big Race
The Story of Ping
The Ugly Duckling

Picture Books:

Come Along Daisy!, Jane Simmons
Danny's Duck, June Crebbin
Do Like a Duck Does!, Judy Hindley
Don't Fidget a Feather!, Erica Silverman
Ducks Disappearing, Phyllis Reynolds Naylor
Ducks Like to Swim, Agnes Verboven
Duncan the Dancing Duck, Syd Hoff
Five Little Ducks, Ian Beck
Fix-it Duck, Jez Alborough
It's Quacking Time!, Martin Waddell
Little Quack's Hide and Seek, Lauren Thompson
Quacky Duck, Paul and Emma Rogers
The Surprise Family, Lynn Reiser
Waddle, Waddle, Quack, Quack, Quack, Barbara Anne Skalak
Wow!: It's Great Being a Duck, Joan Rankin

Music/Movement:

"Funny Ducks"
Source: *101 Fingerplays, Stories and Songs to Use with Finger Puppets*, Diane Briggs

Crafts:

"Happy Spring Paper Plate Sign"
Let your spring ducklings announce the arrival of the season. Follow the simple directions for a paper plate duck that will have a "Happy Spring" flower sign hanging below it to announce the coming of a happy season. This fun-filled magazine offers many simple uncomplicated crafts for preschool classes.
Source: *Pack-o-Fun*, April, 2005

"The Ugly Duckling/Swan Puppet"
After enjoying the traditional story of the ugly duckling becoming a beautiful swan, let the children illustrate the tale through this swan puppet. Two paper plates for a body and a tube sock make a great long swan neck. Cover the body with numerous feathers and let the children tell the story again.
Source: *Crafts from Your Favorite Fairy Tale*, Kathy Ross

Activities:

"Duck, Duck, Goose"
Have all the children (any number will work here) crouch in a circle in the center of the room. One child will walk around the perimeter of the circle saying, "Duck, Duck, Duck . . ." until he taps one child and says, "Goose." The "goose" must get up and chase the child around the circle and tag him before he reaches the empty spot left in the circle. If he fails to reach the child in time he must go around the circle again.

For a variation of this game, try asking the children to waddle like a duck around the circle instead of running when trying to catch the goose.

"Feather Relay"
Mark a game area three or four feet across by placing two pieces of string across the floor. Divide teams A and B each in half and line them up behind each string racing their teammates.

Provide one feather to each team. The goal is to get it across the game field to their teammate by blowing on it and not letting it touch the ground. Of course, the first team to have all their team members complete this will win.
Source: *Things to Make and Do for Thanksgiving*, Lorinda Bryan Cauley

Songs:

(Audio) "Ducks Like Rain"
Source: *Rise and Shine*, Raffi

30 Birds: Owls

Topical Calendar Tie-in:

March 14

"First National Bird Reservation in the U.S."—Visit a bird sanctuary and study the bird's life through the molting process, nesting, feeding, and more.

Videos:

The Happy Owls
The Owl and the Pussycat
Owl Moon
Big Owl's Bath (on "Kipper: Water Play)

Picture Books:

The Barn Owls, Tony Johnston
Bear's New Friend, Karma Wilson
Billywise, Judith Nicholls
Hoot, Jane Hissey
Hoot and Holler, Alan Brown
Hush-a-bye Babies, Jane Slingsby
Little Owl, Piers Harper
Little Owl and the Star: A Christmas Story, Mary Murphy
Oliver's Wood, Sue Hendra
Owl Babies, Martin Waddell
The Owl Who Was Afraid of the Dark, Jill Tomlinson
Owliver, Robert Kraus
Sleepy Little Owl, Howard Goldsmith
What Game Shall We Play?, Pat Hutchins
Whoo-oo is it?, Megan McDonald

Music/Movement:

"Mr. Owl"
Source: *Picture Book Activities*, Trish Kuffner

Crafts:

"Envelope Owl Wall Hanging"
Turn a simple envelope into a beautiful wall hanging of this bird of the night. Open all the flaps of an envelope leaving the top one folded down for the head. On the top flap add eyes and beak and have the children draw feet on the lower portion of the envelope. Add feathers by folding brown candy wrappers from boxed candy and giving in layers on the body. For a final touch, cut fringes around the wings and tail feathers (left, right, and bottom flaps).
Source: *Crafts to Make in the Fall*, Kathy Ross

"Wise Old Owl"
A wise old owl gets wise by listening to what goes on around him and asking questions when he needs to know something. Ask the children what question an owl asks *(Whoooooo!)*. Let's turn our class into wise old

owls. This craft requires a paper plate base. Follow the instructions offered by using craft feathers, tempera paints, and construction paper to make a mask that covers the upper portion of the child's face.

Source: *Little Hands Paper Plate Crafts*, Laura Check

Activities:

"Animal Blind Man's Bluff"

This animal rendering of "Blind Man's Bluff" has the blind man blindfolded and standing in the center of a group of animals. Talk about different types of animals like the owl who sees well at night but is almost blind during the day. Your blind man can be the owl who stands with his pointer stick in the center blindfolded as the animals move around. He will need to discover "whoooo" he has selected by a variety of animal clues offered. See this book for engaging clues to the different animals.

Source: *Fun and Games for Family Gatherings*, Adrienne Anderson

"Magic Owl Feathers"

Review with your class the lifestyle of the owl. Along with this explain how birds molt yearly and you might even see their feathers laying around the area where they live. Add to your lesson the "Magic (Owl) Feathers" exercise offered in this wacky activity book. All you will need is a dish pan, feathers, and a large turkey baster. Children will enjoy trying to see how many feathers they can displace using the baster. To them it is magic; later they will understand a little about science.

Source: *101 Easy Wacky Crazy Activities*, Carole H. Dibble and Kathy H. Lee

Songs:

(Audio) "Owl Lullaby"

Source: *Sharon, Lois and Bram Sing A to Z*

31 Birds: Penguins

Topical Calendar Tie-in:

January 14

"Penguin Awareness Day"—This day is celebrated at Jenkinson's Aquarium in New Jersey, to allow children to learn all about the African Penguin families. Set your own day aside to learn about this tuxedoed bird.

Videos:

The Adventures of Scamper the Penguin
Antarctic Antics
The Cold Blooded Penguin
Little Penguin's Tale
The Pebble and the Penguin

Picture Books:

The Emperor Lays an Egg, Brenda Z. Guiberson
The Emperor Penguin's New Clothes, Janet Perlman
The Little Penguin, A.J. Wood
Lost and Found, Oliver Jeffers
A Mother's Journey, Sandra Markle
Penguin and Little Blue, Megan McDonald
Penguin Post, Debi Gliozi
A Penguin Pup for Pinkerton, Steven Kellogg
Penguins!, Gail Gibbons
Quickly, Quigley, Jeanne M. Gravois
Solo, Paul Geraghty
Splash!: A Penguin Counting Book, Jonathan Cheste and Kirsty Melville
Tacky and the Winter Games, Helen Lester
Tacky Locks and the Three Bears, Helen Lester
Tina and the Penguin, Heather Dyer
Your Pet Penguin, Bobbie Hamsa

Music/Movement:

"Penguin Walking All Around"
Source: *Totally Tubeys!*, Priscella Morrow

Crafts:

"Adelie Penguin"
I am a bird. I can't fly but I love to swim. What am I? Our formal-looking penguin friends can be re-created with these uncomplicated instructions by Judy Press. With the use of toilet-paper tubes, white and black paper, markers, and glue we can fashion a version of the penguin that stands on its own.
Source: *At the Zoo! Explore the Animal World with Craft Fun*, Judy Press

"Penguin Pete"
Pack-O-Fun magazine is chock full of wonderful uses of everyday products to make simple creations for young children. This issue illustrates a penguin re-created with the use of old peanut cans covered in black paper.

Add a white stomach area, some google eyes, and an orange beak of construction paper. Feet and black side flippers can be made of craft foam and glued to the figure. You now have a penguin container for many uses. If it's Valentine's Day, the magazine suggests adding candy hearts to the front of the penguin and using the can to carry Valentine cards.

Source: *Pack-O-Fun* magazine, February, 2006

Activities:

"Penguin Race"

Who won the race in the North Pole? Discuss the race to explore the northern regions. Now let's try another type of race, a Penguin Race. Each team should have at least 3 players and are given a ball the same size. Have the children hold the ball between their knees as they try to reach the "North Pole" across the room and back in order to pass the ball to the next player. The actions you will see mimic the moves of penguins.

Source: *Putting on a Party*, Lori Bonner

"Iceberg Thaw"

Here's a cold race with only 2 simple rules. Who can melt their ice cube first without using their mouth and no other help other than the clothing they are wearing. Watch children as they have fun thinking of various ways to get that frigid square to melt. Be sure to have some hot refreshments ready at the end of this event. BRRRRRR!

Source: *Putting on a Party*, Lori Bonner

Songs:

(Audio) "Penguins"

Source: *Rainbow Plane*

32 Birthdays

Topical Calendar Tie-in:

June 27

"Happy Birthday to You"—On this date in 1859, schoolteacher Mildred J. Hill composed the melody to this familiar song. Can you actually have a birthday party for a birthday song? Try it.

Videos:

Happy Birthday Moon
A Letter to Amy
Princess Scargo and the Birthday Pumpkin
Winnie the Pooh and a Day for Eeyore

Picture Books:

Billy's Bucket, Kes Gray
Birthday Blizzard, Bonnie Pryor
The Birthday Doll, Jane Cutler
The Birthday Swap, Loretta Lopez
Creepy-Crawly Birthday, James Howe
Five Little Monkeys Bake a Birthday Cake, Eileen Christelow
Gotcha!, Gail Jorgensen
Happy Birthday, Sam, Pat Hutchins
Henry's Happy Birthday, Holly Keller
Hilda Hen's Happy Birthday, Mary Wormell
If You Give a Pig a Party, Laura Numeroff
A Letter to Amy, Ezra Keats
The Mouse, the Cat and Grandmother's Hat, Nancy Willard
Some Birthday!, Patricia Polacco
What's Cookin'?: A Happy Birthday Counting Book, Nancy Coffelt

Music/Movement:

"My Birthday"

Here are the candles *(hold fingers up)*
Sitting on my cake *(form cake with fist and candles above it)*
It's my favorite I asked my mom to bake
I'll make a wish and blow them out,
(blow at fingers and lower each one as they're blown out)
I'll get that wish I have no doubt.

Crafts:

"Bubble Wrap Paper"

Create your own bubble wrapping paper for birthday presents or other gift times. Use those leftover bubble wrap sheets for more than popping the bubbles. Tape it to the table; paint it with different colors, then pat your paper on top of it to lift of the bubble paint colors. Let it dry and set it aside to wrap your favorite gifts, cover books, or anything you can think of. Helpful hints and seasonal suggestions are offered in this book.

Source: *101 Great Gifts from Kids*, Stephanie R. Mueller and Ann E. Wheeler

"Styroblock Print Invitations"
The Styrofoam trays from various food products are perfect for using with young children when you want to do prints. Children can sketch their own scene for the front of a birthday invitation by pressing lines into the Styrofoam. Add liquid soap (just a drop) to paints and let the children paint over their scene. Gently place it on paper and rub it into the paper. After lifting it off, let your new scene dry before mounting it on the cards.

Source: *I Can Make Art So Easy to Make!*, Mary Wallace

Activities:

"Musical Parcel"
Choose a small prize, such as a chocolate bar or a small toy, and wrap it in layers of tissue or wrapping paper. Have the children sit in a circle and pass the gift around the circle. When the music stops, that child should remove one layer of wrap. Continue until it is completely uncovered. A similar game follows.

"Chinese Fortune Game"
Try this simple activity, similar to the Chinese second birthday celebration. Collect a number of objects such as books, cassettes, pens, computer disks, etc. And place them on a table. Each child is blindfolded and permitted to select an object that will predict his or her future. (Example: A computer disk may indicate a future computer programmer.) This book includes a list of suggestions on games, crafts, and activities from other cultures.

Source: *Happy Birthday Everywhere*, Arlene Erlbach

Songs:

(Audio) "The Unbirthday Song" and "Happy Birthday Waltz"

Source: *Happy Birthday!*

33 Boats/Ships

Topical Calendar Tie-in:

September 16

"Mayflower Day"—This day denotes the anniversary of the departure of the Mayflower from Plymouth, England, heading out to reach Provincetown, Massachusetts. Stories of the rough storms and deprivation passengers encountered make this an excellent history lesson along with a good lesson on planning ahead.

Videos:

The Island of the Skog
The Little Red Lighthouse and the Great Gray Bridge
Little Tim and the Brave Sea Captain
Little Toot

Picture Books:

Alexander and the Magic Boat, Katharine Holabird
Baby's Boat, Jeanne Titherington
Boats, Anne Rockwell
Boats on the River, Peter Mandel
Captain Duck, Jez Alborough
Dinosailors, Deb Lund
Don't Rock the Boat!, Sally Grindley
Emily and the Golden Acorn, Ian Beck
Farmer Enno and His Cow, Jens Rassmus
Funtime Rhymes: On The Water
I Love Boats, Flora McDonnell
I'm Mighty!, Kate and Jim McMullan
Little Bear's Little Boat, Eve Bunting
Louise Builds a Boat, Louise Pfanner
Pigs Ahoy!, David McPhail
Sailboat Lost, Leonard Everett Fisher

Music/Movement:

"Boats Sail On"
Sung to: "This Old Man"

This small boat
It has oars
We must row to get to shore
So lets row, row, row, row
(pretend to row boat while sitting on floor)
Faster let us go.
I just found it has a hole.
(point to hole in bottom of boat)

This old boat.
It has sails
We pull hard to raise these sails,
(show children how to pull rope to raise sails)
And the wind blows hard
The faster we will go
At least this time no one must row.

This big boat
We turn it on.
It doesn't need oars or sails to run

We just turn the key
(pretend turning key to start engine)
And the engine starts to roar
Watch us as we leave the shore.
(Wave to everyone on the shore.)

Crafts:

"Origami Sailboat"
The ancient art of origami is a craft technique without the use of glue or scissors. What a great idea for young children. Unfortunately many of the thousands of dazzling figures that are usually created are too complicated for young children. Here's one that will work with a little patience. The author has you start with a four-inch square to make this fabulous sailboat. Of course you could use an eight-inch version when working with smaller hands. Create your own sailboat and then let the children decorate their boat with crayons and stickers.

Source: *Paper and Paint: Hands-On Crafts for Everyday Fun*, Phillip C. McGraw and Vincent Douglas

"Bath Craft"
Don't throw away those individual plastic soda bottles. Those bottles will make a perfect catamaran for you little girl's Barbie dolls or your young boy's action figures. Cut oval seat openings in each bottle in preparation or the program. Distribute the bottles to each child and allow them to decorate the bottles with paint or stickers and set them to dry. Suggestions for banding your boats together are offered in this source. Supply a small children's swimming pool for the children to test their new boats. You might suggest that they bring a small doll or toy no larger than Barbie to the program so they can actually launch them that day. This is an ideal toy to make bath time fun once more.

Source: *Family Fun Boredom Busters*, Deanna F. Cook (editor)

Activities:

"Rocking Boat"
While singing the song indicated below or "Row the Boat," children can pair up. Have two children sit on the floor facing each other. Legs should be spread with feet touching their partner's feet. They may then rock back and forth as a boat would rock. An alternate version can be having the children pretend to row oars and move themselves around the room as if rowing down the river.

"Lifeboat"
This is a nice twist on the familiar game of musical chairs. With the usual circle of chairs and some nautical music, you can begin the game. Instead of halting the music as a signal to rush for a chair, children wait to hear the captain yell, "To the lifeboats!" This is a fun, simple addition to any party with a seafaring theme. Try having the children dress the part as well.

Source: *Putting on a Baby*, Lori Bonner

Songs:

(Audio) "A Sailor Went to Sea"

Source: *Playtime Favorites*

34 Careers: Dentist/Teeth

Topical Calendar Tie-in:

June 2

"I Love My Dentist Day"—This is a day for going to the dentist to get and maintain a happy, healthy smile. Find a way to thank the dentist, who helps you keep those teeth looking nice.

Videos:

Dr. DeSoto
George Washington's Teeth
Goofy over Dental Health
The Toothbrush Family: A Visit from the Tooth Fairy

Picture Books:

Calico Cat's Sunny Smile, Donald Charles
Clarabella's Teeth, Ann Vrombaut
Dear Tooth Fairy, Pamela Duncan Edwards
Dr. DeSoto Goes to Africa, William Steig
Dr. Kranner, Dentist with a Smile, Alice K. Flanagon
Freddie Visits the Dentist, Nicola Smee
Grandpa's Teeth, Rod Clement
Harry and the Dinosaurs Say "Raahh!," Ian Whybrow
I Have a Loose Tooth, Sally Noll
Loose Tooth, Lola M. Schaefer
Milo's Toothache, Ida Luttrell
Tooth Fairy's First Night, Anne Bowen
Vera Goes to the Dentist, Vera Rosenberry
What Does a Dentist Do?, Heather Miller

Music/Movement:

"The Dentist"

Sung to: "The Farmer in the Dell"

The dentist cleans my teeth.
The dentist cleans my teeth.
He scrubs them clean
I rinse them out
We make a real great team.

Crafts:

"My Tooth Pouch"

Using felt, have the children trace and cut out two forms of a tooth. They may then glue eyes on that are easily obtainable at any craft store and put a smile on with markers.

Have the children glue the sides of the tooth together, leaving the upper portion open. (Use fabric glue that can be purchased at a craft store.)

The children now own their own tooth holder, where they may place their tooth and put under their pillow. The tooth fairy may exchange the tooth for money in the pouch later.

"Toothpaste Airplane"
This imaginative craft can be used as a vehicle to begin a lesson on transportation or a classroom discussion on brushing your teeth. A special pattern is made available to check the dimensions of your toothpaste box to ensure that it will work. Patterns are also made available for your propellers, wings, etc.

Let the children use this new airplane to store their own personal toothpaste for brushing each day.

Source: *Rainy Day Projects for Children*, Gerri Jenny and Sherrie Gould

Activities:

"Good Nutrition"
Prepare flashcards or flannel board pictures of different types of foods. Discuss good nutrition and have the children pick out what foods help to make happy teeth.

You might also be able to borrow a dentist's teeth mold to illustrate proper brushing methods. If this is not available to you, try getting a dentist's aide to visit your group to talk to the children.

"Toothbrush Painting"
Cut out large forms of a tooth for each child. Using white tempera paint as toothpaste, have the children practice the proper method of brushing. Dentists can be encouraged to donate real toothbrushes for this activity.

Songs:

(Audio) "Tiger with a Toothbrush"
Source: *We're on Our Way*
"Brush Your Teeth"
Source: *Singable Songs for the Very Young*

35 Careers: Firefighters

Topical Calendar Tie-in:

October 8

"Great Chicago Fire Anniversary"—According to legend, Mrs. O'Leary's cow kicked over the lantern in her barn to start the great Chicago fire that burned three and a half square miles of the city. Use this anniversary to discuss with children the importance of fire safety around their family as well as around animals.

Videos:

Curious George
Dot the Fire Dog
Draghetto
Firehouse Dog
Helpful Little Fireman
Hercules

Picture Books:

Daisy the Firecow, Viki Woodworth
Even Firefighters Hug Their Moms, Christine Kole Maclean
Fighting Fires, Susan Kuklin
Firebears: The Rescue Team, Rhonda Gowler Greene
Firefighters, Norma Simon
Firefighters A to Z, Chris L. DeMarest
Firefighters to the Rescue!, Kersten Hamilton
The Firefighters' Thanksgiving, Maribeth Boelts
Firehouse Dog, Amy and Richard Hutchings
Fireman Small, Wong Herbert Yee
Fireman Small: Fire Down Below!, Wong Herbert Yee
Fire Stations, Jason Cooper
Fire Trucks, Hope Irvin Marston
Hello, Fire Truck!, Marjorie Blain Parker
Protecting Your Home, Ann Owen
Three Little Firefighters, Stuart J. Murphy

Music/Movement:

"The Brave Firefighters"
Source: *Little Hands Fingerplays and Action Songs*, Emily Stetson and Vicky Congdon

Crafts:

"Rescue Ladder for Beanbag Animals"
Build your fireman's rescue latter out of two yardsticks and a collection of Popsicle sticks. Be sure to keep the spaces between steps wide enough that your beanbag animals can poke through. Allow the children to decorate their ladder with crayons, markers, and stickers. Your animals can climb up to the top of a chair on your ladder to make their rescue and the ladder can also be used as a storage area for your beanbag animals.
Source: *The Absolute Best Play Days: From Airplanes to Zoos (and Everything in Between!)*, Pamela Waterman

"Firefighter's Hat and Ax"

Many children get great enjoyment pretending to be the firemen they see every day on television or in their neighborhood. The source below gives instructions on how to make such things as hats and axes out of cardboard tubes and construction paper. There are many items related to firefighters than can be made with the use of paper and boxes. Instructions are also available for a fire hose, fire extinguisher, fire alarm box, a fire hydrant, an oxygen tank and mask to create an entire unit. Note: You can have the children practice using their ax to break doors and save their friends by using newspaper strung between chairs for walls and doors. Children will enjoy smashing through to save the day.

Source: *Be What You Want to Be!*, Phyllis and Noel Fiarotta

Activities:

"Firefighter Relay Races"

"Fire, Fire, call the fire department!" Here's the chance for young children to become the firemen that they admire so much. This game is a water relay race that has each team trying to put out their pretend fire before the other team. Red and orange paper flames are used to illustrate the flames on empty bins. Set up special alarms to get this game going. You might even want to dress for the part.

Source: *It's Great to Be Three: The Encyclopedia of Activities for Three-Year Olds*, Kathy Charmer and Maureen Murphy (editors)

"Occupational Musical Chairs"

Musical chairs is a game well known to us all. Tape a picture depicting a different occupation to each chair and begin the music. When it ends let the child without a chair select one and tell the class about the occupation he sees depicted. Once this is done have him remove the chair and begin again.

Source: *The Giant Encyclopedia of Circle Time and Group Activities for Children 3 to 6*, Kathy Charner

Songs:

(Audio) "I Want to Be a Fireman"

Source: *My Favorite Kidsongs Collection #3*

36 Careers: Letter Carriers/Post Office

Topical Calendar Tie-in:

January 8–14

"Universal Letter Writing Week"—Start the New Year off with a letter-writing campaign to friends, new and old, all around the world. This is a good time to start that special pen pal program that keeps everyone in touch with life in other cultures or countries.

Videos:

The Mail Song (Barney's: You can be Anything)
Postman Pat

Picture Books:

Delivering Your Mail, Ann Owen
Good-bye, Curtis, Kevin Henkes
Hail to Mail, Samuel Marshak
Here Comes the Mail, Gloria Skurzynski
In My Neighborhood: Postal Workers, Paulette Bourgeois
Larabee, Kevin Luthardt
Pink Magic, Donna Jo Napoli
Penguin Post, Debi Gliori
The Postman's Palace, Adrian Henri and Simon Henwood
Snowshoe Thompson, Nancy Smiler Levinson
Somebody Loves You, Mr. Hatch, Eileen Spinelli
To the Post Office with Mama, Sue Farrell
Toddle Creek Post Office, Uri Shulevitz
Tortoise Brings the Mail, Dee Lillegard
What Does a Mail Carrier Do?, Lisa Trombauer

Music/Movement:

"The Mail Carrier"
Source: *1001 Rhymes and Fingerplays*, Totline Staff

Crafts:

"Pop-Up Cards"
After a discussion of the various items that a mail carrier delivers to the child's home, it's time to create some of these items. Greeting cards are something the children always remember receiving. This source gives samples of various pop-up cards children can create for their friends and family members.
Source: *Incredibly Awesome Crafts for Kids*, Sara Jane Treinen

"Valentine Mail Vest"
On Valentine's Day children give and receive cards. Try having them delivered by a special mail carrier wearing a mail vest to carry the cards. This simple vest is constructed from brown grocery bags with a special pocket in the front to hold the mail. Although this source illustrates the vest for a Valentine celebration it can easily be adapted for a discussion on careers, specifically on mail carriers.
Source: *Crafts for Valentine's Day*, Kathy Ross

Activities:

"Musical Envelopes"

Everyone enjoys getting mail and children love it most of all. Let's deliver those envelopes with a familiar game titled "Musical Envelopes." Prepare 6 to 8 envelopes, each having inside them a different stunt, penalty or pantomime that the holder will have to perform. The object of the game is to discover who will "pay the Piper" or have to perform their stunt. As the children sit in a circle, begin passing one envelope around when the music begins. When the music stops, whoever is holding the envelope keeps it and the music resumes with the next envelope passing around. Continue until all envelopes have been delivered, at which time anyone holding an envelope must stand one at a time and follow the instructions given to them in the envelope. Miss Campbell's book also offers an adaptation of this game which includes letters and a gift for a party member.

Source: *Perfect Party Games*, Andrea Campbell

"Fruit Flavored Stamps"

After playing such a fun game as "Musical Letters" you will need to explain to children that letters of course cannot be mailed without stamps. Today we will be making our own pretend fruit-flavored stamps to put on envelopes that we will deliver to friends and family. You will need fruit-flavored gelatin and hot water to make the flavored glue for your stamps. Children might cut out glossy pictures from magazines to create their stamps. Follow the simple measurements supplied in this book and the children will enjoy licking those stamps and sending things to friends.

Source: *The Mudpies Activity Book: Recipes for Invention*, Nancy Blakey

Songs:

(Audio) "The Mail Must Go Through"

Source: *Disney's Children's Favorites, Vol. 1*

37 Careers: Police Officers

Topical Calendar Tie-in:

May 19

"National Children and Police Day"—This special day has been set aside for the express purpose of giving children a chance to say "thank you" to the police officers who have helped them and an opportunity for police officers to build a friendly relationship with schoolchildren.

Videos:

Make Way for Ducklings
Officer Buckle and Gloria
The Police Station
Sergeant Murphy's Day Off
I Wanna Be a Police Officer

Picture Books:

Aero and Officer Mike: Police Partners, Joan Plummer Russell
In My Neighborhood: Police Officers, Paulette Bourgeois
I Want to be a Police Officer, Dan Liebman
Jess and the Stinky Cowboys, Janice Lee Smith
Keeping You Safe: A Book About Police Officers, Ann Owen
My Dog is Lost!, Ezra Keats
Officer Brown Keeps Neighborhoods Safe, Alice K. Flanagan
Officer Buckle and Gloria, Peggy Rathmann
Police Cat, Enid Hinkes
Police Dogs, Frances E. Ruffin
Police Officers Protect People, Carol Greene
Police Patrol, Katherine K. Winkleman
Police Stations, Jason Cooper
Sammy, Dog Detective, Colleen Stanley Bare
Sherman Crunchley, Laura Numeroff and Nate Evans

Music/Movement:

"I'm a Police Officer"
Sung to: "I'm a Little Teapot"
Source: *Little Hands Fingerplays and Action Songs*, Emily Stetson and Vicky Congdon

Crafts:

"Police Officer Hat"
This paper plate version of a police officer's hat requires no cutting at all. You will need two paper plates, a stapler, and glue. While the folding procedure for this craft is above preschool children some of the older children might like to attempt it with some guidance. Step-by-step directions are offered and result in a wonderful hat. Younger children should be encouraged to paint or color the paper plates first and perhaps make an insignia to go on the front of the hat.
Source: *Little Hands Paper Plate Crafts*, Laura Check

"Career Dominoes"
For career day or any other time you are working on your community helpers unit you will find this craft a fun way to pull the unit together. Supply the children with precut cardboard dominoes approximately four inches by six inches with the two sections already marked off. Ask them to look through magazines and cut out illustrations of the different types of careers you have discussed together along with pictures of items those professionals would need to do their work (badge, gun, etc.). Have them paste their pictures randomly on the domino pieces. I would then laminate them so they would last longer. Now you are ready to play an amusing game of "Career Dominoes" and see how much the children really remember from the lesson.

Activities:

"Prisoner's Base"
This game is over 600 years old. Popular in England, it was banned by Edward III because it was so popular it became bothersome. It's a form of tag that can be played on a playground or large room area. Corners of the room are sectioned off for home bases and prisons for each team. Designate the first players out to be the police and the others the criminals to be captured. As more players enter the field it can get crowded and hilarious. Check this great game book for rules of play.

Source: *Run, Jump, Hide, Slide, Splash: The 200 Best Outdoor Games Ever*, Joe Rhatigan and Rain Newcome

"Police Safety Program"
Invite the local police department to send a representative to speak to the children about their job and to encourage the children to look to the police for help when they need it. The local police departments can usually be counted on to speak to parents and children at programs on the following topics:

- Strangers
- Bicycle and Traffic Safety
- Dangers of Drugs
- Fingerprinting of Children

Songs:

(Audio) "Mr. Policeman"

Source: *My Favorite Kidsongs Collection #3*

38 Character Traits: Cleanliness

Topical Calendar Tie-in:

May 26–April 1
"National Cleaning Week"—This week serves as a reminder to do your spring cleaning. Set a separate day aside to work on a specific task. Let's all do our share!

Videos:

Alexandria's Clean-up, Fix-up Parade
The Berenstain Bears and the Messy Room
Clean Your Room, Harvey Moon
Franklin is Messy
Harry the Dirty Dog
Keeping House
I Stink!

Picture Books:

The Backwards Watch, Eric Houghton
Bernard's Bath, Joan Elizabeth Goodman
Big Red Tub, Julia Jarman
Casey in the Bath, Cynthia DeFelice
Clean Your Room, Harvey Moon!, Pat Cummings
The Dirty Little Boy, Margaret Wise Brown
Fritz and the Mess Fairy, Rosemary Wells
Messy Bessey's School Desk, Patricia and Frederick McKissack
Mr. Blewitts Nose, Alastair Taylor
Mrs. McBloom, Clean Up Your Classroom, Kelly DiPucchio
Mrs. Potter's Pig, Phyllis Root
No More Water in the Tub!, Tedd Arnold
Pigsty, Mark Teague
The Raggly, Scraggly, No-Soap, No-Scrub Girl, David F. Birchman
Soap and Suds, Diane Paterson
Tidy Titch, Pat Hutchins
To the Tub, Peggy Perry Anderson
Tumble Tower, Anne Tyler
When the Fly Flew in . . ., Lisa Westberg Peters

Music/Movement:

"Rub-a-Dub-Dub"
A nice variation on the song with a child in the bathtub washing up for the night.
Source: *Storytimes for Two-year-olds, 2nd edition*, Judy Nichols

Crafts:

"Bath Powder"
Let Mom finish off her bathtime experience with this specially prepared bath powder made by her child. You will find here a recipe for this bath powder using cornstarch and perfume oil that gives is a special "feel" and an aroma that is pleasing. Provide a variety of oils so that the children

may pick out the aroma that they believe suits their mother. Put the final product in a salt shaker and decorate the container.

Source: *The Mudpies Activity Book: Recipes for Invention*, Nancy Blakey

"Octopus Duster"

Make cleaning fun with this duster made from old tub socks. Follow these simple directions to decorate the sock to resemble an octopus that can clean the dust from your toys or electrical appliances.

Source: *101 Great Gifts from Kids*, Stephanie R. Mueller and Ann E. Wheeler

Activities:

"Bathtime Memory Game"

Try a familiar memory game with the children. Collect a number of items that would be easily recognizable to the children from their bathtime experiences. Display them and discuss their uses. Follow this with a little memory exercise by removing one or more objects, ask the children to open their eyes and identify the missing objects and their use.

Source: *More Picture Book Story Hours: From Parties to Pets*, Paula Gaj Sitarz

"Clothespin Fumble"

Try this game that might keep children in training to help them hang the clean clothes for Mom. It requires a little dexterity, especially when the child is blindfolded. With a clothesline spread across the room let the blindfolded child take a clothespin and try to put it on the clothesline with the use of only one hand.

Source: *Making Children's Parties Click*, Virginia W. Musselman

Songs:

(Audio) "Clean it Up"

Source: *Buzz Buzz*

"Everybody Wash"

Source: *Splish Splash Bath Time Fun*

39 Character Traits: Helpfulness

Topical Calendar Tie-in:

January 17

"Customer Service Day"—Here's a day to exhibit the best we have to offer. Whether you are a helper in your classroom or just selling lemonade at your home stand, now is the time to learn how to be helpful and make your friends and customers happy. Help a friend today.

Videos:

Alexandria's Clean-up, Fix-up Parade
Dragon Tales: Let's Work Together
The Elves and the Shoemaker
Horton Hatches an Egg
The Little Red Hen
Lyle, Lyle Crocodile

Picture Books:

Big Help!, Anna Grossnickle Hines
Bunny Tails, Barbara Brenner, William Hooks and Betty Boegehold
Can I Help?, Marilyn Janovitz
Chestnut Cove, Tim Egan
Dad, Aren't You Glad?, Lynn Plourde
The Farmer in the Dell, John O'Brien
Helpful Betty to the Rescue, Michaela Morgan
Helpin' Bugs, Rosemary Lonborg
Hopper's Treetop Adventure, Marcus Pfister
Is Susan Here?, Janice May Udry
Mrs. McBloom, Clean Up Your Classroom, Kelly DiPucchio
One Duck Stuck, Phyllis Root
One Up, One Down, Carol Snyder
A Really Good Snowman, Daniel J. Mahoney
You and Me, Little Bear, Martin Waddell

Music/Movement:

"Humpty's New Ears"
Source: *The Complete Resource Book for Toddlers and Twos*, Pam Schiller

Crafts:

"Helpful Hand Magnet"
Children can enjoy helping with chores at home if it's approached correctly. Make a game out of the event or let them suggest how they think they can help by making their own chore chart and leave a section next to each chore where a parent can place a sticker when the chore is accomplished. This chart can be hung on the refrigerator with a very special "Helpful Hand Magnet" made by the children themselves. Trace or copy on a copy machine the child's hand and reinforce the paper by laminating it. Distribute macaroni craft letters to help the children glue on the message "I can help." Add a magnet to the back and hang your chart and magnet on the refrigerator.
Source: *The Big Book of Christian Crafts*, Kathy Ross

"Helping Hands Napkin Holder"
Napkin holders are always something Mom can use with pride to the delight of her child. Use the base of a box for the stand. Children can trace their hand out of beautifully designed material for the sides. At every mealtime the child can set the table with a sure sign that he helped with his own hands, seen holding the napkins.

Source: *Gifts to Make for Your Favorite Grown-up*, Kathy Ross

Activities:

"Laundry Matching"
Young children enjoy being included in activities that adults do as part of their everyday workload. Here's a chance for parents at home to get help with the laundry and for teachers and librarians to introduce children to responsibility, classifying objects, and recognizing likenesses and differences. Gather a basketful of clothes of all types. Try including some really goofy-looking outfits for humor. A few variations on how to match clothes (going into the wash, by size, by color, etc.) are offered in this book source. You might even try a matching and sorting game by teams where each team must correctly match items by color *and* get them onto one of their teammates before the other team.

Source: *Mister Rogers' Playtime*, Fred Rogers

"Family Chores"
Initiate a discussion among the children about different types of chores that family members are responsible for in their home. Be sure to steer children into including nontraditional roles in the family (Dad babysits, Mom does plumbing, etc.).

After the discussion begin a pantomime session where children mimic these chores for the class to guess. An excellent list of suggestions is supplied in the book cited here.

Source: *More Picture Book Story Hours: From Parties to Pets*, Paula Gaj Sitarz

Songs:

(Audio) "The More we are Together"

Source: *Toddlers Sing 'N Learn*

40 Character Traits: Kindness

Topical Calendar Tie-in:

February 6
"Pay-a-Compliment Day"—Try the most basic act of kindness and pay a compliment to a friend today. Better yet, try paying a compliment to someone who has given you a difficult time. Set this day aside to mend friendships and start new ones. Try to teach children the "Golden Rule."

Videos:

Alejandro's Gifts
Andy and the Lion
Horton Hatches an Egg
Mufaro's Beautiful Daughter
The Story of Jumping Mouse

Picture Books:

Because of You, B.G. Hennesy
The Best Night Out with Dad, Lisa McCourt
Eddie's Kingdom, D.B. Johnson
Glenna's Seeds, Nancy Edwards
How Kind!, Mary Murphy
I'm Gonna Like Me, Jamie Lee Curtis and Laura Curnell
Mr. Wolf's Pancakes, Jan Fearnley
One Snowy Night, M. Christina Butler
Piggy and Dad Go Fishing, David Martin
Red Hen and Sly Fox, Vivian French
Sam and the Lucky Money, Karen Chinn
The Spiffiest Giant in Town, Julia Donaldson
Three Good Blankets, Ida Luttrell
Three Kind Mice, Vivian Sathie
Tree of Birds, Susan Meddaugh

Music/Movement:

"Friends"
Source: *Songs, Poems, and Fingerplays: Preschool/Kindergarten*, Ada Goren and Allison E. Ward (editors)

Crafts:

"Friendship Light Catcher"
Kindness, caring, and friendship are characteristics that can be discussed during "Random Act of Kindness Week." This craft can make a nice addition to the lesson. Let each child trace their friend's hand on paper. After cutting out the shapes, cross the hand shapes so the fingers look like they are holding each other and color in the shapes made by the fingers crossing each other. With Ms. Hauser's secret liquid ingredient you can turn this into a light catcher. When the result is taped to a window the light will create a wonderful light catcher and spread the word of fairness and brotherhood. Check this book for that everyday special touch.
Source: *Little Hands Celebrate America!*, Jill Frankel Hauser

"Certificates of Kindness"
After a discussion on what services the children can perform to be kind and helpful to their parents, try creating a certificate booklet. Let the children select two or three services they would like to do for their parents (sweep the floor, make a bed, help dad wash the car, etc.). Distribute drawing paper and crayons to the children and allow them to draw themselves doing chores for their parents. Because of the age of the children you will have to write the accompanying phrase describing the pictures (Examples: wash the dishes, make my bed).

After each is done, design a cover and staple the coupons together along with a note to the parents:

Dear Mom and Dad:
You always help me with so many things. Now it's my turn. Here are some coupons for you to use when you need help. Pick the one you need help with, and give it to me. I promise to help you then.
Love,

Activities:

"Love Your Neighbor"
This is a standard circle game with the person who is "It" in the center. Player One (It) will approach someone in the circle and ask the question "Do you love your neighbor?" If the person asked says "yes," the players on either side of him must try to switch places with Player One, who will also try to take one of those empty spaces. The person left with no place to go becomes the new Player One. If the person asked replies, "No," then he is asked whom he does love, which requires some kind of reply such as, "Anyone with blue eyes," "Anyone who loves soccer," etc. Pandemonium occurs as everyone whom this refers to must find a new spot in the circle. Remind all children that no comments are to be made that are unkind.
Source: *Win-Win Games for All Ages*, Josette and B. Luvmour

"Used Dryer Sheets Flower Sachet"
Mom takes care of us, takes us to fun places and cleans our house. Now it's time to do something special for Mom. Have children gather those leftover dryer sheets after their moms finish drying the clothes to make special scented flower sachets. After presenting these to their moms in a specially designed bowl, they can surprise them with the best part of the gift. Kathy Ross let's us know that we can use these to shine chrome appliances in the kitchen.
Source: *All New Crafts for Earth Day*, Kathy Ross

Songs:

(Audio) "Little Cabin in the Wood"
Source: *Wee Sing: Children's Songs and Fingerplays*

41 Character Traits: Laziness

Topical Calendar Tie-in:

March 22
"International Goof-off Day"—Here's a day for some good-natured laziness and silliness. Take time for you to be pampered. Take this day to accomplish nothing, no tests, no lessons, nothing except maybe a little fun and relaxation that everyone needs once in a while.

Videos:

The Ant and the Grasshopper
Horton Hatches an Egg
The Little Red Hen
Rip Van Winkle
Tops and Bottoms

Picture Books:

Famous Seaweed Soup, Antoinette Truglio Martin
How Leo Learned to Be King, Marcus Pfister
Jamie O'Rourke and the Big Potato, Tomie dePaola
Lazy Lion, Mwenye Hadithi
The Lazy Scarecrow, Jillian Powell
Lizard's Guest, George Shannon
The Man Who Was Too Lazy to Fix Things, Phyllis Krasilovsky
The Pixy and the Lazy Housewife, Mary Calhoun
Poof!, John O'Brien
Roses Sing on New Snow: A Delicious Tale, Paul Yee
Slobcat, Paul Geraghty
Tommy DoLittle, John A. Rowe
Tom's Tail, Arlene Dubanevich
The Very Sleepy Sloth, Andrew Murray

Music/Movement:

"The Funny, Fat Walrus"
Source: *Too Many Rabbits and other Fingerplays*, Kay Cooper

Crafts:

"Wacky Door Decree"
Are you feeling a little lazy and want to be alone? Make yourself this wacky doorknob hanger to keep people away. Some suggested messages are offered in this delightful craft book. Clip letters from newspapers or magazines for variety.
Source: *60 Super Simple Crafts*, Holly Herbert

"Jumping Grasshopper"
The class can use this source to make a familiar lazy character from the story *The Grasshopper and the Ant*. The grasshopper is constructed from half of an egg carton and a rubber ball placed inside it to help it hop across the room. This is a nice craft to do in conjunction with this favorite fairy tale.
Source: *Crafts for Kids Who are Wild about Insects*, Kathy Ross

Activities:

"Fast Brains"

Are you the hare or the tortoise? While your body could be the lazy tortoise your brain is as lightning quick as the hare. On a warm day when your class seems too lazy to learn, don't give up. Take them outside and test the "speed of their brains," senses, and reactions with activities such as "Wobble test," "Eyeball," and "Quick Reactions." These blindfold activities will be enjoyed by all!

Source: *Science Fun at Home*, Chris Maynard

"Sleeping Bag Ball"

Here's the height of laziness in ball games. Try this event at your next bedtime program. Let the children bring their sleeping bags and try to play catch with a ball and the edge of their sleeping bag. Don't bother to get up. It's against the rules. Other lazy events are offered here too. In addition to the ones offered in this book try other games in a lazy manner. Try basketball from a seated position or Frisbee with a string attached to reel it back. What other lazy events can you think of today?

Source: *Perfect Kids' Parties*, Karen Famini, Karen Large, Vicky Shiotsu, and Rozanne Lanczak Williams

Songs:

(Audio) "Lazy Mary Will You Get Up?"

Source: *Morning Magic*, Joanie Bartels

42 Circus and Circus Animals

Topical Calendar Tie-in:

July 31–August 5

"National Clown Week"—The first week in August has been appointed a time to celebrate the humor of the circus clown. Trace the career of Emmett Kelley, a well-known professional clown, and the diverse styles of clown characters throughout history. Let the children develop their own clown styles through makeup and costume.

Videos:

Circus Baby
Curious George Rides a Bike
If I Ran the Circus
Kipper's Circus (on "Kipper: Imagine That)

Picture Books:

Barnyard Big Top, Jill Kastner
The Best Night Out with Dad, Lisa McCourt
The Circus, Heidi Goennel
Circus Caps for Sale, Esphyr Slobodkina
Circus Parade, Harriet Ziefert
Circus Train, Jos A. Smith
Dr. Seuss's All Aboard the Circus McGurkus!, Dr. Seuss
Engelbert Joins the Circus, Tom Paxton
Henrietta Saves the Show, John Prater
Little Monkey Says Good Night, Ann Whitford Paul
Liverwurst is Missing, Mercer Mayer
My Mother's Secret Life, Rebecca Emberley
You See a Circus, I See . . ., Mike Downs
Zorina Ballerina, Enzo Giannini

Music/Movement:

"Let's Head to the Circus"
Sung to: "London Bridge"

The circus train is coming to town,
Coming to town, coming to town.
The circus train is coming to town.
Let's have some fun!

The circus clowns jump and fall,
spray some water, make some noise.
The circus clowns make me laugh.
Let's have some fun!

The elephants march side to side,
Side to side, side to side.
The elephants trumpet loud and clear.
Let's have some fun!

(Repeat first verse)

Crafts:

"Dancing Clown"
Precut pieces are suggested for this craft. Pages 46 and 47 of the source book can be copied on a copy machine to help make patterns for each of these pieces. A bright and amusing clown can be constructed out of inexpensive materials such as construction paper, tape, markers, glue, and rubber bands. The source below will give you full instructions along with a full-page, color illustration of how your final product should look. The hands and shoes are connected to the body with rubber bands. A rubber band is also attached to the top of the hat so that you can bounce the clown up and down. I suggest that the top rubber band be connected to a stick for easier handling.

Source: *Rainy Day Surprises You Can Make*, Robyn Supraner

"Clown Wall Pocket"
A decorative wall hanging for a child to keep his special mementos can be constructed by following the step-by-step illustrations in this source. All that is required is paper plates, crayons, glue, and colored construction paper. An additional page is supplied with nine clown face pictures that can be enlarged and displayed as examples for the children to follow.

Source: *Paper Plate Art*, Maxine Kinney

Activities:

"Elephant, Elephant, LION!!!!"
Try this adapted version of the familiar game of "Duck, Duck, Goose." The children will softly say elephant but of course will yell "LION" and hope the lion cannot catch them and eat them before they go around the circus tent (children in the circle) to get to the empty space left by the lion.

"Pin the Nose on the Clowns"
This is a new twist on an old party game. Make your own party game but give the children five chances to be a winner. "Pin the Tail on the Donkey" becomes now "Pin the Nose on the Clowns" when five paper plates are designed as various clown faces and used for targets on a single wall. Have the children help you create the faces for their own circus celebration.

Source: *Cups and Cans and Paper Plate Fans*, Phyllis Fiarotta and Noel Fiarotta

Songs:

(Audio) "The Circus is Coming to Town"

Source: *My Favorite Kidsongs Collection #1*

43 Clocks/Telling Time

Topical Calendar Tie-in:

December 29

"Tick Tock Day"—We always say we will get around to it someday. This day is to remind you that time does run out. Teach people to schedule their time and not procrastinate. The clock is running. Try teaching children time management through timed contest events reminding them that that clock is ticking!

Videos:

Dorothy and the Clock
Rock and Learn: Telling Time
Telling Time
Tick-Tock: All About the Clock

Picture Books:

The Backwards Watch, Eric Houghton
Brown Rabbit's Day, Alan Baker
Cluck O'Clock, Kes Gray
The Completed Hickory Dickory Dock, Jim Aylesworth
Game Time, Stuart J. Murphy
Get Up and Go!, Stuart J. Murphy
It's About Time!, Stuart J. Murphy
I.Q. It's Time, Mary Ann Fraser
Lunchroom Lizard, Daniel Kirk
Mouse Tells the Time, Nicola Moon
There's a Cow in the Road, Reeve Lindbergh
The Snowman Clock Book, Raymond Briggs
Telling Time with Big Mama Cat, Dan Harper
Tell the Time with Thomas, Christopher Awdry
Tuesday, David Wiesner
What Time Is It, Dracula?, Victor Ambros

Music/Movement:

"Hickory Dickory Dock"
Source: *Playtime Rhymes*, Priscilla Lamont (illustrator)

Crafts:

"Cookie Sheet Clock"
Using Styrofoam trays from fruit or vegetables and cookie sheets children can create their own clock to learn to tell time. Use it for lessons on time, as well as reminding children when something needs to be done. Look for more fun ideas in this great source.
Source: *Creative Fun for 2-to-6 Year Olds: The Little Hands Big Fun Craft Book*, Judy Press

"Tell the Time by the Sun"
Discuss the many ways we can tell time, including the use of a sundial. Make your own sundial out of yellow poster board so it looks like the

sun. Cut out a triangle from a three-inch square and paste it standing up on the face of the sundial. To make it into a clock draw a line at the edge of the shadow on the clock as each hour passes.

Source: *The Ultimate Show-Me-How Activity Book*

Activities:

"What's the Time, Mr. Wolf?"

Indicate a safe area for the children. One child is selected to be the wolf standing with his back to the others. While he wanders through the room, the other children follow closely, teasing him by asking, "What's the time, Mr. Wolf?" He may say any number of times until he suddenly turns stating "dinnertime." The children scatter hoping to get home safely before being tagged. Other variations are also offered.

Source: *The Picture Rulebook of Kids' Games*, Roxanne Henderson

"Tick Tock"

After hiding a ticking alarm clock somewhere in the room the children are instructed to locate it. They may begin when you say, "Tick" but must freeze when you say, "Tock." Guess what they say when they find it? This game and other related activities can be found in this book.

Source: *The Giant Encyclopedia of Theme Activities for Children 2 to 5*, Kathy Charner

Songs:

(Audio) "Paper Clocks"

Source: *Learning Basic Skills Through Music, vol. II*

44 Clothing

Topical Calendar Tie-in:

August 9

"National Underwear Day"—Every August, representatives of the underwear industry go to New York City to model and sell the newest styles of underwear. Many still petition to make this day an officially recognized day. Children love to talk about what might be "unmentionable." Create a program around clothes but don't forget your underwear, as Froggie did in the children's book *Froggie Gets Dressed* by Jonathan London.

Videos:

Charlie Needs a Cloak
Corduroy
The Emperor's New Clothes
The Hat
Joseph Had a Little Overcoat
The Mitten
A Pocket for Corduroy
You Forgot Your Skirt, Amelia Bloomer!

Picture Books:

Bit by Bit, Steve Sanfield and Susan Gaber
Daisy Gets Dressed, Clare Beaton
Finklehopper Frog, Irene Livingston
A Fox Got My Socks, Hilda Offen
Jamela's Dress, Niki Daly
Jeremy's Muffler, Laura F. Nielsen
Joseph Had a Little Overcoat, Simms Taback
Max's New Suit, Rosemary Wells
The Most Beautiful Kid in the World, Jennifer A. Ericsson
Mr. Tuggle's Troubles, Lee Ann Blankenship
Mrs. Toggle's Beautiful Blue Shoe, Robin Pulver
My Best Shoes, Marilee Robin Burton
One Mitten, Dristine O'Connell George
Shoe Baby, Joyce Dunbar
Under My Hood I Have a Hat, Karla Kuskin

Music/Movement:

"Matching my Socks"

Sung to: "Three Blind Mice"

Red, blue, green.
Red, blue, green.
Here's how they match.
Here's how they match.

They swirl and mix in the washing machine.
And always come out squeaky clean.
But now I have to sit and match them again.
Red, blue, green.
Red, blue, green.

Crafts:

"Dish-it-Up Chef's Hat"
Clothing can sometimes identify a career. Bring in a variety of hats and see if the children can identify who works with that hat. Try making your own chef's hat with the simple instructions offered here. Keep the hat tall so it can keep the cook's head cool while he works. Now put on your hat and let's pretend to be a pizza maker with another available craft offered in this book called "Pizza, Pizza Pie!"

Source: *All Around Town: Exploring Your Community Through Craft Fun*, Judy Press

"Little Shoe Houses"
The little old lady lived in a shoe. I wonder where she found such an unusual house for her family. After discussing all the different kinds of houses people live in and reading this nursery rhyme let the children try to reproduce what they think the little old lady's house actually looked like. You will need newspaper, a large variety of shoes in all styles, a collection of decorating supplies, paints, and glue. Let their imaginations sour. Also offered are additional things to make for a shoe village.

Source: *Making Make-Believe*, MaryAnn F. Kohl

Activities:

"Laundry Matching"
Young children enjoy being included in activities that adults do as part of their everyday workload. Here's a chance for parents at home to get help with the laundry and for teachers and librarians to introduce children to responsibility, classifying objects, and recognizing likenesses and differences. Gather a basketful of clothes of all types. Try including some really goofy-looking outfits for humor. A few variations on how to match clothes (going into the wash, by size, by color, etc.) are offered in this book source. You might even try a matching and sorting game by teams where each team must correctly match items by color *and* get them onto one of their teammates before the other team.

Source: *Mister Rogers' Playtime*, Fred Rogers

"Marathon Dressing"
Relay races are all the rage with young children. Try this elementary dressing race. With a large collection of oversize shirts piled in the middle of the room, the two teams can race to get on the most clothes properly before the whistle blows.

Older students can use an altered version with each member passing the shirt down the line after trying it on, then moving to the next shirt and on and on.

This is a nice game to play after reading *I Can Dress Myself* by Shigeo Watanabe.

Source: *The Big Book of Kids' Games*, Tracy Stephen Burroughs

Songs:

(Audio) "Mary Wore Her Red Dress"

Source: *American Folk Songs for Children*

45 Clothing: Hats

Topical Calendar Tie-in:

April
"Straw Hat Month"—April is a time to set aside your heavier cloth hats in favor of the straw hats of spring and summer. Plan some hat-related events along with decorating the most outrageous hat design of the month.

Videos:

Caps for Sale
The Cat in the Hat (Dr. Seuss Showcase II)
The Hat
How the Trollusk Got His Hat (Mercer Mayer Stories)
Madeline and the Easter Bonnet

Picture Books:

Casey's New Hat, Tricia Gardella
Cowboy Sam and Those Confounded Secrets, Kitty Griffin and Kathy Combs
Do You Have a Hat?, Eileen Spinelli
Felix's Hat, Catherine Bancroft
The 500 Hats of Bartholomew Cubbins, Theodor Geisel
Hats, Kevin Luthardt
Lucy's Summer, Donald Hall
One Snowy Night, M. Christina Butler
The Purple Hat, Tracey Campbell Pearson
Ten Cats Have Hats, Jean Marzollo
This Is the Hat, Nancy Van Laan
Twelve Hats for Lena: A Book of Months, Karen Katz
Uncle Harold and the Green Hat, Judy Hindley
Uncle Lester's Hat, Howie Schneider
What a Hat!, Holly Keller

Music/Movement:

"Hats"
Source: *Storytime for Two-Year-Olds, second edition*, Judy Nichols

Crafts:

"Newspaper Hats"
Make various style large hats from old newspapers. See the source cited here for illustrations on how to size the hat for each individual child's head by using masking tape. After sizing and designing each child's hat, send the child to the design table to decorate it. At the design table, supply easily obtainable materials such as feathers, buttons, markers, stickers, etc. for all to use.
Source: *Making Cool Crafts and Awesome Art*, Roberta Gould

"Printer's Hat"
From this additional source, children can learn about newspaper printers and how they produce newspapers at a printing plant. This is a dramatic

story of a deaf father's heroic feat in saving his coworkers when a fire erupts at the noisy plant. At the end of this story there are instructions for making a "Newspaper Printer's Hat," which is made of old newspapers in a square shape. This is a nice follow-up to the story.

Source: *The Printer*, Myron Uhlberg

Activities:

"Where's My Hat?"

The "Mr. Wind" rhyme offered in this activity can be recited while the action is occurring, setting the atmosphere for the event. One child who is "It" sits in the center of the circle while "Wind" will attempt to secretly steal away its hat while sounding like the wind. While "Wind" returns to his seat and hides the hat behind him, all other players will do the same. Can the first player recover his hat during this stormy game?

Source: *The Complete Book of Activities, Games, Stories, Props, Recipes, and Dances for Young Children*, Pam Schiller and Jackie Silberg

"Hat Grab"

This game is a simple elimination game, with the group divided into two teams, the "grabbers" and the "defenders." Have your teams line up on opposite sides of the room with one or more hats scattered around the area between them. The goal is for a grabber to successfully run onto the field, grab a hat and return to their line before being tagged. If they are tagged they are eliminated. There should only be one grabber and defender on the field at any time.

Source: *Hopscotch, Hangman, Hot Potato and HaHaHa*, Jack Macguire

Songs:

(Audio) "A Silly Hat"

Source: *I Love to Sing with Barney!*

46 Concepts: Color

Topical Calendar Tie-in:

October 22

"National Color Day"—Celebrate color! Now we have a day set aside to recognize how color affects us every day. Designate a different day for each color alone. Today we will wear, decorate, and color only with the color of the day. What can you do with only one color?

Videos:

Freight Train
Harold and the Purple Crayon
Maisy's Colors and Shapes
Planting a Rainbow

Picture Books:

The Big Blue Spot, Peter Holwitz
The Big Orange Splot, Daniel Pinkwater
The Color Box, Dayle Ann Dodds
Lemons Are Not Red, Laura Vaccaro Seeger
The Mixed-Up Chameleon, Eric Carle
My Yellow Ball, Dee Lillegard
The Orange Book, Richard McGuire
The Pink Party, Maryann MacDonald
Priscilla and the Pink Planet, Nathaniel Hobbie
Purple: Seeing Purple Around Us, Sarah L. Schuette
Samuel Todd's Book of Great Colors, E. L. Konigsburg
Soggy Saturday, Phyllis Root
Teeny, Tiny Mouse: A Book About Colors, Laura Leuck
They Thought They Saw Him, Craig Kee Strete
Thinking About Colors, Jessica Jenkins
Warthogs Paint: A Messy Color Book, Pamela Duncan Edwards
What Color Was the Sky Today, Miela Ford

Music/Movement:

"The Colors in my Box"

Sung to: "Farmer in the Dell"

There's colors in my box
There's colors in my box
Hi Ho the Cherrio
There's colors in my box.

The Yellow takes the blue,
The Yellow takes the blue,
They hug together merrily
And now there's green too.

The white takes the red,
The white take the red,
They hug together merrily
And pink appears instead.

(Repeat verse 1)

Crafts:

"Story Pictures"
In conjunction with *The Chalkbox Story* by Don Freeman listed above, the children may be given black construction paper and colored chalk to create their own picture as they have seen in the story read to them.

These pictures may later be displayed in the library or classroom.

"Color Caterpillar"
Build this special color caterpillar to help each child identify their colors. Using a half strip from an egg carton, children can add the caterpillar features and a pull string to make it a toy. Simply cut a number of circles in assorted colors to glue to each section of the caterpillar.

Also found in this source is a gratifying activity in which the children create a rainbow to a song sung to "The Farmer in the Dell."

Source: *The Giant Encyclopedia of Circle Time and Group Activities for Children 3 to 6*, Kathy Charner

Activities:

"Plate Color Relay"
This activity can be used with even 2-year-olds. Children get to color two sets of paper plates on a single side to make the game pieces. Don't worry if they don't color neatly as long as they enjoy the process of creating the game. These plates can be used for flashcards to practice color recognition for this game. Children can place their creations upside down on a table, and then see how many colors they can identify as they turn them over. For older children, have the children try to play it as a memory game, trying to match the two colors that are mixed up on the kitchen table.

Source: *Quick and Fun Games for Toddler*, Grace Jasmine

"Color Tag"
Now we have a game of tag that has one simple rule: You cannot be tagged if you are touching someone or something that is the color that has been called out. The player that is it will call out the color and then let the children run for their lives.

Source: *101 Best Games*, Eulalia Perez

Songs:

(Audio) "Put a Little Color on You"

Source: *Can a Cherry Pie Wave Goodbye?*

47 Concepts: Shapes

Topical Calendar Tie-in:

August 23

"National Hula-Hoop Championship Day"—Let's all pay homage to the hula-hoop, the most perfect circular toy available for children. Check out shapes in everyday life and begin with your own hula hoop championship to celebrate the perfect circle.

Videos:

Clifford's Fun with Shapes
Maisy's Colors and Shapes
The Village of Round and Square Houses

Picture Books:

Baby Snake's Shapes/Las Formas de Bebe Serpiente, Nancy Twinem
A Circle is Not a Valentine, H. Werner Zimmermann
First Shape Book, Ann Montague-Smith
Kitten Castle, Mel Friedman and Ellen Weiss
Little Cloud, Eric Carl
Peter Rabbit's Rainbow Shapes and Colors, Beatrix Potter
Round and Around, James Skofield
Round is a Mooncake, Roseanne Thong
Shapes, Ann Peat
Shapes, Gwenda Turner
The Shapes Game, Paul Rogers
Silly Shapes, unknown
The Silly Story of Goldie Locks and the Three Squares, Grace Maccarone
There's a Square, Mary Serfozo
What Shape is That, Piggy Wiggy?, Christyan and Diane Fox
When a Line Bends . . . A Shape Begins, Rhonda Gowler Greene
Whose Shadow is This: A Look at Animal Shapes—Round, Long and Pointy, Claire Berge

Music/Movement:

"The Shape Song"
Source: *Early Learning Skill Builders: Colors, Shapes, Numbers and Letters,* Mary Tomczyk

Crafts:

"Shape Snakes"
This is a nice addition to your lesson on shapes and a good way to use up all your precut shapes so you don't have to store them. Kathy Ross suggests you use those triangles, squares, circles, and rectangles to create your own shapely snakes that are cute and bendable. Let them adorn the desks of your students or help the children hunt for similar shapes in their classroom during a shape hunt. Check for specific directions to make these lovable creations in the source book.
Source: *Triangles, Rectangles, Circles, and Squares*, Kathy Ross

"Shape Turkey"
This particular craft can be used around the Thanksgiving holiday or simply during a lesson on shapes. This large turkey is constructed of six different size circles of various colors and a triangle for his beak. It's easy enough to construct and add dimension to the picture.
Source: *175 Easy-to-Do Thanksgiving Crafts*, Sharon Dunn Umnik

Activities:

"Tangram Contest"
Take a square and cut it into seven pieces of various sizes and shapes. You now have an ancient form of Chinese puzzle that can be used to create a large variety of artwork. Challenge each child to place these pieces on another sheet of colored paper to form such things as houses, boats, arrows, animals, or other familiar objects. The source offered here gives simple directions on forming your tangram. Now try and challenge your class to see how many different illustrations they can create out of the same puzzle.
Source: *Traditional Crafts from China*, Florence Temko

"Mailbox Shape Sorting"
Set up your own post office with mailboxes corresponding to the different shapes the children have learned. Distribute to the class a number of envelopes with shapes on the outside. Let the children take turns delivering their envelopes to the correct post box.
Source: *The Giant Encyclopedia of Circle Time and Group Activities for Children 3 to 6*, Kathy Charner

Songs:

(Audio) "Everything has a Shape"
Source: *Sally the Swinging Snake*

48 Concepts: Size

Topical Calendar Tie-in:

June 10, 1902
"Pandora's Arrival"—The arrival of Pandora, a giant panda at the Bronx Zoo in New York, is celebrated with this anniversary. Celebrate that beauty can be seen in large as well as small things in our world.

Videos:

Big Little Bill
Thumbelina
Tom Thumb

Picture Books:

Big and Little, Margaret Miller
Big and Little, Steve Jenkins
Bigger, Daniel Kirk
The Big Seed, Ellen Howard
The Incredible Shrinking Teacher, Lisa Passen
Kidogo, Anik McGrory
Little Big Mouse, Nurit Karlin
Shrinking Mouse, Pat Hutchins
Sizes, Jan Pienkowski
The Smallest Stegosaurus, Lynn Sweat and Louis Phillips
Tall, Jez Alborough
There's a Billy Goat in the Garden, Laurel Dee Gugler
Think Big!, Nancy Carlson
Watch Out Big Bro is Coming, Jez Alborough

Music/Movement:

"Sometimes"
Source: *The Complete Resource Book for Toddlers and Twos*, Pam Schiller

Crafts:

"The Three Bears Puppets"
Have the children trace ready-made patterns or cookie cutters to make the form of the three bears at different sizes. They may then decorate and cut them out by putting on the eyes, nose, and pads for the paws. If time permits, you may cut short pieces of brown yarn to make the body fuzzy.

When completed, put the bears on sticks and have the children act out the story of the Three Bears.

"Giant Sunflower"
A wonderful way to teach the concept of size to children is to have something tangible that they can relate to easily. If you do this lesson in the spring try bringing in a variety of real flowers and show the kids how they grow to a number of different sizes, then bring out the giant sunflower to surprise them with a really large flower.

End the lesson with this wonderful craft in which the children make their own giant sunflower with construction paper, a paper plate center, and real sunflower seeds in the center.

Source: *Cut-Paper Play!*, Sandi Henry

Activities:

"Call-and-Response Game"

This is a chanting adaptation of "Simon Says." The chant included in this text is "What is Big?" which has children chanting the verse and naming large animals with the group repeating unless a small animal is named. Chant slow and fast. Can you get someone to make a mistake and be counted out?

Source: *A Kid's Guide to African American History*, Nancy I. Sanders

"Shadow Hunt"

Take the children on a shadow scavenger hunt. Tell them that we will be looking for different kind of shadows (littlest, roundest, biggest, oddest-looking, etc.). There are many activities you can perform during this hunt. Measure your statues, take paper, and let the children trace the shadows and label them. Take a camera and take pictures of various shadows to be used later for identification games.

Source: *Exploring Summer*, Sandra Harkle

Songs:

(Audio) "Now Tall, Now Small"

Source: *Wee Sing: Children's Songs and Fingerplays*

49 Concepts: Counting

Topical Calendar Tie-in:

February 17

"Great Backyard Bird Count"—Be one of the thousands of volunteers nationwide to track how many birds live near your backyard as well as the diverse variety of birds. The results of this counting aid researchers in watching for birds in trouble. Have your own backyard bird count during the school year.

Videos:

Chicka Chicka 1-2-3
How Much is a Million?
Lentil
One Was Johnny
Over in the Meadow
Really Rosie
Shout it Out Numbers from 1 to 10

Picture Books:

Counting on the Woods, George Ella Lyon
Creepy Crawly Calypso, Tony Langham
Dear Daisy, Get Well Soon, Maggie Smith
How Many, How Many, How Many, Rick Walton
Let's Count It Out, Jesse Bear, Nancy White Carlstrom
Mooove Over!, Karen Magnuson Beil
More Than One, Miriam Schlein
Moving from One to Ten, Shari Halpern
My Granny Went to Market: A Round-the-World Counting Rhyme, Stella Blackstone
My Little Sister Ate One Hare, Bill Grossman
One Hungry Baby, Lucy Coats
One, Two, Three, Count with Me, Catherine and Laurence Anholt
Ten Dogs in the Window, Claire Masurel
Ten Little Fish, Audrey Wood
10 Trick-or-Treaters, Janet Schulman
Where Are My Chicks?, Sally Grindley

Music/Movement:

"First Things"
Source: *Good for You!: Toddler Rhymes for Toddler Times*, Stephanie Calmenson

Crafts:

"I Wonder . . . How Many Petals Do Flowers Have?"
This is a simple sponge art craft. Utilize old sponges cut in the shape of flower petals and poster paint to create delightfully colorful flowers for your classroom. Indicate to each child how many petals he or she will need to complete the project. Crayons can be used for making stems and

leaves. At the completion of the project go back and count together to see if there are enough petals.

Source: *Play and Find Out About Math*, Janice Van Cleave

Craft and Activity:

"Dominoes"

Dominoes is a simple enough game to play with children three to five years of age. It has the advantage of being a game that can be played in a quiet area and with as many children as you like. The children can be helped in making their own set of dominoes in numerous ways:

- Use cut pieces of cardstock or cardboard and use colored sticker dots to add color to each.
- Using the same background, cut sandpaper for dots so that they can be felt as well as seen.
- In place of dots cut out numerals in different colored paper to be glued to the dominoes.
- If you don't want each child to make their own set, have them cooperate in making one giant set for the library or classroom using poster board. Let each domino be one foot by two feet in size. They might wish to paint on the dots or numerals.

Activities:

"Number Charades"

Create two bags, one named "Number Bag" and the other "Action Bag." Put numbers on a piece of paper for the first bag and write an action to be performed on a lot of papers for the second bag. Each child will select one paper from each bag and perform the action indicated the correct number of times shown on the pages drawn at that time.

Source: *Math Play! 80 Ways to Count and Learn*, Diane McGowan and Mark Schrooten

Songs:

(Audio) "1 to 10 Blues"

Source: *Adventures of Catfish Pond*

50 Days of the Week/Months of the Year

Topical Calendar Tie-in:

January 9

"National Thank God It's Monday Day"—Here's a day in celebration of the first day of the week. We celebrate birthdays, religious holidays, and much more. Now it's time to celebrate not just a date on the calendar but a day of the week. Find a variety of ways to celebrate each of the individual days in the week.

Videos:

Chicken Soup with Rice
One Monday Morning
Really Rosie
The Twelve Months

Picture Books:

The Cats of Mrs. Calamari, John Stadler
Come Out and Play Little Mouse, Robert Kraus
Day by Day: A Week Goes Round, Carol Diggory Shields
Dear Daisy, Get Well Soon, Maggie Smith
How Do You Say It Today, Jesse Bear?, Nancy White Carlstrom
January Rides the Wind: A Book of Months, Charlotte F. Otten
Jasper's Beanstalk, Nick Butterworth and Mick Inkpen
Jump into January: A Journey Around the Year, Stella Blackstone
Long Night Moon, Cynthia Rylant
My Best Shoes, Marilee Robin Burton
My Love for You All Year Round, Susan L. Roth
October Smiled Back, Lisa Westberg Peters
Parade Day: Marching through the Calendar Year, Bob Barner
The Story of May, Mordicai Gerstein
Twelve Hats for Lena: A Book of Months, Karen Katz
When This Box is Full, Patricia Lillie

Music/Movement:

"Months of the Year"
Sung to: "Bumping Up and Down in My Little Red Wagon"
Source: *The Instant Curriculum*

Crafts:

"Calendar Bingo"
Bingo is a favorite game for many people and this simple game can be adapted by using the days of the week. The boards can be made of card stock or posterboard. Replace the letters B-I-N-G-O with the words for the days of the week. Since you only have five letters in Bingo to be replaced you might want to differentiate between weekdays and weekend days.

For children just learning to recognize the days of the week, have parts made up beforehand and have them copy a sample board. Bingo chips can be any number of objects, such as buttons, pebbles, pennies, etc.

"Owl Calendar"

Have the children make a special calendar as a gift to their parents on a special day in their family. With the use of reproducible patterns in this book, the child can design a colorful owl who has a calendar dangling just below the branch he's sitting on. This calendar can be hung anywhere in the home for all to enjoy and make use of every day.

Source: *Holiday Gifts and Decorations Kids Can Make for Practically Nothing*, Jerome C. Brown

Activities:

"Paper-Chain Counting Calendar"

Remember those friendship chains or the holiday tree chains that you have made in the past? Now turn it into your own special "Counting Calendar" when a child keeps asking you "How many more days until _______?" Use this special activity to help them keep track of time themselves as any special event comes near. Select the color and décor of your calendar to meet the needs of the event.

Source: *Early Learning Skill Builders: Colors, Shapes, Numbers and Letters*, Mary Tomczyk

"Day of the Week Box"

Special days require special activities. Make each day of your calendar unique with a variety of activities. Help children learn to measure time by days with this special box of activities that families can do together. This source will give you a multitude of time and calendar suggestions for children and their families.

Source: *Early Learning Skill Builders: Colors, Shapes, Numbers and Letters*, Mary Tomczyk

Songs:

(Audio) "Weekly Rap"

Source: *Can a Cherry Pie Wave Goodbye?*

51 Dinosaurs

Topical Calendar Tie-in:

October

"Month of the Dinosaur"—October is the month to promote the scientific awareness of dinosaurs and our past. Search for the variety and sizes of dinosaurs that lived on our planet.

Videos:

Danny and the Dinosaurs
Dazzle the Dinosaur
How Do Dinosaurs Get Well Soon?
Patrick's Dinosaurs
The Mysterious Tadpole
Stanley and the Dinosaurs
T is for Terrible

Picture Books:

Albert Goes Hollywood, Henry Schwartz
Bronto Eats Meat, Peter Maloney and Felicia Zekauskas
Dad's Dinosaur Day, Diane Dawson Hearn
Daniel's Dinosaurs, Mary Carmine
Dinosailors, Deb Lund
Dinosaur Island, Max Haynes
Dinosaur Questions, Benard Most
Dinosaurs Galore!, Giles Andreae
Dinosaur Train, John Steven Gurney
Dinosnores, Kelly DiPucchio
Drumheller Dinosaur Dance, Robert Heidbreder
Four and Twenty Dinosaurs, Benard Most
It's Probably Good Dinosaurs Are Extinct, Ken Raney
Mitchell Is Moving, Marjorie Sharmat
The Smallest Stegosaurus, Lynn Sweat and Louis Phillips
T-Rex, Vivian French

Music/Movement:

"Bringing Home a Baby Dinosaur"
Sung to: "I'm Bringing Home a Baby Bumblebee"
Source: *52 Programs for Preschoolers*, Diane Briggs

Crafts:

"Scale a Dinosaur"
There are a number of types of dinosaurs that children can be introduced to with hard shells, scales, or spikes. Choose one of these types and have a form run off on card stock for the children. Give them paper to cut out scales that can then be glued to the body. If time permits you might want to do a variety of dinosaurs and staple them together for a dinosaur book.

You can also trace the figure of a dinosaur on paper large enough to cover a wall or window. Have the children trace and cut out different colored scales to decorate the creature. This may be a project that a whole school or community may want to become involved in. Have each child write his name on the scale he creates.

"Plate Stegosaurus"
Paper plate crafts can be some of the easiest and cheapest of crafts to deal with in large groups. By using three heavy paper plates, some medium-size shells for scales, and toothpicks for tail spikes children can make a delightful stegosaurus model. It can lead into an exciting unit and this source has a number of crafts for a variety of dinosaurs.
Source: *Crafts for Kids Who are Wild about Dinosaurs*, Kathy Ross

Activities:

"Dinosaur Fun"
Kathy Ross offers three entertaining games here with a dinosaur theme that can be used for birthday parties or to add a little fun to your dinosaur story program. Gather up some balloons and small plastic dinosaurs to play "Hatch the Dinosaur Relay Race. Get gummy dinosaurs and some plastic eggs to go on a "Dinosaur Hunt" or play "Ring the Stegosaurus Game" with pointed ice-cream cones and plastic rings
Source: *The Best Birthday Parties Ever!*, Kathy Ross

"Dizzy Dinosaurs"
This game is similar to the famed musical chairs but with a slight twist. Again have one less chair than players in a single group, but there are a couple of groups this time. The class can be divided into groups of their favorite dinosaurs. When the person who is it calls out the name of the dinosaur all (including himself), scramble for the chairs. Obviously one will be left standing. If you like this, many more activities and crafts on dinosaurs can be found in this source.
Source: *The Children's Party Handbook*, Alison Boteler

Songs:

(Audio) "Dicky, Dicky, Dinosaur"
Source: *Diamonds and Dragons*

52 Dragons

Topical Calendar Tie-in:

April 23

"St. George's Day"—Honor the patron saint of England and the hero of the George and the Dragon legend. Research the wide variety of dragons from the fire-breathing type to the Chinese dragons of fame.

Videos:

Draghetto
Dragon Stew
Frog and Toad Together: Dragons and Giants (Arnold Lobel Video Showcase)
Pete's Dragon
Puff the Magic Dragon

Picture Books:

Chopsticks, Jon Berkeley
The Dragon Pack Snack Attack, Joel E. Tanis and Jeff Grooters
The Dragon Snatcher, M.P. Robertson
Elvira, Margaret Shannon
The Funny Thing, Wanda Gag
The Glitter Dragon, Caroline Repchuk
The Last Dragon, Susan Miho Nunes
The Library Dragon, Carmen Agra Deedy
The Little Girl and the Dragon, Else Holmelund Minarick
Raising Dragons, Jerdine Nolen
Serious Trouble, Arthur Howard
The Tale of Custard the Dragon, Ogden Nash
There's a Dragon in My Sleeping Bag, James Howe
A Treasure at Sea for Dragon and Me, Jean E. Pendziwol
Turnip Soup, Lynne Born Myers
Where's the Dragon?, Jason Hook
Who Wants a Dragon?, James Mayhew

Music/Movement:

"Dragons"

Sung to: "Twinkle, Twinkle little Star"

Dragons, dragons in the air,
Breathing fire here and there.
Up above the castle walls
Fighting knights as they brawl.
Dragons, dragons in the air
Breathing fire here and there.

Crafts:

"All in a Row Fire-Breathing Dragon"

Connect a number of paper plates, painted green, to design a dragon body. Check this useful source for suggestions on adding purple paper scales and legs. For a realistic effect, use yellow, red, and orange paper flames emitting high out of your dragon's mouth. Children will love to use their new puppets to tell any number of dragon stories to friends and family that visit the class.

Source: *Look What You Can Make with Paper Plates*, Margie Hayes Richmond

"Bubble-Print Gila Monster"
The Gila monster is a poisonous lizard that may have in earlier times led to the invention of stories of dragons. This may be due to its large lizard size and the way it flicks its tongue out looking like it's breathing fire. Create your own Gila monster using black and brown tempera paint and that bubble wrap that you have sitting at home. With the use of these two items you can create the bubbled look of the lizard's skin. It's a great effect.

Source: *Animal Habitats!*, Judy Press

Activities:

"Magical Imprisonment of the Dragon Egg"
This is a basic well-known magic trick of the egg in the bottle. The nice thing is that this book continues with the craze of Harry Potter and his wizards and tries to show you many magical themes in crafts, activities, and stories can be used. This trick is discussed as the "dragon egg" that needs to be imprisoned by magic before it hatches.

Source: *The Book of Wizard Parties*, Janice Eaton Kilby and Terry Taylor

"Dragon Boat Races"
Let's head back to China for the Dragon Boat Festivals. A Chinese poet named Qu Yuan protested against a ruler by drowning himself. When the poet's friends try to save him they race their boats across the river but were too late. Reenact this famous event from China by constructing your own colorful dragon boats and beginning a new race against time.

Source: *International Crafts and Games*, Cynthia G. Adams

Songs:

(Audio) "Puff the Magic Dragon"

Source: *Car Songs*

53 Ecology

Topical Calendar Tie-in:

May

"Clean Air Month"—We all want to breathe fresh clean air. Start a campaign this month to help keep our air clean by promoting such activities as riding a bicycle or walking to work or school.

Videos:

Garbage Day!
Giving Thanks
Recycle Rex
Sing-Along Earth Songs
Trashy Town
Where the Garbage Goes

Picture Books:

The Brave Little Parrot, Rafe Martin
Dirt, Steve Tomecek
Do Ducks Live in the Desert?, Michael Dahl
Earthsong, Sally Rogers
I See a Kookaburra!, Steve Jenkins and Robin Page
Mason Moves Away, Amy Crane Johnson
A Most Unusual Lunch, Robert Bender
Mouse in a Meadow, John Himmelman
A Possible Tree, Josephine Haskell Aldridge
The Salamander Room, Anne Mazer
The Seed and the Giant Saguaro, Jennifer Ward
Whale, Judy Allen
What We Can Do About Litter, Donna Bailey
Where Does the Garbage Go?, Paul Showers
Wild in the City, Jan Thornhill
The World that Jack Built, Ruth Brown

Music/Movement:

"Mother Earth"
Source: *52 Programs for Preschoolers*, Diane Briggs

Crafts:

"Make an Earth Day Crown"
Celebrate Earth Day every April 22nd with this special craft for little ones. Using construction paper, create a crown for each child. Using old magazines let each child locate illustrations of various flowers to cut out and glue on the peak of the crown. Draw on the stems and leaves where needed. For an extra challenge, see how many children can find pictures of insects to paste around the flowers. Now your class is all set for a special trip outside to clean up the schoolyard or some other special Earth Day mission.
Source: *Little Hands Fingerplays and Action Songs*, Emily Stetson and Vicky Congdon

"Eco-Envelopes"
Here's a unique idea to help the earth. Recycle old junk mail, calendars, catalogs, etc. by making them into envelopes. These colorful envelopes can actually be used for mail as long as they are not smaller than 3½" by 5". For exact size, children can trace old envelopes.
Source: *Ecology Crafts for Kids*, Bobbe Needham

Activities:

"The Litterbug"
This game is a variation of "Duck, Duck, Goose" and should be preceded by a discussion that we are all responsible for keeping our community clean. This can encompass as many children as you may need. Have all the children stand in a circle facing inward except one, the Litterbug. The Litterbug walks around the exterior of the circle until he drops a piece of paper, can, or other designated item behind one child.

The child in the circle who has the "garbage" dropped by him picks it up and attempts to return it to the Litterbug by tagging him with it before he gets around the circle and back to the empty spot. If he succeeds, he returns to the circle, if not, he becomes the Litterbug.

"Recycling Relay"
Form two teams each with a large pile of trash in front of them consisting of paper, plastic, and aluminum items. At the other side of the room are boxes labeled in the same three categories. Each child takes one piece of trash and places it in the appropriate container. The first team to get all trash in the correct containers wins.
Source: *Great Parties for Kids*, Nancy Fyke, Lynn Nejam, and Vicki Overstreet

Songs:

(Audio) "R-E-C-Y-C-L-E"
Source: *This Pretty Planet*

54 Emotions

Topical Calendar Tie-in:

March 3

"I Want You to be Happy Day"—Commit this entire day to the project of reminding people to be caring and helpful to other people, friends and strangers alike. Set a good example all day, be the first to say hello with a smile, and count how many grumpy people brighten up, surprised that someone cared to say hello.

Videos:

Jim's Dog Muffins
Disney Presents Mickey Loves Minnie
The Mountains of Love
Owen
There's Something in My Attic
When Sophie Gets Angry—Really, Really Angry

Picture Books:

The Bear Under the Stairs, Helen Cooper
Even if I Spill My Milk?, Anna Hines
The Frog Who Wanted to Be a Singer, Linda Goss
Goldie is Mad, Margie Palatini
I Love You So Much, Carl Norac
I Love You with All My Heart, Noris Kern
Let's Talk About Being Shy, Marianne Johnston
Misery Moo, Jeanne Willis and Tony Ross
Mommy's Best Kisses, Margaret Amastas
Pip's Magic, Ellen Stoll Walsh
Sam's Worries, Mary Ann MacDonald
There's a Dragon Downstairs, Hilary McKay
What Are You So Grumpy About?, Tom Lichtenheld
Winter Woes, Marty Kelley

Rhyme/Movement:

"If You're Crying"

If you're crying and you're blue *(rub eyes crying)*
Hug a friend. *(motion hugging)*
If you're crying and you're blue
Hug a friend.
If you're crying and you're blue
Hug a friend and he'll hug you.
If you're crying and you're blue
Hug a friend.
(Rhyming text—No music required)

Crafts:

"Stress Relief Fun"

Emotions can run high sometimes for children as well as adults. Talk to the children about making something special to give to a friends or maybe

Dad or Mom after their hard day at work. Let's make a sock stress reliever. Find an old sock to be decorated. Following instructions offered in the source, fill the sock with sand and tie it off. Be sure to follow instructions clearly to avoid leakage. When the toy is completed, have the children squeeze it and tell you how it makes them feel. Try rolling it across your arm, neck, etc. Relax and enjoy your new toy!

Source: *101 Great Gifts from Kids*, Stephanie R. Mueller and Ann E. Wheeler

"Happy/Sad Face Stick Puppets"
The children can construct a reversible face puppet to help them display the emotions they feel. Using a paper plate, have the children draw a sad face on one side with crayons or markers and a happy face on the opposite side. Give them some yarn to glue to the top and sides of the paper plate to form the hair. Mount the plate on a popsicle stick for ease of handling.

Activities:

"Face Puzzles"
Practice identifying facial expressions and feelings with this simple puzzle activity. After discussing with the children what a face looks like when it is sad, happy, angry, etc. pass out paper plates and get them to draw the face. Be sure each is unique and easily identifiable. Now cut them into 3 or 4 pieces and mix them up. How fast can the child reassemble and identify each emotion?

Source: *Quick and Fun Games for Toddlers*, Grace Jasmine

"Feelings"
During a discussion of how children feel about different situations, the children may use their new mask puppets to demonstrate their answers by holding them up to their faces.

As you read some of the stories listed above to the children, let them use their masks to express the feelings of the characters in the tale.

Songs:

(Audio) "I'm in the Mood"

Source: *Rise and Shine*, Raffi

55 Endangered Animals

Topical Calendar Tie-in:

September 22

"Elephant Appreciation Day"—This is a time to honor the largest and most noble endangered land animal. Elephants, hunted for their tusks, are becoming endangered. Encourage the fight to save this animal and read about the many ways the elephant has helped mankind throughout history.

Videos:

Hot Hippo
How the Elephant Got His Trunk
How the Rhinoceros Got His Skin
Whales
The White Seal

Picture Books:

Condor's Egg, Jonathan London
Do the Whales Still Sing?, Dianne Hofmeyr
A Garden of Whales, Maggie S. Davis
Giant Pandas, Gail Gibbons
Going on a Whale Watch, Bruce McMillan
Hungry Hyene, Mwenye Hadithi and Adrienne Kennaway
Jaguar, Helen Cowcher
Jaguar in the Rainforest, Joanne Ryder
The Kangaroos' Great Escape, Rebecca Johnson
No DoDos: A Counting Book of Endangered Animals, Amanda Wallwork
Otter's Under Water, Jim Arnosky
Rhinoceros Mother, Toshi Yoshida
A Safe Home for Manatees, Priscilla Belz Jenkins
Swim the Silver Sea, Joshie Otter, Nancy White Carlstrom
Tilly and the Rhinoceros, Sheila White Samton

Music/Movement:

"Mr. Owl"
Source: *Picture Book Activities*, Trish Kuffner

Crafts:

"Eagle"
This book aids the children in making a picture of the majestic eagle. Using paints and both handprints they will be able to show the eagle with his feathers spread wide and proud. Parents may be squeamish about painting the children's palms for this craft, but the kids will be delighted.
Source: *Hand-Print Animal Art*, Carolyn Carreiro

"Foot and Hands Macaw"
Macaws are beautiful parrots whose habitat is the humid rain forest. They are gradually becoming rare due to habitat loss and hunting and trapping.

Design your own colorful macaw using various colored construction paper, your foot, and your hands. Trace your foot for the body, then your hands several times in a selection of colors to develop the bird's beautiful plumage.

Source: *Crafts for Kids who are Wild about Rainforests*, Kathy Ross

Activities:

"Clean up an Oil Spill"

Animals become endangered for many reasons, including the carelessness of the human race. We hear many times on the television news reports of oil tankers having accidents and spilling their cargo into the ocean. The results are that many birds and ocean life die and could become part of the endangered list in the future. A wonderful science experiment is offered in this book that illustrates to children how difficult it is to clean up an oil spill. With the use of drinking straws and string to make booms and cotton balls and cornstarch, children will see how long it takes to clean up a small spill let alone a large disaster.

Source: *Awesome Ocean Science!*, Cindy A. Littlefield

"Catch Me"

For a lesson on endangered animals, help the children list a variety of animals and, along with "man," what animals hunt them. Have the children make stick puppets of the animals listed. Help the class remember which animals hunt each other by playing this simple game. Let each child become his or her selected animal and repeat the rhyme "Catch Me" offered in the source here.

Source: *Creative Resources for the Early Childhood Classroom, 4th edition*, Judy Herr and Yvonne Libby Larson

Songs:

(Audio) "The Baby Elephant Song"

Source: *Fun at the Zoo!*, Oklin Bloodworth

56 Environment

Topical Calendar Tie-in:

April 22
"Earth Day"—This day is planned with the express purpose of purifying the oceans, land, and air for this earth for future generations. Learn what you can do to help save the planet you live on today.

Videos:

Alexandria's Clean-Up, Fix-Up Parade
Aunt Ippy's Museum of Junk
Giving Thanks
The Lorax
Sing-Along Earth Songs

Picture Books:

And Still the Turtle Watched, Sheila MacGill-Callahan
The Berenstain Bears Don't Pollute (Any More), Stan and Jan Berenstain
Celebrating Earth Day, Janet McDonnell
Cloud Boy, Rhode Montijo
The Great Trash Bash, Loreen Leedy
It's My Earth, Too, Kathleen Krull
Mother Earth, Nancy Luenn
Mousekin's Lost Woodland, Edna Miller
My Brother Needs a Boa, Anne Weston
Rainforest, Helen Cowcher
The Umbrella, Jan Brett
Welcome to the Greenhouse, Jane Yolen
What to Do about Pollution . . ., Anne Shelby
Where Once There Was a Wood, Denise Fleming

Music/Movement:

"I am a Volcano"
Source: *52 Programs for Preschoolers*, Diane Briggs

Crafts:

"Bag Saver"
Ask children to save their old tissue boxes and recycle them into storage space for Mom's grocery bags. They can paint and decorate it to their taste but be sure to see this source for an adorable look that's easy to create.
Source: *Every Day Is Earth Day*, Kathy Ross

"Pebble Jewelry"
With the use of barrettes, old flat bracelets or hair combs, pebbles, and a little paint children can design their own jewelry with recycled materials. They don't need to add more trash to the environment.

"Shell Butterfly Magnets"
Collect shells and twigs or pipe cleaners to be used to make beautiful butterflies when glued together. Each one can be painted differently and magnets put on the back so they can be placed on a refrigerator.

You will even find recipes and other ideas in this source for making your own: Natural dyes, recycled paper, natural clay and dough, pastes and glues, finger paints and homemade yarn.

Source: *EcoArt!*, Laurie Carlson

Activities:

"Three Rs Rangers"

Duplicate and have the children color the recycling reminder notification provided in this source. Next, why not lead the children in a tour of the school, library, or other location in search of violations? They can then leave their notices to encourage everyone to reduce, reuse, and recycle.

Source: *The Best of the Mailbox, Book 1: Preschool/Kindergarten edition*, Margaret Michel

"Nature Bingo"

Distribute to every child a sheet of construction paper folded into nine squares. If possible take the children out-of-doors so that they can see the many wonders of nature. Ask them to draw a picture of something they see in each of the squares on their paper. Now you are ready to play Nature Bingo!

Source: *Sunny Days and Starry Nights*, Nancy Fusco Castaldo

Songs:

(Audio) "Big Beautiful Planet"

Source: *Rise and Shine*, Raffi

57 Ethnic Groups: Native Americans

Topical Calendar Tie-in:

June 15

"Native American Citizenship Day"—Commemorate the day in 1924 when Congress passed legislation recognizing the citizenship of Native Americans. Learn what you have to do today to become a U.S. citizen.

Videos:

Dancing with the Indians
Giving Thanks
Hiawatha
Knots on a Counting Rope
Princess Scargo and the Birthday Pumpkin

Picture Books:

And Still the Turtle Watched, Sheila MacGill-Callahan
Bear with Me, Ann Rhiannon
Crazy Horse's Vision, Joseph Bruchac
Dancing with the Indians, Angela Shelf Medearis
Dreamcatcher, Audrey Osofsky
Eagle Boy, Richard Lee Vaughan
Giving Thanks, Jonathan London
Giving Thanks: A Native American Good Morning Message, Chief Jake Swamp
Grandmother's Dreamcatcher, Becky Ray McCain
Green Snake Ceremony, Sherrin Watkins
How the Indians Bought the Farm, Craig Kee Strete and Michelle Netten Chacon
Knots on a Counting Rope, Bill Martin, Jr., and John Archambault
My Navajo Sister, Eleanor Schick
The Rattlesnake Who Went to School, Craig Kee Strete
The Star People: A Lakota Story, S. D. Nelson

Rhyme/Movement:

"Indian Life"

(Rhyming text—No music required)
This is the teepee *(make pointed form with 2 hands)*
Painted and tall.
This is the Indian who makes it his home.
(cross arms and sit Indian style)
This is his bow and arrow used to get some food.
(pretend to shoot arrows)
This is his Indian tribe, he'll never be alone.
(spread arms out to include all in the room.)

Crafts:

"Navajo Bracelet"

Navajo jewelry is often hammered out of silver and decorated with blue-green gem stones. It is believed to bring health, happiness, and good luck.

Try making a simple version to fit a child's wrist by cutting loops from toilet-paper tubes and covering it with aluminum foil. Once your bracelet is formed give the children shapes suggested in this book for an original Navajo bracelet.

Source: *Little Hands Celebrate America!*, Jill Frankel Hauser

"Navajo Hogan"

This is a simple craft that can be completed with very young children. Use one egg cup off an egg carton for the base of your hogan. Leaving one space clear for the entrance, cover the rest of the cup with strips of masking tape overlapping for a bark appearance. Now the children can use brown markers to color the tape. This can lead to an entire Navajo village if you like. Instructions for simple Plains Indian tepees are also available in this source.

Source: *Kids Celebrate!*, Maria Bonfanti Esche and Clare Bonfanti Braham

Activities:

"The Rock Game"

This Native American game was used to perfect tracking skills and can be helpful in practicing the use of the various senses. Gather an assortment of rocks with different shapes sizes and colors. There are two parts to this activity. Once the rocks have been distributed to each child they must try to memorize the rock by sight, feel, and smell. When they are collected and tossed onto the floor again the children will be first asked to identify their rock by one sense and then a second time when one sense is denied them. Track that stone and bring it back to your home. Some suggested safety rules to control the game are also offered to make this a fun experience for all.

Source: *Native American Games and Stories*, James Bruchac and Joseph Bruchac

"Navajo Code Talkers"

During World War II the Americans had difficulty sending messages to their troops because their instructions were intercepted by the Japanese who were very adept at deciphering secret codes. They needed to come up with a better way to send military instructions and this came from a group of Navajo soldiers who entered the military and brought with them their very complex Navajo language. It involved not only word phrases but voice tones and much more. Read to the children the story of this part of Native American history from Ms. Sklansky's book and then have the children try to develop their own secret code using instructions offered in the same book. This is a fun way to learn American history.

Source: *Zoom Fun with Friends*, Amy E. Sklansky

Songs:

(Audio) "Strength of Blue Horses"

Source: *The Day I Read a Book*

58 Exercise/Physical Fitness

Topical Calendar Tie-in:

September 30

"Family Health and Fitness Month"—On this day families gather together to become involved in locally organized health and fitness events to promote healthy families. Check out your local libraries, recreations centers, and fitness centers for events in your area that your family can become involved in or start your own special event.

Videos:

Chicken Fat: The Youth Fitness Video
Curious George at the Mini Marathon
Elmocize
Fitness fun with Goofy
How to Exercise
Kids Can Jump!

Picture Books:

Babar's Yoga for Elephants, Laurent deBrunhoff
Bearobics: A Hip-Hop Counting Story, Vic Parker and Emily Bolam
Dinosaurs Alive and Well!, Laurie Krasny Brown and Marc Brown
Hamster Camp: How Harry Got Fit, Teresa Bateman
Let's Exercise, Elizabeth Vogel
Old Mother Hubbard's Dog Needs a Doctor, John Yeoman and Quentin Blake
Olympics!, B. G. Hennessy
Tacky and the Winter Games, Helen Lester
Tiffany Dino Works Out, Marjorie Sharmat
Toddlerobics, Zita Newcome
Toddlerobics: Animal Fun, Zita Newcome
A Yoga Parade of Animals, Pauline Mainland

Music/Movement:

"On My Head"

Source: *The Eensy Weensy Spider: Fingerplays and Action Rhymes*, Joanna Cole and Stephanie Calmenson

Crafts:

"Ice Skater"

There are many forms of exercise that we can introduce to children. Here's one winter sport that many may like. Discuss how ice skating became an Olympic event and of how everyone wishes to look good when they perform.

Construct Olympic ice skaters from layers of folded paper plates, chenille sticks, etc. These graceful skaters are bendable and make a great bulletin board display also.

Source: *Look What You can Make with Paper Plates*, Margie Hayes Richmond

"Tracing Wheels"
Bicycling is a favorite form of exercise for many average adults and children, as well as Olympic hopefuls. Consider exploring with your class the many ways the wheel is used in our lives through exercise in bicycling and roller skating to pizza cutters in cooking. Gather an assortment of wheel types to be used to make some artwork by toddlers.

Source: *Creative Resources for the Early Childhood Classroom, 4th edition*, Judy Herr and Yvonne Libby Larson

Activities:

"Yoga for Children: The Tree"
Get into fitness with this fantastic book on Yoga for children. It requires no special athletic skills and is perfect for stretching and warm-up exercises for ages 3 and up. You will find an entire chapter on yoga stances for seasons and nature. This particular pose is called "The Tree." Children begin with the mountain pose and gradually develop the growth of the tree by standing on one foot and moving their arms with palms together up toward the sky. Switch and try the other foot. If the children have difficulties standing on one foot have them stand touching a wall with one hand for support until they get more proficient. There is a wide variety of positions the children will enjoy creating in this book.

Source: *Yoga Games for Children*, Danielle Bersma and Marjoke Visscher

"Fling-A-Ma-Jig"
Let's get a little exercise with this flying Frisbee. As the weather gets warmer it's time to take our toys outside and get a little exercise at the same time. Make your own Fling-a-ma-jig out of paper plates (preferably plastic plates), some markers, glue, and glitter. Get outside and team up for some fresh air and to see who can throw them the farther than their friends and who can catch the most Frisbees. Look at this source for an important point in the construction that will allow the air to lift that Frisbee higher and higher when thrown.

Source: *Easy Art Fun! Do-it-Yourself Crafts for Beginning Readers*, Jill Frankel Hauser

Songs:

(Audio) "Jumpstart for the Queen of Hearts"

Source: *Castles, Knights and Unicorms*

59 Fairy Tales and Nursery Rhymes

Topical Calendar Tie-in:

November 19

"Mother Goose Parade"—This celebration of children is held annually in California with a parade of Mother Goose rhymes and fairy-tale characters. Ask children to pick their favorite character to imitate and create your own parade and demonstration. Traditionally held the Sunday before Thanksgiving.

Videos:

And the Dish Ran Away with the Spoon
The Gingerbread Boy
Harold's Fairy Tale
Henny Penny
Little Red Riding Hood
Rumpelstiltskin
Some Mother Goose Rhymes
The Ugly Duckling
Wynken, Blynken and Nod

Picture Books:

Babushka's Mother Goose, Patricia Polacco
Dragon Kites and Dragonflies: A Collection of Chinese Nursery Rhymes, Demi
The Giant and the Beanstalk, Diane Stanley
Grandmother's Nursery Rhymes, Nelly Palacio Jaramillo
The Hat, Jan Brett
Joe Giant's Missing Boot: A Mothergooseville Story, Toni Goffe
Little Bo Peep Can't Get to Sleep, Erin Dealey
Mama Goose: A New Mother Goose, Liz Rosenberg
Mother Hubbard's Cupboard: A Mother Goose Surprise Book
Once Upon a Time, John Prater
Piggie Pie!, Margie Palatini
Riddledy Piggledy: A Book of Rhymes and Riddles, Tony Mitton
The Three Bears, Paul Galdone
The Three Billy Goats Gruff, Peter Asbjornsen
The Three Little Pigs, Paul Galdone

Music/Movement:

"Eat Your Gingerbread Boy"
Sung to: "Row, Row, Row, Your Boat"
Source: *Totally Tubeys!*, Priscella Morrow

Crafts:

"The Gingerbread Man"
Following the readings of *The Gingerbread Man*, let the children make their own man out of construction paper. Distribute brown construction paper and precut patterns or use large cookie cutters of the gingerbread man to be traced. After tracing and cutting these forms out, you can decorate the cookie in one of two suggested ways:

- Use colored chalk as icing to draw clothes on and sticker dots for eyes, nose and buttons.
- Cut clothes out of paper and glue it on. Use real raisins or small hard candies for eyes, nose and buttons.

(NOTE: Emphasize that the food is decorative and not edible.)

"Candlestick Craft"

After teaching the children the nursery rhyme "Jack Be Nimble," you can create your own candlestick to jump over. Paper plates and toilet paper rolls make up the main materials needed to develop this craft and have the children practice the rhyme again.

Source: *The Giant Encyclopedia of Circle Time and Group Activities for Children 3 to 6*, Kathy Charner

Activities:

"Blackbirds in a Pie Game"

You can build your own four and twenty blackbirds baked in a pie for this nursery rhyme game. Cut 24 little blackbirds out of paper and place in a pie tin. Create the top of the pie from another tin but cut out the pie air holes first. With your pie complete have each child role a die to determine how many birds they may remove from the pie on their turn. If the player forgets to say "may I?" he must return the birds. The winner is the person with the most birds.

Source: *Music Crafts for Kids*, Noel Fiarotta and Phyllis Fiarotta

"Cinderfella"

After hearing the well-known story of Cinderella, the children might want to try a relay game based on this familiar fairy tale. Split your class into two teams. Have the boys seated in chairs with the girls behind them. All the boys' shoes have been collected and placed in a pile on the other end of the room. Also some humorous pairs have been placed in the pile (large size, baby size, etc.). At the bell, the girls must run to the pile and find their prince's shoes and get them to fit on their feet. If the child is of the age that can tie shoes, you can also require that they be tied before they are done. The team to win is the first to complete the task. Now try switching places.

Source: *Perfect Party Games*, Andre Campbell

Songs:

(Audio) "Gingerbread Man"

Source: *C is for Cookie*, Sesame Street

60 Family Life

Topical Calendar Tie-in:

April 10
"National Siblings Day"—Salute your brother or sister with this momentous day recognizing the bond between family siblings. Here is a day to hug and do something special for your brother or sister just because they are there for you.

Videos:

Alexander and the Terrible, Horrible, No Good, Very Bad Day
A Chair for My Mother
Company's Coming
I'll Fix Anthony
Peter's Chair
The Relatives Came

Picture Books:

Beware of the Aunts!, Pat Thomson
Dad, Aren't You Glad?, Lynn Plourde
Froggy's Day with Dad, Jonathan London
I Want a Brother or Sister, Astrid Lindgren
Lots of Dads, Shelley Rotner and Sheila M. Kelly
My Baby Brother, Harriet Hains
My Little Sister Ate One Hare, Bill Grossman
Night Shift Daddy, Eileen Spinelli
Octopus Hug, Laurence Pringle
Once There Were Giants, Martin Waddell
The Surprise Family, Lynn Reiser
Take Time to Relax, Nancy Carlson
There's a Dragon in My Sleeping Bag, James Howe
What Mommies Do Best/What Daddies Do Best, Laura Numeroff
When Daddy Took Us Camping, Julie Brillhart

Music/Movement:

"Family Fun"
Source: *The Complete Resource Book for Toddlers and Twos*, Pam Schiller

Crafts:

"Playing Cards Photo Frame"
Here's an inspiring use of old playing cards. Kathy Ross leads us step by step through this simple craft turning old playing cards into a four-page foldout photo holder that can fit in Dad's wallet. Fathers will be proud to show off their baby's picture in something so unique and humorous.
Source: *All New Crafts for Earth Day*, Kathy Ross

"Nutshell Families"
Here's a fun craft that children may create after discussing various types of animal families. Collect as many, intact, walnut shell halves as you are able. If you would like to make a whale family that includes a mother,

father, and one baby you will need two walnut shells and one pistachio shell. Paint them gray, add wiggly eyes and add a spout using gray or white paper. Connect them together with a long string and the child can pull them across the table. This same setup can be used to make ladybug families or any other.

Source: *Crafts from Recyclables*, Colleen van Blaricom

Activities:

"Talking Stick"

When people get excited about a particular task they tend to talk all at once. Here's a way to get children to remember to listen when they need to and talk up when they normally would be too shy to speak. It is also an opportunity for children to get parents to listen to them when they need to speak. Have the children create a "talking stick" out of rain sticks or walking sticks, or they can design one from a stick found in the yard. Instructions for making sticks is found in the "I've Got Rhythm" portion of the book cited here. The class can use the talking sticks to help create stories or plays. Good starting points are offered in the source book.

Source: *Show Time! Music, Dance and Drama Activities for Kids*, Lisa Bany-Winters

"Rakhi"

Hindi families celebrate a special festival called Raksha Bandhan. During this holiday families renew their special bonds for each other in special ways. A sister will show her love and respect for her brother by tying a special braided bracelet (rakhi) on his wrist, and in return her brother promises to always protect her. Directions for making this caring symbol of family respect are offered in this book. This would make a wonderful craft to introduce to children for use in their own family and a nice way to teach them to express positive feelings for others.

Source: *International Crafts and Games*, Cynthia G. Adams

Songs:

(Audio) "Reuban and Rachel"

Source: *Wee Sing: Sing-Alongs*

61 Family Life: Mothers

Topical Calendar Tie-in:

July 23
"Parent's Day"—Salute the men and women across this country who are dedicated parents. Help children realize the many things that their parents do for them, possibly by having them help Mom or Dad with all their responsibilities for the entire day.

Videos:

Are You My Mother?
George Washington's Mother
Is Your Mama a Llama?
Monster Mama
Space Case

Picture Books:

Baby Snake's Shapes, Twinem, Neecy
Brave Little Raccoon, Erica Wolf
Earthsong, Sally Rogers
Five Minutes Peace, Jill Murphy
I Love You, Little One, Nancy Tafuri
Just a Minute, Yuyi Morales
Mama Always Comes Home, Karma Wilson
Meredith's Mother Takes the Train, Deborah Lee Rose
Mommy Mine, Tim Warnes
Mommy's Office, Barbara Shook Hazen
A Mother for Choco, Keiko Kasza
Mrs. Chicken and the Hungry Crocodile, Won-Ldy Paye and Margaret H. Lippert
My Mom, Anthony Browne
Rachel's Library, Richard Ungar
Sing Me a Story: Song-and-Dance Tales from the Caribbean, Grace Hallworth
The Way Mothers Are, Miriam Schlein
We're Making Breakfast for Mother, Shirley Neitzel
What Mommies Do Best, Laura Numeroff
When Mama Gets Home, Marisabina Russo
Will You Carry Me?, Heleen Van Rossum

Music/Movement:

"My Mom"
Source: *52 Programs for Preschoolers*, Diane Briggs

Crafts:

"Seeded Pencil Holder"
Any small container may be made into a beautiful pencil holder for Mom on Mother's Day. Collect various types of seeds (melon, bird, sunflower, etc.) to add variety to the design. Rather than trying to glue the seeds directly to the can itself, Phyllis Fiarotta, in her book, suggests cutting a

piece of paper to fit the exterior of the can, then laying the paper flat to add the seeds.

A decorated can of this sort can be used for crayons, or even Mom's or Dad's pencils, needles, or more. For step-by-step illustrated directions, take a look at Fiarotta's book listed here.

Source: *Snips and Snails and Walnut Whales*, Phyllis Fiarotta

"About Our 'Mums'"
This cute spring craft will make every "Mum" smile when she receives it. A large paper flower can be designed with its center having Mom's facial features. On each petal, have the child write (or the teacher can write for them) something the child thinks is special about his or her mom. This is a great time to talk to children about various expressions used in different countries. Explain how children in England often call their mothers "mum," but we have flowers called mums. Talk of other regional expressions in a multicultural lesson.

Source: *The Best of the Mailbox, Book 2: Preschool/Kindergarten edition*, Margaret Michel

Activities:

"Tickle Trunk"
Children enjoy play acting. The "Tickle Trunk" can represent any number of family members. When focusing on mothers, fill it with items that Mom might wear or use in her everyday life. Children will enjoy dressing or acting like Mom in different life situations. This can be expanded to a variety of uses.

Source: *The Preschooler's Busy Book*, Trish Kuffner

"Mother May I?"
This simple game can be played with any number of children. One player (Mother) stands at one side of the room while the other players stand at the other side. The leader states how many steps the children may take to try to reach her. The players must ask her, "Mother, may I?" *before* moving or they return to the beginning of their trip.

Songs:

(Audio) "Tell Me Why?"

Source: *Wee Sing: Sing-Alongs*

62 Farms

Topical Calendar Tie-in:

September 17–23

"National Farm Animals Awareness Week"—Sponsored by the Humane Society of the United States, the purpose of this special day is to educate children about farm animals and how they are raised. In this time of ever disappearing farmlands, this is a chance for children to remember those who raise our farm animals are so important to our lives.

Videos:

Big Red Barn
Henny Penny
The Little Red Hen
The Little Rooster Who Made the Sun Rise
Rosie's Walk

Picture Books:

Barnyard Lullaby, Frank Asch
Chicks and Salsa, Aaron Reynolds
Click, Clack, Splish, Splash, Doreen Cronin and Betsy Lewin
Does a Cow Say Boo?, Judy Hindley
Down on the Farm, Merrily Kutner
Farmer Dale's Red Pickup Truck, Lisa Wheeler
Farmer Duck, Martin Waddell
Farmer Will, Jane Cowen-Fletcher
Heatwave, Helen Ketteman
Inside a Barn in the Country, Alyssa Satin Capucilli
Over on the Farm, Christopher Gunson
Rock-a-Bye Farm, Diane Johnston Hamm
The Rooster Who Lost His Crow, Wendy Cheyette Lewison
Snappy Little Farmyard, Dugald Steer
This Is the Farmer, Nancy Tafuri
When the Rooster Crowed, Patricia Lillie

Music/Movement:

"Farm Animals"
Source: *101 Fingerplays, Stories and Songs to Use with Finger Puppets*, Diane Briggs

Crafts:

"Eggs on a Plate"
Mother hen is protecting her eggs. This book instructs children in how to make their own board game. It will require a spinner that will determine if the eggs stay on or off the game plate, paper eggs, and a main plate showing a mother hen. Help each child make their own boards and let the games begin. Try and save your eggs.
Source: *The Usborne Book of Games and Puzzles*, Alastair Smith (editor)

"Farm Collage"
Young children love the cutting and pasting that's needed to make collages. Cut a barn out of red construction paper for the base of your creation. Let the children search for various farm animals in magazines, etc. and paste on your barn frame.

Activities:

"Farmer is Coming!"
This old-fashioned game is so simple that the children will feel giddy playing it. The farmhands sit in one room while the farmer counts slowly. When the farmer stops counting the field hands will try to sneak up on the farmer getting as close as they can before he claps his hand and freezes them. When he yells, "The farmer is coming!" everyone must return to their seats before they are tagged by the farmer.

Source: *Old Fashioned Children's Games*, Sharon O'Bryan

"Rooster Romp"
This Mexican party game takes a little stamina. Children pair off to see who can last longer than the other when they have to hop while remaining in a designated position. The goal of the game is for one rooster to snatch the scarf that the other has tucked in a belt or pocket without changing his position or stop hopping. Continue pairing off until there is only one winning rooster at the farm. Complete details are offered in the source book.

Source: *Sidewalk Games*, Glen Vecchione

Songs:

(Audio) "I Had a Rooster"

Source: *Jeremiah Was a Bullfrog*

63 Fish

Topical Calendar Tie-in:

September 23
"Fish Amnesty Day"—Give fish a holiday! Set one day aside each year to give fish a break. Put your fishing rods aside and spend the time reading about them instead of fishing for them. How many species of fish can you represent in an illustrated book of fish?

Videos:

The Fisherman and his Wife
Fish is Fish (5 Lionni Classics)
Jonah and the Great Fish
One Fish, Two Fish, Red Fish, Blue Fish
Swimmy (Leo Lionni's Caldecotts)

Picture Books:

Billy's Bucket, Kes Gray
Carl Caught a Flying Fish, Kevin O'Malley
Fish and Flamingo, Nancy White Carlstrom
A Fish Hatches, Joanna Cole
Flood Fish, Robyn Eversole
The Fool and the Fish, Alexander Nikolayevich Afanasyev
Hooray for Fish!, Lucy Cousins
Little Fish, Lost, Nancy VanLaan
Not Norman: A Goldfish Story, Kelly Bennett
The Rainbow Fish, Marcus Pfister
Rainbow Fish and the Sea Monsters' Cave, Marcus Pfister
Rosie's Fishing Trip, Amy Hest
Ten Little Fish, Audrey Wood
There Once Was a Puffin, Florence Page Jaques
What's it Like to be a Fish?, Wendy Pfeffer

Music/Movement:

"Little Fish"
Sung to: "I'm a Little Teapot"

We are little young fish
We play to win.
Here are our tails *(wiggle hind end)*
And here are our fins *(hands flapping on their sides)*
When we go out swimming *(swim around)*
Watch us spin *(spin)*
We jump and turn and dive back in. *(jump, turn, and dive)*

Crafts:

"Little Fish"
Prepare to make a school of fish out of the simplest of materials. Collect those leftover small cardboard tubes that everyone has at home and wrap them in colored tissue paper leaving excess on either end. One end

becomes a tail and other other the mouth when tucked inside the tube. Add wiggle eyes and shiny paper fins and scales for the brightest of fish. If you are having a party you might even put a special prize inside the fish as a favor. Check this book for fishy invitations, seashell bags, and much, much more from the sea.

Source: *My Party Art Class*, Nellie Shepherd

"Aquarium Collage"

Paper plate crafts are my favorite of all crafts because they are easy to use and inexpensive. If you work where the money you spend on supplies is a top concern (and who doesn't?), these type of crafts are the ones to look for.

Here a child can create their own undersea scene on a paper plate using shell macaroni, small pebbles, yarn, and undersea animal stickers. When complete, staple another plate to it with the center removed and substituted with blue plastic wrap. The effect is astonishing. Don't stop there but see what else this author has to offer for an "undersea" program.

Source: *Hit of the Party*, Amy Vangsgard

Activities:

"Pass the Pufferfish"

This is a fun adaptation of Pass the Parcel and the most desirable part of the game is that every child is a winner. Create a giant puffer fish from a lunch bag, wrapping paper, and an assortment of decorative materials and fill it with lots of little fish that also contain presents. Set some nautical music playing and begin passing that large fish until the music stops. The child who is left with the fish gets to take a fish prize before stepping out of the circle. The crazy illustration of the puffer fish offered in this source will have the children laughing with delight.

Source: *My Party Art Class*, Nellie Shepherd

"Octopus"

This undersea tag game has one player representing the octopus and the remainder of the class the fish who need to get past him to the other side of the ocean. If any fish are caught (tagged) they are absorbed into the octopus becoming part of his tentacles looking for more fish.

Source: *Great Big Book of Children's Games*, Debra Wise

Songs:

(Audio) "My Teacher Turned into a Fish"

Source: *Toddlers Next Steps: Silly Songs*

64 Folktales and Legends

Topical Calendar Tie-in:

November 2

"Daniel Boone's Birthday"—Applaud the birth on this date of an American frontiersman, explorer, and militia officer. This legendary character lived with the Shawnee Indians, was captured by the British, and lived a rugged life on the American frontier.

Videos:

American Tall Tale Heroes
Annie Oakley
It Could Always Be Worse
John Henry
Pecos Bill
Stone Soup

Picture Books:

The Badger and the Magic Fan, Tony Johnston
The Great Ball Game, Joseph Bruchac
How the Ostrich Got Its Long Neck, Verna Aardema
How Snowshoe Hare Rescued the Sun: A Tale from the Arctic, Emery and Durga Bernhard
John Henry, Julius Lester
Just a Minute, Yuyi Morales
Mrs. Chicken and the Hungry Crocodile, Won-Ldy Paye and Margaret H. Lippert
Nathaniel Willy, Scared Silly, Judith Mathews and Fay Robinson
Pecos Bill, Steven Kellogg
People of Corn, Mary-Joan Gerson
The Pied Piper of Hamelin, Michele Lemieux
Sing Me a Story: Song-and-Dance Tales from the Caribbean, Grace Hallworth
William Tell, Leonard Everett Fisher
Zzzng! Zzzng! Zzzng!: A Yoruba Tale, Phillis Gershator

Music/Movement:

"There Was a Princess Long Ago . . ."
Source: *The Playtime Treasury*, Pie Corbett

Crafts:

"Robin Hood's Quiver"
Travel to merry old England and romp through Sherwood forest and to the castles of Maid Marian and Prince John with your own quiver and arrows reminiscent of the days of Robin Hood. You'll find this an excellent craft for lessons on legends or medieval times. Don't look for expensive materials. Here you can use simple paper towel tubes and other cheap items easily found around the house.
Source: *Cups and Cans and Paper Plate Fans*, Phyllis and Noel Fiarotta

"Big Mouth Frog"
Folktales are a lot of fun for everyone. Animals play a large part in folktales and legends of many countries. Some of my favorite stories are ones like "The Frog Prince," "The Foolish Frog," and others like these.

This craft helps the child create a wide-mouthed frog sitting on a lily pad. Add long jumping legs from accordion folded paper strips. Now try "The Foolish Frog" with this delightful creation.
Source: *Cut-Paper Play!*, Sandi Henry

Activities:

"From Fable to Theater"
Create your own theatrical version of famous fables or folktales. Many fables include animal characters so a collection of masks made by your class will be useful in this endeavor. Spend a day play-acting and developing your characters before presentations. Constructive feedback after the performance is essential. Check for recommendations of this and other activities in the source book.
Source: *Summer Activities*, Marc Tyler Nobleman

"Show Time"
I was very excited to locate this book because it is chock full of interactive ideas for children, including the most exciting part, which is the last chapter, "Show Time." You will find a series of short plays for only a few actors based on American folk heroes like Paul Bunyan, a scene from *Alice in Wonderland* and short play versions of familiar fairy tales. Kindergarten teachers looking for a performance must get this book.
Source: *Show Time! Music, Dance and Drama Activities for Kids*, Lisa Bany-Winters

Songs:

(Audio) "Pecos Bill"
Source: *Harmony Ranch*

65 Food/Eating

Topical Calendar Tie-in:

February 28

"International Pancake Day"—Conduct your own special pancake day along with the people of Liberal, Kansas, who annually celebrate with a Pancake Race. Women, wearing the traditional apron and scarf, race a special S-shaped course carrying a pancake in a skillet. Other events include a breakfast parade, talent show, pancake flipping contest, and much more. Celebrate the perfect pancake on this day.

Videos:

Dragon Stew
Frog Goes to Dinner
Green Eggs and Ham (The Cat in the Hat/ Dr. Seuss on the Loose)
Let's Eat! Funny Food Songs
Pete's a Pizza
Stone Soup

Picture Books:

Animal Snackers, Betsy Lewin
The Beastly Feast, Bruce Goldstone
A Chef: How We Work, Douglas Florian
Good for Thought: The Complete Book of Concepts for Growing Minds, Saxton Freymann
Fortune Cookie Fortunes, Grace Lin
The Hungry Thing Returns, Jan Slepian and Ann Seidler
Lunch, Denise Fleming
Mouse Mess, Linnea Riley
No More Cookies!, Paeony Lewis
Our Community Garden, Barbara Pollak
Pete's a Pizza, William Steig
Pickles to Pittsburgh, Ron Barrett
Pie in the Sky, Lois Ehlert
Sheep Out to Eat, Nancy Shaw
Sweet Dream Pie, Audrey Wood
Turnip Soup, Lynne Born Myers

Music/Movement:

"The Carrot Song"
Sung to: "Over in the Meadow"
Source: *Little Hands Fingerplays and Action Songs*, Emily Stetson and Vickey Congdon

Crafts:

"Decorative Boxes and Pretty Jewelry"
With the use of the great variety of grains and pasta available, the children can make their own jewelry or decorate a colorful box to be used for almost anything. Instructions and illustrations for these crafts can be

found in the source below. Suggested grains to use include maize, rice, lentils, pearl barley, macaroni, spaghetti, butterfly pasta, and vermicelli.

Source: *The Fun-To-Make Book*, Colette Lamargue

"Bubble Wrap Dried Corn"

This simple artwork can be utilized in so many lessons on such topics as Thanksgiving, Sukkot, Kwanzaa displays, and much, much more. Seal the end of a cardboard towel tube and wrap it with bubble wrap (bubbles outward). Roll the entire thing in a mixture of glue and water and wrap in a couple of layers of yellow tissue paper tucking the ends inside. Use brown tissue to form the brown husks. For more details and illustrations see this source.

Source: *Crafts to Make in the Fall*, Kathy Ross

Activities:

"Brand-Name Lotto"

Children easily recognize brand names and symbols such as McDonald's Cheerios, and more without realizing they are seeing words. Try creating your own Lotto cards for this game with illustrations from well-known products with the words written below the illustration. Use your new cards to play Match, Pairs and Recall games described in the book below.

Source: *Wow! I'm Reading!*, Jill Frankel Hauser

"Breakfast, Lunch, and Dinner Grouping Game"

Prepare flash cards of items that are normally eaten at these three particular meals. These cards can be used to help recognize food words and also to categorize. Check this book for suggestions on foods for these meals.

Source: *Quick and Fun Games for Toddlers*, Grace Jasmine

Songs:

(Audio) "Healthy Food"

Source: *Sesame Road*

66 Foreign Lands: Africa

Topical Calendar Tie-in:

September 24
"South Africa Heritage Day"—Salute the South African neighborhood, honoring the heritage of this multicultural nation.

Videos:

Hot Hippo
Joshua's Masai Mask
Mufaro's Beautiful Daughters
A Story, A Story
Why Mosquitoes Buzz in People's Ears

Picture Books:

An African Princess, Lyra Edmons
Anansi the Spider, Gerald McDermott
Dr. DeSoto Goes to Africa, William Steig
Kente Colors, Debbi Chocolate
King of Another Country, Fiona French
Lazy Lion, Mwenye Hadithi
Little Elephant's Walk, Adrienne Kennaway
Mama Panya's Pancakes: A Village Tale from Kenya, Mary and Rich Chamberlin
Masai and I, Virginia Kroll
Mother Crocodile, Rosa Guy
Papa, Do you Love Me?, Barbara M. Joosse
Rosebud, Ludwig Bemelmans
A South African Night, Rachel Isadora
The Talking Cloth, Rhonda Mitchell
When Africa Was Home, Karen Williams

Music/Movement:

"Jambo, Rafiki"
Source: *Best of Totline: Volume 2*, compiled by Gayle Bittinger

Crafts:

"African Drum"
Using any cylindrical box, such as an oatmeal box, cut the top and bottom out to make the sides of the drum. These parts will be replaced with pieces of felt and sewn on with yarn.

Decorative designs can be added by using poster paints, crayons, and feathers. The results of your work will give you a workable musical instrument.
Source: *101 Easy Art Activities*, Trudy Aarons and Francine Doelsch; *Sticks and Stones and Ice Cream Cones*, Phyllis Fiarotta

"Beaded Bracelet"
The people of Zimbabwe, South Africa, are well known for their colorful beaded bracelets. Help the children make their own colorful bracelets using string and cereal loops of various colors.

For school-age children you can use plastic beads, but the cereal loops are advisable for preschoolers. This source also provides you with some wonderful rhymes and games to go along with this craft.

Source: *Storytime Crafts*, Kathryn Totten

Activities:

"Mancala"

Create your own version of this board game from the African continent. What you will need are cardboard egg cartons (just the bottom), Styrofoam cups, and dried beans. Dress up your board (egg carton) with paint if you like. This game is for two players with one using the left side of the board and the other the right placing and removing beans according to specific instructions. Make your own boards and have a Mancala tournament. Look for detailed game instructions in the source.

Source: *International Crafts and Games*, Cynthia G. Adams

"Drie Blikkies"

This is a popular South African children's street game. Try this with two teams of each four members minimum. Mark four posts with a circle in the center of the four posts (like the dots on a 5 die). At one post stack three tin cans (Blikkies). Team A places people behind each post and Team B lines up at the center circle. Each Team B member will attempt to topple all the blikkies with a tennis ball. If he's successful he tries to run and tag each post before the other team tags him with the ball. The player of Team A who is posted behind the blikkies tries to get the ball and throw it to each post, in order, to get them to tag the runner out. The team with the most points wins.

Source: *Sidewalk Games around the World*, Arlene Erlbach

Songs:

(Audio) "Colors of Africa"

Source: *Circle Time Activities*, Georgianna Stewart

67 Foreign Lands: China

Topical Calendar Tie-in:

October 18

"Birthday of Confucius"—One of the most famous persons of China was a wise philosopher who also went by the name of Kong Zi. He was known for his wise sayings and his rules to follow in order to have a successful life. Advise your friends with the saying, "Confucius says _______."

Videos:

The Five Chinese Brothers
Lon Po Po
Ming Lo Moves the Mountain
Sam and the Lucky Money
A Story of Ping
Tikki Tikki Tembo

Picture Books:

Beautiful Warrior: The Legend of the Nun's Kung Fu, Emily Arnold McCully
Chinatown, William Low
Chopsticks, Jon Berkeley
The Cricket's Cage, Stefan Czernecki
Daisy Comes Home, Jan Brett
The Dragon's Tale: and Other Animal Fables of the Chinese Zodiac, Demi
The Emperor and the Kite, Jane Yolen
The Emperor and the Nightingale, Meilo So
The Emperor's Garden, Ferida Wolff
The Last Dragon, Susan Miho Nunes
The Pea Blossom, Amy Lowry Poule
Roses Sing on New Snow: A Delicious Tale, Paul Yee
Ruby's Wish, Shirin Yim Bridges
The Waiting Day, Harriett Diller
Wan Hu is in the Stars, Jennifer Armstrong
The Warlord's Kites, Virginia Walton Pilegard

Music/Movement:

"This Is Baby's Trumpet"
Source: *Dragon Kites and Dragonflies: A Collection of Chinese Nursery Rhymes*, Demi

Crafts:

"Hair Sticks"
Girls like to create barrettes, ribbons, or other hair accessories to give themselves a new look. With some of the older children try this look from China. Contact your local Chinese restaurant for donations of chopsticks. With these, some craft floss, glue and beads and fabric paint. You can create some fashionable hair sticks to put through your hair when

formed in a bun. Be as creative as you like by even attaching extra beads or characters to the ends of the sticks.

Source: *Best Friends Forever!*, Laura Tories

"Tangrams"

Take a square and cut it into seven pieces of various sizes and shapes. You now have an ancient form of a Chinese puzzle that can be used to create a large variety of artwork. Challenge each child to place these pieces on another sheet of colored paper to form such things as houses, boats, arrows, animals, or other familiar objects. The source offered here gives simple instructions on forming your tangrams. Now try and challenge your class to see how many different illustrations they can create out of the same puzzle.

Source: *Traditional Crafts form China*, Florence Temko

Activities:

"Clapping Hands"

This clapping game is played similarly to that of "Pease Porridge Hot." It may take some practice with the group but this is a game they will enjoy and practice long after the storyhour program has ended. The actual text of "Pease Porridge Hot" can be located on page 31 of Vinton's book.

Source: *The Folkways Omnibus of Children's Games*, Iris Vinton

"Confucius Relay"

Set up two teams for a relay race of a different type. Each team will be inflating balloons and be given a pair of chopsticks. The children need to get the balloons from one point to another with the use of the chopsticks only (Sorry, no hands or body contact). Depending on the age of your group, try going around obstacles too.

Source: *The Penny Whistle Party Planner*, Meredith Brokaw and Annie Gilbar

Songs:

(Audio) "Chinese Friendship Dance"

Source: *Dances Around the World*, Henry Buzz Glass

68 Fractured Fairy Tales

Topical Calendar Tie-in:

August 14–18

"Weird Contest Week"—Ocean City, New Jersey, is known for its weird contest during this week including artistic pie eating, French fry sculpting, wet T-shirt throwing, etc. Take this week to follow their example by having your own weird contest using children's literature. Take your favorite fairy tale and write it from a different point of view. Example: How do you think the wolf in *Little Red Riding Hood* felt about what happened?

Videos:

Cinder-Elly
Prince Cinders
The Truth About Mother Goose
Jake Gander: Storyville Detective

Picture Books:

Cinderella and Cinderella: The Untold Story, Russell Shorto
Cinderella's Rat, Susan Meddaugh
The Cowboy and the Black-Eyed Pea, Tony Johnston
Fables Aesop Never Wrote, Robert Kraus
Fairytale News, Colin and Jacqui Hawkins
The Frog Prince Continued, Jon Scieszka
Jack and the Beanstalk and the Beanstalk Incident, Tim Paulson
Jack and the Meanstalk, Brian and Rebecca Wildsmith
Mr. Wolf and the Three Bears, Jan Fearnley
Moonstruck: The True Story of the Cow Who Jumped Over the Moon, Gennifer Choldenko
Ruby, Michael Emberley
Rumpelstiltskin's Daughter, Diane Stanley
Somebody and the Three Blairs, Marilyn Tolhurst
The Three Silly Billies, Margie Palatini
The Three Little Wolves and the Big Bad Pig, Eugene Triviza
Who's Afraid of the Big Bad Book?, Lauren Child

Music/Movement:

"Little Rap Riding Hood"
A delightfully modern version of the Little Red Riding Hood story done in rap-style with audience participation. This will take some practice on your part as a leader but it adds a wonderful touch to the program. Try getting some high school students to help you present this story.

Source: *Crazy Gibberish and Other Storyhour Stretches*, Naomi Baltuck

Crafts:

"Jack and the Beanstalk"
In this source you will find a wonderfully imaginative craft for your program on fairy tales. Here it centers on Jack and the Beanstalk by creating a beanstalk and the giant's castle. All are made of toilet paper tubes

connected together. Placed one on the top of each other we make the beanstalk and placed in a group we get the effects of castle turrets. With cotton placed under the castle you will get the appearance of a castle floating in the clouds. Enjoy a wonderful fairy-tale effect.

Source: *175 Easy-to-Do Everyday Crafts*, Sharon Dunn Umnik

"Unique Version of the Classic Tale"
Let the children make their own version of the Gingerbread Man tale. Duplicate on the lower portion of a number of pages the familiar refrain "Run, run, as fast as your can! You can't catch me, I'm the Gingerbread Man." Reserve the upper portion for illustrating animals the children wish to introduce into the story chasing the Gingerbread Man.

Source: *The Best of the Mailbox, Book 1: Preschool/Kindergarten edition*, Margaret Michel

Activities:

"Fractured Nursery Rhymes"
Try changing around your favorite nursery rhymes, act them out and see if the class can guess the name of the original rhyme from your mixed-up demonstration. Examples of such events can be:

- Jack Be Nimble jumping over a pumpkin pie?
- Wee Willie Winkie running up and down in his suit?
- Little Miss Muffet is scared by a dinosaur?

How many can the class guess correctly?

"Cinderella Dressed in Yella"
Jump rope rhymes are popular with children. Let the entire class recite this little fractured Cinderella rhyme and let one child jump rope at a time or any other activity you designate (bounce a ball, play catch, etc.) to determine the number you need to complete the rhyme. The group can count it out. What I like about this activity is that there are no losers and everyone can participate.

Source: *Storytime Crafts*, Kathryn Totten

Songs:

(Audio) "Rapunzel Got a Mohawk"

Source: *Ants*

69 Friendship

Topical Calendar Tie-in:

May 21–27

"National New Friends, Old Friends Week"—Friendship is important to everyone's life. Never stop taking the time to establish new friendships but don't forget the old ones. As the saying goes, "Make new friends but keep the old, one is silver and the other gold." Take this week to welcome new people into your life or classroom and do something special for them.

Videos:

Frog and Toad Are Friends: The Story
Happy Lion
Ira Sleeps Over
Peter's Chair
Petunia

Picture Books:

Alex Is My Friend, Marisabina Russo
Andrew Jessup, Nette Hilton
Copy Crocs, David Bedford
Discovering Friendship, Sharon Kadish
Fox Makes Friends, Adam Relf
Harry and Willy and Carrothead, Judith Caseley
How to Be a Friend: A Guide to Making Friends and Keeping Them, Laurie Krasny Brown and Marc Brown
Little Chick's Friend Duckling, Mary DeBall Kwitz
Mary Ann, Betsy James
Moses Sees a Play, Isaac Millman
My Best Friend, Pat Hutchins
A Splendid Friend, Indeed, Suzanne Bloom
That's What Friends Do, Kathryn Cave
Wanted: Best Friend, A.M. Monson
You're Not My Best Friend Anymore, Charlotte Pomerantz

Music/Movement:

"The More we Get Together"
Sung to: "Did You Ever See a Lassie?"

The more we get together, together, together
The more we get together, the happier we'll be.
For you friends are my friends
And my friends are your friends.
The more we get together, the happier we'll be.
(unknown author)

Crafts:

"A Friendship Chain."
Have each child cut a strip of construction paper (2" x 8" long). To this strip have them glue or draw three pictures of things they like to do with

others. All the links designed may be connected to form a friendship chain with each child's name to display in the library during Brotherhood Week.

"Friendship Paper Quilt"
Create a classroom friendship quilt using construction paper and yarn. Each child can create their own section depicting their family friends or whatever theme the group decides. Connect them with yarn and display in your classroom during parent's visitation day or during Friendship Day if your group meets then.

Source: *Creative Fun for 2 to 6 Year Olds: The Little Hands Big Fun Craft Book*, Judy Press

Activities:

"Unpack Your Bag"
This is a wonderful activity to help a new child feel welcome to the class. Ask the new child and parent to bring to class a bag labeled "All About Me" and to place in the bag various items that are important to the child. In the class each item can be removed and the child can help the teacher explain it's importance. You can also have each child in the class show the new child an item they have brought into the class. This is a terrific ice breaker and way to make new friends.

Source: *The Giant Encyclopedia of Theme Activities for Children 2 to 5*, Kathy Charner

"Mirror Pals"
This skill-builder activity helps children with fine and gross motor skills, taking turns, observations skills, and much more. Friends like to do things together and this is an opportunity for them to do exactly the same thing at the same time as they play the mirror image of their best friend. This is a good team activity that can be used for sundry events with or without audience participation.

Source: *Early Learning Skill Builders: Colors, Shapes, Numbers and Letters*, Mary Tomczyk

Songs:

(Audio) "The More we get Together"

Source: *Best Toddler Tunes, vol., 2*

70 Frogs and Toads

Topical Calendar Tie-in:

May 13
"Preakness Frog Hop"—This event decides Maryland's frog entry in the international frog jumping contest in California. Try having your own human frog jump.

Videos:

A Boy, a Dog and a Frog
Frog and Toad are Friends: The Story (Arnold Lobel Video Showcase)
The Frog Prince
The Frog Princess
Frog Went A-Courtin'
Kipper: The Rainbow Puddle

Picture Books:

The Bird, the Frog, and the Light, Avi
An Extraordinary Egg, Leo Lionni
Felix's Hat, Catherine Bancroft
Finklehopper Frog, Irene Livingston
Froggy's Day with Dad, Jonathan London
Frog Odyssey, Juliet and Charles Snape
The Frog Who Wanted to be Singer, Linda Goss
Grandpa Toad's Secrets, Keiko Kasza
Green Wilma, Tedd Arnold
Growing Frogs, Vivian French
Jump, Frog, Jump, Robert Kalan
Once Upon a Lily Pad, Joan Sweeney
Possum and the Peeper, Anne Hunter
Tadpoles, Betsy James
Toad, Ruth Brown

Music/Movement:

"I'm a Little Brown Toad"
Source: *The Frogs Wore Red Suspenders*, Jack Prelutsky

Crafts:

"Clothespin Polliwog"
A simple polliwog can be constructed out of construction paper and a clothespin. Have 2-inch circles pre-cut from blue construction paper. Each child will then cut the circles in half. Glue the top and bottom to each side of the opening of the clothespin to form the front of the polliwog. Once it is dry you can add features and a tail. By squeezing the clothespin you can open and close the mouth of your polliwog. Try going on a "worm hunt" with your polliwog by tossing rubber bands on a table and using your newly born polliwogs.
Source: *The Best Birthday Parties Ever!*, Kathy Ross

"Frog Puppet"
A manageable craft for someone working with very young children and has tight budgets for supplies. Fold over a paper plate to make a wide-mouthed frog, but don't forget his tongue for catching flies. A simple party noisemaker that expands forward when blown makes a perfect tongue. Check for further instructions and other enjoyable crafts in the source book.

Source: *Crafts from Your Favorite Fairy Tales,* Kathy Ross

Activities:

"Bugs for Lunch"
This game will have young children laughing and competing all day. Talk about what we eat for lunch and what frogs eat. Now we eat with forks, but how do frogs get their lunch? Here's where pictures of a different bugs and party blowers (rollout kind) become the central part of this competition. How many bugs can you eat for lunch when you are the frog?

Source: *It's Great to be Three: The Encyclopedia of Activities for Three-Year-Olds,* Kathy Charmer and Maureen Murphy (editors)

"Froggie in the Puddle"
Practice with the children pretending to be jumping frogs and discuss where frogs reside. To set up a pond, designate certain areas as lily pads for the frogs to sit on. While some children sit on the lily pads the remainder of the group should join hands and circle them as they sing the verse supplied for the game. At the last verse the frogs hop to the children who drop their arms to permit the frogs to leave the pond. Select new frogs and begin again.

Source: *Amazing Alligators and Other Story Hour Friends,* Maxine Riggers

Songs:

(Audio) "Five Little Frogs"

Source: *Singable Songs for the Very Young*

71 Fruit

Topical Calendar Tie-in:

July

"National Blueberries Month"—July is the peak of blueberry harvesting time. Learn about blueberry picking as shown in Robert McCloskey's *Blueberries for Sal*. Discover the many uses of blueberries for jam, pancakes, muffins, and more.

Videos:

Fruit: Close Up and Very Personal
The Grey Lady and the Strawberry Snatcher
Anansi and the Talking Melon

Picture Books:

Albert's Field Trip, Leslie Tryon
Apple Farmer Annie, Monica Wellington
The Apple Pie Tree, Zoe Hall
A Book of Fruit, Barbara Hirsch Lember
Chestnut Cove, Tim Egan
Cider Apples, Sandy Nightingale
A Fruit and Vegetable Man, Roni Schotter
Good Job, Oliver!, Laurel Molk
Mr. Putter and Tabby Pick the Pears, Cynthia Rylant
Oliver's Fruit Salad, Vivian French
The Perfect Orange, Frank P. Fraujo
Watermelon Day, Kathi Appelt
What's so Terrible about Swallowing an Apple Seed?, Harriet Lerner and Susan Goldhor
The Wild Bunch, Dee Lillegard

Music/Movement:

"My Apple" or "Two Red Apples"
Source: *Toddle on Over*, Robin Works Davis

Crafts:

"Printing with Fruit"
Pieces of firm fruit are ideal for making prints on shirts, cloth towels, etc. Slice an apple in half and add generous amounts of paint to the flat surface. Now you can decorate various items that can be given as gifts by pressing the fruit to the surface of the item.
Source: *Exciting Things to Do with Color*, Janet Allen

"Paper Weave Fruit Basket"
Help the children make their own picture of a fruit basket containing their favorite fruit. Weave the base of the basket with various colored strips of paper, then paste on the handle. Fill the basket with pictures of fruit they like or cut the shapes from colored paper.
Source: *Cut-Paper Play!*, Sandi Henry

Activities:

"Fruit Smoothies"

During a multicultural festival, children can celebrate a "Harvest Festival" similar to the one in Portugal called "Festa dos Tabuleiros." Read about this holiday and the way it is celebrated in the book named below along with suggestions on fruit and vegetable invitations. Get together to make "Fruit Smoothies" by closely following the directions supplied and the long list of fruit ingredients. Warning: Be sure that you check with parents to ensure that none of the children have any fruit-related allergies.

Source: *Holidays and Festivals Activities Fun!*, Debbie Smith

"The Fruit Song"

Using the special fruit song found in the source listed here have the children identify various types of fruit and gather them together. Keep singing until their gathered into a fruit salad for the final verse.

Source: *300 Three Minute Games*, Jackie Silberg

Songs:

(Audio) "Apple Juice"

Source: *Wee Sing: In the Car*

72 Gender Roles: Nontraditional

Topical Calendar Tie-in:

November 4

"Sadie Hawkins Day"—Usually observed on the first Saturday in November, this day reverses the traditional roles of man and woman and encourages the women and girls to invite the men they select on a date. The holiday is based on the comic strip "Li'l Abner," established in the 1930s.

Videos:

Mommy's Office
William's Doll
You Forgot Your Skirt, Amelia Bloomer!

Picture Books:

Allie's Basketball Dream, Barbara E. Barber
Beautiful Warrior: The Legend of the Nun's Kung Fu, Emily Arnold McCully
Dulcie Dando, Soccer Star, Sue Stops
A Fire Engine for Ruthie, Leslea Newman
Henry's Baby, Mary Hoffman
Little Granny Quarterback!, Bill Martin, Jr.
Mama Is a Miner, George Ella Lyons
Players in Pigtails, Shana Corey
Playground Problem, Margaret McNamara
Pugdog, Andrea U'Ren
Poor Monty, Anne Fine
The Princess Knight, Cornelia Funke
Punxsutawney Phyllis, Susanna Leonard Hill
Sir Cassie to the Rescue, Linda Smith and Karen Patkau
Thomas's Sitter, Jean Richardson
To Capture the Wind, Sheila MacGill-Callahan
What Daddies Do Best/What Mommies Do Best, Laura Numeroff
When I Grow Up, Jo S. Kittinger

Music/Movement:

"My Mom"

Sung to: "You are My Sunshine"

My mom's the coach now when I play football.
(point to mom)
She loves to help me learn all the plays.
She throws the football as well as all of us.
(pretend throwing a football)
Let's all cheer my mom on this special day!
(everyone cheer and clap for their moms)

Crafts:

"Peacock Fan"

Today many people still see families in the traditional method with the father being the major breadwinner and when it comes to dress the female members of the family wearing the more colorful garments. Talk to children about how things are different in many families and how the animal kingdom also shows the changes in traditional roles. Talk about how in lion prides it is the lioness that usually goes out to bring home the meat and in the bird families it is the male of the species who is the more colorful bird. The peacock itself is known for its colorful plumage but only in the male. This little craft can have the children making their own peacock with simple tail feathers made of folded paper that has been decorated and formed into a fan. Check this source for guidance.

Source: *Easy Art Fun! Do-it-yourself Crafts for Beginning Readers*, Jill Frankel Hauser

"Bear Containers"

You will locate an attractive container craft available in this source. You are provided with a bear template that can be photocopied and enlarged to hold the size of the tube container you have selected. Have the child decorate the wide tube and glue it to the bear's lap, then simply fold the bear up around the tube where shown. These containers can be used to store just about anything (party snacks, paper clips, string, pencils, etc.). This would be a great little gift for Mom's desk at work. Let her have a bear hug from you every day.

Source: *Great Paper Crafts*, Ingrid Klettenheimer

Activities:

"Family Chores"

Initiate a discussion among the children about different types of chores that family members are responsible for in their home. Be sure to steer children into including nontraditional roles in the family also (example: Dad babysits, Mom does plumbing etc.).

After the discussion begin a pantomime session where children mimic these chores for the class to guess. An excellent list of suggestions is supplied in the book listed here for you.

Source: *More Picture Book StoryHours: From Parties to Pets*, Paula Gaj Sitarz

"This is What Daddy Does"

This activity can really relate to any member of the family. Children have curiosity about the types of jobs parents do outside the home. Here's a game to help them describe those jobs or lead to a discussion of each occupation. The child begins with "This is what my daddy (or mother, uncle, etc.) does." He then acts out until someone guesses and becomes the next pantomimer.

Source: *Games to Learn By: 101 Best Educational Games*, Muriel Mandell

Songs:

(Audio) "William's Doll"

Source: *Free to be . . . You and Me*

73 Ghosts

Topical Calendar Tie-in:

August 11–September 9

"People's Republic of China's Festival of Hungry Ghosts"—It is also known as Ghost Month, and according to legend, ghosts roam the earth. Many items, such as, prayers, food, or "ghost money" are offered to appease the spirits and ensure a prosperous year.

Videos:

Georgie
The Ghost with the Halloween Hiccups
The Legend of Sleepy Hollow
Tailypo
Winnie the Witch and the Frightened Ghost (Fran Allison's Autumn Tales of Winnie the Witch)

Picture Books:

Berenstain Bears Go on a Ghost Walk, Stan and Jan Berenstain
The Boo Baby Girl Meets the Ghost of Mable's Gable, Jim May
Davy, Help! It's a Ghost!, Brigitte Weninger
The Ghost's Dinner, Jacques Duquennoy
Good Night, Sleep Tight, Don't Let the Bedbugs Bite!, Diane deGroat
Hank the Clank, Michael Coleman
Little Ghost, Kate Khdir and Sue Nash
Lu and the Swamp Ghost, James Carville
Martin and the Pumpkin Ghost, Ingrid Ostheeren
Skeleton Hiccups, Margery Cuyler
The Teeny Tiny Ghost, Kay Winters
The Teeny Tiny Ghost and the Monster, Kay Winters
Ten Timid Ghosts, Jennifer O'Connell
Woo! The Not-so-Scary Ghost, Ana Martin Larranaga

Music/Movement:

"Hallowe'en Ghost"
Source: *The Big Book of Stories, Songs and Sing-Along*, Beth Maddigan

Crafts:

"Standing Ghost Halloween Decoration"
Stand-up ghosts that you've seen around for decorations are easier to make than you think. Blow up a balloon and place it on an open canning jar that is used as a craft stand. With the use of cheesecloth and liquid starch you can create a stiff ghost. Once it's dry it will stand on its own and you can add facial features. Don't miss this effortless and inexpensive craft. Specific details are available in the source book.
Source: *The Mudpies Activity Book: Recipes for Inventions*, Nancy Blakey

"Ghost Prints"

Here's a craft that can be enjoyed by even the youngest of your group. Just place a scoop of white paint on a surface easily cleaned later and let them have the time of their lives fingerpainting. When this activity has exhausted their energies smooth the paint out and create eyes and a mouth. Place a black paper on the mess to lift off their own ghost print. You think this is simple and fun? Try the many other preschool arts and crafts offered in this source.

Source: *Crafts: Early Learning Activities*, Jean Warren

Activities:

"Telling Campfire Ghost Stories"

This activity is for those school-age children who love to create their own ghost stories. Basic guidelines are offered here, including setting the mood, lighting, and storytelling hints, such as making your story personal, with pauses and more. Try setting up your own storytelling club in the class that will meet on a regular basis and present their stories to the class.

Source: *The Kids' Guide to Nature Adventures*, Joe Rhatigan

"A Ghostly Game"

This ghostly game can be played with any number of people over two. It is a word game that requires that the child at least be able to spell the simple words used. The object of the game is for each player to add a letter to the word to continue the spelling without finishing the word. If a player ends the word on the third letter he becomes a half ghost. Any player that gets three half ghost penalties is eliminated.

Source: *Halloween Holiday Grab Bag*, Judith Stamper

Songs:

(Audio) "Ghostbuster's Theme"

Source: *Halloween Fun*

74 Giants

Topical Calendar Tie-in:

June 28
"Paul Bunyan Day"—Honor the famous American folk hero and his giant ox, Babe, on this noteworthy day. Enjoy folk stories of his adventures and search for other giant or tall tale stories to share with your friends.

Videos:

Frog and Toad Together: Dragons and Giants (Arnold Lobel Video Showcase)
The Giant Devil-Dingo
Jack and the Beanstalk
Mickey Mouse: The Brave Little Tailor (Cartoon Classics Collection, Vol. 6)
The Selfish Giant

Picture Books:

Carolinda Clatter!, Mordicai Gerstein
The Giant, Nicholas Heller
The Giant and the Beanstalk, Diane Stanley
His Royal Buckliness, Kevin Hawkes
Joe Giant's Missing Boot: A Mothergooseville Story, Toni Goffe
Kate's Giants, Valiska Gregory
Mary, Mary, Sarah Hayes
The Little Hen and the Giant, Maria Polushkin
Look Out, Jack! The Giant is Back!, Tom Birdseye
The Mightiest, Keiko Kasza
My Daddy Is a Giant, Carl Norac
Rude Giants, Audrey Wood
The Selfish Giant, Oscar Wilde
The Spiffiest Giant in Town, Julia Donaldson
What Can a Giant Do?, Mary Louise Cuneo

Music/Movement:

"The Giant Stomp"
Source: *The Complete Resource Book for Toddlers and Twos*, Pam Schiller

Crafts:

"Large Tracks"
Bigfoot is the best-known Giant along with the giant in Jack and the Beanstalk. Talk about different giants and about the myth of Bigfoot and how people claim to have seen him and his tracks. Let's now make our own tracks. This craft allows you to make Bigfoot boots out of cardboard that can be tied to the children's shoes. If it's a snowy day you can go outside and make your own tracks.
Source: *Crafts to Make in the Winter*, Kathy Ross

"Stick Figures"
Giants are common characters in children's literature and one enjoyed very much by children. In this book you will find some interesting illustrations

and suggestions for making your own giant stick puppets. Some are made using paper plates, pieces of cloth, or just construction paper but all are amusing. Make them as large as possible then place them on long sticks so the children can make them even bigger by holding them high above their heads while telling their favorite giant stories.

Source: *Great Paper Craft Projects*, Ingrid Klettenheimer

Activities:

"Big and Little Day"

Have a big and little day so that children can look at things from a different perspective. A giant might look at an elephant differently than a mouse would see it. Talk about how different things are viewed and read some stories that offer books from a different perspective. I love the idea offered in this source of having a Big Day when you can wear clothes too big for you, eat large sandwiches, etc. Also offered is a game called "elephant and ant," a large and small sorting game, and a big and little hunt. Check out all the fun offered for this day.

Source: *Shapes, Sizes and More Surprises!*, Mary Tomczyk

"Giant Steps"

A basic game familiar to most children and can be played with three or more people. Remember "Mother, may I?" This is the same type of activity.

Source: *Rain or Shine Activity Book: Fun Things to Make and Do*, Joanna Cole and Stephanie Calmenson

Songs;

(Audio) "The Colossal Giant Drink" and
"The Giant Hot Dog that Ate Ohio"

Source: *Weird and Wacky Songs for Kids*, Bob King

75 Glasses

Topical Calendar Tie-in:

March

"Save Your Vision Month"—Take time to remind everyone of the importance of regular eye exams and eye care. Talk about foods to eat to improve eyesight, and proper distance from televisions and computers. Let children who wear glasses know that too is cool!

Videos:

Arthur's Eyes
Goggles

Picture Books:

All the Better to See You With!, Margaret Wild
Baby Duck and the Bad Eyeglasses, Amy Hest
Boris's Glasses, Peter Cohen and Olaf Landstrom
Bumposaurus, Penny McKinlay
Dog's Don't Wear Glasses, Adrienne Geoghegan
Glasses for D. W., Marc Brown
Glasses, Who Needs 'Em?, Lane Smith
The Good Luck Glasses, Sara London
Goggles, Ezra Jack Keats
Hooray for Grandma Jo!, Thomas McKean
I Need Glasses: My Visit to the Optometrist, Virginia Dooley
Jennifer Jean, the Cross-Eyed Queen, Phyllis Reynolds Naylor
Little Hippo Gets Glasses, Maryann MacDonald
Tracks, David Galef
What Can Rabbit See?, Lucy Cousins

Music/Movement:

"Glasses"
Sung to: "A Tisket, a Tasket"

Some glasses, some glasses
My mommy says I need glasses
I don't want black
I don't want brown
But maybe the pink with polka dots will do.
(Let children enter a color they would like.)

Crafts:

"Sunglasses"
If you prefer using environmentally conscious crafts, here's one for you. A simple pattern is provided in this source for children to create their own sunglasses out of scrap cardboard. Decorate them to each individual's preferences.
Source: *Earth-Friendly Wearables,* George Pfiffner

"Magic Spectacles"
Try looking at the world with rose-colored glasses. With the use of posterboard, red cellophane and popsicle sticks children can make their magical spectacles. Let the children look at various things to see what a difference color can make.

Source: *Never-Be-Bored Book*, Judith Logan Lobne

Activity:

"A Collection of Goggles"
Gather a collection of eyeglasses that people wear (reading glasses, swimming goggles, sunglasses, motorcycle goggles, etc.) and place them in a location where children can try them on for size. Children love to pretend. You might supply a mirror and drawing paper and let the children draw self-portraits in their favorite glasses.

"Tide's Out!"
Explore your seashore coastlines searching for the number of hidden sea creatures that inhabit the tide pools in your area. Many marine animals attach themselves to the rocky areas beneath the water. Let's take a look at these rocky residences with a special "spy glass or eyeglass viewer" made out of an empty can, plastic wrap, and a rubber band. Once your viewer is created lower the plastic-wrapped end into the water and you will have a clear and fantastic view of the creatures below the surface of the water. Search for any lost items that may be found below the water and see how many different items you can locate.

Source: *Awesome Ocean Science!*, Cindy A. Littlefield

Songs:

(Audio) "Harry's Glasses"

Source: *Nobody Else Like Me*

76 Grandparents

Topical Calendar Tie-in:

July 23

"Gorgeous Grandma Day"—Here's a day to devote to those grandmothers who keep themselves young and in good shape for themselves and for their families. Help Grandma stay young and beautiful through exercise, activities, and the love of her family.

Videos:

Grandpa
Song and Dance Man
Spot Visits His Grandparents
What's Under the Bed?

Picture Books:

40 Uses for a Grandpa, Harriet Ziefert
A Busy Day for a Good Grandmother, Margaret Mahy
Again!, John Prater
Eleanor, Arthur and Claire, Diana Engel
Grandfather's Dream, Holly Keller
Grandpa's Garden Lunch, Judith Caseley
Grandpa's Teeth, Rod Clement
Grandma According to Me, Karen M. Beil
Granny and Me, Robin Ballard
Little Granny Quarterback!, Bill Martin, Jr.
Lucky Pennies and Hot Chocolate, Carol Diggory Shields
My Friend Grandpa, Harriet Ziefert
My Grandpa Is Amazing, Nick Butterworth
Supergrandpa, David M. Schwartz
Valerie and the Silver Pear, Benjamin Darling

Music/Movement:

"Grandma's Going to the Grocery Store"
A nice rhyme that requires audience response to the leader's queries.
Source: *Crazy Gibberish and Other Storyhour Stretches*, Naomi Baltuck

Crafts:

"Coupon Box for Grandma"
Most grandmothers are still willing to collect coupons to save money these days. Gather together old cereal boxes that will cut down to a third of their size. These can be covered with decorative shelving paper or with regular construction paper and then decorated with stickers by the children. Don't stop now. Explain to the children that Grandma might want to organize her coupons in various ways, such as types of foods. Help them make dividers to put in the box with pictures of food groups on each divider.

"Orizomegami"
Orizomegami is a paper-dying technique similar to the tye-dying of T-shirts when that was a trend. Ms. Lewis offers directions for using paper towels

and food coloring to create numerous styles and shapes that can be used in greeting cards and other crafts. Orizomegami adds pizzazz behind any cut-out paper design. Let the children use this technique to make unique greeting cards for Grandparent's Day. Try it for starry nights, Valentine hearts, bookmarks, and more that are shown in this source. Easy, inexpensive, and beautiful.

Source: *The Jumbo Book of Paper Craft,* Amanda Lewis

Activities:

"Grandma is Strange"
My grandma likes very odd things. For example, she likes to pet porcupines but doesn't like dogs, she likes pears but doesn't like apples, etc. Children will eventually guess that Grandma only likes things that start with the letter P. You might only mention things that are square or only purple, etc. The child guessing the oddity must answer in a specific way to win. Check this source for this secret ending and other ways to play this game.

Source: *Summer Fun! 60 Activities for a Kid-Perfect Summer,* Susan Williamson

"Stamp-it Picnic Tablecloth"
Grandmothers are special people. They love to receive gifts made especially for them by their grandchildren. Even more than receiving gifts, they have the patience, and time, to help children make those special gifts. Develop a Grandparent's Day program where children can work on a project with a grandparent. This special project includes easily found checked tablecloths or placemat paint (an item children love) and flat craft sponges in different shapes. This is a sure winner!

Source: *Hey Kids! Come Craft with Me,* Mary Engelbreit

Songs:

(Audio) "I'm My Own Grandpa"

Source: *A Child's Celebration of Silliest Songs*

77 Handicaps

Topical Calendar Tie-in:

July 20

"Special Olympics Day"—Special Olympics is an international gathering of children and adults with mental retardation or physical handicaps. Programs include a variety of sports training events and competitions. Take a day to assist in a day of sports events for these special friends.

Videos:

Apt. 3
The Play

Picture Books:

Alex Is My Friend, Marisabina Russo
Arnie and the New Kid, Nancy Carlson
Cakes and Miracles: A Purim Tale, Barbara Diamond Goldin
Dad and Me in the Morning, Pat Lakin
Discovering Friendship, Sharona Kadish
Harry and Willy and Carrothead, Judith Caseley
Ian's Walk: A Story about Autism, Laurie Lears
The Little Lame Prince, Rosemary Wells
Listen for the Bus: David's Story, Patricia McMahan
Lucy's Picture, Nicola Moon
My Buddy, Audrey Osofsky
Silent Lotus, Jeanne M. Lee
A Story of Courage, Joel Vecere
We Go in a Circle, Peggy Perry Anderson
With the Wind, Liz Damrell

Music/Movement:

"Roll Along"

Sung to "Row, Row, Row the Boat"

Roll, roll, roll along in my brand new chair.
(pretend to roll wheels on chair)
I may not be able to walk,
But my chair will get me there.

Roll, roll, roll along
(pretend to roll wheels on chair)
Let's play basketball
I will pass the ball to you.
(throw ball to friend)
but be careful *you* don't fall.

Crafts:

"Blind Artist"

Children can be taught that people with handicaps are very capable people who learn to rely on the senses available to them. Give each child in turn a large piece of paper and blindfold her. Call out an item for the child to draw, or simply give her an item to taste or smell, then ask her to draw what she thinks the item is that has been presented.

"Texture Pictures"
After reading *Lucy's Picture* by Nicola Moon, the children will be excited about creating their own pictures using scraps, twigs, sand, and other items that add texture to their creation. Have the children close their eyes and tell you what each scrap feels like to them before adding it to their own illustration.

Activities:

"Hearing—Whispering Down the Lane"
This is the ever popular telephone game. Tell children they must whisper only. The first child begins by whispering a statement which is passed along until the last child calls out the final result. You may not repeat the statement. At the end, discuss how hearing impaired people have difficulty even hearing loud voices even as they had a hard time in "Whispering Down the Lane."

Source: *Kids' Celebrate!*, Maria Bonfanti Esche and Clare Bonfanti Braham

"Steal the Treasure"
Children can get a small understanding of needing to rely closely on their hearing senses when their vision is taken away from them in this game. A child is placed in a chair and blindfolded. Treasure coins are scattered on the floor around him. One to three thieves at a time are instructed to try to steal the coins without being heard. If the Great Detective in the chair can accurately point to a thief, that thief is eliminated.

Source: *Great Theme Parties for Children*, Irene N. Watts

Songs:

(Audio) "Walking on My Wheels"

Source: *Nobody Else Like Me*

78 Holidays: Chanukah

Topical Calendar Tie-in:

December 14–21
"Chanukah" is the Feast of Lights, a festival of eight days celebrating the victory of the Maccabees over Syrians and the dedication of the Temple of Jerusalem

Videos:

Hanukkah
In the Month of Kislev
Lamb Chop's Special Chanukah
Liar, Liar, Pants on Fire
Shalom Sesame: Chanukah

Picture Books:

Biscuit's Hanukkah, Alyssa Satin Capucilli
A Blue's Clue's Chanukah, Jessica Lissy
The Borrowed Hanukkah Latkes, Linda Glaser
By the Hanukkah Light, Sheldon Oberman
The Eight Nights of Chanukah, Leslea Newman
Hanukkah, Oh Hanukkah, Susan L. Roth
Hanukkah Lights, Hanukkah Nights, Leslie Kimmelman
Inside-Out Grandma: A Hanukkah Story, Joan Rothenberg
It's Hanukkah Time!, Latifa Berry Kropf
Lots of Latkes: A Hanukkah Story, Sandy Lanton
The Miracle of the Potato Latkes, Malka Penn
A Picture Book of Hanukkah, David Adler
Runaway Dreidel!, Leslea Newman
The Trees of the Dancing Goats, Patricia Polacco
The Ugly Menorah, Marissa Moss
What Is Hanukkah?, Harriet Ziefert

Music/Movement:

"Five Little Dreidels"
Source: *101 Fingerplays, Stories and Songs to Use with Finger Puppets*, Diane Brigs

Crafts:

"Dreidel Gift Bag"
A simple Chanukah holiday gift bag can be made for the children using shopping bags, poster paint, and basic decorations. This one can be made to look like a simple dreidel. Need crafts for other Jewish holidays? Look in this great source.
Source: *The Jewish Holiday Craft Book*, Kathy Ross

"Candle Candy Holders"
Here is a delightful party favor for some sweet Hanukkah treats. Use simple toilet paper tubes to be decorated for this special holiday. Place some candy treats in red tissue paper and tape it closed. Simply stuff the

tissue into the tube leaving the top sticking out to form the flame of your Hanukkah candles. Find this and other simple Hanukkah crafts in this source.

Source: *Hanukkah Crafts*, Karen E. Bledsoe

Activities:

"Eight Candles Match-Up"
A version of the Lotto game designed for Chanukah, this will be easy for any age. You will need to create a Lotto board with numbers 1 to 8 and a Star of David on it as shown in the book listed. Card pieces that will be placed facedown on the table will have illustrations of the menorah with various numbers of candles lit. Want something for older children? Check this same source for a board game offered called "To the Temple," where the object of the game is to be the first to reach the Holy Temple of Jerusalem. Your dreidel will tell you how many spaces you move forward, and the board gives you directions to continue the game.

Source: *Hanukkah: Festival of Lights*, Arthur Friedman

"Live Dreidel Game"
Add a little variety to the holidays with this live dreidel game. Follow the instructions to create a belt for a child to wear. This is a special belt with pockets to hold the Hebrew letters. The child wearing the belt is the dreidel and is unaware of which letter is in each pocket. Turn on your music and the human dreidel will begin to spin and collapse onto one of the letters. Keep score as you would when playing with a toy dreidel.

Source: *Crafts for Hanukkah*, Kathy Ross

Songs:

"I'm a Little Latke"

Source: *Candle, Snow and Mistletoe*, Sharon, Lois and Bram

79 Holidays: Christmas

Topical Calendar Tie-in:

December 16–24

"Las Posadas," a nine-day celebration leading up to Christmas, is usually held in Mexico and in some areas of the United States. Las Posadas is a reenactment of the night of the birth of Jesus. Parents and children wander their familiar neighborhoods knocking on neighbors, doors looking for shelter as Mary did that famous night. When they are finally offered shelter, everyone goes into the house and celebrates through a variety of party events.

Videos:

Arthur's Christmas Cookies (Arthur Celebrates the Holidays)
The Bear Who Slept through Christmas
The Elves and the Shoemaker
The Little Drummer Boy
The Mole and the Christmas Tree
Morris' Disappearing Bag
The Twelve Days of Christmas
A Visit from St. Nicholas

Picture Books:

A Christmas Star Called Hannah, Vivian French
Christmas Trolls, Jan Brett
Claude the Dog, Dick Gackenbach
The Feathered Crown, Marsha Hayles
Gingerbread Mouse, Katy Bratun
How Santa Got His Job, Stephen Krensky
Lyle at Christmas, Bernard Waber
Merry Christmas Geraldine, Holly Keller
The Oldest Elf, James Stevenson
One Snowy Night, M. Christina Butler
Paddington Bear and the Christmas Surprise, Michael Bond
The Perfect Present, Michael Hagu
Snowbear's Christmas Countdown, Theresa Smythe
Tree of Cranes, Allen Say
What Could be Keeping Santa?, Marilyn Janovitz

Music/Movement:

"Santa Visit"
Sung to: "Eeensy, Weensy Spider"

The roly poly Santa climbed down the chimney flue
He passed out the presents he brought for me and you.
He peeked in and watches me sleeping in my bed.
Then the roly poly Santa kissed me on my head!

Crafts:

"Craft Stick Reindeer"
This basic triangle reindeer face is simple enough for the youngest child to come away with a good feeling about his work. With the use of three craft sticks formed into a triangle, two wiggle eyes, a pom-pom nose, and a string to hang this ornament on the tree everyone can create Santa's reindeer faces for the holiday. Use a red pom-pom so you don't forget the most famous reindeer, Rudolph.

Source: *Christmas Parties: What Do I Do?*, Wilhelminia Ripple

"Pine Cone Wreath"
A beautiful and simple Christmas wreath can be constructed using very inexpensive materials such as mat board (or cardboard), glue, pine cones, and ribbon. Put out a box of various beads and glitter and children will be delighted with the variety of wreaths they will produce.

Source: *One-Hour Holiday Crafts for Kids*, Cindy Groom Harry and staff

Activities:

"Antler Toss"
Santa's reindeers fly in teams of two, and you can team up in pairs for this special holiday ring toss game. Distribute to each child reindeer antler headbands to wear and have them sit on chairs facing each other. You may supply rings or as this source suggests make some out of pipe cleaners. At the start of the jingle bells, have each team member attempt to toss the rings onto their partner's antlers. Each ring will give them a point. How many points do you think would be the perfect number for a winner on Christmas Day?

Source: *Christmas Parties: What Do I Do?*, Wilhelminia Ripple

"Santa's Coming"
Santa's coming to deliver your Christmas presents. Have you been a good boy or girl? Will you get a present or will you get some coal? In this circle activity children will be offered treats but are eliminated if they receive the coal. Decorate a group of small boxes equal to the amount of children playing the game that can be easily opened without ripping the wrapping. In one box put a lump of coal and in the remainder of the boxes put a small collection of such things as stickers, lollipops, tattoos, bookmarks, etc. Each box should have a different surprise. Play some fun Christmas music and begin passing the boxes until the music stops. At this time each child opens the boxes and takes out one surprise for himself. The child with the coal is eliminated, but make sure he gets at least something for his efforts. In secret, switch the coal with the contents of one of the other boxes and continue the game.

Songs:

(Audio) "Kris Kringle's Jingle Bell Band"

Source: *Rhythms on Parade*, Hap Palmer

80 Holidays: Easter

Topical Calendar Tie-in:

April 16
"Easter Sunday"—Usually the first Sunday following the first full moon after the vernal equinox, this holiday commemorates the Resurrection of Jesus Christ.

Videos:

The Beginners Bible: The Story of Easter
The Easter Bunny
The First Easter Rabbit
Funny Little Bunnies
Madeline and the Easter Bonnet
Max's Chocolate Chicken

Picture Books:

The Bunny Who Found Easter, Charlotte Zolotow
Coriander's Easter Adventure, Ingrid Ostheeren
The Easter Chick, Geraldine Elschner
Easter Egg Disaster, Karen Gray Ruelle
Easter Parade, Irving Berlin
Easter Surprise, Catherine Stock
The Great Easter Egg Hunt, Michael Garland
Happy Easter Day!, Wendy Watson
Humbug Rabbit, Lorna Balian
Owen's Marshmallow Chick, Kevin Henkes
Peter Rabbit's Happy Easter, Grace Maccarone
Queen of Easter, Mary Engelbreit
The Story of the Easter Bunny, Katherine Tegen
Winnie the Pooh: The Easter Bear?, Ann Braybrooks

Music/Movement:

"Bunny Hop"
Sung to: "A Tisket, a Tasket"

A hoppin', a hoppin', the bunnies went a hoppin'
(hop like bunnies)
They hopped on down and hid some eggs
(pretend to hide eggs)
For all the kids to find them.

A hoppin', a hoppin', the bunnies went a hoppin'.
(hop like bunnies)
They packed that basket with candy and eggs
And hid it in my house so I can find them.
(hand over eyes searching for baskets)

Crafts:

"Easter Egg Mats"

Eggs, eggs, everywhere! Children love to decorate Easter eggs. Try this uncomplicated holiday craft that children can take home to decorate their Easter tables. Parents will be happy to include their children's craft in their holiday events. Use colorful craft foam to trace egg shapes. Next cut a variety of shapes and designs to be glued on the eggs for decoration. Suggestions for designs are offered in this source. These egg mats or coasters will add a festive mood to your table.

Source: *Easy Crafts to Make Together: 750 Family-Fun Ideas*, Carol Field Dahlstrom (editor)

"Boxy Bunny"

Make your own Easter treat basket with the use of the bottom half of a half-gallon milk carton, a cardboard tube, construction paper, plastic grass, and cotton balls. This Easter craft book gives you a number of good possibilities but this Boxy Bunny has many uses and can be made by young children out of inexpensive materials. Check it out for this year's holiday program.

Source: *Fun-to-Make Crafts for Easter*, Tom Daning

Activities:

"Ring-Toss Rabbit"

Construct your own ring-toss game for the Easter holidays. This book demonstrates the construction of an Easter bunny stand that can be used for tossing paper rings on his hand or ears. Determine points for where the children connect with the bunny.

Source: *Fun-to-Make Crafts for Easter*, Tom Daning

"Easter Egg Hockey"

This is a game that will require a large area, such as a gym or outdoor play space. The class can be divided into two teams. Use boxes for your goal areas and a large plastic Easter egg for the ball. Here's the twist, though: The children may not touch the egg with any part of their body. They must touch the egg only with the cardboard Easter eggs they have previously decorated. If anyone touches it the other team gains a point. A surefire hit for any group.

Source: *Creative Games for Young Children*, Annetta Dellinger

Songs:

(Audio) "Little Bunny Foo Foo"

Source: *Animal Song Favorites*, Kidsongs

81 Holidays: Fourth of July

Topical Calendar Tie-in:

November 22
"What Do You Love About America Day"—This day occurs annually the day before Thanksgiving. While many people complain about their life in America, take this time instead to let everyone know what you like about this great country.

Videos:

Star-Spangled Banner
Independence Day
Yankee Doodle

Picture Books:

Apple Pie 4th of July, Janet S. Wong
Fourth of July, Janet McDonnell
Fourth of July Bear, Kathryn Lasky
Fourth of July Mice!, Bethany Roberts
A Fourth of July on the Plains, Jean VanLeeuwen
Fourth of July, Sparkly Sky, Joan Holub
The Fourth of July Story, Alice Dalgliesh
Happy 4th of July, Jenny Sweeney!, Leslie Kimmelman
Hats off for the Fourth of July!, Harriet Ziefert
Hurray for the Fourth of July, Wendy Watson
Independence Day, Marc Tyler Nobleman
Looking for Uncle Louie on the Fourth of July, Kathy Whitehead
Phoebe's Parade, Claudia Mills

Music/Movement:

"Wave, Wave, the Flag"
Sung to: "Row, Row, Row Your Boat"
Source: *Fun with Mommy and Me*, Dr. Cindy Bunin Nurik

Crafts:

"Statue of Liberty Crown"
A symbol of hope and freedom for people coming to our country, the Statue of Liberty should be an intrinsic part of the Fourth of July celebrations. Follow the directions in this source to create a Statue of Liberty crown out of paper plates and complete it by painting it gold and maybe adding a little glitter, which children enjoy. Wear your Liberty crown for a patriotic parade on the birthday of our nation.
Source: *Star Spangled Crafts*, Kathy Ross

"Fiery Fireworks"
These colorful fireworks are a perfect craft for the very young child. Made out of painted toilet paper rolls and colored tissue paper, the child can decorate it with a world of sticker stars. These paper firecrackers are good for decorations or hiding special treats at Fourth of July picnics.
Source: *My Party Book*, Marion Elliot

Activities:

"Firecracker Boom"

Ms. Feldman's group card game offers children a safe method of celebrating the Fourth of July with firecrackers. Well, not real firecrackers, but illustrations on a stack of cards mixed with others. This game is easily adapted to teach children to identify any category of items you are working with today (food, clothes, furniture, etc.), but watch out for the firecracker card because that's when the fun begins!

Source: *Transition Tips and Tricks for Teachers*, Jean Feldman

"Capture the Flag"

The Fourth of July holiday is a celebration of our independence from Great Britain. This did not happen without some battles and controversy. This is a good time for a little history lesson followed by an enjoyable team game called "Capture the Flag." Let the children divide up into two teams, each with a flag from his team's adopted country. The goal of this game is to cross the yard or room to retrieve the other team's flag from its hiding place and carry it back to home base. Look for directions on this team game and variations using other props in this source book.

Source: *Great Games!*, Sam Taggar and Susan Williamson

Songs:

(Audio) "The United States"

Source: *Wee Sing: In the Car*

82 Holidays: Groundhog Day/Shadow

Topical Calendar Tie-in:

February 2

"Groundhog's Day"—Discuss the ancient belief that if the groundhog sees his shadow we will have six more weeks of winter. Can you see your shadow? Have a shadow dancing or shadow painting party for everyone.

Videos:

The Boy with Two Shadows
The Spirit of Punxsutawney: Groundhog Day
Tale of the Groundhog's Shadow

Picture Books:

Geoffrey Groundhog Predicts the Weather, Brice Koscielniak
Go to Sleep, Groundhog!, Judy Cox
Gregory's Shadow, Don Freeman
Great Fuzz Frenzy, Janet Stevens and Susan Stevens Crummel
Gretchen Groundhog, It's Your Day!, Abby Levine
Groundhog Gets a Say, Pamela Curtis Swallow
It's Groundhog Day!, Steven Kroll
My Shadow, Robert Louis Stevenson
Punxsutawney Phyllis, Susanna Leonard Hill
Return of the Shadows, Norma Farber
Shadow Night, Kay Chrao
Shadows, April Pulley Sayre
Shadows are About, Ann Whitford Paul
Shadowville, Michel Bartalos

Music/Movement:

"The Little Groundhog"
Sung to: "Little White Duck"

The little groundhog's sleeping in the ground.
(pretend to sleep on ground)
The little groundhog's sleeping in the ground.
He stretched and pushed up to take a peek,
(stretch and slowly rise up)
He saw his shadow.
The news is bleak.
(look and move back into the hole to sleep)
Now there's eight more weeks of winter in my future.
Eight more weeks of snow and ice and shiver.

Crafts:

"Shadow Painting"
A shadow of a creature has appeared before you. What is he? Let the children paint their own shadow creatures using sponges, black paint, and animal stencils. If you are one of those schools that have Ellison machines and have cut out animal shapes for crafts, I hope you didn't throw away

the portion of the paper that was left. Never throw anything out! You now have a ready-made stencil that children can tape to a large sheet of paper and sponge paint on to make shadow artwork.

"Paperbag Groundhog"

Help your groundhog predict an early spring or a long winter. After discussing this with the children have them make their own groundhog on a hill to make their own predictions. Fold a paper plate in half, color brown, and cut a small hole in the bottom. This will be your hill. Add a sun to the topside then cut a groundhog shape out of a paper bag. With your groundhog attached to a straw, he can now pop in and out of the hill you created to make his predictions. For more details and illustrations of this craft see the source book.

Source: *Kids' Celebrate*, Maria Bonfanti Esche and Clare Bonfanti Braham

Activities:

"Groundhog"

After teaching children the legend of the groundhog and his shadow, this game can add a little fun to the lesson. Each child and teacher will be given a cloud and a sun to hold up whenever the teacher holds her illustration above her head. The groundhog (student in the center of the circle) closes his eyes and waits for instructions to come out of his hole. When he opens his eyes and looks around the circle and finds clouds, he must choose a child (a shadow) to be the next groundhog. If he sees the sun he will cover his eyes and climb back into his hole. During each round the children can be taught the delightful rhyme offered by Ms. Silberg, titled "Groundhog, Groundhog."

Source: *The Complete Book of Activities, Games, Stories, Props, Recipes and Dances for Young Children*, Pam Schiller and Jackie Silberg

"Shadow Dancing"

Let your shadow dance across your parking lot on any sunny day. This exciting and artistic activity will require the children to team up and will also turn your parking lot into an artistic museum. Nancy Blakey offers a recipe for "Shadow Dancing Paint" which is inexpensive, easy to mix, and best of all, "is biodegradable and will wash off cement or asphalt with water." Mix your paints with several colors and put them into small jars with lids. Distribute sponge-tip paintbrushes or just small sponges. Put on the music while one of your teammates dances and ends in a dance position, leaving his or her shadow on the ground. Quickly his teammates grab their sponges and dip them into the paints, making a portrait where his shadow now lies.

Source: *Go Outside!*, Nancy Blakey

Songs:

(Audio)"Here's a Little Groundhog"

Source: *Holiday Piggyback Songs*

83 Holidays: Halloween

Topical Calendar Tie-in:

October

"Halloween Safety Month"—Everyone should gather to plan a month to educate children and parents about safe methods of trick-or-treating for Halloween night. Ghosts and goblins run the streets, but first show Mom candy before you eat.

Videos:

Arthur's Halloween (Arthur Celebrates the Holidays)
Georgie
The Ghost with the Halloween Hiccups
Halloween
The Pumpkin Who Couldn't Smile

Picture Books:

The Best Halloween of All, Susan Wojciechowski
Five Little Pumpkins, Iris Van Rynbach
Fright Night Flight, Laura Krauss Melmed
Halloween Mice!, Bethany Roberts
Halloween Sky Ride, Elizabeth Spurr
Here They Come!, David Costello
In the Haunted House, Even Bunting
Let's Celebrate Halloween, Peter and Connie Roop
Luther's Halloween, Cari Meister
Plumply, Dumply Pumpkin, Mary Serfozo
Rattlebone Rock, Sylvia Andrews
Sheep Trick or Treat, Nancy Shaw
This is the Pumpkin, Abby Levine
The Ugly Pumpkin, Dave Horowitz
When the Goblins Came Knocking, Anna Grossnickle Hines
Witch Mama, Judith Caseley

Music/Movement:

"Trick or Treat"
Sung to: "Three Blind Mice"

Trick or treat, trick or treat
Trick or treat, trick or treat
Put on your costume it's Halloween night
We'll hunt for candy until morning light
While witches, ghosts and bats fly by
It's Halloween night.
It's Halloween night.

Crafts:

"Jack-o'-Lantern Surprise"

Pop-up surprises are forever an enjoyable craft for children. Strive to make the most original pumpkin face of a paper plate that the children have painted orange. Follow the step-by-step instructions offered to make a pocket pumpkin with a surprise ghost inside that can pop up at any time. I can see this craft having the dual purpose of a pop-up surprise and a storage area for special treats.

Source: *The Mailbox: October Arts and Crafts Preschool–Kindergarten*, Ada Goreen, Mackie Rhodes, and Jan Trautman (editors)

"A Haunted Woods"

Halloween's a time when children enjoy spooky events and stories. Let them create their own eerie scene by designing a haunted woods as a background for a story they want to tell later. With the use of black crepe paper for trees and cotton stretched across the scene for clouds you get the effect of trees at night. Add eyes to the trees for a spooktacular effect.

Source: *Making Pictures: Spooky Things*, Penny King and Clare Roundhill

Activities:

"Monster Munch"

Most monsters are not picky eaters but this one definitely is in this beginning letter sound game. Construct a Monster face with a large mouth cut into it out of an old cereal box. The monster now begins to munch on some silly "monster food" that is determined by what is the first item placed in his mouth. If a car is put in the mouth, the child can only feed the monster items that begin with that first letter sound. Look for more fun offered like "Sound Hunt," "Same Sound Bags," and "In the End" offered in the source book.

Source: *Wow! I'm Reading!*, Jill Frankel Hauser

"Witch Hunt"

"We're going on a witch hunt,
A witch hunt, a witch hunt.
We're going on a witch hunt
Be careful, where can she be?"

Hide a witch's hat, a bat, and a black cat somewhere in the room. Encourage the children to quietly search for the hidden items. If they find the black cat they should cry out "meow" and sit down where they are. If they find the bat they should fly to their seat with it, because they are safe this round and can't be eliminated. Whoever finds the witch's hat should quickly put it on and try to catch (tag) one of the other children in the room. The first one tagged by the witch or her black cat (who can only tag from his seated position) is out of the game. Continue with the next round.

Songs:

(Audio) "What Can We Be for Halloween"

Source: *Holiday Songs for all Occasions*

84 Holidays: Kwanzaa

Topical Calendar Tie-in:

December 26–January 1

"Kwanzaa"—This holiday is recognized as the traditional African harvest festival. It stresses the unity of the black family, with a communitywide harvest feast (Karamu) on the seventh day, created by Dr. Maulana Karenga in 1966.

Videos:

Holidays for Children: Kwanzaa
Seven Candles for Kwanzaa

Picture Books:

Celebrating Kwanzaa, Diane Hoyt-Goldsmith
The Gifts of Kwanzaa, Synthia Saint-James
Habari Gani? What's the News?, Sundaira Morninghouse
Iwani's Gift at Kwanzaa, Denis Burden-Patmon
K is for Kwanzaa: A Kwanzaa Alphabet Book, Juwanda G. Ford
Kente Colors, Debbi Chocolate
Kwanzaa, Janet Riehecky
Kwanzaa, A. P. Porter
Kwanzaa, Deborah M. Newton Chocolate
Kwanzaa, Dorothy Rhodes Freeman and Dianne M. Macmillan
A Kwanzaa Celebration, Nancy Williams
My First Kwanzaa Book, Debra M. Chocolate
Seven Candles for Kwanzaa, Andrea Davis Pinkney
Seven Days of Kwanzaa, Ella Grier
The Story of Kwanzaa, Donna L. Washington

Music/Movement:

"Holiday Candles all in a Row" or "Kwanzaa Today"
Source: *Toddle on Over*, Robin Works Davis

Crafts:

"Pumpkin Trivet"
Since Kwanzaa is a harvest festival, any fruit or vegetable shape can be used to create a delightful trivet for Mom. Pack in a supply of old bottle caps, cardboard, and orange spray paint, and you will see some delightful results from even the youngest child with this craft.
Source: *Crafts for Kwanzaa*, Kathy Ross

"Kwanzaa Hug Card"
Here's an item that is simple and can be adapted to any season or situation. Using simple construction paper and yarn, children can create a beautiful greeting card with hands folded over. Open them wide to get a big hug from the friend that sent this lovely card to you for this holiday.
Source: *Crafts for Kwanzaa*, Kathy Ross

"Kinara"
Make your own paper kinara (or candle holder) to help celebrate this family holiday. The kinara is similar to the menorah in shape but holds only seven candles. The center candle, higher than the other, is a black one. Three places are made on either side of this candle to hold six other candles (3 green to the left and 3 red to the right). It's an African custom to make these things by hand.

Activities:

"Seven Candles Game"
The name of this game is mishumaa saba in Swahili. It is constructed of red, green, and black straws, the colors of the kinara. These colors are an important part of the game because they determine a winner in this take on pickup sticks.

Source: *Kwanzaa Crafts*, Carol Cnojewski

"Togetherness Kwanzaa Meal"
Have the children plan a gathering where elders (not just parents) are invited to share and exchange stories, pictures, and memories. The children can prepare special meals to be served from recipes found in the two books listed here.

Source: *Let's Celebrate Kwanzaa: An Activity Book for Young Readers*, Helen Davis Thompson; and *Kwanzaa: An African-American Celebration of Culture and Cooking,* Eric V. Copage

Songs:

(Audio) "First Fruit"

Source: *Kwanzaa Songs*

85 Holidays: St. Patrick's Day (also includes Elves and Little People)

Topical Calendar Tie-in:

March 17

"St. Patrick's Day"—Take this day to commemorate the patron saint of Ireland and all the legends associated with that Emerald Isle and the wearing of the green.

Videos:

Holidays for Children: St. Patrick's Day
Snow White and the Seven Dwarfs

Picture Books:

It's St. Patrick's Day, Rebecca Gomez
Leprechaun Gold, Teresa Bateman
The Leprechaun in the Basement, Kathy Tucker
Leprechauns Never Lie, Lorna Balian
Let's Celebrate St. Patrick's Day, Peter and Connie Roop
The Littlest Leprechaun, Justine Fontes
Mary McLean and the St. Patrick's Day Parade, Steven Kroll
Patrick's Day, Elizabeth Lee O'Donnell
Seeing is Believing, Elizabeth Shub
Shadows, Deanna Calvert
Shawn O'Hisser, the Last Snake in Ireland, Peter J. Welling
St. Patrick's Day, Mari C. Schuh
St. Patrick's Day, Brenda Haugen
St. Patrick's Day, Gail Gibbons
St. Patrick's Day Shamrocks, Mary Berendes
Tim O'Toole and the Wee Folk, Gerald McDermott

Music/Movement:

"The Leprechaun"
Sung to: "Muffin Man"

Do you know the leprechauns?
The leprechauns, the leprechauns.
Do you know the leprechauns?
Who live on the emerald isle.

Catch yourself a leprechaun
(chase imaginary leprechaun around the room)
A tricky one, the leprechaun.
Catch yourself a leprechaun
To get his pot of gold!
(hold arms around a pot of gold)

But hold on tight and don't let go.
(squeeze arms together to hold him tight)
He'll run away, he'll take his gold.

He'll hop across an old rainbow
And hide for another time.

Crafts:

"Leprechaun Face Mask"

"Erin Go Bragh"—Take a visit to the emerald isle as one of its famous mythical leprechauns. Children can celebrate t. Patrick's Day by disguising themselves as leprechauns. Use the outside ring of a paper plate for the base of your mask. A green hat can be designed and attached to the top portions of the ring. Add a red streamer beard and a band to easily place it on the child's face. Check Ms. Ross' book for further decorations and illustration of your leprechaun hat and ideas for celebrating this special holiday.

Source: *Crafts for St. Patrick's Day*, Kathy Ross

"St. Pat's Harp"

Harps are a well-known Irish symbol to accompany Irish ballads. Trace and precut the shape of a harp from posterboard. Cut a bar long enough to lay across the top of the harp. Punch five holes on the bar and an equal amount on the lower portion of the harp. Decorate the bottom of the harp with a green shamrock. Give each child some long, green yarn to weave through the holes to create the strings of the harp.

Source: *Music Crafts for Kids*, Noel and Phyllis Fiarotta

Activities:

"Gold in the Pot Game"

Look into this book for a variety of games for St. Patrick's Day. This first one had children trying to return the leprechaun's gold back into his pot of gold by tossing it onto an upside-down soup kettle. It takes a little talent to keep those coins from sliding off the other side. When you are finished with this game try some rainbow games suggested such as, "Rainbow Hunt," "Pass the Rainbow Surprise Ball," and "Color the Rainbow Relay."

Source: *The Best Birthday Parties Ever!*, Kathy Ross

"Beep Bop the Shamrock"

Allow the children to bring in their own lunch bags, and they can then decorate them with pictures of shamrocks for this special holiday. Blow them up and have them practice keeping them in the air. Put music on and tell the children when you yell "Beep Bop the Shamrock" everyone should begin. The one to keep it in the air the longest of course wins.

Source: *Creative Games for Young Children*, Annetta Dellinger

Songs:

(Audio) "John, John the Leprechaun"

Source: *One Elephant, Deux Elephants*, Sharon, Lois Bram

86 Holidays: St. Valentine's Day

Topical Calendar Tie-in:

February 14

"St. Valentine's Day"—This is a day for sharing feelings with loved ones or simply starting some new friendships. Make time to spend with your family and your closest friends, and find a way to let them know how much you care.

Videos:

Bee My Valentine
The Best Valentine in the World
A Goofy Look at Valentine's Day
Little Mouse's Big Valentine
One Zillion Valentines

Picture Books:

A Circle Is Not a Valentine, H. Werner Zimmermann
Froggy's First Kiss, Jonathan London
Happy Valentine's Day, Dolores, Barbara Samuels
Heart to Heart, George Shannon
If You'll Be My Valentine, Cynthia Rylant
Little Mouse's Big Valentine, Thacher Hurd
Pigs in Love, Teddy Slater
Queen of Hearts, Mary Engelbreit
Roses Are Pink, Your Feet Really Stink, Diane deGroat
Valentine, Carol Carrick
Valentine's Day, Miriam Nerlove
Valentine's Day: Stories and Poems, Caroline Feller Bauer
The Valentine Express, Nancy Elizabeth Wallace
Valentine Mice!, Bethany Roberts
Will You Be My Valentine?, Steven Kroll

Music/Movement:

"Valentine's Day Hugs"
Sung to: "Hokey Pokey"

You put your right arm out.
You put your left arm out.
You bring those arms together
And you squeeze with all your might.

You hug and say "I love you"
And you spread it all around.
That's what this day's about.

Crafts:

"Love Bugs"

Make a simple love bug mounted on a heart card as a special Valentine's card for that special friend. These silly bugs are simple to make by crushing kitchen foil to form the body and gluing small pieces of colored tissue over the body. Legs are formed using pipe cleaners and the effects are finalized by cutting paper wings to place on their back with decorative hearts. This same craft can easily be used to make ladybugs. Check this source for a variety of illustrations for your love bugs.

Source: *Valentine Things to Make and Do*, Rebecca Gilpin

"Valentine Bear"

Make your own huggable Valentine bear with the patterns supplied in this book. Children will be able to put together this simple bear, add paw prints and a large heart on his stomach. This book supplies a large number of holiday patterns that children can enjoy.

Source: *Cut and Create! Holidays*, Kim Rankin

Activities:

"Hug Tag"

Valentine's Day is a day for love and caring for other people. Children like to play a game of tag. Try "Hug Tag" in which children are tagged and become frozen. They must stay this way until someone cares enough to help them. Can you guess how? Check it out in this source book.

Source: *Creative Resources for the Early Childhood Classroom, 4th edition*, Judy Herr and Yvonne Libby Larson

"Rakhi"

Hindi families celebrate a special festival called Raksha Bandhan. During this holiday, families renew their special bonds for each other in special ways. A sister will show her love and respect for her brother by tying a special braided bracelet (rakhi) on his wrist, and in return her brother promises to always protect her. Directions for making this caring symbol of family respect are offered in this book. Try making the bracelet and reenacting the ritual in your family to show your love and care of the people in your family.

Source: *International Crafts and Games*, Cynthia G. Adams

Songs:

(Audio) "Skinnamarink"

Source: *Car Songs*

87 Holidays: Thanksgiving

Topical Calendar Tie-in:

November 23
"Turkey Free Thanksgiving"—The turkeys want to make a break for it so give them a break and try celebrating Thanksgiving Day without a turkey. Plan a meal and invite a toy turkey to be the guest of honor instead of the main meal. (3rd Thursday in November)

Videos:

Don't Eat Too Much Turkey!
Giving Thanks
One Terrific Thanksgiving
The Pilgrims of Plimoth
Thanksgiving Day

Picture Books:

1, 2, 3 Thanksgiving!, W. Nikola-Lisa
Clifford's Thanksgiving Visit, Norman Bridwell
The Firefighters' Thanksgiving, Maribeth Boelts
Giving Thanks: A Native American Good Morning Message, Chief Jake Swamp
Gracias, The Thanksgiving Turkey, Joy Cowley
I am the Turkey, Michele Sobel Spirn
Silly Tilly's Thanksgiving Dinner, Lillian Hoban
Sometimes It's Turkey, Lorna Balian
The Squirrels' Thanksgiving, Steven Kroll
The Story of Thanksgiving, Nancy J. Skarmeas
Thanks for Thanksgiving, Julie Markes
Thanksgiving is . . ., Gail Gibbons
Thanksgiving with Me, Margaret Willey
A Turkey for Thanksgiving, Eve Bunting
'Twas the Night Before Thanksgiving, Dav Pilkey
The Ugly Pumpkin, Dave Horowitz

Music/Movement:

"The Turkey Strut"
Sung to: "The Hokey Pokey"
Source: *Little Hands Fingerplays and Action Songs*, Emily Stetson and Vicky Congdon

Crafts:

"Here Come the Turkeys Napkin Rings"
Make attractive turkey napkin rings for your family's holiday table. On a strip of construction paper six inches long, glue turkey feathers created by strips of colored paper formed in a loop. When finished, take the entire strip, wrap it around a toilet paper tube and bend the feathers up to form the turkey tail. Make the turkey's head out of curled strips of brown paper. Don't forget his face. This will make an attractive addition

to any family's Thanksgiving table and the children can view it with pride.

Source: *My Very Own Thanksgiving: A Book of Cooking and Crafts*, Robin West

Craft and Activity:

"Turkey Toss"

Here's a Thanksgiving craft and game combination that will have the children laughing if you can keep them from eating their chips before the game begins. A flat illustration of a turkey is created with the use of construction paper and cardboard. The colorful turkey feathers will be added to the board by using cardboard egg carton sections to form cups with numbers in them across the turkey's back. Now the fun begins, when each child receives 5 candy corns to toss at the turkey's tail with hopes of earning the highest score.

Source: *Fun to Make Crafts for Every Day*, Tom Daning (editor)

Activities:

"A Thanksgiving Mix-up"

Children sit in chairs in a circle with one person, "It," standing in the center. Give each child a name that identifies them as something on a Thanksgiving Day dinner table. The person who is It calls out two items, and those two exchange seats. The caller can continue in this manner until he calls, "The dinner table is tipped over," at which time everyone scatters for a different seat including the caller. The person left out is the next caller.

Source: *It's Time for Thanksgiving*, Elizabeth Hough Sechrist and Janette Woolsey

Songs:

(Audio) "Turkey Wobble"

Source: *Holiday Songs for all Occasions*

88 Hospitals/Doctors

Topical Calendar Tie-in:

May 7–13
"National Hospital Week"—This special week always includes May 12th and honors the doctors, nurses and aides that work at our hospitals and help us stay healthy. Take a field trip to a local hospital or invite these wonderful healthcare workers to visit you, bringing some of the equipment they use every day.

Videos:

Curious George Goes to the Hospital
The Hospital
Madeline
Sesame Street Home Video Visits the Hospital

Picture Books:

Barney is Best, Nancy Carlstrom
A Day in the Life of a Nurse, Connie Fluet
Doctors, Dee Ready
Keeping You Healthy: A Book About Doctors, Ann Owen
Kevin Goes to the Hospital, Liesbet Slegers
Maggie and the Emergency Room, Martine Davison
Miffy in the Hospital, Dick Bruna
My Friend the Doctor, Joanna Cole
Next! Please, Christopher Inns
One Bear in the Hospital, Caroline Buchnall
Paddington Bear: Goes to the Hospital, Michael Bond and Karen Jankel
Poor Monty, Anne Fine
Robby Visits the Doctor, Martine Davison
This is a Hospital, Not a Zoo!, Roberta Karim
What Does a Doctor Do?, Felicia Lowenstein

Music/Movement:

"Doctor, Doctor"

(Rhyming text—No music required.)

Doctor, Doctor please help me
Put a banding on my knee.
(pretend putting band-aid on)
Check my ears and my sore throat
(point to ears and then down mouth)
And give me a sweet antidote.
(pretend taking pill)

Crafts:

"Mend my Broken Arm"
Ask the children if any of them have ever broken an arm or leg and had to have a doctor place a cast on it so that it would mend properly. How did this feel and how did they get around? If possible, have some discarded

casts, some crutches, and other props donated from a local hospital on display for the children to see that day. Have some gauze available and pretend to wrap each other's arm as a doctor would do for you. Now we will make our own cast that we can have friends sign or decorate ourselves. Inflate a long stretch balloon that children will pretend is the arm of a friend that has been broken. We will actually use strips of long papier-mâché to go around the balloon leaving the ends open to form a cast. When it is dry paint it white and puncture the balloon. Children can now slip their arm through as a pretend cast and get their friends to sign it or color it.

"First Aid Basket"
This book offers a very helpful use for old plastic or wire mesh crates that are given with gifts or come with fruit at the supermarket. While this book offers gift ideas, they can very nicely be adapted to make a "First Aid Basket" that contains Band-Aids, cotton balls, and other items needed in an emergency. Make a picturesque basket that can decorate your bathroom or bedroom.
Source: *Hey Kids! Come Craft with Me*, Mary Engelbreit

Activity:

"Hospital Helpers"
Transform part of your room into a hospital room, complete with props such as face masks, Band-Aids, play syringe, and some of the other items mentioned on a long list offered in this source. After reading such books as *Madeline* by Ludwig Bemelmans, *Curious George Goes to the Hospital* by H. A. Rey, and others listed above, children can act out what they believe happens at a hospital. Many other suggestions for making this educational experience a great deal of fun is offered in the following source.
Source: *Making Make-Believe*, MaryAnn F. Kohl

"Germs and Doctors"
This form of tag requires no special equipment but children will need a doctor if they get sick (only pretend!). We need a number of children to be doctors in this game and a small number to be germs that infect the other players. Check this source for actual proportions for the teams. If you're infected (tagged) call for that doctor to save you. Check it out!
Source: *Run, Jump, Hide, Slide, Splash: The 200 Best Outdoor Games Ever*, Joe Rhatigan and Rain Newcomb

Songs:

(Audio) "Doctor Knickerbocker"
Source: *Name Games*, Sharon, Lois and Bram

89 Houses/Homes

Topical Calendar Tie-in:

June 25
"Log Cabin Day"—Pay tribute to the homes of history on this day to remember the log cabins of Abraham Lincoln's youth. Build your own log cabin out of Popsicle sticks and discuss the variety of other homes in history, like teepees, mud adobes, etc.

Videos:

The Little House
Madeline and the New House
The Old Mill
This is the House that Jack Built
The Village of Round and Square Houses

Picture Books:

Castles, Caves and Honeycombs, Linda Ashman
Duncan's Tree House, Amanda Vesey
Gingerbread Mouse, Katy Bratun
The Great Blue House, Kate Banks
The Halloween House, Erica Silverman
A House by the Sea, Joanne Ryder
The Magic House, Robyn Harbert Eversole
My House, Lisa Desimini
A New House for the Morrisons, Penny Carter
No Place Like Home, Jonathan Emmett
Robert's Snow, Grace Lin
The Someday House, Anne Shelby
Sunflower House, Eve Bunting
This is Our House, Michael Rosen
Where Does the Teacher Live?, Paula Feder
You See a Circus, I See . . ., Mike Downs

Music/Movement:

"My Little House"
Source: *The Book of Fingerplays and Action Songs*, John M. Feierabend

Crafts:

"Little Shoe Houses"
The little old lady lived in a shoe. I wonder where she found such an unusual house for her family. After discussing all the different kinds of houses people live in and reading this nursery rhyme let the children try to reproduce what they think the little old lady's house actually looked like. You will need newspaper, a large variety of shoes in all styles, a collection of decorating supplies, paints, and glue. Let their imaginations sour. Also offered are additional things to make for a shoe village.
Source: *Making Make-Believe*, MaryAnn F. Kohl

"Realistic Bird Nest"
We've discussed how people live and even how nursery rhyme characters live in the craft above. Now let's discuss the different types of homes that animals live in today. With that help the children make a realist looking bird nest out of water, dirt, twigs, and more. Add a little bird out of pine cones and hazelnuts and add little eggs constructed from round nuts painted colorfully. This makes a terrific spring craft.

Source: *Making Make-Believe*, MaryAnn F. Kohl

Activities:

"Guess Which Room I Am In"
Gather a collection of items that are unique to particular rooms in a house. An example would be the bathroom where you might collect such items as bubble bath, soap, toilet paper, etc., and ask children what these items are used for and where they would find them in the house. If you are in a house you can take a trip to the room to see what else you find there. Now try this game offered here by giving clues to what you have in the box and see if the children can guess the item and then in what room it belongs. Follow this with other games listed in this book.

Source: *Quick and Fun Games for Toddlers*, Grace Jasmine

"House Sounds Guessing Game"
A house is a very busy place with a family in it. Have you ever stopped to just listen and count how many different sounds you hear in your home? Make a recording of sounds from your house and see if the children can guess what they are. For a list of suggestions see this source.

Source: *More Picture Book Story Hours: From Parties to Pets*, Paula Gaj Sitarz

Songs:

(Audio) "Sing Your Way Home"

Source: *Wee Sing: Sing-Alongs*

90 Humor

Topical Calendar Tie-in:

March 31
"National 'She's Funny That Way' Day"—This is the time to discover the humorous nature of women. Name the top 5 ways your mother, sister, wife, or teacher make you laugh every day. Don't forget to return the favor.

Videos:

Caps for Sale
The Day Jimmy's Boa Ate the Wash
The Emperor's New Clothes
Harold and the Purple Crayon
Rosie's Walk

Picture Books:

Ants Can't Dance, Ellen Jackson
April Foolishness, Teresa Bateman
The Cats of Mrs. Calamari, John Stadler
Mr. Tuggle's Troubles, Lee Ann Blankenship
My First Riddles, Judith Hoffman Corwin
My Mom and Dad Make Me Laugh, Nick Sharrot
Never Ride Your Elephant to School, Doug Johnson
No More Water in the Tub!, Tedd Arnold
Nonsense, Sally Kahler Phillips
Serious Trouble, Arthur Howard
Shoo! Scat!, Lois G. Grambling
Sody Sallyratus, Teri Sloat
There Was an Old Woman Who Lived in a Boot, Linda Smith
This is the Teacher, Rhonda Gowler Greene
Too Much Noise, Ann McGovern

Music/Movement:

"Willy the Worm"
Source: *Fall Frolic*, Mary Jo Huff

Crafts:

"Joke Box"

Monkey See, Monkey Do/ Where's the monkey in the zoo?
Open the box and you will see/ The only place the monkey can be.

Decorate a box using any available materials such as colored construction paper, stickers, markers. Allow the children to use their imagination. Inside glue a small mirror to the bottom of the box. Across the open section of the box bottom tape or glue black yarn to form a cage. Design and replace the box cover and you're set for a delightful joke with your friends.

"Crazy Caterpillar"
Crazy critters can be made out of paper plates, boxes, and even egg cartons. A crazy caterpillar is the perfect theme for egg carton crafts. This

book offers instruction on making a goofy-looking caterpillar that also doubles as a planter. Within a week the children can see their seeds sprout up making a grassy back to the caterpillar to give him his fuzzy look. This will also work well in a science lesson on plants.

Source: *Rainy Day Activity Book*, Andrea Pinnington

Activities:

"Spoons"

Here's a game for times when the children are not in the mood to learn anything but just are totally in a silly mood. All the supplies needed are spoons and a deck of cards. Everyone sits in a circle with the spoons in the center. Cards are passed from one person to the next in a specific way so that when a child gets a designated card he must quickly reach for a spoon. (Check this source for specifics.) This is the signal for pandemonium as others try to get a spoon and not be left out and receive a letter. The last person to actually get the word SPOON spelled out is the winner of the game.

Source: *Great Games*, Sam Taggar and Susan Willliamson

"Ha, Ha, Ha"

Laughter is contagious. See if the children can control their laughter during this ridiculously silly game of laughter. The children will feel silly enough when asked to lie on the ground with each other in a pattern supplied in this book and pass along the terms of "Ha," "Ha, Ha," etc., in specific patterns *without* breaking down and actually laughing. Look for specific details of this game and changes for playing again if you can keep a straight face in the source book.

Source: *Hey Mom, I'm Bored!*, Story Evans and Lise O'Haire

Songs:

(Audio) "Laugh with me" and "Ain't it Great to be Crazy"

Source: *I Love to Sing with Barney*

91 Imagination/Pretend

Topical Calendar Tie-in:

September 10
"Swap Ideas Day"—Now's the time to encourage children to use their creative imagination to come up with ideas that can benefit humanity through problem solving. Ask them to share these ideas with others.

Videos:

The Emperor's New Clothes
Harold and the Purple Crayon
In the Night Kitchen
One Monday Morning
A Picture for Harold's Room

Picture Books:

Amazing Grace, Mary Hoffman
The Bear Under the Stairs, Helen Cooper
Chimps Don't Wear Glasses, Laura Numeroff
Do Like a Duck Does!, Judy Hindley
Dragon Scales and Willow Leaves, Terryl Givens
Even Firefighters Hug Their Moms, Christine Kole Maclean
Fancy Nancy, Jane O'Connor
The Hippo-not-amus, Tony and Jan Payne
If Elephants Wore Pants . . ., Henriette Barkow
If I Were Queen of the World, Fred Hiatt
I'm a Jolly Farmer, Julie Lacome
Kate's Giants, Valiska Gregory
Magic Beach, Alison Lester
Noises at Night, Beth Raisner Glass and Susan Lubner
Pete's a Pizza, William Steig

Music/Movement:

"Imagination Zoo"
Source: *It's Great to be Three: The Encyclopedia of Activities for Three-Year-Olds*, Kathy Charmer and Maureen Murphy (editors)

Crafts:

"Boogie Woogie Creatures"
Have the children bring an old glove from home. With this give them each five medium-size pom-poms of various colors to glue to the top of the glove's fingers. To each of these glue felt or craft store eyes. After they have dried, the children may don the gloves and make the creatures dance to music by wiggling their fingers.

"Carnaval Mystery Masks"
Carnaval is celebrated in many countries in a variety of ways. Our most well-known carnival celebration is Mardi Gras in New Orleans, Louisiana. People take this opportunity to mask up and hide their identity pretending to be what they are not. Take a look at the directions in

this book for an assortment of Carnaval mystery masks that can be created along with "Fantastic Hats" used around the world. Step out of yourself for the day and become someone or something else.

Source: *Zany Rainy Days: Indoor Ideas for Active Kids*, Hallie Warshaw and Mark Shulman

Activities:

"Machine"

The target age level for this activity is 5 years and up. Young children have great imaginations. Let them pretend to be various machines for this game encouraging the other team to guess while they perform the functions of the machine they have selected. You might have cards available with sample names (or illustrations) or machines such as pinball machines, bowling pin reset machine, washing machine, etc. Divide your class into 2 groups and let them work as a team giving suggestions to the member of their team who is acting out. The creativity of children will amaze you and this is an activity that works well indoors or out.

Source: *Win-Win Games for All Ages*, Josette and Ba Luvmour

"Match Me, Match Me if You Can"

The Match game gets a unique approach with this team event. Divide your class into two teams of no more than 10 members. Prepare beforehand a large variety of cards portraying a collection of actions or characters (ballerinas, cowboys, taking a bath, cooking, etc.) that team members will be asked to pantomime. Half of each team will be shown cards portraying the actions they will be performing. Next place the cards facedown on a table after they have been shuffled. At the sound of the bell the actors will begin to pantomime while the remaining half of their team will try to match the cards from the table with their teammate's actions. The team that correctly matches their cards first wins.

Songs:

(Audio) "Imagine That!"

Source: *The Day I Read a Book*

92 Insects

Topical Calendar Tie-in:

June 23–24

"International Butterfly Festival"—Encouraged by the many species of beautiful butterflies found on Mt. Magazine in Arkansas, many people flock to this festival begun in 1997. At least 91 extraordinary butterflies can be found on the mountain's plateau-like summit. Plan your own butterfly festival through paper butterflies, or start your own conservatory

Videos:

The Ant and the Dove
The Caterpillar and the Polliwog
The Grasshopper and the Ants
In the Tall, Tall Grass
Roberto the Insect Architect
Waiting for Wings
Why Mosquitoes Buzz in People's Ears

Picture Books:

Aaaarrgghh! Spider!, Lydia Monks
Bug Safari, Bob Barner
The Bugliest Bug, Carol Diggory Shields
Butterfly Story, Anca Hariton
The Caterpillow Fight, Sam McBratney
Charlie the Caterpillar, Dom DeLuise
Diary of a Spider, Doreen Cronin
Gotcha!, Gail Jorgensen
I Love Bugs!, Philemon Sturges
Insects Are My Life, Megan McDonald
Miss Spider's New Car, David Kirk
Ten Flashing Fireflies, Philemon Sturges
What's That Sound, Woolly Bear?, Philemon Sturges
When the Fly Flew in . . ., Lisa Westberg Peters
Zzzng! Zzzng! Zzzng!: A Yoruba Tale, Phillis Gershator

Music/Movement:

"Little Green Caterpillar"
Source: *Totally Tubeys!*, Priscella Morrow

Crafts:

"Insect's Playground"
Grass can be an insect's playground. Create a grass hat for young children out of green construction paper and strategically place various insects that live in the grass (ladybugs, ants, spiders, etc.) peeking through the blades of grass. This can be used as a religious craft, "God made the grass," with a field trip out in the schoolyard to see which of the insects they can find.
Source: *Crafts to Celebrate God's Creation*, Kathy Ross

"Caterpillar on a Leaf"
Creep, crawl, and fly. Caterpillars are a favorite bug for children's stories. After hearing about this interesting insect help the children make their own caterpillar pin sitting on a green felt leaf. Using yellow tissue paper soaked in a special solution wrap the paper around a plastic straw. Work from both ends to slide the tissue together to make the segments of the caterpillar. Gradually work the tissue off the end of the straw and form it into the position of an arch for the caterpillar. Let it dry hard before gluing it to your felt leaf and add wiggle eyes and green dots.

Source: *Crafts to Celebrate God's Creation*, Kathy Ross

Activities:

"Worm-a-Thon"
In this book you will locate a good recipe for playdough. Once this is made you can divide your class into teams each with their own bowl of playdough. Yell "Ready, set, go!" and off go the team members, rolling playdough into worms with each member adding to the tail in an attempt to create the longest worm they've ever seen. A time limit on the project is suggested.

Source: *The Big Book of Kid's Games*, Tracy Stephen Burroughs

"Shoo, Fly!"
Enjoy this circle activity based on the well-known song about flies. It's a simple dance event that parents and even 2-year-olds can do as a group and works well between stories.

Source: *The Complete Book of Activities, Games, Stories, Props, Recipes, and Dances for Young Children*, Pam Schiller and Jackie Silberg

Songs:

(Audio) "Shoo Fly"

Source: *Circle Time Activities*

93 Insects: Bees

Topical Calendar Tie-in:

July 10

"Don't Step on a Bee Day"—This unusual holiday is designated to remind children and adults who love to run barefoot during the summer that they must watch not to "step on a bee." Bees do not just travel from flower to flower but through clover in our grass. Discuss what to do if you get stung by a bee.

Videos:

Bea's Own Good
The Berenstain Bears Save the Bees (The Berenstain Bears on the Truth)
The Little Dog and the Bees

Picture Books:

The Bee, Lisa Campbell Ernst
The Bee and the Dream, Jan Freeman Long
Bees, Susan Ashley
The Bumblebee Queen, April Pulley Sayre
Buzz, Janet S. Wong
"Buzz, Buzz, Buzz," went Bumblebee, Colin West
Buzzy, the Bumblebee, Denise Brennan-Nelson
The Flower of Sheba, Doris Orgel and Ellen Schecter
Gran's Bees, Mary Thompson
Happy Bees!, Arthur Yorninks
Honey in a Hive, Anne Rockwell
Honeybee's Party, Joanna and Paul Galdone
The Honey Makers, Gail Gibbons
King Solomon and the Bee, Dalia Hardof Renberg
The Magic Schoollbus: Inside the Beehive, Joanna Cole
Mr. Bumble, Kim Kennedy

Music/Movement:

"Buzz, Buzz"
Sung to: "Row, Row, Row Your Boat"

Buzz, Buzz, Buzz the bees
All around the hive
(have children buzz circling a hive)
Making honey all day long
For when the Queen arrives.

Crafts:

"Flying Bumblebee"
A paper plate craft featuring a "Fluttering Ladybug" is featured in this source and along with making a delightful craft for children can also make a wonderful springtime decoration for your library. Take this craft and make a variation by switching insects. A ladybug can be substituted

with a bumblebee depending on the topic you are dealing with that day. Minimal cost and skills are required to create this project.

Source: *Fun to Make Crafts for Every Day*, Tom Daning (editor)

"Bumble Bee"
A simple bumblebee can be constructed using folded black construction paper for wings, pipe cleaners, and yellow pom-poms for it's body. This engaging little craft will have the children buzzing all over your room.

Source: *The Giant Encyclopedia of Theme Activities for Children 2 to 5*, Kathy Charner

Activities:

"Buzzzz"
This bumblebee game helps the children develop breath control. Divided into two teams of bees they will have to invade another bee's territory to tag them and get back to his own hive. There's only one catch buzzing like a bee in a continuous breath. Check this source for details of the game and setup requirements.

Source: *Sidewalk Games*, Glen Vecchione

"Bee Clock"
Try out this little experiment to see when bees will arrive or what will attract them. This special exercise recommends you attract bees with sugar water or cola for a couple of days documenting the time they actually arrive. Try the third day with a different product suggested in this activity and see if they arrive just as quickly. A section called "a bit about bees" has some funny facts about how bees communicate to others that they have located food. Check it out!

Source: *The Kids' Guide to Nature Adventures*, Joe Rhatigan

Songs:

(Audio) "If You're a Bee"

Source: *Happy Bees*

94 Insects: Ladybugs

Topical Calendar Tie-in:

May 28

"Freeing the Insects Day"—Also known as Insect-Hearing Festival, this Japanese festival has vendors selling insects in tiny bamboo cages. These pets are kept near the house so that their music can be heard during the night. Then on a day late in August, people gather in a park to release them and listen to the freed insects burst into their individual sounds.

Videos:

Ladybug, Ladybug, Winter is Coming

Picture Books:

Bright Beetle, Rick Chrustowski
Bubba and Trixie, Lisa Campbell Ernst
Daddy Is a Doodlebug, Bruce Degen
Eye Spy a Ladybug!, Melinda Lilly
The Grouch Ladybug, Eric Carle
Ladybug, Emery Bernhard
Ladybug, Karen Hartley and Chris Macro
Ladybugs, Claire Llewellyn
Ladybugs: Red, Fiery and Bright, Mia Posada
A Ladybug's Life, John Himmelman
Lara Ladybug, Christine Florie
Lenny's Lost Spots, Celia Warren
Spotted Beetles: Ladybugs in Your Backyard, Nancy Loewen
The Very Lazy Ladybug, Isobel Finn and Jack Tickle

Music/Movement:

"Ladybug"

A new slant on the old Ladybug rhyme.

Source: *Once Upon a Childhood: Fingerplays, Action Rhymes, and Fun Times for the Very Young*, Dolores Chupela

Crafts:

"Ladybug and Buggy Riddles"

This refreshing source for library storyhour program includes a pattern for making a ladybug with movable wings. Patterns are easily photocopied so that the children can decorate it with sticker dots or use crayons. This will make a great prop when reciting the rhyme "Ladybug" or answering the "buggy riddles" supplied in the same source.

Source: *Library Storyhour from A to Z*, Ellen K. Hasbrouck

"The Ladybug"

Hand art is a fun way for children to create colorful animals or insects. Have them paint the palm of their hand and imprint it on the paper to create a bug body. Use black thumbprints to create the spots on the ladybug's back.

A palm print done with green paint can be placed below the bug for a leaf. When all is dry children can add outlines and such features as antennae and legs. Try this source for many animal art creations done in this way.

Source: *Hand-Print Animal Art*, Carolyn Carreiro

Activities:

"Ladybug Bingo"

The source cited here provides a full page of bingo cards with ladybugs each with different number of dots on the card instead of just numbers. Cut the card in half and have the children color their ladybugs. One half of the board is cut up to create markers that match the ladybugs on their board. Now you're ready to play. Children roll dice to determine which ladybug to cover. This wonderful counting game can be found in the source book.

Source: *Kids Celebrate!*, Maria Bonfanti Esche and Clare Bonfanti Braham

"Ladybug Game"

This is an uncomplicated game that the youngest children can handle. The children can partner with another child or a parent to begin. As they recite the rhyme they perform the actions first facing each other, then back to back until they fly away to find another partner and begin again.

The children will love moving from one person to the next until they end up finally with their original partner.

Source: *Storytime Craft*, Kathryn Totten

Songs:

(Audio) "Hello Ladybug"

Source: *Piggyback Planet Songs for a Whole Earth*

95 Kindergarten

Topical Calendar Tie-in:

August

"Get Ready for Kindergarten Month"—Entry into kindergarten sometimes can be difficult for young children and even more so for the parents of those children. Take this month to prepare for kindergarten not only educationally but emotionally. Celebrate this special event. For tips to help smooth this transition, try www.kindergartenrocks.com.

Videos:

Everybody Knows That
Mister Rogers' Neighborhood: Going to School
Morris Goes to School
Richard Scarry's Sally's First Day at School

Picture Books:

Amanda Pig, Schoolgirl, Jean Van Leeuwen
Benjamin Bigfoot, Mary Serfozo
Big David, Little David, S.E. Hinton
Boomer Goes to School, Constance McGeorge
Born in the Gravy, Denys Cazet
Countdown to Kindergarten, Alison McGhee
Harry and Tuck, Holly Keller
Miss Bindergarten Celebrates the 100th Day of Kindergarten, Joseph Slate
Miss Bindergarten Has a Wild Day in Kindergarten, Joseph Slate
My Mom Made Me Go to School, Judy Delton
Rachel Parker, Kindergarten Show-off, Ann Martin
Red Day, Green Day, Edith Kunhardt
School Isn't Fair!, Patricia Baehr
The Twelve Days of Kindergarten, Deborah Lee Rose
What Will Mommy Do When I'm at School?, Dolores Johnson

Music/Movement:

"School Days"
Source: *More Picture Book Story Hours: From Parties to Pets*, Paula Gaj Sitarz

Crafts:

"Everything-in-its-Place Plates"
During the kindergarten year children learn many basic skills including how to keep their supplies in a neat and orderly manner. Help them with this skill by making their own "everything-in-its-place" holder. This cute multipocket holder is made using paper plates, paints, and decorative materials. Children can use it to keep their crayons, pencils, and paper where they can always find them easily.
Source: *Look What You Can Make with Dozens of Household Items!*, Kathy Ross

"First Day Poster"
Let the children show their parents what they accomplished on their first week or month of kindergarten. Each day supply the child with a two-inch white square and ask them to illustrate something they did today. If they did finger painting they might just want to put a thumbprint on it. If they cut out things let them draw a picture of scissors, etc. At the end of the week or month give the child a large, colored poster board for them to glue their squares onto. Label it "My Kindergarten Accomplishments."

Activities:

"Show Time"
I was very excited to locate this book because it is chock full of interactive ideas for children, including the most exciting part, which is the last chapter, "Show Time." You will find a series of short plays for only a few actors based on American folk heroes like Paul Bunyan, a scene from *Alice in Wonderland,* and short play versions of familiar fairy tales. Kindergarten teachers looking for a performance must get this book.

Source: *Show Time! Music, Dance and Drama Activities for Kids,* Lisa Bany-Winters

"Unpack Your Bag"
This is a wonderful activity to help a new child feel welcome to the class. Ask the new child and parent to bring to class a bag labeled "All About Me" and to place in the bag various items that are important to the child. In the class each item can be removed and the child can help the teacher explain it's importance. You can also have each child in the class show the new child an item they have brought into the class. This is a terrific ice breaker.

Source: *The Giant Encyclopedia of Theme Activities for Children 2 to 5,* Kathy Charner

Songs:

(Audio) "Kindergarten Wall"

Source: *Mail Myself to You*

96 Kites

Topical Calendar Tie-in:

March 27
"Kite Flying Day"—March winds bring May flowers and a favorite activity of spring, kite flying. Break out those kites and watch them fly high. Let's go fly those kites!

Videos:

Berenstain Bears Go Fly a Kite
Dorothy and the Kite
Spot's Windy Day (Spot Goes to the Farm)
Kites Sail High

Picture Books:

Anatole Over Paris, Eve Titus
Angel's Kite, Alberto Blanco
A Carp for Kimiko, Virginia Kroll
Catch the Wind!: All About Kites, Gail Gibbons
Curious George Flies a Kite, Margaret Rey
The Emperor and the Kite, Jane Yolen
Hamlet and the Enormous Chinese Dragon Kite, Brian Lies
The Kite, Mary Packard
Lucky Song, Vera B. Williams
Mike's Kite, Elizabeth MacDonald
Moonlight Kite, Helen E. Buckley
Rabbit's Birthday Kite, Maryann MacDonald
The Sea-Breeze Hotel, Marcia Vaughan and Patricia Mullins
Someone Bigger, Jonathan Emmett
The Warlord's Kites, Virginia Walton Pilegard

Music/Movement:

"The Kite"
Source: *Fun with Mommy and Me,* Dr. Cindy Bunin Nurik

Crafts:

"Wind Bags"
Gather those plastic grocery bags that are piling up in your house and throw them to the wind. Use these bags as a simple kite by adding 2-foot lengths of ribbon to the bottom for a kite tail, and cover the bag images with stickers or with marker designs. Add a good length of string and take your wind bags out for a run as they open and soar through the air.
Source: *Family Fun Boredom Busters,* Deanna F. Cook (editor)

"Let's Go Eat a Kite"
When the children have now built up an appetite from playing with their wind bags take them inside for a special kite treat. Take a piece of bread cut into the shape of a kite and pass out peanut butter and jelly to the children. Let them divide the shape into four parts filling opposite parts with jelly and the remaining sections with peanut butter. Add a curled

slice of peeled carrot for the tail. Note: Be sure to determine if any of your children in your group has any peanut allergies before doing this craft. If that is the case, look for tasty alternatives such as other flavored jams to use.
Source: *Family Fun Boredom Busters*, Deanna F. Cook (editor)

"A Diamond Kite"
Make use of recycled plastic bags to design your own colorful diamond kite. With the youngest of children you may need to precut the shape, while older children can learn to measure for the correct shape. For the best results use acrylic paints for colorful artwork. If that is unavailable this source gives alternatives when using poster paint.
Source: *My First Paint Book*, Dawn Sirett

Activities:

"Kite Puzzle"
Puzzles are always fun to work. Try making your own puzzles out of kites purchased from local stores. If you have multiple kites you can challenge a couple teams of children to try to find the correct pieces to reassemble the parts. This and other kite adventures are offered in the source book.
Source: *Kids' Outdoor Parties*, Penny Warner

"Kite Run"
The children should be escorted outdoors in order to demonstrate and play with their newly made kites. Whenever possible children should be given a chance to show off their new creations, and this will give you an opportunity to demonstrate the correct way to use these kites.

Songs:

(Audio) "My Kite"
Source: *Piggyback Songs*

97 Libraries

Topical Calendar Tie-in:

March 1–7

"Return the Borrowed Books Week"—Here's a week to remember to return those books you borrowed from the library or a friend. Clean off your shelves to prepare for those books to be returned to you. Visit your local library now to return those books.

Videos:

Andy and the Lion
Arthur's Lost Library Book
Curious George Goes to the Library (Curious George Goes to Town)
The Library
Locked in the Library
Wild About Books

Picture Books:

Author's Day, Daniel Pinkwater
Beverly Billingsly Borrows a Book, Alexander Stadler
Carlo and the Really Nice Librarian, Jessica Spanyol
Clarence the Copy Cat, Patricia Lakin
Edward and the Pirates, David McPhail
I'm Going to New York to Visit the Lions, Harriet Ziefert
The Librarian from the Black Lagoon, Mike Thaler
Libraries Take Us Far, Lee Sullivan Hill
The Library Dragon, Carmen Agra Deedy
Lucy's Quiet Book, Angela Shelf Medearis
Maisy Goes to the Library, Lucy Cousins
Rachel's Library, Richard Ungar
Red Light, Green Light, Mama and Me, Cari Best
Sophie and Sammy's Library Sleepover, Judith Caseley
Storyhour—Starring Megan!, Julie Brillhart
Stuart Little: Stuart at the Library, Susan Hill
Tomas and the Library Lady, Pat Mora
A Visit to the Library, B. A. Hoena
What Happened to Marion's Book?, Brook Berg
Wild About Books, Judy Sierra

Music/Movement:

"The Books Are Coming Home Again"
Sung to: "The Ants Go Marching"

The books are coming home again, Hurrah, Hurrah.
The books are coming home again, Hurrah, Hurrah.
Maisy and Clifford climb onto the shelves,
Thomas the train says, "The Library's the next stop."
And they all sit waiting to go
  Out again
  And be read to a friend.

Crafts:

"Bookbug Bookmarks"
A simple bookmark can be made by each child as a memento of their library visit. They may be made using the following materials: colored paper, crayons, large pom-poms, and small eyes. Each child may decorate their precut bookmark as they wish. They will then be given a pom-pom to glue on as the bookbug's head and then eyes to glue on that.

"Bubble-Printed Notebook"
Explain to children how books are purchased and prepared for their use only after they are protected with special covers, due date pockets, etc. Now it's time for the children to design their own book covers for their precious books at home.

In a tub of cold water add a large amount of dishwashing liquid and swish until you get a great deal of suds. Drip different colors of food colorings over the suds, then place a large sheet of typing paper on top of it. After removing the paper place it aside to dry or later use for colorful book covers.

Source: *Ultimate Show-Me-How Activity Book*

Activities:

"Book Hunt"
Want a unique way of getting children to notice the new books that come into the library? Try this book hung technique. Gather the new books you want to display and put a nametag on each book with the name of each child attending the library that day then hide the books somewhere in the library. When the children arrive inform them that there is a book hidden in the library with their name on it. They are to spend the same time locating the book and then going to a corner to read or look through the book. End your program with a "Show and Tell," where each child gets to report on their special book. Look for a vast variety of book ideas in this encyclopedia of activities.

Source: *It's Great to Be Three: The Encyclopedia of Activities for Three-Year-Olds*, Kathy Charmer and Maureen Murphy (editors)

"A Walking Tour"
A short walking tour of the library is essential in this program. Such topics as the following should be covered:

- Location of books at the child's level
- Book care
- What's available at the library (besides books)
- Library manners
- A visit to the public library is suggested.

Songs:

(Audio) "At the Library"

Source: *We're On Our Way*

98 Machines

Topical Calendar Tie-in:

August

"National Inventors Month"—Designate this month to honor inventors and their inventions throughout history. Visit your local library to discover how even the simplest item was invented, such as the stapler, paper clip, etc.

Videos:

Big Rigs
Drummer Hoff
I Wanna Be a Heavy Equipment Operator
Kipper: The Flying Machine
Mike Mulligan and the Steam Shovel
Simple Machines

Picture Books:

Bam, Bam, Bam, Eve Merriam
The Busy Building Book, Sue Tarsky
Construction Zone, Tana Hoban
The Crazy Crawler Crane and Other Very Short Truck Stories, Mittie Cuetara
The Day Veronica Was Nosy, Elizabeth Laird
Edison's Fantastic Phonograph, Diana Kimpton
Fire Trucks, Carol K. Lindeen
Leonardo and the Flying Boy, Laurence Anhold
The Magic Sewing Machine, Sunny Warner
The Night Worker, Kate Banks
Road Builders, B. G. Hennessy
Mowing, Jessie Haas
The Rusty, Trusty Tractor, Joy Cowley
Sydney's Star, Peter H. Reynolds
Tough Trucks: The Crane, Frances Ann Ladd
Trash Trucks!, Daniel Kirk

Music/Movement:

"Pound Goes the Hammer"
Source: *Storytimes for Two-Year-Olds*, Judy Nichols

Crafts:

"Machine Sculpture"
Collect a variety of machine parts in preparation for your class creating their own machine sculpture. Items such as pipes, clock parts, calculators, etc. will suffice. Using heavy tape let the children connect them as they see fit. You may even want to spray paint it later.

A flat sculpture can be designed using nails, wood, and other flat objects. Let the children name their pieces of art and display them prominently in your classroom.

Source: *Good Earth Art*, Mary Ann F. Kohl and Cindy Gainer

"Gadget Printing"
Children really enjoy making prints of various items. In this source you will find instructions on creating a paint pad for each child to use. Next allow them to select various gadgets or simple machines (potato mashers, forks, combs, etc.) to dip into the paint pad and press on paper. Their artwork will be the envy of everyone.
Source: *Crafts: Early Learning Activities*, Jean Warren

Activities:

"Machine"
The target age level for this activity is 5 years and up. Young children have great imaginations. Let them pretend to be various machines for this game encouraging the other team to guess while they perform the functions of the machine they have selected. You might have cards available with sample names (or illustrations) or machines such as pinball machines, bowling pin reset machine, washing machine, etc. Divide your class into 2 groups and let them work as a team giving suggestions to the member of their team who is acting out. The creativity of children will amaze you and this is an activity that works well indoors or out.
Source: *Win-Win Games for All Ages*, Josette and Ba Luvmour

"Machine Hunt"
Tour your class or house with your group in search of a variety of simple machines (typewriters, record player, computers, etc.). If you don't have a lot in your room hang pictures where children can find them. Once you collect whatever they can find discuss their many functions.

Songs:

(Audio) "My Favorite Machine
Source: *Piggyback Songs*

99 Magic

Topical Calendar Tie-in:

October 31

"Magic Day"—This day of magic and fun is celebrated annually on the anniversary of the birth of Harry Houdini.

Videos:

The Amazing Bone
The Magic Fishbone
Rumpelstiltskin
The Sorcerer's Apprentice
Strega Nonna
Sylvestor and the Magic Pebble
Molly and the Magic Wishbone

Picture Books:

Alice the Fairy, David Shannon
Berry Magic, Teri Sloat
But Not Kate, Marissa Moss
Cinder Apples, Sandy Nightingale
Dragon Snatcher, M.P. Robertson
A Fairy in a Dairy, Lucy Nolan
Hamster Camp: How Harry Got Fit, Teresa Bateman
Laura's Secret, Klalus Baumgaret
The Magic Backpack, Julia Jarman and Adriano Gon
The Magic Hat, Mem Fox
The Magic Sewing Machine, Sunny Warner
Rabbit Surprise, Eric L. Houch, Jr.
The Toy Brother, William Steig
Uncle Harold and the Green Hat, Judy Hindley
The Witch's Walking Stick, Susan Meddaugh
The *Wizard, the Ugly and the Book of Shame*, Pablo Bernasconi

Music/Movement:

"Magic Words"

(Rhyming text—No music required)
If I can wave my wand in the air,
I'd make all troubles disappear.
I'd make my Mom queen for a day,
And my littler brother would never disobey.
Mom says she knows some magic too.
It's those special words "please and thank you."

Crafts:

"Flower Garden"

Make a bouquet or a wall of flowers in your library from the children that could be displayed that week or begin your own garden in the classroom. Use paper petals and centers out of cupcake cups. Relate the craft to the book *The Flower Faerie* by Frank Asch.

"Secret Letters in Invisible Ink"
Here's a magical way to send messages to friends and family. It will require an adult to open the message so make sure the child picks a friend they want to share their secrets with today. Take that old computer paper and some lemon juice to send the message. To discover what the message says later each child will need to press the message with a steam iron so make sure a responsible adult assists with this part of the project to avoid any injuries.

Source: *Days of Knights and Damsels: An Activity Guide*, Laurie Carlson

Activities:

"Magical Imprisonment of the Dragon Egg"
This is a basic well know magic trick of the egg in the bottle. The nice thing is that this book continues with the craze of Harry Potter and his wizards and tries to show you many magical themes in crafts, activities, and stories that can be used. This trick is discussed as the "dragon egg" that needs to be imprisoned by magic before it hatches.

Source: *The Book of Wizard Parties*, Janice Eaton Kilby and Terry Taylor

"Magical Fun"
After reading the story *The Well-Mannered Balloon* by Nancy Willard you may want to teach the children a little magic trick with balloons. This magical secret children can perform at any of their parties to wow their friends. Give each child a balloon to blow up for their trick. Each child is provided with a long needle that they will use to puncture the balloon. Tell them that we will secretly place a small piece of Scotch tape at the back of the balloon where your friends can't see. If you place the needle through the Scotch tape the balloon will not puncture. After withdrawing the balloon, show your friends it's a real balloon by breaking it in a different location. The children will enjoy working up a little dialog that they can use for this event.

Songs:

(Audio) "Magical Music" or "Make Believe"

Source: *Imagine That!*, Jim Valley and friends

100 Manners/Etiquette

Topical Calendar Tie-in:

March 1–7

"Write a Letter of Appreciation Week"—The art of letter writing to show appreciation for a gift received or help obtained from a friend has become a lost art. Teach your children how to express their appreciation and illustrate their best manners by reminding them to send that thank-you note when needed.

Videos:

Barney's Best Manners
Character Builders: Politeness and Joy
Circus Baby
The Selfish Giant
Time for Table Manners

Picture Books:

The Bad Good Manners Book, Babette Cole
Bee Polite and Kind, Cheri J. Meiners
Big Black Bear, Wong Herbert Yee
The Child's World of Manners, Sandra Ziegler
It's Your Turn Now: A Story About Politeness, Cindy Learney
Kitty Princess and the Newspaper Dress, Emma Carlow and Trevor Dickinson
Manners, Aliki
Mind Your Manners, Peggy Parish
Monster Manners, Bethany Roberts
Mother May I?, Lynn Plourde
Pass the Fritters, Critters, Cheryl Chapman
Please Say Please!: Penguin's Guide to Manners, Margery Cuyler
Rude Mule, Pamela Duncan Edwards
Say Please, Virginia Austin
Time for Bed, the Babysitter Said, Peggy Perry Anderson
What's the Magic Word?, Kelly DiPucchio
Wipe Your Feet!, Daniel Lehan

Music/Movement:

"BURP!"

BURP! Pardon me for being so rude.
It wasn't me, it was my food!
It didn't like it down below
And just popped up to say hello!

Source: *Schoolyard Rhymes*, Judy Sierra

Crafts:

"Please—and Thank You!"

Encourage good manners through example. It's important to talk about what are good manners and what to do in different situations. After such discussions tell the children that we are going to make our own manners game. With the use of an old individual milk carton and some magazine pictures depicting different situations the children can make large dice to roll when it's their turn. Can they remember what to do in each situation? Look for further instructions for this lesson in the source book.

Source: *The Little Hands Playtime! Book*, Regina Curtis

"Craft Stick Coasters"

Have a conversation with your class about how you would feel if someone mistreated your toys or favorite desk. Continue the lesson with how we should treat other people's property. Have the children make coasters our of Popsicle sticks that will be decorative but will keep their mom's furniture free of those ugly glass rings that occur from soda bottles, milk glasses, etc. They can give these to their moms to let her know they care.

Source: *Craft Stick Mania*, Christine M. Irvin

Activities:

"Mother, May I?"

This game is one that is familiar to most children. The leader may be another child or the teacher. The children begin at one end of the room and try to reach the leader by taking the amount of steps that the leader says they may take. The child must first remember to say, "Mother, May I?" before taking those steps or he will have to return to the beginning of the course. The child who reaches the leader first becomes the new leader.

"May I?" Hopscotch"

Supplies needed for this game are limited to a piece of chalk and some sort of pavement. Great! It saves on money. Draw a large square divided into six boxes (3 next to each other) numbered for the children. The object is to hop from one square to the next, getting all the way to the end without landing on any of the lines. The child must look up at the sky as he jumps and stops after each try to ask "May I?" If the child is successful in reaching his goal, he will be given permission to proceed by the rest of the group.

Different variations are suggested such as hopping backwards, etc. Try this and many other children's action games explained in detail in this source.

Source: *Children's Traditional Games*, Judy Sierra and Robert Kaminski

Songs:

(Audio) "Manners"

Source: *Circle Time Activities*

101 Mixed-up Creatures

Topical Calendar Tie-in:

April

"Appreciate Diversity Month"—This new national observance honors all diversity that exits within the workplace, schools, and communities. Celebrate diversity among children's literature also with multicultural books and even actual mixed-up literary characters.

Videos:

The Lorax
The Pig's Picnic
The Zax (Cat in the Hat/Dr. Seuss on the Loose)

Picture Books:

Albie's Trip to the Jumble Jungle, Robert Skutch
Beasty Bath, Robert Neubecker
Casey in the Bath, Cynthia DeFelice
Cock-a-Doodle Moooo!: A Mixed-Up Menagerie, Keith DuQuette
The Gruffalo, Julia Donaldson
I Love You, Stinky Face, Lisa McCourt
A Most Unusual Lunch, Robert Bender
Moo Who?, Margie Palatini
A Mother for Choco, Keiko Kasza
My Cat, the Silliest Cat in the World, Gilles Bachelet
Nonsense, Sally Kahler Phillips
Silly Suzy Goose, Petr Horacek
A Twisted Tale, Carolyn Fisher
Zoodles, Bernard Most

Music/Movement:

"Mistakes"
Source: *Let's Get Ready for Kindergarten*, Laura Townsend

Craft:

"Imaginary Creatures"
With the popularity of the Wuzzles, a simple mix-up of animals' parts can make a popular craft. Cut up illustrations of different types of animals and allow the children to mix and match the parts to create their own characters.

When they've selected the parts they want to match, help them mount them on large construction paper. They can then color them if needed or leave them as they are. Ask each child to identify what animal each part really belongs to.

"Mixed-Up Magazine"
A variation of the first craft suggestion is this one in which the children cut various pictures from magazines. You will of course need a head and body to identify your creature, but his limbs, etc., may even be made of odd items, such as baseball bats, clubs, etc.

Younger children love to mix and match and cut and paste. This is sure to be a success.

Source: *Preschool Art*, Mary Ann Kohl

Activities:

"Z is for Zigzag"

Prepare to mix up as many animals as you can find. Allow the children to find animals they think should be paired off. Pleated papers will help you guide the construction of your crazy character. This takes a little skill with the final product viewed from one side showing one animal and from the other a different animal. Flatten it out and what a mix-up! Start a card party and have the children send off mystery messages to friends with this same technique.

Source: *The Kids' Can Do it Book*, Deri Robins, Meg Sanders and Kate Crocker

"Backward Party"

People can be pretty mixed-up creatures sometimes just as other creations can be. Try celebrating the art of silliness by having your own backwards party. Do everything in reverse. This very useful source will give you everything you need from backward invitations, straws and crafts, to such games as "Goose, Goose Duck" and "Backward Pulling Races." So come one and all to a great party but don't forget: "Come in backwards."

Source: *Hit of the Party*, Amy Vangsgard

Songs:

(Audio) "Boogie Man Boogie"

Source: *Monster Teaching Time*

102 Money

Topical Calendar Tie-in:

February 12

"Lost Penny Day"—Take all those pennies you have been saving and put them back into circulation. Take them and give them to a shelter or a group that assists the homeless or the Humane Society. Pennies can add up and make the difference for someone.

Videos:

The Adventures of Two Piggy Banks: Learning to Save
Alexander, Who Used to Be Rich Last Sunday
If You Made a Million
Sam and the Lucky Money

Picture Books:

Argo, You Lucky Dog, Maggie Smith
Benny's Pennies, Pat Brisson
Bunny Money, Rosemary Wells
Deena's Lucky Penny, Barbara deRubertis
Follow the Money, Loreen Leedy
How Much is That Doggie in the Window?, Iza Trapani
Jelly Bean for Sale, Bruce McMillan
Mama Bear, Chyng Feng Sun
Pass the Buck, Michael Dahl
Pennies, Suzanne Lieurance
The Penny Pot, Stuart J. Murphy
Pigs Will Be Pigs, Amy Axelrod
Sam and the Lucky Money, Karen Chinn
Save, Spend or Donate?, Nancy Loewen
You Can't Buy a Dinosaur with a Dime, Harriet Ziefert

Music/Movement:

"Money"

A penny for some candy,
A nickel for a pickle
No a dime, the cost begins to climb.

Quarters, pennies, nickels, dimes
Are dropped in here for spending times.
Plink, Plank, Plink, Plank
I will fill my piggy bank.

Crafts:

"Dangling Coin Saver"

This is a very special bank children can use to save their money for the Christmas holidays. Shaped like a turkey it could be made before the Thanksgiving holiday and used for decoration as well as a bank. The body is constructed of a toilet paper tube with the various features added. For preschoolers, you will need to precut most materials.

Source: *Holiday Paper Projects*, E. Richard Churchill

"Penny Rubbings"
Relate this to Lincoln's birthday with the children making special posters or greeting cards with decorations from penny rubbings. The children can use pencils to rub both front and backs of the pennies on lightweight paper.

"Design Your Own Dollar"
Older children can create their own dollar on paper (9 x 4 inches). After discussing the meanings of the symbols on a dollar bill, let the children design their own with words and pictures they believe should be on our American money.

Source: *Kids Celebrate!*, Maria Bonfanti Esche and Clare Bonfanti Braham

Activities:

"Penny Waterfall Game"
Although this is called the "Penny" waterfall game it can be used with any coins you are currently teaching about in your program. Fill a container almost to the top with water and distribute coins of choice to each of the children playing. The object of the game is to roll your coin down a path (waterfall) into the water container without causing the water to spill over the top. Variations for this game are also offered in this source that will help the children with counting. Have the children count how much money actually went into the container before the game was completed. It's a simple game with minimal supplies and maximum uses.

Source: *365 Games Toddlers Play*, Sheila Ellison

"Musical Money"
This is a variation of the musical chairs game, with children passing around little cups with coins in them. When the music stops, the children left holding the cups need to identify the coin they have in their cup. It is a nice educational, yet fun, game with no losers. It lends itself to many variations and some more of these can be found in the source where this was located.

Source: *The Giant Encyclopedia of Theme Activities for Children 2 to 5*, Kathy Charner

Songs:

(Audio) "I Got a Dime"
Source: *Bigger than Yourself*

"How Much Is That Doggie in the Window"
Source: *Great Big Hits!*, by Sharon, Lois and Bram

103 Monsters

Topical Calendar Tie-in:

October 27

"Frankenstein Friday"—Celebrate the "mother" and "father" of the Frankenstein monster, Mary Shelley and Boris Karloff. Use this day to introduce the original Frankestein stories along with other well-known monsters of movie and literature fame.

Videos:

Kipper: The Purple Park Monster
Leo, the See-Through Crumbpicker
Monster Mama
Tailypo
There's a Nightmare in My Closet

Picture Books:

After-School Monster, Marissa Moss
All for One, Jill Murphy
The Ghost Family Meets its Match, Nicola Rubel
Go Away Big Green Monster!, Ed Emberley
Goodnight, Baby Monster, Laura Leuck
The House that Drac Built, Judy Sierra
Monster Brother, Mary Jane Auch
Monsters Party All Night Long, Adam J. B. Lane
The Monsters' Test, Brian J. Heinz
No Such Thing, Jackie French Koller
Orso, the Troll Who Couldn't Scare, Brad Thiessen
The Scariest Monster in the Whole Wide World, Pamela Mayer
Seven Scary Monsters, Mary Beth Lundgren
The Teeny Tiny Ghost and the Monster, Kay Winters
Three-Star Billy, Pat Hutchins

Music/Movement:

"Monster Run"
Sung to: "Hickory Dickory Dock"

The ghosts soar up in the night.
The witches fly by on their brooms.
The skeleton rattles his bones,
And they all
Rush back into their tombs!

Crafts:

"Hairy Monster"
Children love to pretend to be monsters, the goofier the better. Here's a hairy creation the children can wear in their next performance of a monster story. It's made very simply using large, brown grocery bags cut up in strips. Attach toilet tissue tubes for two-inch eyes that bug out. The more

curled strips you add to your monster's body the hairier he will look. Check this source for a reliable illustration of the final craft.

Source: *Fun with Paper Bags and Cardboard Tubes*, F. Virginia Walter

"Bubble-Print Gila Monster"

The Gila monster is a poisonous lizard that may have in earlier times led to the invention of stories of dragons. This may be due to its large lizard size and the way it flicks its tongue out looking like it's breathing fire. Create your own Gila monster using black and brown tempera paint and that bubble wrap that you have sitting at home. With the use of these two items you can create the bubbled look of the lizard's skin. It's a great effect.

Source: *Animal Habitats!*, Judy Press

Activities:

"Monster Munch"

Most monsters are not picky eaters but this one definitely is in this beginning letter sound game. Construct a monster face with a large mouth cut into it out of an old cereal box. The monster now begins to munch on some silly "monster food" that is determined by what is the first item placed in his mouth. If a car is put in the mouth the child can only feed the monster items that begin with that first letter sound. Look for more fun offered like "Sound Hunt," "Same Sound Bags," and "In the End" offered in the source book.

Source: *Wow! I'm Reading!*, Jill Frankel Hauser

"Costume Party"

Have a "Worst Monster Competition." Allow the children to come dressed as a scary or humorous monster. Let them parade for the group to any eerie music available and award paper ribbons in various categories. (Suggestion: At this age all should get some type of award.)

Songs:

(Audio) "The Monster Mash"

Source: *Personality Hit Parade*

104 Moving

Topical Calendar Tie-in:

September 24
"National Good Neighbor Day"—Build a world that cares by showing appreciation of your new neighbors when you move into a new neighborhood. Plan a block party to get to know each other. The same can be done in school to get to know all the children in neighboring classes.

Videos:

A Chair for My Mother
Ira Says Goodbye

Picture Books:

The Best Ever Good-Bye Party, Amy Hest
Good-bye, House, Robin Ballard
The Gunniwolf, Wilhelmina Harper
I'm Not Moving, Mama, Nancy Carlstrom
I Want to Go Home, Alice McLerran
Jamaica's Blue Marker, Juanita Havill
Leaving Home with a Pickle Jar, Barbara Dugan
The Leaving Morning, Angela Johnson
Mason Moves Away, Amy Crane Johnson
A New House for Mouse, Petr Horack
Little Dog Lost, Inga Moore
Mary Ann, Betsy James
Moving Day, Robert Kalan
Mr. Chips, Laura Kvasnosky
Red Fox on the Move, Hannah Gifford
Seeds, George Shannon
To Annabella Pelican from Thomas Hippopotamus, Nancy Patz

Music/Movement:

"Moving"
Sung to: "Where is Thumbkin?"

We are moving,
Let's get packing, *(pretend to fill boxes)*
Box those clothes
And those toys

Say hello to new friends. *(wave hello)*
Hug and call your old friends. *(hug pretend friend)*
What a joy! What a joy!

Crafts:

"Orizomegami"
Orizomegami is a paper-dying technique similar to the tie-dying of T-shirts when that was a trend. Ms. Lewis offers directions for using paper towels and food coloring to create numerous styles and shapes that can be used in greeting cards and other crafts. Orizomegami adds pizzazz behind any

cut-out paper design. Let the children use this technique to make their own notices to friends to inform them than they are moving. Parents often send out cards, "I'm Moving." Let the children be included in the process by using this technique to make cards for their friends. Try it for starry nights, Valentine hearts, bookmarks, and more that are shown in this source. Easy, inexpensive, and beautiful.

Source: *The Jumbo Book of Paper Crafts*, Amanda Lewis

"My Most Awesome Room"

Oftentimes when parents are preparing to move they neglect to include the children in decisions that affect their life a great deal. The move itself can be traumatic but to all children the fear of where they fit into this new home can induce stress. Here is an activity you can suggest to parents who have informed you they are moving and also to parents who are now introducing a new student into your classroom. Allow children to have a large amount of input into how their new room is to be designed. Work on mapping out your room with large paper and multicolored paper for beds, rugs, desks, etc. Look for other useful suggestions in the source book.

Source: *Summer Fun!: 60 Activities for a Kid-Perfect Summer*, Susan Williamson

Activities:

"Racing Colors"

"Racing Colors" is a simple board game that children can play using their own toy race cars, or even their favorite Thomas the Tank engine collection as playing pieces. The board is set up in three parts specifically divided by color. Children will find out who gets to move ahead by the colors they pull from the game bag. Let the children race to the end of the board. This game can be adapted for a lot of uses. I would think you can talk about moving and place houses at the finish line and see which child can reach his new home before his friends.

Source: *Early Learning Skill Builders: Colors, Shapes, Numbers and Letters*, Mary Tomczyk

"Junk Shop Relay"

When preparing to move from one house to another we usually find we've collected a large amount of junk, as well as, treasures. Tell the children we will be practicing moving all that junk and treasure so we will be able to help Mom and Dad if we ever need to move to another house or just from one room to another.

For this ridiculous relay you will need two of each item (hat, toy, cup, etc.). Line the children up and start them passing the items. At intervals the leader can call out wacky commands to slow things down, such as, "Put the hat on your head," "Feather—tickle someone," and more.

Source: *World's Best Outdoor Games*, Glen Vecchione

Songs:

(Audio) "So Long, It's Been Good to Know You"

Source: *Gonna Sing My Head off!*, Kathleen Krull

105 Music

Topical Calendar Tie-in:

September 15

"International Sing Out Day"—Sing out! This is a time to break out in song to express your feelings and have some fun. Sing out loud and strong to get your point across to a friend. This fun way of communicating as in old movies can be a challenge but the nice thing is people have a hard time arguing if they are singing, so Sing Out!

Videos:

The Bremen Town Musicians
Frog Went A-Courtin'
Keeping House
Lentil
Musical Max
Really Rosie

Picture Books:

Anatole and the Piano, Eve Titus
Bravo, Tanya, Satomi Ichikawa
Brother Billy Bronto's Bygone Blues Band, David F. Birchman
Carolinda Clatter!, Mordical Gerstein
Creepy Crawly Calypso, Tony Langham
Daddy's Little Girl, Bobby Burke and Horace Gerlach
Fiddle-I-Fee, Will Hillenbrand
Fog, Susi L. Fowler
The Frog Who Wanted to Be a Singer, Linda Goss
The Heart of the Wood, Marquerite Davol
J.B.'s Harmonica, John Sebastian
Musical Max, Robert Kraus
Music in the Night, Etta Wilson
There's a Hole in the Bucket, Nadine Bernard Westcott

Music/Movement:

"Let's Play Music"
Sung to: "The Wheels on the Bus"

The drums in the band go bam, bam, bam
Bam, bam, bam
Bam, bam, bam
The drums in the band go bam, bam, bam
All around the room.

The bells in the band go ding, ding, ding . . . etc.
The blocks in the band go tap, tap, tap . . . etc.
The horns in the band go beep, beep, beep . . . etc.

Crafts:

"Little Lyre"
Mythology tells us that the god Hermes made a lyre from a scooped out shell of a tortoise and used it the charm the other gods. Paper plates are cheap but very versatile. With the use of paper plates, wooden skewers, black wool, some glue, scissors and markers each child can design their

own turtle shell lyre. This is a good springboard for programs on musical instruments and mythology both.

Source: *Crafts for Kids: Myths and Takes Book*, Greta Speechley

"Pan Pipes"

Here's a musical instrument even your three-year-olds can handle. Supply each child with four cardboard tubes each one inch shorter than the other. Allow them to paint them each different colors and let them dry while you tell other stories. When they are dry tape them together in a row with colorful tape. Plug one end with plastein. Now the children are ready to play their pipes by blowing into the open ends.

Source: *Fun with Paper Bags and Cardboard Tubes*, F. Virginia Walter

Activities:

"Musical Envelopes"

Everyone enjoys getting mail and children love it most of all. Let's deliver those envelopes with a familiar game titled "Musical Envelopes." Prepare 6 to 8 envelopes, each having inside them a different stunt, penalty, or pantomime that the holder will have to perform. The object of the game is to discover who will "pay the Piper" or have to perform their stunt. As the children sit in a circle, begin passing one envelope around when the music begins. When the music stops whoever is holding the envelope holds on to it and the music resumes with the next envelope passing around. Continue until all envelopes have been delivered at which time anyone holding an envelope must stand one at a time and follow the instructions given to them. Miss Campbell's book also offers an adaptation of this game which includes letters and a gift for a party member.

Source: *Perfect Party Games*, Andrea Campbell

"Christmas Match to Music"

Although this is written as a Christmas game it can easily be altered for other holidays or events. Cut out paper Christmas ornaments and cut them in half. Distribute the portions among the children sitting in the circle. One child is selected to sit in the center of the circle with his portion of an ornament and will try to locate his matching portion before the group finishes singing the Christmas song (or other song) that they chose.

This and many comparable games are offered in this excellent source.

Source: *The Best of the Mailbox, Book 1: Preschool/Kindergarten edition*, Margaret Michel

Songs:

(Audio) "The Upward Trail"

Source: *Wee Sing: Sing-Alongs*

106 Mythical Creatures

Topical Calendar Tie-in:

February 28

"National Tooth Fairy Day"—Why shouldn't the tooth fairy have her own day? On this day honor the nightly work of this mythical creature that gathers our teeth and does who knows what with them? Have children determine and illustrate what they believe the tooth fairy does with all those teeth.

Videos:

The Dragon and the Unicorn
The Elves and the Shoemaker
Little Toot and the Loch Ness Monster
Pegasus
The Three Billy Goats Gruff

Picture Books:

Alice the Fairy, David Shannon
Cock-a-Doodle Moooo!: A Mixed-Up Menagerie, Keith DuQuette
Feliciana Meets d'Loop Garou, Tynia Thomassie
Franklin and the Tooth Fairy, Paulette Bourgeois
The Ghosts' Trip to Loch Ness, Jacaues DuQuennoy
Goblin Walk, Tony Johnston and Bruce Degen
Max and Ruby's First Greek Myth: Pandora's Box, Rosemary Wells
The Midnight Unicorn, Neil Reed
The Mystery in the Bottle, Val Willis
Princess Jessica Rescues a Prince, Jennifer Brooks
Runnery Granary, Nancy Farmer
Tooth Fairy's First Night, Anne Bowen
Trouble with Trolls, Jan Brett
Unicorn Dreams, Dyan Sheldon and Neil Reed
Unicorns! Unicorns!, Geraldine McCaughrean

Music/Movement:

"Once Upon a Time"
Source: *Finger Tales*, Joan Hilyer Phelps

Crafts:

"Loch Ness Monster"
"Nessie," better known as the Loch Ness Monster, is one of the more familiar mythical creatures that children hear about along with the Abominable Snowman and the Unicorn. This is a great craft for lessons on mythical creatures or an addition to a lesson on Scotland. Follow these simple instructions for fashioning a stick puppet of the monster and place him in the Loch Ness made of paper plates. Let him swim away and disappear from sight as he has done to so many people trying to catch sight of this shy creature.
Source: *Around the World Art and Activities*, Judy Press

"Torn Paper Mermaid"
Locate a reproducible picture of a mermaid and give each child their own copy. After the children color it give them green tissue paper to create scales for the mermaid's tail. Have them simply tear small pieces and glue them overlapping to give the effect of scales on a fish.

Activities:

"Soft Fuzzy Things of Death"
Although you might not be too comfortable with the title of this ancient game and I would probably lighten it up to a freeze event for young children rather than death, it is a popular event. It is a basic twist on dodgeball, but where you can't really get hurt because the item thrown at you is "a soft fuzzy thing." Learn how to make this item with yarn and practice the rules of the game in this book of games from all over.

Source: *Run, Jump, Hide, Slide, Splash: The 200 Best Outdoor Games Ever*, Joe Rhatigan and Rain Newcomb

"Sphinx Riddles"
Tell the children about the story behind the mythical sphinx with the wings of a bird and the claws of a griffin. She would ambush travelers who would have to solve her important riddle in order to move on or be destroyed by her at once. Collect a variety of riddles to be used for this game. Divide the class in two teams who will try to get past the sphinx. Select one child to be sphinx. As the travelers approach the sphinx one at a time the sphinx draws a riddle from the box to ask. If the player knows the answer he moves on and gains a point for his team. If he doesn't know the answer he is eliminated from the game. The game continues until all players have had a chance or one team is totally eliminated. The team with the highest points wins. Continue with another sphinx.

Songs:

(Audio) "The Unicorn"

Source: *The Child's Collection of the World*

107 Names

Topical Calendar Tie-in:

March 6

"Fun Facts about Names Day"—Celebrate names, their origins and meanings. Visit the local library and try to discover the meaning of your name or such fun facts as: Does Barbie have a last name? or What was the name of the White House before it was named the White House?, etc.

Videos:

Chrysanthemum
Rumpelstiltskin
Tikki Tikki Tembo

Picture Books:

Ananse and the Lizard, Pat Cummings
Chrysanthemum, Kevin Henkes
Eleanor, Ellatony, Ellencake, and Me, C. M. Rubin
From Anne to Zach, Mary Jane Martin
George Foreman: Let George Do It!, George Foreman and Fran Manushkin
How I Named the Baby, Linda Shute
I am Rene, the Boy, Rene Colato Lainex
A Lion Named Shirley Williamson, Bernard Waber
Long Night Moon, Cynthia Rylant
Names for Snow, Judi K. Beach
Nothing, Mick Inkpen
The Old Woman Who Named Things, Cynthia Rylant
The Other Emily, Gibbs Davis
Paco and the Witch, Felix Pitre
A Perfect Name, Charlene Costanzo

Music/Movement:

"Letters, Letters Everywhere"
Sung to: "Alphabet Song"

(Suggestion: Make a flannel board for a child named Sean and add the letters of his name to the board as you sing the song. Later have the children make their own name letters for the board.)

ABCDEFG
Where are the letters that are me?
S is the leader
E follows behind.
A jumps into the row and
N gets in line.
Letters letters everywhere.
I found these and made them mine.

Crafts:

"Name Snake"
Ssssslither through this craft as you make your own name snake. Children will have a wonderful time learning to spell their name while creating this slippery reptile out of boxes. While the source of this craft suggests matchboxes, small boxes will do here. Cover each box with green construction paper then add red construction paper strips in a zigzag shape to the tops to form a stripe on the snake. The length of the snake will depend on the child's name. Have the child arrange the boxes in the correct order and connect them with short strips of red ribbon. The final box will become the snake's head with the addition of eyes and a red forked tongue.

Source: *Look and Make: Presents*, Rachel Wright

"Name Sculptures"
Let children generate their own creative nameplate for their door. This source gives wonderful instructions for making your own salt clay or baker's dough. These require no baking, but simply harden as they dry in the air. Acrylic paints make the best use of color for this craft. An easy and colorful activity that the children will want to do again and again.

Source: *Make Gifts!*, Kim Solga

Activities:

"New-Neighbor Games"
Trade a name allows each child to print his name on many strips of paper. The children may trade their strips with their newly made friends and create a friendship chain with these strips. They should try to get one strip from everyone in the room by trading off one of theirs. They should be sure to keep trading until they are sure they don't have any duplicate names in their possession. The first to do this is the winner.

They can then chain them together with glue or tape to create their own chain friendship belt.

"Name Ball"
This is a simple game that requires that the children pay attention and can easily get to know each other. They should form a circle with one child in the center. The center child will toss a ball in the air calling the name of a child in the circle. That child will attempt to catch the ball before it hits the ground.

Source: *Making Children's Parties Click*, Virginia W. Musselman

Songs:

(Audio) "The Name Game"

Source: *Shaking a Tailfeather*

108 Night

Topical Calendar Tie-in:

August 11

"Night of the Shooting Stars"—Since the year 830, a meteor shower known as "The Perseids" (because it begins in the constellation Pereus) arrives every year on this night. Watchers can see as many as 60 meteors an hour cross the sky.

Videos:

The Berenstain Bears in the Dark
Goodnight, Gorilla
Moon Man
Owl Moon
Stars! Stars! Stars!

Picture Books:

And If the Moon Could Talk, Kate Banks
Bayou Lullaby, Kathi Appelt
Brave Little Raccoon, Erica Wolf
The Deep Blue Sky Twinkles with Stars, Cindy Szekeres
Kate, the Cat and the Moon, David Almond and Stephen Lambert
Lights Out!, John Himmelman
Little Rabbit Goes to Sleep, Tony Johnston
Moonfall, Susan Whitcher
The Night Eater, Ana Juan
The Night Worker, Kate Banks
Polar Bear Night, Lauren Thompson
Quiet Night, Marilyn Singer
The Story of the Milky Way, Joseph Bruchac and Gayle Ross
Ten Flashing Fireflies, Philmon Sturges
Twinkle, Twinkle, Little Star, Iza Trapani

Music/Movement:

"The Moon"

Source: *Once Upon a Childhood: Fingerplays, Action Rhymes and Fun Times for the Very Young*, Dolores Chupela

Crafts:

"Silvery Moon"

"By the light of the silvery moon" children can make their own nighttime mobile out of what every librarian keeps in stock, paper plates. Cut out the center of your paper plate and use it to create a crescent moon to be covered in aluminum foil. The rim can represent the sky. Hang the moon in the center of your night circle with string to create a mobile children will love to hang in their bedroom window. Check this craft book for an illustration of your craft and suggestions for the night sky.

Source: *Art Starts for Little Hands*, Judy Press

"Sun and Moon Masks"

This is an easy paper craft that children can do and later use to act out stories about the sun and the moon. This is a pair of characters that always belong together. This can even lead into a great discussion on other pairs the children are familiar with (cat and dog, stars and stripes, etc.).

Source: *Paper Fun for Kids*, Marion Elliot

Activities:

"Falling Star Dust"

"When you wish upon a star" you will need your magical star dust to try to make that wish come true. Star (or meteor) particles have entered the earth's atmosphere while meteors have passed by us. These particles are made of nickel and iron and can be attracted by magnets. Visit a sandy beach and try to collect some of these particles with the use of a magnet and string. Visit this book source for more information on collecting and observing these particles.

Source: *Go Outside!*, Nancy Blakey

"Musical Sleeping Bags"

Remember musical chairs? Try musical sleeping bags. The same rules apply with all sleeping bags or beach towels, etc. in a circle. Try this game as a preview to settling down for a nighttime story.

Source: *Super Slumber Parties*, Brooks Whitney

Songs:

(Audio) "Ev'ry Night When the Sun Goes In"

Source: *Wee Sing: Sing-Alongs*

109 Noise/Sounds

Topical Calendar Tie-in:

October 14, 1947
"First official flight to break the sound barrier." Discuss with the children the effects sound can have on various items.

Videos:

Lentil
Mr. Brown Can Moo! Can You? (Dr. Seuss's ABC)
Musical Max
Noisy Nora

Picture Books:

As Quiet as a Mouse, Hilda Offen
Do Monkeys Tweet?, Melanie Walsh
Don't Make a Sound, Mary Packard
Granny Greenteeth and the Noise in the Night, Kenn and Joanne Compton
Let's Go Home, Little Bear, Martin Waddell
The Listening Walk, Paul Showers
Meow!, Katya Arnold
The Noise Lullaby, Jacqueline K. Ogburn
Nonna's Porch, Rita Gray
Oh, What a Noisy Farm, Harriet Ziefert
Possum and Peeper, Anne Hunter
Quiet Night, Marilyn Singer
Shhh!, Jeanne Willis and Tony Ross
Too Much Noise!, Ann McGovern

Music/Movement:

"I'm a Very Noisy Person!" and **"I'm a Very Quiet Person!"**
Source: *Good for You!: Toddler Rhymes for Toddler Times*, Stephanie Calmenson

Crafts:

"Native American Shaker"
The noisy craft can be used for a Thanksgiving celebration or a unique addition to a multicultural event. Children can learn Native American dances and use this shaker to add to the music. With the use of a plastic soda bottle, some tissue paper, markers, and unpopped popcorn you can let the music begin.
Source: *November Arts and Crafts: Preschool–Kindergarten*, Mackie Rhodes and Jan Trautman (editors)

"Noisy Goblin"
A noisy little goblin for Halloween celebrations or simply to use for musical activities can be created out of small milk cartons. Place some dried beans inside, seal, and attach a popsicle stick handle. The exterior of the

box can be decorated as a goblin (depicted in this source) or any other character you may wish during the year.

Source: *175 Easy-to-Do Halloween Crafts*, Sharon Dunn Umnik

Activity:

"Music of the Night"

The summer nights are full of sounds both from nature and from unnatural (human-made) sources. This game encourages children to learn to sit quietly and try to list in a variety of ways *all* the sounds that they hear in the night. How often do these sounds repeat themselves? Who or what make these sounds? Check here for ways of cataloging these sounds and safety suggestions for this activity.

Source: *The Everything Kids' Nature Book*, Kathiann M. Kowalski

"Sound Count"

Little children love to make noise so give them a chance to do so through this simple activity for 30–36 months of age. You can use a variety of noises to help the children practice counting. Display all types of items that can make noise such as musical instruments, toys, or more. With the use of dice you can determine how many sounds a child must make in a row. Follow directions for this and other very basic games found in this book.

Source: *365 Games Toddlers Play*, Sheila Ellison

Songs:

(Audio) "Let Ev'ryone Clap Hands"

Source: *Wee Sing: In the Car*

110 Old Age

Topical Calendar Tie-in:

March 22

"As Young as You Feel Day"—This day reminds everyone that you are only as young as you feel, so stop acting your chronological age and get out there and act as young as you want to be. Visit your grandparents and remind them that they can be young and have fun with you today.

Videos:

Alejandro's Gift
The Bremen Town Musicians
Cloudy with a Chance of Meatballs
Wilfrid Gordon McDonald Patridge

Picture Books:

Can You Do This, Old Badger?, Eve Bunting
Dancing Granny, Elizabeth Winthrop
A Fruit and Vegetable Man, Roni Schotter
The Grannyman, Judith Byron Schachner
Great Aunt Martha, Rebecca C. Jones
Henry and Mudge and the Great Grandpas, Cynthia Rylant
Hooray for Grandparents' Day, Nancy Carlson
Mrs. Peachtree's Bicycle, Erica Silverman
Remember That, Leslea Newman
Stranger in the Mirror, Allen Say
Sunshine Home, Allen Say
There Was an Old Woman Who Lived in a Boot, Linda Smith
Verdi, Janell Cannon
When I am Old with You, Angela Johnson
William's Ninth Life, Minna Jung
The Woman Who Saved Things, Phyllis Krasilousky

Music/Movement:

"Grandma, Grandma"
Source: *The Big Book of Stories, Songs, and Sing-Alongs*, Beth Maddigan

Crafts:

"Skidproof Slipper Socks"
Remember those socks with grippers that children wore as infants so that they wouldn't slip? Well we all need that kind of help at some time or other. Let's make some special socks for Grandma or Grandpa when they are walking around the house. Design these jazzy safety socks with special markers and puffy paint. Show your grandparents how much you care and love them. Directions are offered in the source book.
Source: *Perfect Kids' Parties*, Vicky Shiotsu and Rozanne Lanczak Williams

"The Old Woman in the Shoe"
Make the old woman's shoe home using construction paper, crayons, and tape or staples. A child's conception of the old woman's shoe may vary with what they think the shoe should look like. Patterns of various types of shoes can be made available for tracing. After the completion of the craft, show the children the illustrations of this story.

Activities:

"Newspaper Log"
Community service projects are a wonderful way for children to learn responsibility and respect for the elderly. Discuss the fact that many of our senior community live on a fixed income and also need more help in dealing with daily chores. How can children help with this problem? Have them gather the newspapers that the seniors need to recycle and return them as "newspaper logs" that can now be used to heat their house.

Source: *All New Crafts for Earth Day*, Kathy Ross

"Catch the Cane"
Take an item that children normally associate with elderly people, the cane, and turn it into a easy catch it if you can game. While everyone forms a circle, let one child remain in the center holding the cane upright on the floor. When he is ready he will call out a number and release the cane for that other person to catch.

Source: *Making Children's Parties Click*, Virginia W. Musselman

Songs:

(Audio) "This Ole Man"

Source: *Mother Goose Songs*

111 Parties

Topical Calendar Tie-in:

February 28
"Mardi Gras"—Celebrated the two weeks leading up to Lent, this event allows people to set aside restraint in favor of masked parties, parades, and other celebrations. The climax is Fat Tuesday.

Videos:

Beneath the Ghost Moon
The Berenstain Bears and Too Much Birthday
Little Bear: Parties and Picnics
Spot Goes to a Party
Dora: Super Silly Fiesta

Picture Books:

Andrew's Amazing Monsters, Kathryn Hook Berlan
Badger's Bring Something Party, Hiawyn Oram
Block Party Today!, Marilyn Singer
Brave Horace, Holly Keller
Cassandra Who?, Iris Hiskey
Halloween Party, Linda Shute
The Hippo Hop, Christine Loomis
If You Give a Pig a Party, Laura Numeroff
Jeremy's Tail, Duncan Ball
Lizzy's Dizzy Day, Sheila Keenan
Miss Spider's Tea Party, David Kirk
The Pink Party, Maryann MacDonald
Slumber Party, Judith Caseley
Some Birthday!, Patricia Polacco
The Spaghetti Party, Doris Orgel

Music/Movement:

"Min's Birthday"
Source: *The Moon in the Man*, Elizabeth Honey

Crafts:

"Pretty Party Plates"
Planning a classroom party? Have the children help you with the decorations and also create their own party plates. Using paper plates for the center have the child actually create a decorative placemat attached to the back of the plate. One example offered by the author is flower petals with the plate as the center of the flower. This book is a must-see for examples of art for the very young when budgets are tight. When aren't they?
Source: *My Party Book*, Marion Elliot

"Party Hats"
Party hats are traditional in children's parties. Try some of these colorful hats in simple designs forged from paper, glitter, feathers, etc. This is a

simple craft that can be completed by even the youngest of children. Bright color illustrations are offered in this source to guide you.

Source: *The Grolier Kids Craft Paper Craft Book*, David Hancock, Jill Hancock, Ann Murray, Lyn Orton, Cheryl Owen, and Lynda Watts

Activities:

"Rooster Romp"

This Mexican party game takes a little stamina. Children pair off to see who can last longer than the other when they have to hop while remaining in a designated position. The goal of the game is for one rooster to snatch the scarf that the other has tucked in a belt or pocket without changing his position or stop hopping. Continue pairing off until there is only one winning rooster at the farm. Complete details are offered in the source book.

Source: *Sidewalk Games*, Glen Vecchione

"Lantern Riddles"

This two-part activity is used in China for the Lantern Festival. You will need to develop a collection of hanging lanterns based on the animals of the zodiac and suspend special riddles cards from the bottom of the lanterns. Now let's see how many riddles your partygoers can actually solve without help from their friends. Directions for the constructions of your mobiles are offered in this source along with an assemblage of riddles to use.

Source: *Moonbeams, Dumplings and Dragon Boats*, Nina Simonds, Leslie Swartz, and the Children's Museum

Songs:

(Audio) "My Hair Had a Party Last Night"

Source: *Totally Zany*

112 Pets

Topical Calendar Tie-in:

October 15

"Wishbone for Pets"—This program allows lovers of pets and pet sitters to have a special money-raising event for their favorite animal friends. This event is held around Thanksgiving with all proceeds going to a local pet-related charity, so that we can say thank you for all the unconditional love our pets have given to us.

Videos:

Arthur's Pet Business
Frog Goes to Dinner
Jim's Dog, Muffins
"Let's Get a Pup!" said Kate
The Mysterious Tadpole
Pet Show!

Picture Books:

Aaaarrgghh! Spider!, Lydia Monks
Any Kind of Dog, Lynn Reiser
Be Gentle!, Virginia Miller
Daddy, Could I Have an Elephant, Jake Wolf
Furry, Holly Keller
I Took My Frog to the Library, Eric A. Kimmel
I Wanna Iguana, Karen Kaufman Orloff
Moonbear's Pet, Frank Asch
Mr. Green Peas, Judith Caseley
The New Puppy, Lawrence Anholt
An Octopus Followed Me Home, Dan Yaccarino
The Perfect Pet, Margie Palatini
Pick a Pet, Diane Namm
The Queen's Goat, Margaret Mahy
Slithery Jake, Rose-Marie Provencher

Music/Movement:

"My Pets"
Source: *101 Fingerplays, Stories and Songs to Use with Finger Puppets*, Diane Brigg

Crafts:

"Paper Plate Pets"
Looking for the perfect pet? These crazy critters require no feeding, no grooming, and no walking, but they do take some imagination. Break out your large paper plates to fold in half for the mouth, and then follow instructions and illustrations from this book to make the silliest or scariest pets the children have ever seen. For younger children, you might want to have precut paper squares for teeth or tongues and extra large circles for

eyes. Pom-poms make good nostrils if they are the large size. Parents can help with making crazy curled hair and more.

Source: *Better Homes and Gardens Big Book of Kids' Crafts*, Dan Rosenberg (editor)

"Pebble Pets"

Collect as many smooth stones of various sizes as you can find, because once the children begin, they may want to make several pets to take home. This is reminiscent of the "Pet Rock" craze of earlier years. For suggestions on how to color them, just see this source.

Source: *The Grolier Kids Crafts Book*, Cheryl Owen and Anna Murray

Activities:

"A 4-H Pet Show"

Invite your local 4-H group to bring their pets to the program and speak to the children about these animals. These pets may include hamsters, rabbits, ducks, etc. This will allow small children an opportunity to see and touch animals they may have never touched before.

"Dog and Flea Game"

Fleas love to hop on a dog. Here's a little game that takes a little skill but children will love to try again and again to succeed. Make your dog from an oatmeal box covered with a brown sock. Add features and floppy ears but leave the top open.

The fleas are made of small rubber balls covered in tissues.

Are you ready to play? Tell the children to see how many fleas they can get into the dog by bouncing them on the ground and letting them hop into his top.

Source: *Crafts for Kids Who are Wild about Insects*, Kathy Ross

Songs:

(Audio) "My Neighbor's Dog"

Source: *Shake a Leg*, Norman Foote

113 Pirates

Topical Calendar Tie-in:

September 19

"Talk like a Pirate Day"—Now we have a day where everyone can swash their buckles and put on their eye patch and talk like a pirate saying "Arrr, matey, where's my gold?" Learn about famous pirates like Bluebeard and even a few infamous lady pirates like Ann Bonny.

Videos:

Kipper: Pirates
The Pirate Adventure (Raggedy Ann and Andy)
Pirate Island

Picture Books:

Alvin the Pirate, Ulf Lofgren
Andy's Pirate Ship: A Spot the Difference Book, Philippe Dupasquier
Bubble Bath Pirates!, Jarrett J. Krosoczka
Do Pirates Take Baths?, Kathy Tucker
Edward and the Pirates, David McPhail
Emily and the Golden Acorn, Ian Beck
Henry and the Buccaneer Bunnies, Carolyn Crimi
How I Become a Pirate, Melinda Long
Mimi and Gustav in Pirates!, Denis Woychuk
Olive's Pirate Party, Roberta Baker
Pigasus, Pat Murphy
Pirates: Robbers of the High Seas, Gail Gibbons
To Capture the Wind, Sheila MacGill-Callahan
Tough Boris, Mem Fox
The Trouble with Uncle, Babette Cole
Wild Will, Ingrid and Dicter Schubert

Music/Movement:

"One-Eyed Pirate" or **"Parrots on a Pirate"**
Source: *52 Programs for Preschoolers: the Librarians Year Round Planner*, Dianne Briggs

Crafts:

"Spyglass"
"Ships Ahoy!" Pirates and other seafarers have spotted ships across the ocean with a spyglass. Help the children create their own pirate spyglass with these uncomplicated instructions. You will only need construction paper and paper towel tubes and toilet paper tubes. You will be able to simulate the operation of spyglass once it is constructed. Sail your ships and see what you can see. You might also turn this simple craft into a kaleidoscope by adding colored plastic wrap or cellophane to the end.
Source: *The Absolute Best Play Days: From Airplanes to Zoos (and Everything in Between!)*, Pamela Waterman

"Parrot Puppet"
What is a pirate without his trusty parrot sitting on his shoulder? Create your own pirate's friend from toilet paper tubes, feathers, and more. Patterns for the parrot's features are supplied in this source and can be reproduced on colored paper to make the results more realistic.
Source: *Hit of the Party*, Amy Vangsgard

Activities:

"Smuggle the Gold"
"Ahoy Mates! Where's my gold?" This great variation of the well known game of tag will be enjoyed by children of all ages. The change here is that no one knows who really plays the part of "it" but the person himself. "It" is the smuggler on the ship hiding the treasure in his hand. Let the children stand in a circle with their hands behind them. As the teacher goes around the circle pretending to pass a small treasure to each child, along the way she actually leaves the treasure with someone. To begin the game shout, "Smugglers, ahoy!. Everyone will run around trying to tag before being tagged. Can you find the smuggler? What happens when you find him? What happens if you find the wrong person? Check Deanna Cook's boredom buster ideas to end this and other games.
Source: *Family Fun Boredom Busters*, Deanna F. Cook (editor)

"Save Peter Pan/Tiger Lilly from Captain Hook"
The children form a protective circle around the child to be protected (Peter Pan or Tiger Lilly). Another child representing Captain Hook attempts to break through this circle to tag Peter Pan and in this way becoming the new Pan. See this and dozens of other beguiling games in the source book.
Source: *Hit of the Party*, Amy Vangsgard

Songs:

(Audio) "Pirate Story"
Source: *A Child's Garden of Songs*

114 Plants/Seeds

Topical Calendar Tie-in:

April 13
"International Plant Appreciation Day"—Plants are important to our everyday life. Imagine a world without plants! We would have no cotton shirts, toilet paper, and many other daily items that they give us. Take this day to show your appreciation by giving a friend a house plant to care for each day.

Videos:

The Empty Pot
Frog and Toad Together: The Garden (Arnold Lobel Video Showcase)
Harold and His Amazing Green Plants
Jack and the Beanstalk
The Little Red Hen
Tops and Bottoms

Picture Books:

The Carrot Seed, Ruth Krauss
The Enormous Carrot, Vladimir Vagin
Jack's Garden, Henry Cole
The Leaf Men, William Joyce
Meow Monday, Phyllis Root
Our Community Garden, Barbara Pollak
A Plant Called Spot, Nancy J. Peteraf
The Pumpkin Man and the Crafty Creeper, Margaret Mahy
Seeds, George Shannon
Seeds! Seeds! Seeds!, Nancy Elizabeth Wallace
Something Is Growing, Walter Lyon Krodop
Sunflower, Miela Ford
The Surprise Garden, Zoe Hall
The Tiny Seed, Eric Carle
Toot and Puddle: Wish You Were Here, Holly Hobbie

Music/Movement:

"We Plant the Seeds"
Sung to: "The Farmer in the Dell"
Source: *Fun with Mommy and Me*, Dr. Cindy Bunin Nurik

Crafts:

"Hanging Flowers"
Make your own hanging gardens with this enchanting hanging flower. Draw a large petal on construction paper and cut it out. Trace around it six times to create the petals that you will glue to the back of a paper plate around the exterior to form a flower. Here's where the fun begins. Get children to crunch tightly formed balls out of tissue paper squares left on the table. (Nice chance to have an impromptu basketball game.) When the balls are gathered, instruct the children to glue them to the front of

the plate until the whole plate is covered in bright buds. Add a loop to hang in an appropriate are for display.

Source: *Look and Make: Presents*, Rachel Wright

"Fern Print"

This craft will have to be completed in two steps so you will need to plan ahead. Step one is the gathering and pressing of a variety of ferns. This can be done as a group or you can supply these for the children. The second step will involve arranging your collection in a picture perfect design that can be mounted and framed for special gifts.

Source: *Nature's Art Box*, Laura C. Martin

Activities:

"A Seedy Experiment"

Find an assortment of seed experiments that are offered in this nature book. Gathering seeds and sorting them to be examined later with magnifying glasses can be an interesting class assignment. Have them sort the seeds they find into different storage compartments. Look for "what seeds birds are eating," "pine cones and other seeds," and my favorite experiment offered, the best way to collect seeds is with your socks. Take a look because the children will love the fun of the search.

Source: *The Kids' Guide to Nature Adventures*, Joe Rhatigan

"Growing Flowers"

Calming music may be played while allowing the children to pretend they are seeds all curled up. As the teacher circulates around the room, the child that's touched on the head pretends to grow into a type of flower he or she likes best.

Later have the children tell what kind of flower they are and how it feels to grow like a flower.

Songs:

(Audio) "Plant a Seed"

Source: *We Have a Dream: Friends Around the World*

115 Poetry

Topical Calendar Tie-in:

April 10–16

"Young People's Poetry Week"—The Children's Book Council sponsors this special week of events encouraging children to enjoy poetry. Read it, write it, and enjoy it. Try sponsoring your own poetry week featuring local readers reading such poets as Shel Silverstein, Jack Prelutsky, Frost and others. Follow this with a chance for children to write and present their own hilarious poems.

Videos:

Beast Feast
Casey at the Bat
McElligot's Pool
Madeline
The Owl and the Pussycat

Picture Books:

Beneath the Ghost Moon, Jane Yolen
Boo to a Goose, Mem Fox
Casey at the Bat, Ernest Lawrence Thayer
Five Little Monkeys Play Hide and Seek, Eileen Christelow
A Frog in the Bog, Karma Wilson and Joan Rankin
Miss Mary Mack, Mary Ann Hoberman
Poetry Speaks to Children, Elise Paschen
Rosie's Fishing Trip, Amy Hest
Roses are Pink, Your Feet Really Stink, Diane deGroat
Shoe Baby, Joyce Dunbar
The Tale of Custard the Dragon, Ogden Nash
Teddy Bear, Teddy Bear, Timothy Bush
To Market, To Market, Anne Miranda
Who Swallowed Harold?, Susan Pearson

Music/Movement:

"Rainwear"

Sung to: "It's Raining, It's Pouring"

It's raining , it's pouring *(flutter fingers downward like rain)*
The puddles are now forming.
I pulled on my boots *(pull on boots)*
And ran hot foot
To jump in the puddles this morning. *(jump into puddles)*

It's raining, it's pouring *(flutter fingers like rain)*
This umbrella is so boring *(hold up umbrella)*
When I hold it up high
But it drips down my back
When it's pouring.

Crafts:

"Giant Brain"
This craft can be used during a poetry event or for a Halloween program. Look up your favorite Frankenstein or monster poem to read. You might try "Horror Movie Marathon" from *Sailing off to Singapore*, which talks about the brain that wouldn't die, the blob, etc. After poems on such creepy characters, try this crafty costume from Kathy Ross and greet the "Great Brain" using, of all things, pantyhose.
Source: *Make Yourself a Monster! A Book of Creepy Crafts*, Kathy Ross

"Shadow Box Scene"
Introduce your group to poetry and your favorite poets in a fun way through these shadow box scenes. After a reading of a chosen poem give the children a paper plate. Ask them to illustrate their favorite part of the poem either through crayons, markers, or cut-outs glued on the plate.

Add a second plate on top of it facing the opposite way and with the center cut out to give the picture a three-dimensional look. Finally, let the children decorate the frame.
Source: *Paper Plate Art*, Maxine Kinney

Activities:

"Rhyming Treasure Hunt"
Introduce children to the fun of poetry starting with familiar nursery rhymes, and then continue with silly poems by such authors as Shel Silverstein and Jack Prelutsky. Now make a game out of rhyming with this special treasure hunt. Give each child a bag and let them search the house or classroom for items that rhyme (shoe, glue, picture of a zoo) etc. If they can't find a match for an item, they are offered other options in the instructions for this game. Along with the treasure hunt you will also find directions for a "Rhyme Challenge," "Toss-a-Rhyme," and "Rhyme Sort." Move from these fun filled events to introducing other types of poet and their works.
Source: *Wow! I'm Reading!*, Jill Frankel Hauser

"Poems to Songs"
Turn poetry into song with this lesson in rhythm. Hand out a variety of rhythm instruments for children to use while speaking nursery rhymes like "Old King Cole," "Humpty Dumpty," and more offered in this book. Move on to a variety of poems that children are already familiar with today.
Source: *Show Time! Music, Dance and Drama Activities for Kids*, Lisa Bany-Winters

Songs:

(Audio) "Love Poem"
Source: *Sing A to Z*, Sharon, Lois and Bram

116 Pop-Mania

Topical Calendar Tie-in:

January 30

"Bubble Wrap Appreciation Day"—Here's a day just to be silly and have fun. It's a day to celebrate the invention of bubble wrap, learn its history and uses. Learn snapping etiquette and spend the day snapping bubble wrap with coworkers, classmates, and friends. Also learn the use of bubble wrap in art.

Videos:

Hot-Air Henry
The Mole and the Chewing Gum

Picture Books:

Bubbles, Bubbles, Kathi Appelt
Bubble Trouble, Stephen Krensky
Bubble Trouble, Joy N. Hulme
Heatwave, Helen Ketteman
Jolly Snow, Jane Hissey
Popcorn, Alex Moran
Pop! Went Another Balloon! Keith Fanilkner
Strega Nona Takes a Vacation, Tomie dePaola
Tubtime, Elvira Woodruff
The Well-Mannered Balloon, Nancy Willard

Music/Movement:

"Pop, Pop, Pop!"
Source: *The Book of Fingerplays and Action Songs*, John M. Feierabend

Crafts:

"Bubble Makers"
Bubbles are a sure success at any time when dealing with young children. Here you will find methods of making easy bubble wands and pipes from styrofoam trays, soda bottles, and other throwaway items. Need a recipe for the bubble mixture? That's supplied here too. Fill your room with a cloud of bubbles and this is sure to be a big hit.
Source: *Earth-Friendly Outdoor Fun*, George Pfiffner

"Bubble Pop Art"
Here's a simple art project all children will be crazy about. Mix detergent and water in a container and let the children blow bubbles with straws. Let the other children chase the bubbles and catch them on colored paper.

Use crayons or markers to trace the wet circles that appear on the paper. Look for even more exciting variations in this source.
Source: *Good Earth Art*, Mary Ann F. Kohl and Cindy Gainer

Activities:

"Pop-a-Loony"

Decorate your classroom with various balloons. Place a message in each one describing a loony action each child needs to perform. Each child can take a turn selecting a balloon, popping it any way they can, and acting out the loony action it requires. The class can try to guess the mime acted out (monkey eating banana) or the child may simply be required to perform a stunt (close eyes and walk backward).

Source: *Everybody Wins!: Non-Competitive Party Games and Activities for Children*, Jody L. Blosser

"Bubble Bop"

Divide the group in two with one group blowing bubbles and the other group popping them. Add a little music but instruct the children to pop the bubbles only according to your called out instructions. Try "stomp on them," "run backwards," "karate chop," etc., then switch groups.

Source: *Creative Games for Young Children*, Annetta Dellinger

Songs:

(Audio) "Popcorn Calling Me"

Source: *Buzz Buzz*

117 Problem Solving

Topical Calendar Tie-in:

November 19–25

"National Game and Puzzle Week"—Traditionally held Sunday through Saturday of Thanksgiving week, this program is used to increase the appreciation of board games and puzzles. Spend some valuable time with your family problem solving with these brain teasers. For further information write: Frank Beres, National Game & Puzzle Week, P.O. Box 268, Beloit, WI 53512-0268

Videos:

Art Dog
Have You Seen My Duckling?
Katy No-Pocket
Miss Nelson in Missing
Whistle for Willie

Picture Books:

The 13th Clue, Ann Jonas
The Best Vacation Ever, Stuart J. Murphy
Detective LaRue: Letters from the Investigations, Mark Teague
Dot and Jabber and the Mystery of the Missing Stream, Ellen Stroll Walsh
Goggles!, Ezra Jack Keats
Harry and the Lady Next Door, Gene Zion
How to be a Friend, Marc Brown
Jeremy's Tail, Duncan Ball
Jingle Bells, Nick Butterworth
Let's Play, Leo Lionni
The Magic Toolbox, Mie Araki
Too Much Noise!, Ann McGovern
Where Do Balloons Go?: An Uplifting Mystery, Jamie Lee Curtis
Will You Carry Me?, Heleen Van Rossum
You Can't Buy a Dinosaur with a Dime, Harriet Ziefert

Music/Movement:

"Min's Birthday"
Source: *The Moon in the Man*, Elizabeth Honey

Crafts:

"Stick-to-it Puzzle"
Here's a puzzler anyone would enjoy. Children will get a chance to make an original artwork using watercolor techniques provided in this source. When completed, turn their masterpieces into magnetic puzzles by cutting the pieces the same size as self-stick magnets provided. Four separate watercolor techniques are provided: rubber cement-resist painting, crayon-resist painting, wet on wet, and dry brush. Any of these methods can be used with children 4 years and up.
Source: *Better Homes and Garden's Big Book of Kids' Crafts*, Dan Rosenberg (editor)

"Pizza Puzzles"

Make your own puzzle in the shape of a pizza out of cardboard. Add food features on the top with pictures from magazines. Help the children with math puzzles by dividing your pizza in equal parts for the child's math group.

Source: *Good Earth Art*, Mary Ann F. Kohl and Cindy Gainer

Activities:

"Detective Fool"

With everyone seated in a circle, one child is chosen to be "Detective Fool." He's taken from the room and blindfolded. When he returns to the circle everyone will have changed seats. When "Detective Fool" points to someone, that person says, "April Fools" or another appropriate phrase, while disguising his voice. If the detective is able to determine who it is he can change places with him in the circle. You will find this a friendly game for all classes.

Source: *Creative Games for Young Children*, Annetta Dellinger

"The Guessing Game"

Children can use their critical thinking skills in this guessing game. Prepare a large number of envelopes with pictures of items (bus, television, etc.) inside. Write clues to the item on the exterior of the envelope and one at a time read the clues to the group until one little detective calls out the correct answer. Reveal the picture.

Source: *The Best of the Mailbox, Book 2: Preschool/Kindergarten edition*, Margaret Michel

Songs:

(Audio) "Who Put the Bomp?"

Source: *Great Big Hits 2*, Sharon, Lois and Bram

118 Reptiles: Alligators, Crocodiles

Topical Calendar Tie-in:

October 21

"Reptile Awareness Day"—Jenkinson's Aquarium in New Jersey offers this special day to educate children about reptiles and their life. You can try to do the same. Learn how alligators, snakes, and turtles are related. Introduce reptile stories and maybe invite someone from Jenkinson's or your local aquarium or pet store to bring some special friends for the day.

Videos:

Alligator All Around
Cornelius
How the Elephant Got his Trunk
Lyle, Lyle the Crocodile
Mama Don't Allow

Picture Books:

Bill and Pete to the Rescue, Tomi dePaola
Clarabella's Teeth, An Vrombaut
Copy Crocs, David Bedford
Counting Crocodiles, Judy Sierra
Crocodile Listens, April Pulley Sayre
Dial-a-Croc, Mike Dumbleton
Five Little Monkey's Sitting in a Tree, Eileen Christelow
I am a Little Alligator, Francois Crozat
Kapac the Killer Croc, Marcia Vaughan
More Mr. & Mrs. Green, Keith Baker
See You Later, Alligator, Babette McCarthy
The Selfish Crocodile, Faustin Charles and Michael Terry
Where's My Mommy?, Jo Brown
Where's Your Smile, Crocodile?, Claire Freedman
Why Alligator Hates Dog: A Cajun Folktale, J. J. Reneaux

Music/Movement:

"The Alligator"
Source: *Alphabet Art*, Judy Press

Crafts:

"Captain Hook's Crocodile Clothespin"
Disney's Peter Pan and Captain Hook were always battling each other, but the one great fear for Captain Hook was the alligator always looking to eat him. This wonderful Disney Craft book has an assortment of crafts to offer based on all the Walt Disney movie characters that children have come to know and love. Captain Hook will have to watch out after you create a collection of crocodiles and of clothespins, marker, paper, and googly eyes. Be sure it doesn't eat you up.
Source: *Disney's Ten-Minute Crafts for Preschoolers*, Laura Torres

"Make an Alligator Purse"
Create a large construction paper purse in the shape of an alligator. Children can add the features themselves. This can be easily used to demonstrate the story *The Lady with the Alligator Purse* by Nadine Westcott if you give each child paper versions of the story characters.
Source: *The Giant Encyclopedia of Theme Activities for Children 2 to 5*, Kathy Charner

Activities:

"Guarding Gators"
Watch out for the gator invasion. This is an action-packed game of tag that has a player trying to guard his home from an invasion of alligators. How successfully can you defend your turf? Don't let the alligators get past you to your home or be eaten and become one of them yourself. Check the rules for both guard and gators in this swampy experience.
Source: *Hey Mom, I'm Bored!*, Story Evans and Lise O'Haire

"Alligator and Fish"
This activity suggests the use of a sliding board for the game but any type of sliding tools can be used (tubes on a slick surface, skateboard-type items to ride on, etc.) to adapt this for use in a gymnasium. Select a person to be the alligator. He is placed one giant step away from the end of the slide (or sliding area marked). Children will slide down the slide or area marked and tries not to slide into the arms (jaws) of the alligator. The alligator must never move his feet from the area they are planted.
Source: *The Little Witch's Black Magic Book of Games*, Linda Glovach

Songs:

(Audio) "The Smile on the Crocodile"
Source: *Sing Around the Campfire*

119 Reptiles: Snakes

Topical Calendar Tie-in:

March 10–12

"World's Largest Rattlesnake Roundup"—Sweetwater, Texas, runs their annual rattlesnake roundup on this week, offering rattlesnakes on display, snake meat available to eat, information about snakes, and snake hunts. Take this week to learn a little more about these misunderstood reptiles. Have your own snake hunt by hiding illustrations of the variety of snakes throughout your building and getting the children to identify each one they have found.

Videos:

A Boy and a Boa
The Day Jimmy's Boa Ate the Wash
To Bathe a Boa

Picture Books:

The Cactus Flower Bakery, Harry Allard
Hide and Snake, Keith Baker
Slithery Jake, Rose-Marie Provencher
How Snake Got His Hiss, Marguerite W. Davol
Jimmy's Boa and the Bungee Jump Slam Dunk, Trinka Hakes Noble
My Brother Needs a Boa, Anne Weston
Never Fear, Snake My Dear!, Rolf Siegenthaler
Rattlesnake Dance, Jim Arnosky
The Rattlesnake Who Went to School, Craig Kee Strete
Slithery Jake, Rose-Marie Provencher
Small Green Snake, Libba Moore Gray
Snake Hunt, Jill Kastner
Snakes!, David T. Greenberg
Verdi, Janell Cannon

Music/Movement:

"Slither, Slither Little Snake"
Sung to: "Old MacDonald"

Slither, slither little snake
Through the grass and weeds.
(crawl on your stomach)
And shed your skin to make some new
Through the grass and weeds.
With some skin shed here
And some skin shed there,
(shake and shiver skin loose)
Here some skin, there some skin
Everywhere some old skin.
Slither, slither little snake
Through the grass and weeds.

Crafts:

"Baby Rattlesnake"
Based on Mira Reisberg's amusing tale of *Baby Rattlesnake*, this craft would fit with any snake program. With the use of wallpaper scraps children create a colorful snake with wild and fancy patterns. It's delightfully easy with wonderful results.
Source: *Storybook Art*, MaryAnn F. Kohl and Jean Potter

"Slithery Snake"
For children a little older and with more patience try this snake craft made of small plastic cups strung together. Paint it, add eyes, and a long tongue and let it slither across the table as its body swivels back and forth.
Source: *Why Throw It Away? Making Crazy Animals*, Jen Green

Activities:

"Poisonous Snakes"
Parachute games are a colorful way to fill short spans of time between lessons and a way for the children to burn off that excess energy during the day. Cut some short strands of rope and toss them on top of a large parachute that the children are holding. These will represent the "poisonous snakes." Warn everyone that if the rope touches them they have then been "bitten" by snake. The only way to get rid of the poison is to run to the wall and back before rejoining the game. When the teacher yells "snake bite," the children will pop the parachute up and down, attempting to send the snakes to someone other than themselves.
Source: *The Ultimate Playground and Recess Game Book*, Guy Bailey

"Serpent Game"
Playing games with dice and marbles is an activity early Egyptians used for daily entertainment. This serpent dice game requires players to work their way around the sections of a coiled serpent to reach his head. Create your own version of this reptilian game using cardboard, Styrofoam cups, beans, and some crayons. An actual pattern that can be reproduced is offered in the source book.
Source: *International Crafts and Games*, Cynthia G. Adams

Songs:

(Audio) "Sally the Swinging Snake"
Source: *Sally the Swinging Snake*

120 Reptiles: Turtles

Topical Calendar Tie-in:

May 23
"World Turtle Day"—Protect and honor turtles and tortoises around the world. This holiday is sponsored by the American Tortoise Rescue organization in hopes of saving turtles and their habitats.

Videos:

Franklin Is Messy
The Tortoise and the Hare
Thirteen Moons on Turtle's Back
Yertle the Turtle

Picture Books:

Albert's Impossible Toothache, Barbara Williams
Ananse's Feast: An Ashanti Tale, Tololwa M. Mollel
Frog's Best Friend, Marion Dane Bauer
Hi, Harry!, Martin Waddell
How Honu the Turtle Got His Shell, Casey A. McGuire-Turcotte
One Tiny Turtle, Nicola Davies
Tomorrow, Up and Away!, Pat Lowery Collins
The Tortoise and the Hare Race Again, Dan Bernstein
The Turtle and the Moon, Charles Turner
Turtle Bay, Saviour Pirotta
Turtle in the Sea, Jim Arnosky
Turtle Splash! Countdown at the Pond, Cathryn Falwell
Turtle, Turtle, Watch Out!, April Pulley Sayre
What Newt Could Do for Turtle, Jonathan London

Music/Movement:

"Wag, Hop, Hide!"
Source: *Good for You!: Toddler Rhymes for Toddler Time*, Stephanie Calmenson

Crafts:

"Paper Turtle"
Using the large format shown in this book, which is appropriate for the manual dexterity of this age, children can color and glue together the parts of a turtle. Large pieces make it easy for the children to handle the work they're doing. The illustrations in this book can be easily duplicated for use.
Source: *Big and Easy Art*, Teacher Created Materials, Inc.

"Turtle Mousepad"
Almost everyone has a computer at home for children to research homework or just to play each day. Have the children make their own special mousepad for when it is their turn to use the computer. Kathie Stull offers a humorous-looking turtle constructed from green soft-foam sheeting, wiggle eyes, and glue. Patterns are offered for size and children

are given black markers to design the turtle's shell. Place your mousepad at the computer to signal to your family that it's now your turn at the computer.

Source: *20-minute Crafts*, Kathie Stull

Activities:

"Turtle Races"

Slow and steady wins the race. Try this turtle race with materials everyone has on hand, a legal size sheet of lined paper, some quarters and some pennies. Supply each child with a quarter for the turtle's body and a penny for the head and set each turtle up at the starting line of the paper. Each player may take turns tossing two coins for dice to decide how they will move their turtle from line to line racing to the finish line. The source here offers such ideas as: two heads and you move your turtle's head two lines and roll again; two tails and your turn is over and you must slide your turtle's head back on it's body, etc. Check for the list of fun ways to move your turtle to the end of the race. This can easily be adapted to larger playfields by making paper plate turtles with separate body and head and moving them across the entire room at stages. The use of money, of course, will help the children become familiar with various coins.

Source: *Family Fun Boredom Busters*, Deanna F. Cook (editor)

"Racing Colors"

"Racing Colors" is a simple board game that children can play using their own toy race cars as shown or you can adapt it as a follow-up to the story of *The Tortoise and the Hare*. The board is set up in three parts specifically divided by color. Children will find out who gets to move ahead by the colors they pull from the game bag. Instead of cars this time gather some toy turtles and bunny figurines to make the race and maybe add a third mystery character to the mix. Can the tortoise win the race this time?

Source: *Early Learning Skill Builders: Colors, Shapes, Numbers and Letters*, Mary Tomczyk

Songs:

(Audio) "Turtle"

Source: *Animal Alphabet Songs*

121 Royalty

Topical Calendar Tie-in:

January 6

"Epiphany (Three Kings' Day)"—This day is held in honor of the three kings who brought gifts to the baby Jesus. The night before this day, children place boxes of grass by their doors for the kings' camels and the next morning the grass will be eaten and replaced with a thank-you gift. On January 6, a cake is served at the celebration with a tiny plastic baby baked inside. When the cake is sliced and served, the one who gets the baby toy is named the king for the day. Look for this and other ways to celebrate this day at your local library.

Videos:

The Emperor's New Clothes
King Midas and the Golden Touch
One Monday Morning
Ouch!
The Most Wonderful Egg in the World
The Recess Queen
Rumpelstiltskin

Picture Books:

Caterina: The Clever Farm Girl, Julienne Peterson
The Emperor and the Nightingale, Meilo So
If I Were Queen of the World, Fred Hiatt
King of Another Country, Fiona French
The Kiss that Missed, David Melling
Kitty Princess and the Newspaper Dress, Emma Carlow and Trevor Kickinson
A Pie Went By, Carolyn Dunn
The Princess and the Pizza, Mary Jane and Herm Auch
Princess Bee and the Royal Good-night Story, Sandy Asher
The Princess Knight, Cornelia Funke
Princess Penelope's Parrot, Helen Lester
The Queen's Holiday, Margaret Wild
The Queen's Goat, Margaret Mahy
The Quiltmaker's Gift, Jeff Brumbeau
Serious Trouble, Arthur Howard

Music/Movement:

"Royalty"

(Let's get everyone seated with this special royal rhyme.)

This is the king *(boys point to themselves)*
And here is his crown. *(place pretend crown on head)*
Here is his throne.
So let's sit down. *(Boys sit down on floor.)*

This is the queen. *(continue verse for the girls)*
And here his her crown

Here is her throne
So let's sit down.

End by waving your scepters to parents and announcing:
"You may be seated."

Crafts:

"Graham Cracker Castles"
Castles are an integral part of the medieval theme when Knights, dragons, Kings and Queens roamed the landscape. Help the children build those castle walls up against attack by using basic materials at hand (graham crackers, marshmallows, peanut butter, and animal crackers). Finished the lesson? Maybe its time for a snack, so let the children storm the castle and eat it down.

Source: *Bubble Monster and other Science Fun*, John H. Falk, Robert L. Pruitt II, Kristi S. Rosenberg and Tali A. Katz

"Blackbird Pie Puppet"
"Sing a Song of Sixpence" is a familiar nursery rhyme featuring royalty. After dressing up children in their own royal crowns why not make this special craft that will allow you to act out this poem? Make a stick puppet of the blackbird following the pattern offered. Trace the rim of an aluminum pie pan on brown paper to make the top crust of your pie and then glue it to the top of the pan. With slits across the pan and crust you can now let your blackbird pop out of the pie during the repetition of the poem.

Source: *Days of Knights and Damsels: An Activity Guide*, Laurie Carlson

Activities:

"Good Morning Your Majesty"
Try this nice little greeting activity. Select one child to be the king or queen to sit blindfolded on the throne. As each child enters, let him bow and greet the king properly, and the king will attempt to determine who is speaking to him.

Source: *50 Fabulous Parties for Kids*, Linda Hetzer

"Treasure Hunt"
Hide the Queen's treasure (a variety of small items) throughout the room or house. As the children enter give the first child a clue. With each find, the children get a clue to the location of the next prize.

Source: *50 Fabulous Parties for Kids*, Linda Hetzer

Songs:

(Audio) "The Royal Ball"

Source: *Castles, Knights and Unicorns*

122 Safety

Topical Calendar Tie-in:

April 24
"National Playground Safety Week"—This week is dedicated to the safety of children at our local playgrounds. Here's an opportunity for parents, grandparents, and children to help clean up the playground and be sure it is safely monitored. Also, talk to children about strangers and safety at playgrounds.

Videos:

D. W. Rides Again
Fire Safety for Kids
Meeting Strangers: Red Light, Green Light
Mickey Mouse: Safety Belt Expert
The Rescue Rangers' Fire Safety Adventure
Stop, Drop and Roll

Picture Books:

Always be Safe, Kathy Schulz
Axle Annie and the Speed Grump, Robin Pulver
Fire Safety, Nancy Loewen
If I Cross the Street, Stephen Kroninger
I Can Be Safe: A First Look at Safety, Pat Thomas
Keeping You Safe: A Book About Police Officers, Ann Own
Look Both Ways: A Cautionary Tale, Diane Z. Shore and Jessica Alexander
No Dragons for Tea, Jean Pendziwol
Officer Buckle and Gloria, Peggy Rathmann
Playing Outdoors in Winter, Dorothy Chlad
The Sly Fox and the Chicks, Carl Sommer
Stop, Drop and Roll, Margery Cuyler
Traffic Safety, Nancy Loewe
A Treasure at Sea for Dragon and Me, Jean E. Pendziwol
Watch Out for Banana Peels and Other Important Sesame Street Safety Tips, Sarah Albee

Music/Movement:

"Matches"
Sung to: "Did You Ever See a Lassie?"
Source: *It's Great to be Three: The Encyclopedia of Activities for Three-Year-Olds*, Kathy Charmer and Maureen Murphy (editors)

Craft:

"Train Crossing Lights"
Children know all about crossing lights when it comes to the red, green, and yellow street lights displayed at each intersection, but are they familiar with the warning signals displayed at railroad crossings? During your next program on trains don't forget to discuss the safety issue connected with being around trains. Display crossing bars and also the flashing lights that are displayed when trains are coming through. Now let's make

our own train safety crossing lights by adapting the "sunshine ornament" craft offered in this book to our needs. You will need paper plates, crayons (red, yellow, and orange), wax paper, and an iron. This craft will require some adult supervision. Once you make your light, add a handle to the top and use a flashlight to shine behind it when you swing it back and forth.

Source: *Paper and Paint: Hands-On Crafts for Everyday Fun*, Vincent Douglas

Craft & Activity:

"Traffic Light"

A good addition to your traffic safety lesson would be this traffic light craft. Save those cardboard milk cartons. Have an adult cut one side of the carton out and three circles on the opposite side. Wrap the box with black construction paper and punch out the three circle holes. Distribute red, green, and yellow cellophane paper of the type used for Easter baskets. Have the children tape them across the holes in the proper location. Now offer a flashlight to the child who will play the traffic controller. Instruct him to shine the light through the carton to the red light if he wants it to shine and have the children stop. Dim the lights for a better effect and have the other children follow a prescribed traffic route on whatever vehicle they want to ride.

Activity:

"Stop and Go Safety Club"

Pedestrian safety needs to be something we educate our children about at the earliest ages. Even at the age of 3 or 4 a child can be taught about traffic lights, crossing walks, and more. Tell them they are joining a very special club, the "Stop and Go Safety Club," where they get a log book and earn stickers. After presenting children with their books which is blank take them outside to teach them what is to be done at crosswalks and more. Later as you stop at these locations ask them what they should do. If they come up with the correct answer, they come up with a sticker for their book. Repeat this often with many safety issues.

Source: *Quick and Fun Games for Toddlers*, Grace Jasmine

Songs:

(Audio) "Take the Hand of Someone You Love"

Source: *Sing-Along Travel Songs*

123 School

Topical Calendar Tie-in:

May 1

"School Principal's Day"—This day is set aside to honor elementary, middle, and high school principals for their caring and dedication to education. Take the time to say thank you on this day.

Videos:

Emily's First 100 Days of School
Louis James Hates School
Mister Rogers' Neighborhood: Going to School
Morris Goes to School
Spot Goes to School
Starring First Grade
The Teacher from the Black Lagoon

Picture Books:

Back to School for Rotten Ralph, Jack Gantos and Nicole Rubel
Beginning School, Irene Smalls
First Day Jitters, Julie Danneberg
I'll Go to School if . . ., Bo Flood
I. Q. Goes to School, Mary Ann Fraser
Little Bunny's Preschool Countdown, Maribeth Boelts
Lunch Bunnies, Kathryn Lasky
Minerva Louise at School, Janet Morgan Stoeke
Mr. Tanen's Ties Rule!, Maryann Cocca-Leffler
My First Day at Preschool, Edwina Riddell
School Days, B. G. Hennessy
Something Special, Nicola Moon
What Teachers Can't Do, Douglas Wood
When an Elephant Comes to School, Jan Ormerod

Music/Movement:

"School Days"
Sung to: "Hokey Pokey"

The teachers come in, the kids come in
(right hand, fingers up march in, then left hand)
The school bell rings, *(bang on pretend bell)*
And they start a special day.

They take out their books and pens
(open book and pretend to read and write)
And learn to read and write.
That's what it's all about.

Crafts:

"Cardboard Tube Art File"
Protect your artwork or valuable school assignments with ingenious use of cardboard tubes. Kathy Ross offers instructions on making your own

carrying case for school materials made out of old paper-towel tubes, plastic milk caps, and decorative materials. Now this is real use for recycled material!

Source: *All New Crafts for Earth Day*, Kathy Ross

"See, What I Did! Clothespin"

When children begin school they take great pride in displaying their accomplishments for the entire family to see. Assist the children in making their own clip to hold their papers. You will need spring-type clothespins, magnets, and construction paper. Trace the faces supplied to show a little face peering over the papers with pride.

Source: *Rainy Day Projects for Children*, Gerri Jenny and Sherrie Gould

Activities:

"Chalk Walk"

Children of all ages love to write on chalk boards. To settle them down, try this fun team event. This "racing and erasing" game has children taking turns starting a picture with teammates continuing the line until they are able to create a picture of their own. You never know where your teammate will go with your work, since you can't confer with them. Add your own time limits and restrictions on the event. Don't have a bulletin board? Don't worry because you can get a large piece of butcher paper to lie on the floor. This is a fun event for all ages.

Source: *The Laughing Classroom*, Diana Loomans and Karen Kolberg

"Who Stole the Cookie From the Cookie Jar?"

This is a simple game done with a chant that goes as follows:

All: Who stole the cookie from the cookie jar?
Leader: *(pointing to one child)* Did you steal the cookie from the cookie jar?

Child: Who, me?
All: YES, you!
Child: Not me!
All: Not you? Then who? *(pause)*

Repeat this chant, substituting items found at school for the cookie and selecting a new child each time.

Songs:

(Audio) "School Days"

Source: *Sing and Dance*, Jack Grunsky

124 Sea and Seashore

Topical Calendar Tie-in:

August 17

"Sandcastle Day"—One of the most celebrated events honored at the seashore is the art of making sandcastles. Now we have a day dedicated to honoring this art created by both children and adults. Try having your own contest for designing unique styles of sandcastles.

Videos:

Burt Dow: Deep-Water Man
Little Tim and the Brave Sea Captain
Swimmy
In the Swim

Picture Books:

Beach Bunny, Jennifer Selby
A Beach Day, Douglas Florian
Beach Day, Karen Roosa
Beach Play, Marsha Hayles
Famous Seaweed Soup, Antoinette Truglio Martin
A House by the Sea, Joanne Ryder
I Was All Thumbs, Benard Waber
The Mystery in the Bottle, Val Willis
Pigs on a Blanket, Amy Axelrod
The Queen's Holiday, Margaret Wild
Sally and the Limpet, Simon James
Sally Goes to the Beach, Stephen Huneck
Sand Cake, Frank Asch
The Sandcastle, M. P. Robertson
The Twelve Days of Summer, Elizabeth Lee O'Donnell

Music/Movement:

"To the Beach"
Source: *The Big Book of Stories, Songs and Sing-Alongs*, Beth Maddigan

Crafts:

"Painted Seashells"
What can we do with all those seashells our children want to collect when we visit the beach each year? Here are some great ideas. With some newspaper to protect your tables, some clean dry shells of various sizes and 3 or more colors of paint you can make some artwork of your own. Drip 3 colors into the interior of your shell and move it around to create swirls. With shells that have a flat surface on the back you can make magnets. Small shells can make great decorations for boxes, frames, and more. Look in this book for suggestions on paint types, techniques, and additional uses for the shell artwork once it's completed.
Source: *The Kids Can Press Jumbo Book of Easy Crafts*, Judy Ann Sadler

"Shell Necklace or Belt"
With a collection of small shells and some kite string, children can make their own necklaces or belts. Holes in the shells should be done before the program. The shells may be left natural or painted if time permits.

Activities:

"Going for a Swim"
Make your class into new actors to act out this simple actions story by Pam Schiller. Since you are heading for the beach encourage to children to dress and bring in whatever they think they would wear or use at the beach for this event. Let the teacher narrate the story as a group of children act out how they feel the story should be seen. This story can also be used in lessons on seasons, emotions, or even family units. Now try to add your own version of the story.

Source: *The Complete Book of Activities, Games, Stories, Props, Recipes and Dances for Young Children*, Pam Schiller and Jackie Silberg

"Fishing"
Set up a small child's pool in the room (no water, please). Inside have numerous small paper fish with small metal tabs glued near the mouth portion. Give each child a small fishing pole (string and stick with a magnet on it) and let them catch as many fish as they can in a given period of time.

Songs:

(Audio) "The Swim"
Source: *Disney's Dance Along*

125 Seasons: Fall

Topical Calendar Tie-in:

September 30

"Pumpkin Day"—Spend this day learning about all the varieties of pumpkins available and all the so many things to be made out of them. Invite parents to help you demonstrate what can be made with pumpkin besides pumpkin pie this fall. Hold yourself a pumpkinfest while you read *Too Many Pumpkins* by Linda White.

Videos:

Winnie the Pooh and the Blustery Day

Picture Books:

Autumn, Colin McNaughton
Autumn Days, Ann Schweninger
Autumn Walk, Ann Burg
The Cinnamon Hen's Autumn Day, Sandra Dutton
Clifford's First Autumn, Norman Bridwell
Every Autumn Comes the Bear, Jim Arnosky
Fall, Chris L. Demarest
Fall Is Here! I Love It!, Elaine W. Good
Fall Leaves Fall!, Zoe Hall
I Know it's Autumn, Eileen Spinelli
It's Fall!, Linda Glaser
Leaves! Leaves! Leaves!, Nancy Elizabeth Wallace
Possum's Harvest Moon, Anne Hunter
The Seasons: Fall, Nuria Roca
Ska-tat!, Kimberley Knutson

Music/Movement:

"Fall Leaves"

Sung to: "Frere Jacques"

Leaves are falling *(fingers flutter down like falling leaves)*
Leaves are falling.
Floating down.
Floating down.
Red, brown and orange
Falling high in piles
Let's jump right in, *(jump into leaf pile)*
Jump right in.

Crafts:

The leaves are falling everywhere this autumn. Ask parents to take some time with their children to go leaf gathering. Give their child a bag and go on a nature walk. Ask the child to find as many different colors and shapes of leaves as they can during the walk. Take them home or to your classroom to make these two imaginative crafts.

"Leaf-Tailed Squirrel"
Cut out a simple squirrel pattern from brown or tan construction paper or cardstock. Bush up the squirrel's tail by gluing the leaves children have gathered during one of your outings. Add a Popsicle stick if you want to make a puppet out of your creations. This source does offer a pattern for the squirrel and other recommendations for completing this craft.

Source: *The Mailbox: October Arts and Crafts: Preschool–Kindergarten*, Ada Goren, Mackle Rhodes, and Jan Trautman (editors)

"Autumn Leaf Crowns"
Follow your squirrel craft with this crown. Give each child a simple band of construction paper and have them glue the remaining leaves they have gathered to the band to create their own crown. You may also decorate your room by making "Autumn Streamers" and a "Leaf Rainbow" offered in the source listed here. Put on some seasonal music and have your own autumn parade or party.

Source: *Best of Totline: volume 2*, compiled by Gayle Bittinger

Activities:

"Four Season Toss"
Make your own action game for whatever season you are teaching at the present time. Give each child a poster board divided into 12 boxes. Challenge each child to locate twelve pictures from magazines provided that is representative of the season they are learning about in the current lesson, and then paste them in each square Write terms below each picture such as "hoot like at owl," "smile like a jack-o-lantern," etc. (See this source for a list of suggestions for each of the seasons.) Play the game by tossing a coin on the squares to determine what the child will act out for that season. Many more ideas are offered in this creative source.

Source: *Making Make-Believe*, MaryAnn F. Kohl

"Autumn Leaves are Falling Down"
In this source you will locate a cheerful rhyme sung to "London Bridge." After a lesson on the fall season and discussion of the changing of leaf colors the children can mimic these trees by holding up the numerous colored leaves and letting them fall at the appropriate time in the song. This is an activity children will wish to repeat again.

Source: *The Giant Encyclopedia of Circle Time and Group Activities for Children 3 to 6*, Kathy Charner

Songs:

(Audio) "Autumn Leaves"

Source: *Piggyback Songs*

126 Seasons: Spring

Topical Calendar Tie-in:

April 16

"Sechselauten"—This two-day celebration in Switzerland generally held on the third Sunday in April, represents the beginning of spring. Children wear costumes on Sunday and carry the Boogg, a snowman that symbolizes winter and is filled with firecrackers. At 6:00 p.m. someone will ring the town's bells signaling the arrival of spring. On Monday at the same time the bells are rung, the snowman is set on fire, and the firecrackers explode to set off that night's parades and festivities.

Videos:

Frog and Toad are Friends: Spring (Arnold Lobel Video Showcase)
Madeline and the Easter Bonnet
Springtime for Max and Ruby
Miffy's Springtime Adventure

Picture Books:

Arctic Spring, Sue Vyner
A Bunny for all Seasons, Janet Schulman
Caterpillar Spring, Butterfly Summer, Susan Hood
Frog's Best Friend, Marion Dane Bauer
Goose Moon, Carolyn Arden
Hurray for Spring!, Patricia Hubbell
It's Spring!, Linda Glaser
Let's Look at the Seasons: Springtime, Ann Schweninger
Mouse's First Spring, Lauren Thompson
Splish, Splash, Spring, Jan Carr
Spring Break at Pokeweed Public School, John Bianchi
The Story of May, Mordicai Gerstein
Wake Up, It's Spring!, Lisa Campbell Ernst
When Spring Comes, Robert Maass
When Spring Comes, Natalie Kinsey-Warnock

Music/Movement:

"This is the Way We Dress for Spring"
Source: *The Complete Resource Book for Toddlers and Twos*, Pam Schiller

Crafts:

"Spring Flowers"
Brighten someone's day with a bouquet of flowers this spring. You will need only construction paper of various colors, crayons, scissors, glue, and a paper hole punch to create a garden of blossoms to brighten anyone's home. With the hole punch you can create the flower seeds to glue to the center of the flower. Next add petals from strips of paper that are formed into a look to give the flowers dimension. Add a stem and leaves. If you have any plastic containers that can be decorated for pots,

try stapling flowers into the pot and let the children present the plant to their moms for Mother's Day.

Source: *Paper and Paint: Hands-On Crafts for Everyday Fun*, Phillip C. McGraw and Vincent Douglas

"Fluffy Toy Lamb"

After a talk of events that occur in the spring, help the children create their own spring lamb for puppet shows. Use a simple black glove as a base. The fingers will be the feet and the thumb the face with a little eye on it. The rest is simple. Just cover the palm and back of the hand area of the glove with cotton balls and tie a ribbon around the lamb's neck. Why not let the children try them out while singing "Mary had a little lamb?"

Source: *Crafts to Make in the Spring*, Kathy Ross

Activities:

"First Aid for City Trees"

Read the story of *The Giving Tree* by Shel Silverstein to children and then talk about how we can give back to the trees. Trees planted along curbsides need help more than others. Become a nature doctor by adopting a tree to take care of throughout the seasons. This book offers a variety of ways for children to save a tree's life. Discuss what a doctor uses to take care of you and what you will need to take care of a tree as a new nature doctor.

Source: *Summer Fun! 60 Activities for a Kid-Perfect Summer*, Susan Williamson

"The Farmer and His Seeds"

The following activity may be performed while singing the words to the tune of "The Farmer in the Dell."

The farmer plants the seeds.
The farmer plants the seeds.
Hi, ho, the dairy-o.
The farmer plants the seeds. *(bend and pretend to plant)*

The sun comes out to shine, etc. *(make circle with arms)*
The rain begins to fall, etc. *(fingers flutter up and down)*
The plant begins to grow, etc. *(slowly raise up)*
The farmer cuts them down, etc. *(cutting motion)*
And now he grinds it up, etc. *(grinding motion)*
And now he bakes the bread, etc. *(put in oven)*

Songs:

(Audio) "Sing-a-Ling"

Source: *Wee Sing: In the Car*

127 Seasons: Summer

Topical Calendar Tie-in:

June 21
"Summer Solstice"—Note the beginning of the summer season is the longest day of the year.

Videos:

Caillou's Summer Vacation
Frog and Toad are Friends: A Swim (Arnold Lobel Video Showcase)
Summer Picnic

Picture Books:

Alaska's 12 Days of Summer, Pat Chamberlin-Calamar
Caterpillar Spring, Butterfly Summer, Susan Hood
Come to My Party and Other Shake Poems, Heidi B. Roemer
Hotter than a Hot Dog!, Stephanie Calmenson
It's Summer!, Linda Glaser
Leaves! Leaves! Leaves!, Nancy Elizabeth Wallace
Shooting Star Summer, Candice Ransom
Summer, Anna Claybourne
Summer, Ron Hirschi
Summer's End, Maribeth Boelts
Summer: Signs of the Season Around North America, Valerie J. Gerard
A Summery Saturday Morning, Margaret Mahy
The Twelve Days of Summer, Elizabeth Lee O'Donnell
When Summer Comes, Robert Maass

Music/Movement:

"Summer"
Source: *The Big Book of Stories, Songs and Sing-Alongs*, Beth Maddigan

Crafts:

"Talking Sun Puppet"
"Summertime means lots of sunshine." Well, let's take a look at this paper plate creation of the sun. Paint one plate yellow and then arrange orange and yellow hand shapes that the children have traced (or use Ellison Die cuts of hands) around the edges of the plate. Add special eyes and check this book source on instructions for a rubber-band mouth, tube handle, and how to make your sun look like its talking. Let the sun shine on your program.
Source: *Crafts to Make in the Summer*, Kathy Ross

"Four Seasons Clipboard"
Here you will find a seasonal clipboard that children can make for their home refrigerators where the entire family may leave messages to each other. On a piece of heavy colored posterboard have the children fashion four trees for the four corners representing each of the seasons and their changes. Glue two spring-type clothespins to the top for attaching important messages.
Source: *175 Easy-to-Do Everyday Crafts*, Sharon Dunn Umnik

Activities:

"Four Season Toss"
Make your own action game for whatever season you are teaching at the present time. Give each child a poster board divided into 12 boxes. Challenge each child to locate twelve pictures from magazines provided that is representative of the season they are learning in the current lesson, and then paste them in each square. Write terms below each picture such as "buzz like a bee," "melt like ice-cream," etc. (See this source for a list of suggestions for each of the seasons.) Play the game by tossing a coin on the squares to determine what the child will act out for that season. Many more ideas are offered in this creative source.

Source: *Making Make-Believe*, MaryAnn F. Kohl

"Music of the Night"
The summer nights are full of sounds both from nature and from unnatural (human-made) sources. This game encourages children to learn to sit quietly and try to list in a variety of ways ALL the sounds that they hear in the night. How often do these sounds repeat themselves? Who or what make these sounds? Check here for ways of cataloging these sounds and safety suggestions for this activity.

Source: *The Everything Kids' Nature Book*, Kathiann M. Kowalski

Songs:

(Audio) "Mister Sun"

Source: *Sing A to Z*, by Sharon, Lois and Bram

128 Seasons: Winter

Topical Calendar Tie-in:

December 21

"First Day of Winter"—Welcome the snowy season of sledding, building snowmen, and snowball fights. Build your own snow cones for a special treat.

Videos:

Ladybug, Ladybug, Winter is Coming
Little Bear: Winter Tales
Madeline's Winter Vacation
The Snow Day

Picture Books:

Biscuit's Snowy Day, Alyss Satin Capucilli
Dear Rebecca, Winter is Here, Jean Craighead George
The First Day of Winter, Consie Powell
Henrietta's First Winter, Rob Lewis
In Wintertime, Kim Howard
The Last Snow of Winter, Tony Johnston
Little Fern's First Winter, Jane Simmons
Now it Is Winter, Eileen Spinelli
Stormy Weather, Amanda Harvey
The Winter Day, Beverly Komoda
Winter Is, Ann Dixon
A Winter's Tale, Ian Wallace
A Winter Walk, Lynne Barasch
Winter Woes, Marty Kelley

Music/Movement:

"Winter Animal Friends"
Source: *101 Fingerplays, Stories and Songs to Use with Finger Puppets*, Diane Briggs

Crafts:

"Snow Scene"
Make a simple winter scene. Give each child a sheet of black or blue construction paper. Have them cut three different sizes of white circles to glue on to form a snowman. (Pre-cut circles for two- or three-year-olds is advisable.) Use real material of various colors for the scarf and hat. Use chalk to draw the snow on the ground and small, white sticker dots for the snow falling from the sky. Stickers are a popular item in crafts at a young age.

"Sleepy Bear Mitten Hanger"
During the winter season the children could always use a place to hang their mittens to dry. Here's a craft that will have them finally wanting to hang them up without arguing with Mom. Create a sleepy little polar bear face out of a paper plate. Give him a wintery appearance with a snow

cap and add clothespins on a string at the bottom to hang your mittens to dry.

Source: *175 Easy-to-Do-Everyday Crafts*, Sharon Dun Umnik

Activities:

"Snowball Game"
Try this simple dexterity activity. Give each child a ruler and cotton ball. After a discussion on what cotton balls look like (clouds, snowballs, etc.) have the children balance the cotton ball on the ruler while performing various activities called out by the leader. Try such feats as balancing on one foot, holding the ruler above the head, or involve the children in team relay events.

Source: *Focus on Winter*, Rosie Seaman

"Inuit Clay Bird Game"
Here's a game from the frozen north played by Inuit children. When winter comes and it's too cold to go out, this game will make a delightfully simple pastime. Follow simple directions offered here to create 15 small birds out of air-drying clay. It sounds like it might be complicated but these little birds take only a little rolling and pinching of clay that even the youngest child will be able to accomplish. Now let's play the game. Children sitting in a circle will be shaking and tossing these little birds to the floor and depending on their position when they land get to pick them up again. The child with the most birds in the end will win the game.

Source: *Winter Day Play!*, Nancy F. Castaldo

Songs:

(Audio) "Put Another Log on the Fire"

Source: *Sing and Dance*, Jack Grunsky

129 Secrets/Mystery

Topical Calendar Tie-in:

October 1–7

"Mystery Series Week"—This week celebrates super sleuths of literature who appear in mystery series books. Display books in your library or classroom along with mystery clues to be solved. Children love hearing from their favorite characters such as Cam Jansen, Encyclopedia Brown, Nancy Drew, Hardy Boys and more.

Videos:

Art Dog
Franklin and the Secret Club
Tigger, Private Ear
Jake Gander: Storyville Detective
Mystery on the Docks

Picture Books:

The 13th Clue, Ann Jonas
Albert's Halloween: The Case of the Stolen Pumpkins, Leslie Tryon
The Case of the Crooked Candles, Jonathan V. Cann
Cowboy Sam and Those Confounded Secrets, Kitty Griffin and Kathy Combs
The Dark at the Top of the Stairs, Sam McBratney
Ducks Disappearing, Phyllis Reyn Naylor
Gertrude, the Bulldog Detective, Eileen Christelow
Grandpa's Teeth, Rod Clement
The High-Rise Private Eyes: The Case of the Baffled Bear, Cynthia Rylant
Hot Fudge, James Howe
Laura's Secret, Klaus Baumgaret
The Mystery of King Karfu, Doug Cushman
Pearl and Wagner: Three Secrets, Kate McMullan
Secrets, Ellen B. Senisi
Star of the Week, Barney Saltzberg
The Two O'Clock Secret, Bethany Roberts

Music/Movement:

"The Secret"
Source: *The Complete Book of Rhymes, Songs, Poems, Fingerplays and Chants*, Jackie Silberg and Pam Schiller

Crafts:

"Carnaval Mystery Masks"
Caranaval is celebrated in many countries in a variety of ways. Our most well-known carnival celebration is Mardi Gras in New Orleans, Louisiana. People take this opportunity to mask up and hide their identity, pretending to be what they are not. Take a look at the directions in this book for an assortment of carnaval mystery masks that can be created along with

"fantastic hats" used around the world. Step out of yourself for the day and become someone or something else.

Source: *Zany Rainy Days: Indoor Ideas for Active Kids*, Hallie Warshaw and Mark Shulman

"Crayon Magic"
Help the children leave secret mystery messages for their friends and family. Have children leave clues to whomever they want using crayons and watercolor paints. Need a clue how to do this? Check out this wonderful source of a variety of crafts:

Source: *Loo-Loo, Boo, and Art you Can Do*, Denis Roche

Activities:

"Mystery Classmate"
Take photos of all members of the class individually during the first week of school. Have each picture cut in four puzzle like pieces and placed in individual envelopes with an accompanying nametag. Have a poster titled "Mystery Classmate" displayed in your room. Each day put up one piece of the puzzle until someone in the room can guess who the person is in the photo. When the identity is discovered move it and the nametag to a bulletin board that will eventually hold your whole group. This is a fun way to get to know each other.

"Mystery Bundle"
Try wrapping a variety of common objects in tissue paper and tie them securely. Pass these objects around the group and see if they can determine its contents by the shape they see, the touch and/or smell. If you wish to keep score, give one point to each child who discovers he was correct when it is opened.

Source: *Child Magazine's Book of Children's Parties*, Angela Wilkes

Songs:

(Audio) "My Aunt Came Back"

Source: *We Sing: In the Car*

130 Self-Reliance

Topical Calendar Tie-in:

July 27

"Walk on Stilts Day"—Here is a day to walk on stilts, providing you a chance to gain self-confidence through mastering balance and coordination. Enjoy the challenge and feel good about yourself.

Videos:

Do it Yourself (Paddington Bear: Paddington, P.I., vol.2)
Have You Seen My Duckling?
Regina's Big Mistake

Picture Books:

All by Myself, Aliki
Baby Duck's New Friend, Frank and Deven Asch
Bear, John Schoenher
A Cool Kid—Like Me!, Hans Wilhelm
Daisy Gets Dressed, Clare Beaton
Emily Just in Time, Jan Stepian
Good Job, Little Bear, Martin Waddell
Let Me Do It!, Janice Gibala-Broxholm
Little Mo, Martin Waddell
Mudball, Matt Tavares
My Own Big Bed, Anna G. Hines
Palm Trees, Nancy Cote
What Shall We Do, Blue Kangaroo?, Emma Chichester Clark
You Can Do It, Sam, Amy Hest
You Can Do It Too!, Karen Baicker

Music/Movement:

"I Can Do it Myself"
Source: *The Complete Book of Rhymes, Songs, Poems, Fingerplays and Chants*, Jackie Silberg and Pam Schiller

Crafts:

"Color-changer"
Children love to say, "I can do it!" Part of growing up is learning to be self-reliant. Talk to children about how animals also teach their children how to be independent and take care of themselves. One of the most interesting animals is the chameleon who most people think changes color to hide but actually is hidden because of his natural skin color. The chameleon has his own tricks for hiding from strangers. Read more about this interesting animal and his tricks along with a special chameleon art project in this book. Try expanding this project by talking to children about what tricks they would use to hide or escape from strangers if they had to.
Source: *Arty Facts: Animals and Art Activities*, Ellen Rodger (editor)

"Hiking Stick"
Independence is a good thing but sometimes everyone needs something or someone to lean on. Along with your discussion on learning to do things on your own it is important to emphasize that everyone needs a little help sometimes and you shouldn't be to proud to ask for help when you need it. Here's a little craft that can make help attractive. Make your own hiking stick and decorate it as picturesque as your prefer then arrange for a special outing to try out their craft. An uphill trek will show them how useful this little item is for them. Check this source for some cooking tips on decorations and a special activity on measuring what your pace actually is and how fast you walk.

Source: *The Kids' Guide to Nature Adventures*, Joe Rhatigan

Activities:

"I Can Do It"
This is a variation of the game "King of the Hill" that will help children demonstrate what they are capable of doing. It is a wonderful method of illustrating self-reliance and more while having a great deal of fun and laughter.

In a bag, place a large number of papers each listing activities the children need to perform to show growth in their life (Ex: bounce a ball, tie your shoes, put on your own shirt, etc.). These activities can be physical or verbal acts and often change depending on the age of the group playing the game.

Each child sits at the bottom of a flight of stairs. If the child is able to perform the action the leader announces from the paper drawn from the bag he moves up one step. If he is unable to do it he simply waits for his next turn. The first to reach the top of the hill wins. This is a game children will wish to attempt often.

"Stop and Go Game"
This activity helps children practice gross motor skills while enjoying themselves immensely. Make a collection of circles, stop signs, and go circles. Lay out these game pieces across the floor for the children to follow. Instruct the children to follow the signs on the road created by hopping, skipping, jumping, or other skills you mention at that time, and remember to stop with both feet on the stop sign.

Source: *The Giant Encyclopedia of Theme Activities for Children 2 to 5*, Kathy Charner

Songs:

(Audio) "You Know that You Can Do It"

Source: *My Favorite Kid Songs Collection #3*

131 Senses

Topical Calendar Tie-in:

October 21

"Sweetest Day"—The Sweetest Day was designed to do something nice for someone today, something that will make them say, "Oh, that's so sweet!" Try giving some comfort food that tastes sweet and makes you feel good to shut-in or sick neighbors.

Videos:

Apt. 3
King Midas and the Golden Touch
You and Your Sense of Touch

Picture Books:

Ears Are for Hearing, Paul Showers
Feeling Things, Allan Fowler
Forest Friends' Five Senses, Cristina Garelli
Hearing Things, Allan Fowler
I Can Tell by Touching, Carolyn Otto
My First Look at Touch, Jane Yorke
My Five Senses, Margaret Miller
Polar Bear, Polar Bear, What Do You Hear?, Bill Martin, Jr.
Seeing Things, Allan Fowler
Sense Suspense: a Guessing Game for the Five Senses, Bruce McMillan
Seven Blind Mice, Ed Young
Smelling Things, Allan Fowler
Tasting Things, Allan Fowler
What's That Awful Smell?, Heather Tekavec
What Do You Do With a Tail Like This?, Steve Jenkins and Robin Page

Music/Movement:

"Circus Senses Action Verse"
Source: *Holiday Hoopla: Songs and Finger Plays*, Kathy Darling

Crafts:

"Musical Wind Flower"
After a discussion of spring storms and the winds that accompany them ask the children if they have ever seen wind chimes. Demonstrate a variety of wind chime styles and ask the children to close their eyes and see if they can identify the one they hear. Following this demonstration inform the children that they will be making a similar wind chime called a "Musical Wind Flower." Collect large plastic soda bottles and cut about an inch from the bottom of each. The bottom of this bottle will shape the flower when the children fill the indentures with many colors of Play-Doh. Use a hole-punch to add string to the top and three ribbons to the bottom with bells attached to them. This craft allows the children to use their sense of touch with the Play-Doh, their sense of visual beauty, and

ultimately their sense of hearing when they're delighted with the sounds of their project. Let the wind bring music into your life.

Source: *Play-Doh: Fun and Games*, Kathy Ross

"Scented Gifts"

The sense of smell is one of the strongest of our senses especially when we come across a particularly unpleasant odor. Help create some pleasant sensations by giving a scented gift. This source gives you examples of six different designs for sachets, including one for your dog.

Source: *Make Gifts!*, Kim Solga

Activities:

"Touch Hunt"

Play a simple game in which the leader calls out a texture. The children search the room for an item that feels like the texture called out. If the children can read the simple texture words, pass out a list and have your own scavenger hunt. Add a little more difficulty by calling out a texture and a shape together.

Source: *Stop, Look and Listen*, Sarah A. Williamson

"House Sounds Guessing Game"

A house is a very busy place with a family in it. Have you ever stopped to just listen and count how many different sounds you hear in your home? Make a recording of sounds from your house and see if the children can guess what they are. For a list of suggestions see the source book.

Source: *More Picture Book Story Hours: from Parties to Pets*, Paula Gaj Sitarz

Songs:

(Audio) "A Song About Smells"

Source: *What A Day*, Fred Penner

132 Sign Language

Topical Calendar Tie-in:

June 27, 1880

"Birth of Helen Keller"—Celebrate the birthday of Helen Keller, the first deaf-blind person to graduate from college. Helen's use of sign language, taught to her by her teacher Anne Sullivan, served her well and opened up many opportunities to learning.

Videos:

Say, Sing and Sign: Colors
Say, Sing and Sign: Songs
Sign Me a Story

Picture Books:

Amelia Lends a Hand, Marissa Moss
Dad and Me in the Morning, Pat Lakin
Family and Community, Stanley H. Collins
Let's Sign: Every Baby's Guide to Communicating with Grown-ups, Kelly Ault
More Simple Signs, Cindy Wheeler
Moses Goes to a Concert, Isaac Millman
Moses Goes to the Circus, Isaac Millman
Moses Sees a Play, Isaac Millman
My First Signs, Annie Kubler
The Printer, Myron Uhlberg
Sign Language, Karen Price Hossell
Sign Language for Kids, Lora Heller
Some Kids are Deaf, Lola M. Schaefer
What's it Like?: Deafness, Angela Royston

Music/Movement:

"Hand Clapping"
Source: *Fall Frolic*, Mary Jo Huff

Crafts:

"Signs of Love"
The internationally know sign for "I Love You" used by the deaf community is often used by others as well. It's a combination of the letters, I, L, and Y together in one symbol formed by one hand. This craft re-creates this symbol by tracing the child's hand and gluing it on top of two hearts for background. While this craft works well in any lesson on handicaps and the deaf community it can also be used during the Valentine's holiday for a special Valentine card.
Source: *Fun to Make Crafts for Every Day*, Tom Daning (editor)

"Spicy Shapes"
This book offers a recipe for cinnamon dough that can be used to make your spicy shapes, but is not meant to be eaten. The wonderful thing about this is that the final creations will last for years. These can be hung in any area that you want to add that fragrant aroma that will be pleasing

to all. Trace the child's hand in the intentional sign of "I Love You" and send your aromatic gift to your favorite person.
Source: *Grand Activities*, Shari Sasser

Activities:

"Finger Spelling Bee"
Have a collection of pictures or words of items cut from a magazine. Let each child draw one item from the bag and spell it in sign language. Players keep going until one person remains. Of course you are eliminated if you spell incorrectly.
Source: *Finger Spelling Fun*, David A. Adler

"Finger Spelling Telephone"
Played similar to the original telephone game but in this one the child is given a simple message (one word) to spell in sign language. This is passed along until at the final destination the secret word is revealed, hopefully correct.
Source: *Finger Spelling Fun*, David A. Adler

Songs:

(Audio) "Hand Talk"
Source: *Sesame Road*

133 Space and Spaceships

Topical Calendar Tie-in:

May 6
"International Astronomy Day"—This day is observed on a Saturday near the first quarter moon between mid-April and mid-May. Set your sights to the stars and see if you can name those constellations.

Videos:

Company's Coming
I Wanna Be an Astronaut
Moon Man
Magic School Bus: Space Adventures
Stars! Stars! Stars!

Picture Books:

Alistair and the Alien Invasion, Marilyn Sadler
Astronaut Piggy Wiggy, Christyan and Diane Fox
A Brave Spaceboy, Dana Kessimakis Smith
Dmitri, the Astronaut, Jon Agee
Grandpa Takes Me to the Moon, Timothy R. Gaffney
Harold's Trip to the Sky, Crockett Johnson
I Want to be an Astronaut, Byron Barton
It Came from Outer Space, Tony Bradman
Man on the Moon, Anastasia Suen
Space Station Mars, Daniel San Souci
My Brother is from Outer Space (The Book of Proof), Vivian Ostrow
One Day, Daddy, Frances Thomas
This Rocket, Paul Collicutt
Tinker and Tom and the Star Baby, Avid McPhail
A Trip to Mars, Ruth Young

Music/Movement:

"Off We Go"

10 – 9 – 8
The rockets are ready to detonate.

7 – 6 – 5
Let's take this ship for a test drive.

4 – 3
I forgot my helmet, pardon me.

2 – 1
BLAST OFF! See you when we get home!

Crafts:

"Space Alien"
Head off into space and see what you can discover. If you want to be an astronaut this book offers you instructions on constructing an old-fashioned space helmet out of large ice cream containers collected from

your local ice cream parlors. These are just large enough to go over your head. Or maybe you would rather be from the other side of space? Then you can become a space alien with directions for this large one-eyed creature that will fit on the child's head.

Source: *I Can Make That! Fantastic Crafts for Kids*, Mary Wallace

"A Roaring Rocket"

Let's make a glittering silver rocket made of a cardboard tube covered in foil. Add side wings and flames shooting from the end made of colored tissue paper. Add some pizzaz by gluing your rocket to black posterboard, paint a planet beneath it and some spirals with glitter and glue. This outer space scene will attract a lot of compliments.

Source: *Making Pictures Out of this World*, Penny King

Activities:

"Space Walk"

Decorate your room with various colored stars and circles with the names of the planets. Add music to the event as the children walk from star to star and planet to planet. Reward the children with sticker stars and other items as they land on given planets. For further instructions see the source book.

Source: *Celebrate*, Rainbow Publishing Co.

"5–4–3–2–1 Blast Off!"

Try a space-age version of freeze tag or statues. Enjoy an easy game for even the youngest child to enjoy.

Source: *Celebrate*, Rainbow Publishing Co.

Songs:

(Audio) "The Rocket Song"

Source: *I Love to Sing with Barney*

134 Sports

Topical Calendar Tie-in:

March 6–12

"National Cheerleading Week"—Celebrate all the varieties of sports played every day around the world, but let's not forget those cheerleaders who cheer our sports figures to their wins. Celebrate National Cheerleading week by making up your own cheers to urge on sports players, spelling bee champs, or anything that you feel needs a little help to win.

Videos:

Casey at the Bat
Frog and Toad are Friends: A Swim (Arnold Lobel Video Showcase)
Madeline and the Soccer Star
Miss Nelson Has a Field Day
The Olympic Champ
Players in Pigtails
The Tortoise and the Hare

Picture Books:

Allie's Basketball Dream, Barbara E. Barber
Baseball, Football, Daddy and Me, David Friend
The Big Game, Louise A. Gikow
Dulcie Dando, Soccer Star, Sue Stops
Fox Under First Base, Jim Latimer
Game Time, Stuart J. Murphy
Hunter and Stripe and the Soccer Showdown, Laura Malone Elliott
Jimmy's Boa and the Bungee Jump Slam Dunk, Trinka Hakes Noble
Kick, Pass and Run, Leonard Kessler
Little Granny Quarterback!, Bill Martin, Jr.
The Littlest Leaguer, Syd Hoff
Olympics!, B. G. Hennessy
Piggy and Dad Go Fishing, David Martin
Playing Right Field, Willy Welch
Sam the Zamboni Man, James Stevenson
Swish!, Bill Martin, Jr. and Michael Sampson
Take Me Out to the Ball Game, Maryann Kovalski
Ziggy's Blue Ribbon Day, Claudia Mills

Music/Movement:

"I'm a Little Toy"

I'm a little toy that plays a game.
I can be toss, hit or thrown down a lane.
When my team takes the field,
They kick me around.
Can you name me, as I roll around.

Crafts:

"Basketball Toss"

Basketball is a game that even the youngest children can play. Construct a backboard out of oaktag or posterboard. To this attach paper cups with number scores above each. Using ping-pong balls or just crumpled paper, allow the children to score by tossing them in the cups (baskets).

"Olympic Games: The Discus Throw"

Prepare for the Olympic Games with a specially designed 'Discus' for the discus throw event. You will need the sturdier paper plates for this craft in order for them to soar farther through the air. Permit the children to decorate their discus with their own unique logo and then glue two together for extra strength. Now let the games begin.

Source: *Look What You Can Make with Paper Plates,* Margie Hayes Richmond

Activities:

"Balloon Golf"

Here's a sport that will combine eye-hand coordination and large motor skills with a child's love for hitting things. Gather a multicolored collection of balloons, a bucket and some child-size plastic golf clubs. Children will enjoy trying to hit balloons with the clubs to achieve a number of suggested results, such as, distance, aim, and other goals listed in this source.

Source: *Quick and Fun Games for Toddlers,* Grace Jasmine

"Water Balloon Bowling"

Let's take bowling out-of-doors with this water balloon game. You will need at least 7 people for this game since 6 of them will become "human bowling pins" for this event. Instead of a bowling ball fill balloons with water to roll across the grass. Points will be determined by how many feet get wet on our "pins," whether or not the ball breaks, and so on (check this source for scoring). When your turn is over, you become one of the pins and the rotation continues until everyone has had a turn. The person scoring the highest is the winner.

Source: *Go Outside!,* Nancy Blakey

Songs:

(Audio) "The Monkeys Baseball Game"

Source: *Tom Paxton's Fun Animal Songs*

135 Strangers

Topical Calendar Tie-in:

May 25
"National Missing Children's Day"—To inform people of the serious problem of missing children in this country and to educate children on safe procedures at school, home, and while out playing.

Videos:

The Berenstain Bears Learn about Strangers
Learn about Living: Never Talk to Strangers
Little Red Riding Hood
Lon Po Po
Meeting Strangers: Red Light, Green Light
Wings: A Tale of Two Chickens

Picture Books:

Aunt Skilly and the Stranger, Kathleen Stevens
Aware and Alert, Patricia Lakin
Don't Talk to Strangers, Kevi
Elizabeth Imagined on Iceberg, Chris Raschka
A Kid's Guide to Staying Safe on the Streets, Maribeth Boelts
The Lady in the Box, Ann McGovern
Ruby, Michael Emberley
The Sly Fox and the Chicks, Carl Sommer
Stranger Danger, Peggy Pancella
Your Body Belongs to You, Cornelia Spelman

Music/Movement:

"The Stranger"
Two little children walking home from school.
(hold up two fingers walking across other hand)
They meet a tall man lookin' so cool
(bring pointer finger of other hand over to meet others)
The stranger said, "Have an ice cream cone"
(hold out imaginary cone)
"NO" shouted the children. (shout out NO)
And they ran on home. *(have two fingers race over palm)*

Crafts:

"Identification Chart"
Have the children make a frame for their own special identification chart. Include on the chart the children's fingerprints and, if possible, use a Poloroid camera to include their picture. The children may present this chart to their parents as a special gift.

"Thumbprint Cookies"
After having a program full of talks of strangers, safety, and a visit from police officers for emphasis, try lightening up the atmosphere a little with this special treat. Offer some drinks and tell the children we will try doing

our fingerprints in a yummy way by making our own thumbprint cookies. A recipe and directions are offered in this book.

Source: *Summer Fun! 60 Activities for a Kid-Perfect Summer*, Susan Williamson

Activities:

"Contribute to (or Create) a Blog"

This is an extremely useful extension to the lessons on strangers. Discuss the fact that the majority of people you chat with on computers are strangers. After an in-depth discussion on computer safety, chat rooms, etc., talk about the recent resurgence of "blogs," or electronic journals. Check this source for suggestions on creating your own handwritten "blogs" in an assortment of amusing ways in your classroom or throughout your school or library.

Source: *Summer Activities*, Marc Tyler Nobleman

"Police Visitation"

Contact the local police department and arrange for an officer to speak to the parents, as well as the children. Have the police do official fingerprints for later identification. Many fingerprints done at home are done incorrectly and become useless when needed for identifying a lost child.

Police will offer the children many suggestions on protecting themselves from strangers, and some departments have films for this age group that you may not be able to get elsewhere.

Some departments might even have a costume of McGruff, the crime dog, and will be able to have an officer come dressed as the dog. This costume is only sold to law enforcement agencies.

Songs:

(Audio) "Stranger Danger"

Source: *Kindergarten Sing and Learn*

"Better Say No"

Source: *Family Vacation*

136 Toys

Topical Calendar Tie-in:

December

"Safe Toys and Gift Month"—Each December the Prevent Blindness of America group produces a list of toys that are hazardous to children's eyesight. Use this time to help children determine which of their toys are hazardous to their baby siblings and must be put away safely.

Videos:

Alexander and the Wind-Up Mouse (Leo Lionni's Caldecotts)
Corduroy
Ira Sleeps Over
Kipper: The Ball
A Pocket for Corduroy

Picture Books:

Arthur's Honey Bear, Lillian Hoban
Baba Yaga and the Wise Doll, Hiawyn Oram
Baby Duck's New Friend, Frank and Devin Asch
Bea's 4 Bears, Martha Weston
Birthday Doll, Jane Cutler
Cat and Bear, Carol Greene
Eli and the Uncle Dawn, Liz Rosenberg and Susan Gaber
Ellen and Penguin, Clara Vulliamy
A Fire Engine for Ruthie, Leslea Newman
Hoot, Jane Hissey
Little Rabbit Goes to School, Harry Horse
Nothing, Mick Inkpen
Paisley, Maggie Smith
Ten Out of Bed, Penny Dale
The Toymaker, Martin Waddell

Music/Movement:

"My Toy Box"
Source: *It's Great to be Three: The Encyclopedia of Activities for Three-Year-Olds*, Kathy Charmer and Maureen Murphy (editors)

Crafts:

"Italian 'Piggy in the Pen'"
This is a toy that tests your skills. The "pig" in this toy is a ping-pong ball, and you must try to get it in the round cylinder while it's still attached with a cord. This is a toy that can be taken anywhere (even the car) to amuse children.

Ms. Fiarotta's book will supply you with step-by-step instructions and a full-page illustration of the toy itself.
Source: *Sticks and Stones and Ice Cream Cones*, Phyllis Fiarotta

"My Toy Box"
Children need a special place to store their favorite toys. This source provides you with step-by-step illustrated guidelines for making your own colorful toy box. Any child three and up would be able to design their own with a little adult supervision. The exterior, and main portion of the box, is covered with torn strips of colored paper dipped in a glue solution and placed on the box overlapping. This will need to be stored overnight to dry so be sure you have the time and storage area to do it, but it's sure worth it.

Source: *I Can Make Toys*, Mary Wallace

Activities:

"Fling-A-Ma-Jig"
Let's get a little exercise with this flying Frisbee. As the weather gets warmer it's time to take our toys outside and get a little exercise at the same time. Make your own fling-a-ma-jig out of paper plates (preferably plastic plates), some markers, glue, and glitter. Get outside and team up for some fresh air and to see who can throw them the farthest than their friends and who can catch the most Frisbees. Look at this source for an important point in the construction that will allow the air to lift that Frisbee higher and higher when thrown.

Source: *Easy Art Fun! Do-It-Yourself Crafts for Beginning Readers*, Jill Frankel Hauser

"Alien Out!"
Alien Out is a new version of the "Old Maid" card game with which youngsters are familiar. Make your own card game here by cutting 21 small cards out of card stock or posterboard. Now have the children draw illustrations of people, animals, shapes, flowers, toys, or whatever other category you would like. The twenty-first card should be a picture of an alien. Now start your card came using the rules provided by the author of this book but be sure not to be the one left holding the alien card.

Source: *Easy Art Fun! Do-It-Yourself Crafts for Beginning Readers*, Jill Frankel Hauser

Songs:

(Audio) "Toyland"

Source: *Jazz Baby, Volume 2*

137 Toys: Balloons

Topical Calendar Tie-in:

October 4

"Balloons Around the World"—On this day, balloon twisting and sculpting artists donate their time to a charity in the community. Follow their lead and use something you are talented at doing and either raise money for an organization or try making someone's life brighter through your entertainment.

Videos:

Hot-Air Henry
Teddy Bear's Balloon Trip
James and the Red Balloon and Other Thomas Adventures
Kipper: Arnold's Balloon Trip

Picture Books:

Altoona Baboona, Janie Bynum
Beaten By a Balloon, Margaret Mahy
Benjamin's Balloon, Alan Baker
The Grumpalump, Sarah Hayes
The High-Rise Private Eyes: The Case of the Troublesome Turtle, Cynthia Rylant
Hot Air: The (Mostly) True Story of the First Hot-Air Balloon Ride, Marjorie Priceman
Mine's the Best, Crosby Bonsall
Miss Eva and the Red Balloon, Karen M. Glennon
My Red Balloon, Eve Bunting
Nathan's Balloon Adventure, Lulu Delacre
Swollobog, Alastair Taylor
The Well-Mannered Balloon, Nancy Willard
Where Do Balloons Go?: An Uplifting Mystery, Jamie Lee Curtis
You Can't Take a Balloon into the Museum of Fine Arts, Jacueline Preiss Weitzman
You Can't Take a Balloon into the Metropolitan Museum, Jaqueline Preiss Weitzman and Robin Preiss Glasser

Music/Movement:

"Balloons, Balloons"
Sung to: "Alphabet Song"

Red and purple, green and blue,
These are the colors over you.
Blow them up and let them go
Balloons fly up and lift and flow.
Red and purple, green and blue,
I've got one for me and you.

Crafts:

"Ballimp"
A simple "Great Year" blimp can be constructed using a long-style balloon. Add features, such as side wings made of cardboard and attach with rubber cement. Decorate as desired, then see how far you can fly your newly made blimp.

Source: *How to Make Snoop Snappers and Other Fine Things*, Robert Lopshire

Activities:

"Dinosaur Fun"
Kathy Ross offers three entertaining games here with a dinosaur theme that can be used for birthday parties or to add a little fun to your dinosaur story program. Gather up some balloons and small plastic dinosaurs to play "Hatch the Dinosaur Relay Race." Get gummy dinosaurs and some plastic eggs to go on a "Dinosaur Hunt" or play "Ring the Stegosaurus Game" with pointed ice cream cones and plastic rings

Source: *The Best Birthday Parties Ever!*, Kathy Ross

"Avenue Goals"
Avenue is played sitting down so is suitable as an indoor game that works best with an air-filled balloon (not helium). Divide the children into two groups that will sit opposite each other about 2 to 5 feet apart on the floor forming the Avenue between them. Players count off from one end of the line forming two teams. One end of the avenue is the goal for the first team while the opposite site is the goal for the remaining team. Begin with the balloon placed in the center. Each child tries to move the balloon down the avenue by patting or blowing it but they mustn't leave the line. The balloon may not be held or thrown. Watch the excitement as the balloon veers off target moving me unexpected directions.

Source: *Great Big Book of Children's Games*, Debra Wise

Songs:

(Audio) "Hot Air Balloon"

Source: *Alligator in the Elevator*, Rick Charette

138 Trains

Topical Calendar Tie-in:

April 29, 1900

"Anniversary of Casey Jones' Death"—The famed engineer of the Illinois Central's Cannonball Express. Enjoy the classic folk song about his well-known train ride.

Videos:

Casey Jones
Freight Train
The Little Engine that Could
Trains

Picture Books:

All Aboard! A True Train Story, Susan Kuklin
Cecil Bunions and the Midnight Train, Betty Paraskevas
Circus Train, Jos A. Smith
Engine, Engine Number Nine, Stephanie Calmenson
Here Comes the Train, Charlotte Voake
I Love Trains!, Philemon Sturges
Inside Freight Train, Donald Crews
New Baby Train, Woody Guthrie
The Owl Who Became the Moon, Jonathan London
Shortcut, Donald Crews
The Story of the Little Red Engine, Diana Ross
That's Not My Train . . ., Fiona Walt
The Train Ride, June Crebbin
Window Music, Anastasia Suen

Music/Movement:

"Rainbow Train"
Source: *The Big Book of Stories, Songs and Sing-Alongs*, Beth Maddigan

Crafts:

"Picnic Train"
Don't throw away those boxes! As librarians or teachers we tend to save everything for use in crafts. Now Ms. Pinnington offers a great use for those leftover small cereal boxes, juice boxes, and matchboxes. With one of each a child can cover the boxes with blue paper and glue them together as shown in Ms. Pinnington's book to form a train engine. Add decorative wheels, windows, and more. With the top of the cereal box cut off this train now has an area to place picnic treats and a pull-out section to hide candy. Children will be enthralled with this delightful train invention.
Source: *Rainy Day Activity Book*, Andrea Pinnington

"Train Crossing Lights"
Children know all about crossing lights when it comes to the red, green, and yellow street lights displayed at each intersection but are they familiar with the warning signals displayed at railroad crossings? During your

next program on trains don't forget to discuss the safety issue connected with being around trains. Display crossing bars and also the flashing lights that are displayed when trains are coming through. Now let's make our own train safety crossing lights by adapting the "Sunshine Ornament" craft offered in this book to our needs. You will need paper plates, crayons (red, yellow, and orange), wax paper, and an iron. This craft will require some adult supervision. Once you make your light add a handle to the top and use a flashlight to shine behind it when you swing it back and forth.

Source: *Paper and Paint: Hands-On Crafts for Everyday Fun*, Vincent Douglas

Activities:

"Choo-Choo Train"

As the children recite a given verse, they chug along with another child attaching himself to the train each time. When the train is complete, they go under the bridge (a stick going up and down). Those who are touched by the stick are out of the game and must return to the station.

Source: *New Games to Play*, Juel Krisvoy

"Playing Train"

Look for details on this delightful creative dramatic activity in the source indicated below. Children get the whole train experience with everyone pretending to be ticket agents, conductors, engineers, and passengers. Suggestions for realistic props are given and children actually have to have a destination in mind. During the trip, children learn meanings of "one-way," "round-trip," etc.

Source: *Kid's Celebrate*, Maria Bonfanti Esche and Clare Bonfanti Braham

Songs:

(Audio) "Little Red Caboose"

Source: *Buzz, Buzz*

139 Transportation

Topical Calendar Tie-in:

August 14–20
"National Aviation Week"—Offered annually the week of Orville Wright's birthday, this holiday honors the world of aviation. Celebrate with your own paper airplane competition.

Videos:

Beep! Beep!
Curious George Rides A Bike
Freight Train
Steamboat Willie
The Wheels on the Bus
Wings: A Tale of Two Chickens

Picture Books:

Christina Katerina and the Great Bear Train, Patricia Lee Gauch
Daisy's Taxi, Ruth Young
Delivery Van, Betsy and Giulio Maestro
Friday's Journey, Ken Rush
Here Come's the Train, Charlotte Voake
I Fly, Anne Rockwell
In the Driver's Seat, Max Haynes
Maxi, the Hero, Debra and Sal Barracca
A Mouse's Tale, Pamela Johnson
The Neighborhood Trucker, Louise Bordon
On the Go, Ann Morris
A Rainbow Balloon, Ann Lenssen
This Is the Way We Go to School, Edith Baer
Train Song, Diane Siebert
Where's That Bus, Eileen Browne
Zip, Whiz, Zoom!, Stephanie Calmenson

Music/Movement:

"Here Comes the Choo-Choo Train"
Source: *Storytimes for Two-Year-Olds*, Judy Nichols

Crafts:

"Speeding Along"
Build your own car stick puppet to be used in a puppet show. Using cardboard, colored paper, glue, and a hole-punch you can produce the vehicle of your dreams. Place it on a garden stick and it becomes a puppet to help you tell some of the stories you are fond of today.
Source: *The Grolier Kids Crafts Puppet Book*, Lyn Orton

"Toothpaste Airplane"
This imaginative craft can be used as a vehicle to begin a lesson on transportation or a discussion on brushing your teeth. A special pattern is made available to check the dimensions of your toothpaste box to ensure

that it will work. Patterns are also made available for your propellers, wings, etc.

Let the children use this new airplane to store their own personal toothpaste for brushing each day.

Source: *Rainy Day Projects for Children*, Gerri Jenny and Sherrie Gould

Activities:

"The Plane without a Pilot"
Travel by air can be a little difficult if you don't have a pilot. In this game your pilot must guide you from the ground. Let the children pair off one being the pilot and the other the plane. Your pilot is grounded and must stay in the same place at all times while your plane can fly anywhere but blindfolded. Let your pilot guide his plane to an agreed upon landing spot with code words. Be sure not to let anyone crash into each other. Give every child a chance to be both pilot and plane.

Source: *101 Best Games*, Eulalia Perez

"Car Wash and Gas Station"
For very small children this activity will be a blast and you can get some of your class toys cleaned at the same time. Discuss various means of transportation including the family car. Setup stations such as a "Gas Station," a "Garage," and a "Car Wash" area so that children can discuss what happens to a car at these locations. Give some buckets of real water and toy cars and the children won't mind getting wet while these clean the cars.

Source: *The Instant Curriculum*, Pam Schiller and Joan Rossano

Songs:

(Audio) "Goin for a Ride"

Source: *Sing-Along Travel Songs*

140 Trees

Topical Calendar Tie-in:

April 28
"Arbor Day"—The last Friday in April, a day set aside to celebrate trees and their importance in our lives and to this world.

Videos:

Arbor Day
The Giving Tree
The Great Kapok Tree
It's Arbor Day, Charlie Brown
The Legend of Johnny Appleseed

Picture Books:

Be a Friend to Trees, Patricia Lauber
The Bee Tree, Patricia Polacco
A Busy Year, Leo Lionni
The Elephant Tree, Penny Dale
The Growing Up Tree, Vera Rosenberry
Leaf Jumpers, Carole Gerber
A Possible Tree, Josephine Aldridge
The Never-Ending Greenness, Nei Waldman
Night Tree, Eve Bunting
Our Tree Names Steve, Alan Zweibel
Someday a Tree, Eve Bunting
A Tree for Me, Nancy Van Laan
Tree of Cranes, Allen Say
What's So Terrible about Swallowing an Apple Seed?, Harriet Lerner and Susan Goldhor
Why Do Leaves Change Color?, Betsy Maestro

Music/Movement:

"Five Little Leaves"
Source: *Head, Shoulders, Knees, and Toes and Other Action Rhymes*, Zita Newcome

Crafts:

"Paper Pine Trees"
Judy Press offers two craft options for making trees in this book. After identifying a collection of leaves and the trees they have come from try making your own tree forest made of pine trees from construction paper, Popsicle sticks, and a cardboard egg carton base. Next, head for Australia and make the Macrozamia Tree (similar in look to the palm tree) out of corrugated cardboard tubes. This second tree plan can be adjusted to represent a variety of trees with leaves. Illustrations are offered in the source book.
Source: *Vroom! Vroom! : Making 'Dozers, 'Copters, Trucks and More*, Judy Press

"My Friendship Tree"
Family trees are a common craft in many classes. Unfortunately with so many diverse family makeups this can be a difficult project. Many children may be uncomfortable perhaps only showing one parent or other ways their family is different. Try a variation called a "Friendship Tree," where children can include all types of friends which include family. Hand out posterboard with a picture of a tree with many branches, and children may cut out numerous colored leaves. On each leaf they can draw a picture of something each friend likes to do.
Source: *Rain Day Play!*, Nancy Fusco Castaldo

Activities:

"Yoga for Children: The Tree"
Get into fitness with this fantastic book on yoga for children. It requires no special athletic skills and is perfect for stretching and warm-up exercises for ages 3 and up. You will find an entire chapter on yoga stances for seasons and nature. This particular pose is called "The Tree." Children begin with the mountain pose and gradually develop the growth of the tree by standing on one foot and moving their arms with palms together up toward the sky. Switch and try the other foot. If they have difficulty standing on one foot, have them stand touching a wall with one hand for support until they get more proficient. There is a wide variety of positions the children will enjoy creating.
Source: *Yoga Games for Children*, Danielle Bersma and Marjokek Visscher

"Feed the Wildlife Tree"
This source offers some wonderful ideas for making adorable decorations to be hung on outdoor trees for the benefit of our beautiful wildlife. Cookie cutter shapes from bread, orange halves with seeds sprinkled on them, and other suggestions are offered. Take the class on an excursion outdoors to hang their treats on their own wildlife tree. Let them observe the tree each day and take note of what creatures make an appearance.
Source: *Great Parties for Kids*, Nancy Flyke, Lynn Nejam and Vicki Overstreet

Songs:

(Audio) "I'm a Nut"
Source: *Kids Silly Song Sing-a-Longs*

141 Weather: Rain

Topical Calendar Tie-in:

March

"National Umbrella Month"—Celebrate the invention of a versatile item that's used by many and discuss the variety of wet weather gear that are needed by children.

Videos:

The Cat in the Hat (Dr. Seuss Showcase II)
Cloudy with a Chance of Meatballs
Come on, Rain!
A Letter to Amy
Rain
A Rainbow of My Own

Picture Books:

Bamboo and Friends: The Rainy Day, Felicia Law
Bumpa Rumpus and the Rainy Day, Joanne Reay and Adriano Gon
Cat and Mouse in the Rain, Tomek Begacki
Down Comes the Rain, Franklyn Branley
I Love the Rain, Margaret Park Bridges
It's Raining, It's Raining, Kin Eagle
Mudball, Matt Tavares
The Puddle, David McPhail
Puddles, Jonathan London
Rain, Manya Stojic
Rain Drop Splash, Alvin Tresselt
Rain Romp, Jane Kurtz
The Rains Are Coming, Sanna Stanley
That Sky, That Rain, Carolyn Otto
Soggy Saturday, Phyllis Root
Splish! Splash!: A Book About Rain, Josepha Sherman

Music/Movement:

"The Rain comes Down"
Sung to: "Mulberry Bush"

The rain comes down *(fingers float down like rain)*
The flowers grow up
(one hand grows up through circle of other hand pantomiming flower growing)
The rain comes down
The umbrellas go up *(open the umbrella)*
The rain comes down
And we all dress up in
Boots, coat and rain cap.
(put on each piece of clothing)

Crafts:

"Raindrop Painting"

Reproduce the sound of rain falling on the roof. Talk about how rain makes puddles, streams, and more. If you have a space to work that can be easily cleaned try having the children make their own artwork with the use of aluminum pie tins that have holes in them, paper, and tempera paints. Make some original rain creations.

Source: *The Little Hands Playtime! Book*, Regina Curtis

"Pitter Patter Rain Stick"

Rainsticks for centuries have been used in ceremonial rituals by tribes in South America to bring rain to areas of the desert that needed it. Held by one end and tilted to one side, small pebbles trickle down to make the sound of rain falling from the sky. Today they're also used for anything from musical uses to decorations.

Create your own with aluminum foil, uncooked rice, long cardboard tubes, and stickers. Tear off another foil sheet one and a half times the length of the tube and create a snakelike strip that is pushed into the tube along with the rice. Seal the other end and decorate with stickers.

Source: *Crafts to Make in the Spring*, Kathy Ross

Activities:

"Rain Check"

Rain accumulates everywhere with puddles in your yard, in cups, toys left outside, etc. Use the opportunity after a rainy day to have some fun with simple rain experiments. Develop your own rain gauge to measure rain collection. The most fun offered in Mr. Maynard's book is making our own water filter with basic materials. Would you drink water from puddles? Show children how their water gets filtered.

Source: *Science Fun at Home*, Chris Maynard

"Water Puddle Game"

Spring brings rain and often produces many puddles for kids to play in that day. Discuss with the children proper dress for this weather. Now try this obstacle game. Place around the room blue paper puddles of various sizes. Encourage the children to make their way through this obstacle course without getting "wet." Add variety by having them hop through, skip, jump, etc.

Source: *Focus on Spring*, Rosie Seaman

Songs:

(Audio) "Rain: It's Raining, It's Pouring;"
"Rain on the Green Grass"
"If all the Raindrops were Gumdrops"

Source: *Sing Around the Campfire*

142 Weather: Snow

Topical Calendar Tie-in:

November 14, 1965

"Artificial snow introduced to America"—This was the first use of artificial snow (bleached cornflakes, white sand, and plastic shavings) by the film industry.

Videos:

Brave Irene
Frosty the Snowman
Snowflake Bentley
The Snowman
The Snowy Day

Picture Books:

The Biggest Snowball Fight, Angela Shelf Medearis
Emily's Snowball: The World's Biggest, Elizabeth Keown
Emmett's Snowball, Ned Miller
The Golden Snowflake, Francoise and Frederic Joos
Little Fern's First Winter, Jane Simmons
Names for Snow, Judi K. Beach
Ralph's Frozen Tale, Elise Primavera
Snow Angel, Jean Marzollo
Snow, Uri Shuevitz
Snow, Manya Stojic
Snowballs, Lois Ehlert
The Snow Speaks, Nancy White Carlstrom
Snowy Day!, Barbara M. Joosse
Straight to the Pole, Kevin O'Malley
The Tiny Snowflake, Arthur Ginolfi

Music/Movement:

"Snowflakes"

Sung to: "Pop Goes the Weasel"

Round and round the snowflakes spin *(spin around)*
Falling to the ground. *(fall down)*
Making such a pretty sight,
Covering all the ground. *(lay down on floor)*

Gather up the snowflakes tight
Bunch them into a ball.
Prepare to have a snowball fight.
BAM!—what a fall! *(pretend to get hit with snowball!)*

Crafts:

"Snow Cones"

Why not try a little refreshment at your storyhour. If you're able to obtain an ice crusher, have the children make their own snow cones. Use canned juices for flavor.

"Wooden Spoon Snowman"
Snowmen or snowwomen are familiar creatures to children during the winter season. Try using old ice cream spoons painted white for the snowman's body then simply add the scarf, hat, and features from felt. Add a string to the top and you have a tree ornament or a safety pin to the back and the child can wear it.

Source: *Christmas Ornaments Kids can Make,* Kathy Ross

Activities:

"Snow Removal Race"
If we have a bad winter parents will be complaining about having to need to remove all the snow. In this game the children will never complain about the job. Popped popcorn is used to represent snow scattered on plastic wrap. Children from each team will need to remove the snow by eating all the popcorn but this game has special requirements for how this will be done that can be as exhausting as shoveling but fun too. This game is not for preschoolers but can be adjusted to meet the needs of that age.

Source: *Fun and Games for Family Gatherings,* Adrienne Anderson

"Ice-Cube Color Painting"
Develop your own art activity room for children on a snowy day. It's too snowy and icy to go outside so let's move indoors. You can still bring the weather with you by setting up a refreshment table to make snow cones with flavored juices, another area for winter games and a final ice activity table where children can use partially frozen ice cubes and other materials recommended in this book to make their own art work. Watch as the ice cubes melt and make some interesting effects. This book also recommends two excellent books to read aloud on this fun-filled day.

Source: *Early Learning Skill Builders: Colors, Shapes, Numbers and Letters,* Mary Tomczyk

Songs:

(Audio) "Snowflakes Falling from Sky"

Source: *Piggyback Songs*

143 Weather: Storms

Topical Calendar Tie-in:

March 11

"Blizzard of '88"—This is the anniversary of a record snowstorm that hit the northeastern part of the United States. Encourage children to find out how frostbite affects their body, write or tells stories of snowstorms they have experienced or hear about and how it affects the community. How can you help a friend during a snowstorm?

Videos:

Brave Irene
Cloudy with a Chance of Meatballs
The Old Mill

Picture Books:

City Storm, Mary Jessie Parker
Franklin and the Thunderstorm, Paulette Bourgeois
How Thunder and Lightning Came to Be, Beatrice Orcutt Harrell
Hurricane!, Jonathan London
Hurricane, David Wiesner
Just You and Me, Sam McBratney
Molly and the Storm, Christine Leeson
One Stormy Night, Ruth Brown
Outside, Inside, Carolyn Crimi
Rainflowers, Ann Turner
Rain Song, Lezlie Evans
Rainy Day Dream, Michael Chesworth
Ruby's Storm, Amy Hest
The Storm, Anne Rockwell
Storm Boy, Paul Owen Lewis

Music/Movement:

"April Clouds"
Source: *School Days*, Pam Schiller

Crafts:

"Musical Wind Flower"
After a discussion of spring storms and the winds that accompany them ask the children if they have ever seen wind chimes. Demonstrate a variety of wind chime styles and ask the children to close their eyes and see if they can identify the one they hear. Following this demonstration inform the children that they will be making a similar wind chime called a "Musical Wind Flower." Collect large plastic soda bottles and cut about an inch from the bottom of each. The bottom of this bottle will shape the flower when the children fill the indentures with many colors of Play-Doh. Use a hole-punch to add string to the top and three ribbons to the bottom with bells attached to them. This craft allows the children to use their sense of touch with the Play-Doh, their sense of visual beauty, and

ultimately their sense of hearing when they're delighted with the sounds of their project. Let the wind bring music into your life.

Source: *Play-Doh: Fun and Games*, Kathy Ross

"Cloudy with a Chance of ______."

After reading the story *Cloudy with a Chance of Meatballs* by Judi Barrett, discuss with the children various storms that they have experienced. Give the children a larger piece of construction paper and let them draw houses, etc. for scenery. Add their own type of storm by gluing cups in the sky, rice, beans, etc. for a strange storm of their own.

Source: *Literature Based Art Activities*, Darlene Ritter

Activities:

"Where's My Hat?"

The "Mr. Wind" rhyme offered in this activity can be recited while the action is occurring setting the atmosphere for the event. One child who is "It" sits in the center of the circle while "Wind" will attempt to secretly steal away its hat while sounding like the wind. While "Wind" returns to his seat and hides the hat behind him all other players will do the same. Can the first player recover his hat during this stormy game?

Source: *The Complete Book of Activities, Games, Stories, Props, Recipes, and Dances for Young Children*, Pam Schiller and Jackie Silberg

"Mud Painting"

Now here's an event for your group to participate in after a stormy day if you are not afraid of a little mud. Turn it into an expression of art on your sidewalk or parking lot.

Source: *The Preschooler's Busy Book*, Trish Kuffner

Songs:

(Audio) "It Ain't Gonna Rain"

Source: *The Cat Came Back*, Fred Penner

144 Westward Ho!

Topical Calendar Tie-in:

February 10–12

"Gold Rush Days"—This yearly community event reveres the life in the Old West with rodeos, parades, and gold panning. Celebrate a time when pioneers discovered gold and moved to the western part of the country.

Videos:

Pecos Bill
I Wanna Be a Cowboy

Picture Books:

Boss of the Plains: The Hat that Won the West, Laurie Carlson
A Campfire for Cowboy Billy, Wendy K. Ulmer
Casey's New Hat, Tricia Gardella
The Cowboy and the Black-eyed Pea, Tony Johnston
Cowboy Bunnies, Christine Loomis
Cowboy Rodeo, James Rice
Cowboys, Glen Rounds
Cowpokes, Caroline Stutson
Do Cowboys Ride Bikes?, Kathy Tucker
Going West, Jean Van Leeuwen
Mathew the Cowboy, Ruth Hooker
Moony B. Finch, the Fastest Draw in the West, David McPhail
Tyrannosaurus Tex, Betty G. Birney
A Wild Cowboy, Dana Kessimakis Smith and Laura Freeman
Yippee-Yay!: A Book About Cowboys and Cowgirls, Gail Gibbons
The Zebra Riding Cowboy, Angela Shelf Medearis

Music/Movement:

"The Cowboy's at the Ranch"
Sung to: "Farmer in the Dell"

The cowboy's at the Ranch.
The cowboy's at the Ranch,
Yee-haaa the cowboy yells
The cowboy's at the Ranch.

The cowboy gets the horse *(pull on the reins)*
The cowboy gets the horse
Neigh snorts the horse today.
The cowboy gets the horse.

The cowboy saddles the horse. *(saddle horse)*
The cowboy saddles the horse.
Neigh snorts the horse with rage. *(snort angrily)*
The cowboy saddles the horse.

The cowboy rides the horse. *(gallop)*
The cowboy rides the horse.

Yeehaaa the ranch hands yell
The cowboy rides the horse.

Crafts:

"Cowboy Face Mask"
Let the children ride the plains with this amusing cowboy face mask. It consists of a large ten gallon hat and mask all in one piece. Children will be happy with the large size of this hat and be ready to start playing cowboy games almost instantly. This is a surefire hit.
Source: *Paper Fun for Kids*, Marion Elliot

"Hobby Horse"
Help children build their own hobby horses for their westward adventure. All that is required is a large cardboard to be like the type used in gift wrapping, a paper bag for a head, some markers, and masking tape. You might even wish to get yarn to add reins for the child to hold. Happy Trails!
Source: *The Month by Month Treasure Box*, Sally Patrick, Vicky Schwartz, and Pat Lo Presti

Activities:

"Wild West Target Practice"
Using a collection of soda cans you can set up an appealable target for the children to aim at. Set it upon a table or your own homemade western fence. Fill small socks with beans to create beanbags and see how many targets a child can topple, in a row. This source makes available to the instructor quite a few games, crafts, and reproducible patterns for your own Wild West party.
Source: *Hit of the Party*, Amy Vangsgard

"Trouble on the Trail"
Read about cattle drives and their obstacles. Set up a mini obstacle course to represent the trail drive that the class will travel. Decide on a trail boss, a cowboy, a cattle rustler, and the remainder of the class can be cattle. See if the trail boss and cowboy can get their cattle past the obstacles set up (see book for suggestions) and avoid being tagged by the cattle rustler.
Source: *Kickin' Up Some Cowboy Fun*, Monica Hay Cook

Songs:

(Audio) "Home on the Range"
Source: *Car Songs*

145 Witches

Topical Calendar Tie-in:

March 12, 1692
"Salem Witch Trials"—The Salem trials began on this date with the first accusation against Martha Corey for practicing witchcraft.

Videos:

Hansel and Gretel
Strega Nonna
Teeny-Tiny and the Witch Woman
There's a Witch Under the Stairs
The Witch's Hat
The Wizard

Picture Books:

Baba Yaga and the Wise Doll, Hiawyn Oram
The Candy Witch, Steven Kroll
CinderHazel: The Cinderella of Halloween, Deborah Nourse Lattimore
I Know I'm a Witch, David A. Adler
Little Green Witch, Barbara Barbieri McGrath
Little Witch Learns to Read, Deborah Hautzig
Meredith the Witch Who Wasn't, Dorothea Lachner
Paco and the Witch, Felix Pitre
A Perfect Pork Stew, Paul Brett Johnson
Piggie Pie!, Margie Palatini
Room on the Broom, Axel Scheffler
Snow White and the Seven Dwarfs, Jacob Grimm
Strega Nonna Meets her Match, Tomie dePaola
The Surprise in the Wardrobe, Val Willis
The Witches' Supermarket, Susan Meddaugh
The Witch with a Twitch, Layn Marlow

Music/Movement:

"Little Witches"
Source: *Fun with Mommy and Me*, Dr. Cindy Bunin Nurik

Crafts:

"Bad Hair Day Pin"
Try a discussion on how everyone's hair is not only different in color but in texture, length, and style. Show a variety of hairstyles that have been used down the span of the centuries. It will bring some laughs to the children to see what their parents thought was a cool hairstyle. We all have bad hair days so try this pin craft using plaster of paris to make a "Bad Hair Day" pin to let your friends know that you have a sense of humor about it. Add this to your Halloween program by painting the face green and adding a witch hat to your pin with the hair off to the sides. Witches have bad hair days every day.
Source: *Wearable Art with Sondra*, Sondra Clark

"Halloween Stick Puppet"
A stick puppet is something that can be made with construction paper and tongue depressors without too much difficulty. Check this source for some wild Halloween crafts including this colorful, wild-eyed witch that reminds me of a crazy cartoon witch from old Bug's Bunny cartoons.
Source: *175 Easy-to-Do Halloween Crafts*, Sharon Dunn Umnik

Activities:

"Witch Hunt"
"We're going on a witch hunt,
A witch hunt, a witch hunt.
We're going on a witch hunt
Be careful, where can she be?"

Hide a witch's hat, a bat, and a black cat somewhere in the room. Encourage the children to quietly search for the hidden items. If they find the black cat they should cry out "meow" and sit down where they are. If they find the bat they should fly to their seat with it because they are safe this round and can't be eliminated. Whoever finds the witch's hat should quickly put it on and try to catch (tag) one of the other children in the room. The first one tagged by the witch or her black cat (who can only tag from his seated position) is out of the game. Continue with the next round.

"Which Witch is Which?"
This is a nice party game that can be used in children's parties or programs, as well as adult parties. This is a Halloween Tic-Tac-Toe game with play pieces made with illustrations of famous television witches. With children's parties you could also make pieces from famous children's book witches. Use these pieces and create a large tablecloth board to be used in the game. Check out instructions for unique playing piece materials and some witchy videos also in this source:
Source: *Halloween Parties*, Lori Hellander

Songs:

(Audio) "Witch Doctor"
Source: *Funny 50's and Silly 60's*

146 Zoos

Topical Calendar Tie-in:

July 1
"First U.S. Zoo Anniversary"—This day celebrates the opening of the Philadelphia Zoological Society, the first U.S. zoo.

Videos:

Goodnight Gorilla
Happy Lion's Treasure
If I Ran the Zoo
Leo the See-Through Crumbpicker
The Mole in the Zoo

Picture Books:

Alligator Baby, Robert Munsch
Animals at the Zoo, Rose Greydanus
Anthony and the Aardvark, Lesley Sloss
At the Zoo, Douglas Florian
The Baby Beebee Bird, Diane Redfield Massie
The Boy Who Loved Bananas, George Elliott
Cyril the Mandrill, Francesca Greco
Dancing Granny, Elizabeth Winthrop
Goodnight, Gorilla, Peggy Rathmann
My Visit to the Zoo, Aliki
Out and About at the Zoo, Kathleen W. Deady
Tarzanna, Babette Cole
Tuscanini, Jim Propp
Zoo Dreams, Cor Hazelaar
Zoo-Looking, Mem Fox
Zoo Parade, Harriet Ziefert and Simms Taback

Music/Movement:

"Zoo Antics"
Sung to: "The Ant's Go Marching"

The animals were hopping through the zoo
WATCH OUT! WATCH OUT!
The animals were hopping through the zoo
WATCH OUT! WATCH OUT!
The animals were hopping through the zoo.
We stopped to see the Kangaroos
And we all started hopping
Down the road, to get out of the rain.

The animals were climbing up in the trees
WATCH OUT! WATCH OUT!
The animals were climbing up in the trees
WATCH OUT! WATCH OUT!
The animals were climbing up in the trees

We stopped to see a lot of monkeys
And we all started climbing
Up in the trees to get out of the rain.

The animals were diving into the pool.
WATCH OUT! WATCH OUT!
The animals were diving into the pool.
WATCH OUT! WATCH OUT!
The animals were diving into the pool
Penguins thought it was really cool
When we all started diving
Down into the pool at the end of the zoo!

Crafts:

"Berry Busy Zoo"

Plastic berry baskets make the perfect zoo cages for your children's miniature animals. Set up signs and a little door on it. Gather a collection of these berry baskets and set up a full zoo table. Add trees, water areas where needed, etc. Also available in this book are instructions for cornstarch clay (Funclay) that you could use to form animals. Read *Goodnight Gorilla!* and let the animals go back to their cages.

Source: *Making Make-Believe,* by MaryAnn F. Kohl

"Egg Carton Zoo"

This is another method of creating amusing zoo animals. These are constructed from empty egg cartons. Build a zoo full of creatures, such as, armadillos, giraffes, a crab, rabbit, cricket, and more.

Source: *Likeable Recyclables,* Linda Schwartz

Activities:

"Zoo Races"

The tortoise and the hare are not the only animals that like to race. Try thinking of all the different types of animals you see at the zoo and pair them up for that legendary race. Fill your zoo first with animals by having each child display the actions of an animal that the class can guess. Once your zoo is filled, pair off those animals for the race of the century.

Source: *Early Learning Skill Builders: Colors, Shapes, Numbers and Letters,* Mary Toriczyk

"Zoo Game"

Using the reproducible zoo animals in the source provided here. Trace them on black construction paper to create the shadows. Follow the instructions provided to play your own zoo animal match up game matching the animal to his own shadow. Also provided for you are other amusing zoo activities, snacks, crafts and even a zoo chant.

Source: *Seasonal Activities for 3-Year-Olds,* by Carol L. Van Hise

Songs:

(Audio) "Going to the Zoo"

Source: *Jeremiah Was a Bullfrog*

Part IV:

Finding Aids Storytellers Can Use Every Day

1 Index to Picture Book Authors

NOTE: Numbers are program numbers, not page numbers.

A

B

C

D

E

F

G

K

L

N

O

R

T

U

V

W

2 Index to Picture Book Titles

NOTE: Numbers are program numbers, not page numbers.

B

C

D

E

F

G

H

I

J

M

N

Q

T

U

V

W

Y

Z

3 Index to Music/Movement

NOTE: Numbers are program numbers, not page numbers.

Y

Z

4 Index to Crafts

NOTE: Numbers are program numbers, not page numbers.

5 Index to Activities

NOTE: Numbers are program numbers, not page numbers.

6 Index to Song Titles

NOTE: Numbers are program numbers, not page numbers.

About the Author

Carolyn Cullum has worked as a System Coordinator for Children's Services in a public library in New Jersey for the past 25 years. Her past experiences include working with children as an elementary school teacher for five years, as a school librarian, and as a Sunday school teacher with her local church.

She has a B.A. in elementary education and an M.L.S in library service as well as an educational media specialist certification. She spoke to the Edison Kindergarten Teacher's Association illustrating the use of children's fiction books in science and math lessons in the classroom, along with hands-on demonstrations of crafts. She presented a variety of stories at the New Jersey Association of Kindergarten Teachers Convention. Cullum has spoken to local PTA groups, high school parenting classes, elementary school auditorium programs, as well as colleges. She has also appeared on local cable television shows in Edison, New Jersey, to present a variety of stories using props and demonstrate craft ideas that were offered in the first edition of *The Storytime Sourcebook*. Cullum has also served as a senior judge for an organization titled FCCLA (Family, Career and Community Leaders of America) for a statewide high school storytelling event titled "Storybook Ethics" for the past 10 years.